DocBook 5: The Definitive Guide

DocBook 5: The Definitive Guide

Norman Walsh
edited by Richard L. Hamilton

O'REILLY®

Beijing · Cambridge · Farnham · Köln · Sebastopol · Taipei · Tokyo

DocBook 5: The Definitive Guide
by Norman Walsh; edited by Richard L. Hamilton

Published by O'Reilly Media, Inc., 1005 Gravenstein Highway North, Sebastopol, CA 95472.

O'Reilly books may be purchased for educational, business, or sales promotional use. Online editions are also available for most titles (*http://my.safaribooksonline.com*). For more information, contact our corporate/institutional sales department: 800-998-9938 or *corporate@oreilly.com*.

Editor: Mike Loukides
Production Editor: Sarah Schneider
Proofreader: Audrey Doyle

Indexer: Ellen Troutman Zaig
Cover Designer: Karen Montgomery
Interior Designer: David Futato
Illustrator: Robert Romano

Printing History:

May 2010:	*DocBook 5: The Definitive Guide.*
October 1999:	*DocBook: The Definitive Guide.*

RepKover.
This book uses RepKover™, a durable and flexible lay-flat binding.

ISBN: 978-0-596-80502-9

M

1273686696

Table of Contents

Part II. Reference

Part III. Appendixes

Preface

DocBook provides a system for writing structured documents using XML. It is particularly well suited to books and papers about computer hardware and software, though it is by no means limited to them. Because it is a large and robust format, and because its main structures correspond to the general notion of what constitutes a book, DocBook has been adopted by a large and growing community of authors. DocBook is supported "out of the box" by a wide range of tools, both open source and commercial. In short, DocBook is an easy-to-understand and widely used schema. Worldwide, hundreds (perhaps thousands) of organizations use DocBook for millions of pages of documentation in a wide variety of print and online formats.

Why Read This Book?

This book is designed to be the clear, concise, normative reference to the DocBook schema. This book is the official documentation for DocBook.

We hope to answer, definitively, all the questions you might have about all the elements and attributes in DocBook. In particular, we cover the following subjects:

Getting started with DocBook
> With around 400 elements, DocBook can be a bit overwhelming at first. We get you up to speed quickly.

Writing DocBook documents
> Where should you start and what should you do?

Parsing and validating DocBook documents
> After you've written a document, how can you tell if it really conforms to the DocBook schema?

Publishing DocBook documents
> After you've written one, what do you do with it? We introduce some popular free tools you can use to publish DocBook documents in print and various electronic formats.

Customizing the schema
> Many individuals and corporations have created custom schemas based on Doc-Book. We show you how to write a "customization layer" to tailor DocBook for your content.

Understanding the elements
> Each element is extensively documented, including the intended semantics and the purpose of all its attributes. An example of proper usage is included for most elements.

Using the DocBook stylesheets
> The DocBook XSL Stylesheets, part of the DocBook project (*http://docbook.sf .net/*) at SourceForge (*http://sourceforge.net/*), have become the de facto standard way to process DocBook. This book contains a brief description about using the stylesheets, but for detailed information we recommend Bob Stayton's excellent book, *DocBook XSL: The Complete Guide* [Stayton07].

Getting more information
> Finally, we direct you to other places you can go for information about DocBook, XML, and other relevant topics.

This Book's Audience

We expect that most readers will have some familiarity with XML. Even if your experience goes no further than writing a few HTML pages, you're probably in good shape. If you're not already familiar with XML, there are many popular books, including Erik Ray's *Learning XML* [Ray03]. For a list of other resources, consult Appendix C.

 The previous edition of this book described some of the SGML-specific features available to users of the DocBook DTD versions 4.x and earlier. In this edition, we don't cover SGML at all. Starting with DocBook V5.0, DocBook is normatively an XML vocabulary.

Organization of This Book

This book is divided into three parts.

Part I, *Introduction* is an introduction to DocBook and includes the following chapters:

Chapter 1, Getting Started with DocBook
> Provides an overview of DocBook, including a history of the schema and a description of what is new in DocBook V5.0

Chapter 2, Creating DocBook Documents
> Describes how to get started creating books, sets of books, articles, and other documents using DocBook

Chapter 3, Validating DocBook Documents
> Describes how to validate DocBook instances and how to interpret common validation errors

Chapter 4, Publishing DocBook Documents
> Provides a high-level overview of DocBook publishing

Chapter 5
> Describes how to customize the DocBook schema, including examples of common customizations

Part II, *Reference*, is a complete reference guide to the DocBook elements.

Part III, *Appendixes*, contains installation instructions, a discussion of DocBook variants and future directions, a list of resources, an interchange checklist, and a copy of the GNU Free Documentation License:

Appendix A, Installation
> Describes how to install the DocBook schema and stylesheets

Appendix B, DocBook Variants and Future Directions
> Describes DocBook variants and discusses future directions

Appendix C, Resources
> Lists websites, books, and other resources

Appendix D, Interchanging DocBook Documents
> An interchange checklist; includes things to consider when sharing DocBook documents with others

Appendix E, GNU Free Documentation License
> A copy of the GNU Free Documentation License

At the end of this book you'll find a Glossary on page 515 and an Index.

Conventions Used in This Book

The following typographical conventions are used in this book:

Italic
> Indicates new terms, URLs, email addresses, filenames, and file extensions.

`Constant width`
> Used for program listings, as well as within paragraphs to refer to element and attribute names, program examples, attribute value literals, start- and end-tags, and source code example text.

`Constant width bold`
> Shows commands or other text that should be typed literally by the user.

Constant width italic

> Shows text that should be replaced with user-supplied values or by values determined by context. An example is *filename*, where the word "filename" is a placeholder for the actual filename.

   This icon signifies a tip, suggestion, or general note.

   This icon indicates a warning or caution.

Using Code Examples

This book is here to help you get your job done. In general, you may use the code in this book in your programs and documentation. You do not need to contact us for permission unless you're reproducing a significant portion of the code. For example, writing a program that uses several chunks of code from this book does not require permission. Selling or distributing a CD-ROM of examples from O'Reilly books does require permission. Answering a question by citing this book and quoting example code does not require permission. Incorporating a significant amount of example code from this book into your product's documentation does require permission.

We appreciate, but do not require, attribution. An attribution usually includes the title, author, publisher, and ISBN. For example: "*DocBook 5: The Definitive Guide* by Norman Walsh; edited by Richard L. Hamilton. Copyright 2010 Norman Walsh, ISBN: 978-0-596-80502-9."

If you feel your use of code examples falls outside fair use or the permission given above, feel free to contact us at *permissions@oreilly.com*.

Safari® Books Online

Safari Safari Books Online is an on-demand digital library that lets you easily search over 7,500 technology and creative reference books and videos to find the answers you need quickly.

With a subscription, you can read any page and watch any video from our library online. Read books on your cell phone and mobile devices. Access new titles before they are available for print, and get exclusive access to manuscripts in development and post feedback for the authors. Copy and paste code samples, organize your favorites, download chapters, bookmark key sections, create notes, print out pages, and benefit from tons of other time-saving features.

O'Reilly Media has uploaded this book to the Safari Books Online service. To have full digital access to this book and others on similar topics from O'Reilly and other publishers, sign up for free at *http://my.safaribooksonline.com*.

How to Contact Us

Please address comments and questions concerning this book to the publisher:

O'Reilly Media, Inc.
1005 Gravenstein Highway North
Sebastopol, CA 95472
800-998-9938 (in the United States or Canada)
707-829-0515 (international or local)
707-829-0104 (fax)

We have a web page for this book, where we list errata, examples, and any additional information. You can access this page at:

http://www.oreilly.com/catalog/9781449389604

To comment or ask technical questions about this book, send email to:

bookquestions@oreilly.com

For more information about our books, conferences, Resource Centers, and the O'Reilly Network, see our website at:

http://www.oreilly.com

Acknowledgments

This book wouldn't exist, there wouldn't have been any point in writing it, were it not for DocBook's enthusiastic support from an entire community of writers, engineers, managers, and other users. My thanks to you all.

It also wouldn't exist if my wife was not so understanding and supportive. Writing a book invariably takes more time and effort than one imagines, time first borrowed from, then begged for, and eventually stolen from other activities. Thank you, Deb!

And, to conclude a series, it also wouldn't exist were it not for Dick Hamilton's encouragement and hard work. Dick first persuaded me to complete a second edition in print, then offered to publish it. He negotiated with O'Reilly, agreed to edit it, and wrote more of it than he could be persuaded to take credit for. Thank you, Dick.

Several sections in this book use material from DocBook V5.0: The Transition Guide, (*http://docbook.org/docs/howto/*) also known as the "DocBook How-to." Thanks to Jirka Kosek and Michael Smith for their work on the How-to.

Thanks to Nancy Harrison, Scott Hudson, Mauritz Jeanson, Jirka Kosek, and Larry Rowland for their technical review of the book.

Thanks to Bob Stayton for being Secretary to the Technical Committee, and to Scott Hudson for chairing the eLearning and Publisher's Subcommittees and for being the driving force behind those two initiatives. Thanks also to the entire DocBook Technical Committee for contributing time every month to the continued maintenance of DocBook.

Introduction

## CHAPTER 1

Getting Started with DocBook

This chapter provides an overview of DocBook, starting with its history. It includes a description of DocBook V5.0 and the changes from DocBook V4.x to V5.0.

A Short DocBook History

DocBook is more than 15 years old. It began in 1991 as a joint project of HaL Computer Systems and O'Reilly & Associates (as O'Reilly Media, Inc. was then called). Its popularity grew, and eventually it spawned its own maintenance organization, the Davenport Group. In mid-1998, maintenance moved to a Technical Committee of the Organization for the Advancement of Structured Information Standards (OASIS).

DocBook's roots are in *SGML*, where it was defined with a Document Type Definition, or DTD. DocBook was released as both an SGML and an *XML* vocabulary starting with V4.1. The V4.x versions of DocBook, like the versions that came before them, were also defined with a DTD. Starting with DocBook V5.0, DocBook is exclusively an XML vocabulary defined with RELAX NG and Schematron.

The HaL and O'Reilly Era

The DocBook DTD was originally designed and implemented by HaL Computer Systems and O'Reilly & Associates around 1991. It was developed primarily to facilitate the exchange of UNIX documentation originally marked up in *troff*. Its design appears to have been based partly on input from SGML interchange projects conducted by the Unix International and Open Software Foundation consortia.

When DocBook V1.1 was published, discussion about its revision and maintenance began in earnest in the Davenport Group, a forum created by O'Reilly for computer documentation producers. DocBook V1.2 was influenced strongly by Novell and Digital.

In 1994, the Davenport Group became an officially chartered entity responsible for DocBook's maintenance. DocBook V1.2.2 was published simultaneously. The founding sponsors of this incarnation of Davenport include the following people with their affiliations at that time:

- Jon Bosak, Novell
- Dale Dougherty, O'Reilly & Associates
- Ralph Ferris, Fujitsu OSSI
- Dave Hollander, Hewlett-Packard
- Eve Maler, Digital Equipment Corporation
- Murray Maloney, SCO
- Conleth O'Connell, HaL Computer Systems
- Nancy Paisner, Hitachi Computer Products
- Mike Rogers, SunSoft
- Jean Tappan, Unisys

The Davenport Era

Under the auspices of the Davenport Group, the DocBook DTD began to widen its scope. It was now being used by a much wider audience and for new purposes such as direct authoring with SGML-aware tools and publishing directly to paper. As the largest users of DocBook, Novell and Sun had a heavy influence on its design.

In order to help users manage change, the new Davenport charter established the following rules for DocBook releases:

- Minor versions ("point releases" such as V2.2) could add to the markup model, but could not change it in a backward-incompatible way. For example, a new kind of list element could be added, but it would not be acceptable for the existing itemized list model to start requiring two list items inside it instead of only one. Thus, any document conforming to version *n*.0 would also conform to *n.m*.
- Major versions (such as V3.0) could both add to the markup model and make backward-incompatible changes. However, the changes would have to be announced in the last major release.

  In 2009, the Technical Committee updated this policy to allow backward-incompatible changes in a major version, provided the change is announced in a major or minor release at least six months in advance.

- Major version introductions must be separated by at least a year.

V3.0 was released in January 1997. DocBook's audience continued to grow, but many of the Davenport Group stalwarts became involved in the XML effort, and development slowed dramatically. The idea of creating an official XML-compliant version of DocBook was discussed, but not implemented at that time.

In July 1998, the sponsors moved the standards activities from the Davenport Group to OASIS, forming the OASIS DocBook Technical Committee with Eduardo Gutentag of Sun Microsystems as chair.

The OASIS Era

The OASIS DocBook Technical Committee (*http://www.oasis-open.org/docbook/*) is continuing the work started by the Davenport Group. The transition from Davenport to OASIS was very smooth, in part because the core team remained essentially the same.

DocBook V3.1, published in February 1999, was the first OASIS release. It integrated a number of changes that had been "in the wings" for some time. In March 2000, Norm Walsh became chair of the Technical Committee.

In February 2001, OASIS made DocBook SGML V4.1 and DocBook XML V4.1.2 official OASIS Specifications (*http://lists.oasis-open.org/archives/members/200102/msg00000.html*).

In October 2005, the DocBook Technical Committee released the first beta test version of DocBook V5.0. Development of the DocBook 4.x series continued in parallel with the development of V5.0. In October 2006, the DocBook Technical Committee released DocBook V4.5, the last release planned in the 4.x series.

In 2008, the Publisher's Subcommittee was chartered to develop and maintain official variants of DocBook in support of the publishing industry. The subcommittee focuses on schema customizations to support: periodicals as regularly published technical notes or journals, book publishing (such as business, legal, medical, and other non-technical domains), educational textbooks, and other document types as appropriate for this industry.

DocBook V5.0 became an official Committee Specification in June 2009 and became an official OASIS Standard in October 2009. The Technical Committee continues DocBook development to ensure that the schema will continue to meet the needs of its users.

DocBook V5.0

DocBook V5.0 represents a major step forward for DocBook. The differences between DocBook 4.x and V5.0 are quite radical in some aspects, but the basic idea behind DocBook is still the same, and almost all element names are unchanged. Because of this it is very easy to become familiar with DocBook V5.0 if you know any previous version of DocBook.

What's New in DocBook V5.0?

In V5.0, DocBook has been rewritten as a native RELAX NG grammar ("An introduction to the RELAX NG schema language" [RNG-Intro] is an excellent introduction to the grammar). The objectives were to produce a schema that:

1. "Feels like" DocBook. Most existing documents should still be valid or it should be possible to transform them in simple, mechanical ways into valid documents.
2. Enforces as many constraints as possible in the schema. Some additional constraints are expressed with Schematron rules.
3. Cleans up the content models.
4. Gives users the flexibility to extend or subset the schema in an easy and straightforward way.
5. Can be used to generate XML DTD and W3C XML Schema versions of DocBook.

Under the ordinary operating rules of DocBook evolution, the only backward-incompatible changes that could be made in DocBook V5.0 were those announced in DocBook V4.0. In light of the fact that this is a complete rewrite, the Technical Committee gave itself the freedom to make "unannounced" backward-incompatible changes for this one release.

Renamed and removed elements

A number of elements have been removed from DocBook. Some have been replaced by simpler, more versatile alternatives. Others have been removed because they were no longer needed, and still others have been renamed. Table 1-1 lists the elements that have been renamed for DocBook V5.0.

Table 1-1. Renamed elements

Old name	New name
sgmltag	tag
bookinfo, articleinfo, chapterinfo, *info	info
authorblurb	personblurb
collabname, corpauthor, corpcredit, corpname	orgname
isbn, issn, pubsnumber	biblioid
lot, lotentry, tocback, tocchap, tocfront, toclevel1, toclevel2, toclevel3, toclevel4, toclevel5, tocpart	toc, tocdiv, and tocentry
graphic, graphicco, inlinegraphic, mediaobjectco	mediaobject and inlinemediaobject
ulink	link
ackno	acknowledgements

The following elements were removed from DocBook V5.0 without direct replacements: action, beginpage, highlights, interface, invpartnumber, medialabel, modespec, structfield, and structname. If you use one or more of these elements, Table 1-2 contains suggestions for recoding them in DocBook V5.0.

Table 1-2. Recommended mapping for removed elements

Old name	Recommended mapping
action	Use `<phrase remap="action">`.
beginpage	Remove: beginpage is advisory only and has tended to cause confusion. A processing instruction or comment should be a workable replacement if one is needed.
highlights	Use abstract. Note that because highlights has a broader content model, you may need to wrap contents in a para inside abstract.
interface	Use menuchoice or one of the "gui*" elements (guibutton, guiicon, guilabel, guimenu, guimenuitem, or guisubmenu).
invpartnumber	Use `<biblioid class="other" otherclass="medialabel">`. The productnumber element is another alternative.
medialabel	Use `<citetitle pubwork="`*mediatype*`">`, where *mediatype* is the type of media being labeled (e.g., cdrom or dvd).
modespec	No longer needed. The current processing model for olink renders modespec unnecessary.
structfield, structname	Use varname. If you need to distinguish between the two, use `<varname remap="`*structname or structfield*`">`. In some contexts, it may also be appropriate to use property for structfield.

Linking and cross-referencing

In DocBook 4.x the id attribute is used to assign a unique identifier to an element. In DocBook V5.0 this attribute is renamed xml:id, and its usage is consistent with *xml:id Version 1.0* [XML-ID], a W3C Recommendation.

The biggest change in linking is that now nearly any inline element, not just xref or link, can be the source of a link. For example, consider the following DocBook 4.x example:

```
<section id="dir">
  <title>DIR command</title>
  <para>...</para>
</section>

<section id="ls">
  <title>LS command</title>
  <para>This command is a synonym for
    <link linkend="dir"><command>DIR</command></link> command.
  </para>
</section>
```

In DocBook V5.0, this can be written as the following:

```
<section xml:id="dir">
  <title>DIR command</title>
  <para>...</para>
</section>

<section xml:id="ls">
  <title>LS command</title>
  <para>This command is a synonym for
    <command linkend="dir">DIR</command> command.
  </para>
</section>
```

In addition, the `href` attribute from the XLink namespace was added to the same set of inline elements as `linkend`. The following example shows how you can use `href`. Note that you need to declare the XLink namespace in your document instance to use this attribute:

```
<article xmlns="http://docbook.org/ns/docbook"
         xmlns:xl="http://www.w3.org/1999/xlink" version="5.0">
  <title>Test article</title>

  <para>
    <application xl:href="http://www.gnu.org/software/emacs/">Emacs</application>
    is my favourite text editor.</para>

    ...
</article>
```

The `ulink` element was removed from DocBook V5.0. It can be replaced by the `link` element using the XLink `href` attribute.

The XLink `href` attribute may contain a fragment identifier to create a link within a document. For example:

```
<command xl:href="#dir">DIR</command>
```

 XLink references are not expected to be checked during validation, but `linkend` references are.

Uniform info elements

DocBook versions earlier than DocBook V5.0 use unique elements for block information. For example, a `book` element would contain a `bookinfo` element. This was done to support different content models for different block elements. DTDs only allow one content model for each element, so a different element name was required for each block's information element.

RELAX NG does not have this limitation. An element can have a different content model in different contexts. Therefore, the array of info elements (`articleinfo`, `bookinfo`, etc.) has been replaced with a single `info` element.

Required title and version attributes

DocBook V5.0 requires the `title` attribute on large block elements such as `article`. The written specification for earlier versions of DocBook noted this, but the DTD could not enforce this constraint. With RELAX NG, this constraint can now be enforced in the schema.

DocBook V5.0 no longer requires a Document Type Declaration. However, because processors may need to know the version of an instance, DocBook V5.0 has added the `version` attribute, which must appear on the root element of a DocBook document. The `version` attribute may also appear on other elements, and mixing of versions is allowed.

Additional constraints

HTML and CALS tables
> DocBook 4.x did not prevent mixing of CALS and HTML table elements in a single table, even in cases where the result might be unusable. DocBook V5.0 specifically prohibits mixing.

Co-constraints
> DocBook V5.0 enforces co-constraints such as the constraint that the `otherclass` attribute on `biblioid` may appear if, and only if, the `class` attribute exists and has the value `other`.

Data types
> DocBook V5.0 uses some data types; for example, the `col` attribute on `tgroup` is defined as a positive integer. In some cases, the data type for a particular value may constrain it further than that value was constrained in prior releases.

Table of contents

Prior to DocBook V5.0, the markup for tables of contents was clumsy and difficult to use. Although nearly all tables of contents are generated automatically, there are still cases where a table may need to be created or edited manually. Therefore, DocBook V5.0 introduces a simpler, recursive structure. See the `toc`, `tocdiv`, and `tocentry` reference pages for details and an example.

Constraint definitions using Schematron

DocBook V5.0 uses rule-based validation for certain constraints using Schematron. These constraints, such as the requirement that the root element of a document have a `version` attribute, are easier to express in a rule-based language than in a schema language, even one as flexible as RELAX NG.

Accessibility

Inline and block annotations are allowed in most contexts. Inline annotations use the `alt` element, and block annotations are supported by the new **annotation** element.

Finally in a Namespace

All DocBook V5.0 elements are in the namespace *http://docbook.org/ns/docbook*. XML namespaces are used to distinguish between different element sets. In the past few years, almost all new XML grammars have used their own namespace. It is easy to create compound documents that contain elements from different XML vocabularies. Consider this simple article marked up in DocBook V4.5:

```
<!DOCTYPE article PUBLIC '-//OASIS//DTD DocBook XML V4.5//EN'
                         'http://www.oasis-open.org/docbook/xml/4.5/docbookx.dtd'>
<article>
  <title>Sample article</title>
  <para>This is a really short article.</para>
</article>
```

The corresponding DocBook V5.0 article will look very similar:

```
<article xmlns="http://docbook.org/ns/docbook" version="5.0">
  <title>Sample article</title>
  <para>This is a really short article.</para>
</article>
```

The only change is the addition of a default namespace declaration (`xmlns="http://docbook.org/ns/docbook"`) on the root element (and a **version** attribute, which is described in the next section). This declaration applies the namespace to the root element and all nested elements. Each element is now uniquely identified by its local name and namespace.

> The namespace name *http://docbook.org/ns/docbook* serves only as an identifier. This resource is not fetched during processing of DocBook documents, and you are not required to have an Internet connection during processing. If you access the namespace URI with a browser, you will find a short explanatory document about the namespace. In the future, this document will probably conform to (some version of) RDDL and provide pointers to related resources.

Relaxing with DocBook

For more than a decade, the DocBook schema was defined using a DTD. However, DTDs have serious limitations, and DocBook V5.0 is thus defined using a powerful schema language called RELAX NG. Thanks to RELAX NG, it is now much easier to create customized versions of DocBook, and the content models are now cleaner and more precise.

Using RELAX NG has an impact on the document prolog. Example 1-1 shows the typical prolog of a DocBook 4.x document. The version of the DocBook DTD (in this case V4.5) is indicated in the Document Type Declaration (<!DOCTYPE>) that points to a particular version of the DTD.

Example 1-1. DocBook V4.5 document

```
<?xml version="1.0" encoding="utf-8"?>
<!DOCTYPE article PUBLIC '-//OASIS//DTD DocBook XML V4.5//EN'
                         'http://www.oasis-open.org/docbook/xml/4.5/docbookx.dtd'>
<article lang="en">
  <title>Sample article</title>
  <para>This is a very short article.</para>
</article>
```

In contrast, DocBook V5.0 does not depend on DTDs anymore. Instead of the Document Type Declaration, the version attribute identifies the DocBook version, as shown in Example 1-2.

Example 1-2. DocBook V5.0 document

```
<?xml version="1.0" encoding="utf-8"?>
<article xmlns="http://docbook.org/ns/docbook" version="5.0" xml:lang="en">
  <title>Sample article</title>
  <para>This is a very short article.</para>
</article>
```

DocBook V5.0 is built on top of existing XML standards as much as possible. For example, the lang attribute is superseded by the standard xml:lang (*http://www.w3.org/ TR/REC-xml/#sec-lang-tag*) attribute.

Another fundamental change is that there is no direct indication of the schema used. In Chapter 3, you will learn how you can specify a schema to be used for document validation.

> Although we recommend the RELAX NG schema for DocBook V5.0, there are also DTD and W3C XML Schema versions available (see "Where to Get the Schemas" on page 12) for tools that do not yet support RELAX NG.

Why Switch to DocBook V5.0?

The simple answer is "because DocBook V5.0 is the future." Apart from this marketing blurb, there are also more technical reasons:

DocBook 4.x is feature-frozen

DocBook V4.5 is the last version of DocBook in the 4.x series. Any new DocBook development, like the addition of new elements, will be done in DocBook V5.0. It is only a matter of time before new elements are added into DocBook V5.0, but they are not likely to be back-ported into DocBook 4.x. DocBook 4.x will be in maintenance mode and errata will be published if necessary.

DocBook V5.0 offers new functionality
DocBook V5.0 provides significant improvements over DocBook 4.x. For example, there is general markup for annotations, a new and more flexible system for linking, and unified markup for information sections using the info element.

DocBook V5.0 is more extensible
Having DocBook V5.0 in a separate namespace allows you to easily mix DocBook markup with other XML-based languages such as SVG, MathML, XHTML, or even FooBarML.

DocBook V5.0 is easier to customize
RELAX NG offers many powerful constructs that make customization much easier than it would be using a DTD (see Chapter 5).

Schema Jungle

Schemas for DocBook V5.0 are available in several formats at *http://www.oasis-open .org/docbook/xml/5.0/* (or the mirror at *http://docbook.org/xml/5.0/*). Only the RELAX NG schema is normative, and it is preferred over the other schema languages. For your convenience there are also DTD and W3C XML Schema versions provided for DocBook V5.0. However, neither the DTD nor the W3C XML schema can capture all the constraints of DocBook V5.0. This means that a document that validates against the DTD or XML schema is not necessarily valid against the RELAX NG schema, and thus may not be a valid DocBook V5.0 document.

DTD and W3C XML Schema versions of the DocBook V5.0 grammar are provided as a convenience for users who want to use DocBook V5.0 with legacy tools that don't support RELAX NG. Authors are encouraged to switch to RELAX NG-based tools as soon as possible, or at least to validate documents against the RELAX NG schema before further processing.

Some document constraints can't be expressed in grammar-based schema languages like RELAX NG or W3C XML Schema. To define these additional constraints DocBook V5.0 uses Schematron. We recommend that you validate your document against both the RELAX NG and Schematron schemas.

Where to Get the Schemas

The latest versions of schemas can be obtained from *http://docbook.org/schemas/5x .html*. At the time this was written the latest version was 5.0. Individual schemas are available at the following locations:

RELAX NG schema
http://docbook.org/xml/5.0/rng/docbook.rng

RELAX NG schema in compact syntax
    http://docbook.org/xml/5.0/rng/docbook.rnc
DTD
    http://docbook.org/xml/5.0/dtd/docbook.dtd
W3C XML Schema
    http://docbook.org/xml/5.0/xsd/docbook.xsd
Schematron schema with additional checks
    http://docbook.org/xml/5.0/sch/docbook.sch

These schemas are also available from the mirror at *http://www.oasis-open.org/docbook/xml/5.0/*.

DocBook Documentation

Detailed documentation about each DocBook V5.0 element can be found in DocBook Element Reference on page 83 in this book.

DocBook XSL: The Complete Guide [Stayton07] by Bob Stayton is the essential reference for the DocBook stylesheets.

Backward Compatibility

Whether you're just getting started with DocBook, or curating a collection of tens of thousands of DocBook documents, one question that you have to consider is "how stable is DocBook?" Will the documents that you write today still be useful tomorrow, or next year, or in the next century?

This question may seem particularly pertinent if you're in the process of converting a collection of DocBook 4.x documents to DocBook V5.0 because we introduced a number of backward-incompatible changes in V5.0.

The DocBook Technical Committee understands that the community benefits from the long-term stability of the DocBook family of schemas. We also understand that DocBook must continue to adapt and change in order to remain relevant in a changing world.

All changes, and especially changes that are backward incompatible (changes that make a currently valid document no longer valid under a new version of the schema), have a cost associated with them. The technical committee must balance those costs against the need to remain responsive to the community's desire to see DocBook grow to cover the new use cases that inevitably arise in documentation.

With that in mind, the DocBook Technical Committee has adopted the following policy on backward-incompatible changes. This policy spells out when backward-incompatible changes can occur and how much notice the technical committee must provide before adopting a schema that is backward incompatible with the current release.

This policy allows DocBook to continue to change and adapt while simultaneously guaranteeing that existing users will have sufficient advance notice to develop reasonable migration plans.

With respect to schema changes, the technical committee asserts that the following points will always apply:

- A point release (X.1 to X.2, X.2 to X.3, X.1 to X.1.2, etc.) *will not* contain any backward-incompatible changes.
- A major release (X.1 to Y.0, X.2 to Y.0, X.1.2 to Y.0, etc.) *may* contain backward-incompatible changes if:
  — the change was announced in the release notes for the previous version (major or minor) and
  — the change was announced in a release that occurred at least six months previously.

By these rules, the technical committee can announce, in V5.1, for example, its plans to make a backward-incompatible change in V6.0. Then, in V6.0, if it's been at least six months since V5.1 was released, it can make that change.

As a general rule, the technical committee tries to avoid backward-incompatible changes.

## CHAPTER 2

Creating DocBook Documents

This chapter explains in concrete, practical terms how to make DocBook documents. It's an overview of all the kinds of markup that are possible in DocBook documents. It explains how to create several kinds of DocBook documents: books, sets of books, chapters, articles, and reference manual entries. The idea is to give you enough basic information to actually start writing. The information here is intentionally skeletal; you can find the details in the reference section of this book.

Making an XML Document

An XML document consists of an optional XML declaration, an optional Document Type Declaration, which includes an optional internal subset, and a document (or root) element. We'll discuss each of these in turn.

In XML vocabularies like DocBook, which are defined with RELAX NG (and also in the case of vocabularies defined with W3C's XML Schema), it is common to omit the Document Type Declaration entirely. The Document Type Declaration associates a document with a particular Document Type Definition (DTD).

An XML Declaration

XML documents often begin with an XML declaration that identifies a few simple aspects of the document, for example:

```
<?xml version="1.0" encoding="utf-8"?>
```

Identifying the version of XML ensures that future changes to the XML specification will not alter the semantics of this document. The encoding declaration tells the processor what character encoding this document uses. It must match the actual encoding that you use. The complete details of the XML declaration are described in the W3C standard, *Extensible Markup Language (XML) 1.0* [XML].

If your document uses XML 1.0 and an encoding of either utf-8 or utf-16, the XML declaration is not required. But it is never wrong to include it. If you do not include an

XML declaration, your document must conform to XML 1.0. If you want to use XML 1.1, you must include an XML declaration and specify `version="1.1"` in it.

The XML declaration is syntactically similar to a processing instruction, but it is not one. The XML declaration, if it is present, must be absolutely the first thing in your document and it may not appear anywhere else.

A Document Type Declaration

XML documents don't require a DTD, and if you are using RELAX NG, often they will not include one. Historically, DocBook XML documents have almost always had one.

The Document Type Declaration identifies what the root element of the document will be and may specify the DTD that should be used when parsing the document. A typical Document Type Declaration for a DocBook V4.5 document looks like this:

```
<?xml version='1.0'?>
<!DOCTYPE book PUBLIC "-//OASIS//DTD DocBook XML V4.5//EN"
                "http://www.oasis-open.org/docbook/xml/4.5/docbookx.dtd">
```

This declaration indicates that the root element will be `book` and that the DTD used will be DocBook V4.5, identified with both its public and system identifiers. In this example, the DTD is identified with an HTTP URI. System identifiers in XML must be URIs. Almost all systems accept filenames and interpret them locally as `file:` URLs, but it's always correct to fully qualify them.

You can specify a DTD for DocBook V5.0 documents:

```
<?xml version='1.0'?>
<!DOCTYPE book PUBLIC "-//OASIS//DTD DocBook V5.0//EN"
                "http://www.oasis-open.org/docbook/xml/5.0/docbook.dtd">
```

But the limited constraints that can be expressed in DTDs mean that the resultant document may or may not *really* be valid DocBook V5.0. The normative schema for DocBook V5.0 is the RELAX NG grammar with its Schematron annotations.

The only reason to use a DTD with DocBook V5.0 is if your editing environment (or other tool) requires one, for example, for syntax-directed editing. If you're using a tool that requires DTDs, check with the vendor, as maybe a more recent version is available that supports RELAX NG.

An Internal Subset

Even if you aren't using the DTD version of DocBook V5.0, you may still want to use a Document Type Declaration to provide local declarations such as entities:

```
<?xml version='1.0'?>
<!DOCTYPE book [
<!ENTITY nwalsh "Norman Walsh">
<!ENTITY chap1 SYSTEM "chap1.xml">
```

```
<!ENTITY chap2 SYSTEM "chap2.xml">
]>
```

These declarations form what is known as the internal subset. In this example, the DTD has been omitted, but the two are not mutually exclusive. If you are using a DTD (which is technically known as the *external subset*), you can include the internal subset immediately after the DTD:

```
<?xml version='1.0'?>
<!DOCTYPE book PUBLIC "-//OASIS//DTD DocBook V5.0/EN"
               "http://www.oasis-open.org/docbook/xml/5.0/docbook.dtd" [
<!ENTITY nwalsh "Norman Walsh">
<!ENTITY chap1 SYSTEM "chap1.xml">
<!ENTITY chap2 SYSTEM "chap2.xml">
]>
```

When both are specified, the internal subset is parsed *first*. If multiple declarations for an entity occur, the first declaration is used. This means that declarations in the internal subset override declarations in the external subset.

The Document (or Root) Element

All XML documents must have exactly one root element, although it may have sibling comments and processing instructions. If the document has a Document Type Declaration, the root element usually immediately follows it:

```
<?xml version='1.0'?>
<!DOCTYPE book [
<!ENTITY nwalsh "Norman Walsh">
<!ENTITY chap1 SYSTEM "chap1.xml">
<!ENTITY chap2 SYSTEM "chap2.xml">
]>
<book xmlns="http://docbook.org/ns/docbook" version="5.0">…</book>
```

The important point is that the root element must be physically present immediately after the Document Type Declaration. You cannot place the root element of the document in an external entity.

Physical Divisions: Breaking a Document into Separate Files

The rest of this chapter describes how you can break documents into logical chunks, such as books, chapters, sections, and so on. Before we begin, and while the subject of the internal subset is fresh in your mind, let's take a quick look at how to break documents into separate files.

Actually, we've already told you how to do it. If you recall, in the preceding sections we had declarations of the form:

```
<!ENTITY name SYSTEM "filename">
```

If you refer to the entity *name* in your document after this declaration, the system will insert the contents of the file *filename* into your document at that point. So, if you've got a book that consists of three chapters and two appendixes, you might create a file called *book.xml*, which looks like this:

```
<!DOCTYPE book [
<!ENTITY chap1 SYSTEM "chap1.xml">
<!ENTITY chap2 SYSTEM "chap2.xml">
<!ENTITY chap3 SYSTEM "chap3.xml">
<!ENTITY appa SYSTEM "appa.xml">
<!ENTITY appb SYSTEM "appb.xml">
]>
<book xmlns="http://docbook.org/ns/docbook" version="5.0">
<title>My First Book</title>
&chap1;
&chap2;
&chap3;
&appa;
&appb;
</book>
```

You can then write the chapters and appendixes conveniently in separate files.

Documents that you reference with external parsed entities cannot have a Document Type Declaration. For example, Chapter 1 might begin like this:

```
<chapter xml:id="ch1"><title>My First Chapter</title>
<para>My first paragraph.</para>
...
```

But it must not begin with its own Document Type Declaration:

```
<!DOCTYPE chapter>
<chapter xmlns="http://docbook.org/ns/docbook"
         xml:id="ch1">
<title>My First Chapter</title>
<para>My first paragraph.</para>
...
```

It is also possible to construct documents from different files using XInclude. Recasting the previous example using XInclude yields:

```
<book xmlns="http://docbook.org/ns/docbook"
      xmlns:xi="http://www.w3.org/2001/XInclude" version="5.0">
<title>My First Book</title>
<xi:include href="chap1.xml"/>
<xi:include href="chap2.xml"/>
<xi:include href="chap3.xml"/>
<xi:include href="appa.xml"/>
<xi:include href="appb.xml"/>
</book>
```

Notice that we can completely omit the Document Type Declaration in this case, but we must declare the XInclude namespace.

The essential trade-offs between external parsed entities and XInclude are:

- XInclude can be used in a document that does not have a Document Type Declaration. Many web services applications (ones that rely on SOAP, anyway) forbid a Document Type Declaration and therefore cannot use entities of any sort.

- The documents *referenced by* XInclude are complete, free-standing XML documents. They can declare their own local entities using a Document Type Declaration. Documents referenced by external parsed entities cannot have a Document Type Declaration. If they use entities, those entities must be declared in the document that does the including.

- External parsed entities can have multiple top-level elements. They are not required to be "single rooted." XIncluded documents must be wholly well-formed XML.

- All XML validators support external parsed entities. (Validators that do not *are not* conformant XML processors.) XInclude is a separate specification and may or may not be supported by tools.

- The XML validator expands entities and therefore "sees" the entire document. This means that ID/IDREF links can freely cross entity boundaries. Because XIncluded documents are free-standing, a document containing an IDREF that crosses a document boundary cannot be valid. It can be well-formed, and processors can do the right thing, but the validator cannot determine that the document is valid. What's more, the same ID value can occur in several XIncluded documents without causing a validity error. This may cause subsequent processing to fail.

- As time passes, the use of DTD-based mechanisms like entities is diminishing. If you have an eye on the future, to the extent that it is practical, it is probably better to use XInclude than entities.

Logical Divisions: The Categories of Elements in DocBook

DocBook elements can be divided broadly into these categories:

> Sets
> Books
> Divisions, which divide books
> Components, which divide books or divisions
> Sections, which subdivide components
> Meta-information elements
> Block elements
> Inline elements

In the rest of this section, we'll describe briefly the elements that make up these categories. This section is designed to give you an overview. It is not an exhaustive list of every element in DocBook.

For more information about any specific element and the elements that it may contain, consult the reference page for the element in question.

Sets

A set contains two or more books. It's the hierarchical top of DocBook. You use the set tag, for example, for a series of books on a single subject that you want to access and maintain as a single unit, such as the manuals for series of computer systems or the documentation (tutorial, reference, etc.) for a programming language. Sets are allowed to contain other sets, though this is not common.

Books

A book is probably the most common top-level element in a document. The DocBook definition of a book is very loose and general. Given the variety of books authored with DocBook and the number of different conventions for book organization used around the world, any attempt to impose a strict ordering of elements would make the content model extremely complex. Therefore, DocBook gives you free rein. You can use a local customization (see Chapter 5) if you want to impose a more strict ordering for your applications.

A book consists of a mixture of the following elements:

Dedication
> The dedication pages almost always occur at the front of a book.

Navigational components
> There are a couple of component-level elements designed for navigation: toc, for Tables of Contents and Lists of Titles (for lists of figures, tables, examples, etc.); and index, for indexes.

Divisions
> Divisions are the first hierarchical level below book. Divisions contain parts and references. A part contains components. A reference contains refentrys. These are discussed more thoroughly in "Making a Reference Page" on page 36.

> Books can contain components directly and are not required to contain divisions.

Components
> These are the chapter-like elements of a book.

Components

Components are the chapter-like elements of a book or part: preface, chapter, appendix, glossary, and bibliography. An article can also occur at the component level. We describe articles in more detail in "Making an Article" on page 36. Components generally contain block elements and/or sections, and some can contain navigational components and refentrys.

Sections

There are several flavors of sectioning elements in DocBook:

sect1, sect2, sect3, sect4, sect5
> The sect1...sect5 elements are sectioning elements. They can occur in most component-level elements. These numbered section elements must be properly nested (sect2s can only occur inside sect1s, sect3s can only occur inside sect2s, and so on). There are five levels of numbered sections.

section
> The section element is an alternative to numbered sections. The section element is recursive, meaning that you can nest it to any depth desired.

simplesect
> In addition to numbered sections, there is the simplesect element. It is a terminal section that can occur at any level, but it cannot have any other sectioning element nested within it.
>
> A distinguishing feature of simplesect is that it does not occur in the Table of Contents.

bridgehead
> A bridgehead provides a section title without any containing section.

refsect1...refsect3
> These elements, which occur only in refentrys, are analogous to the numbered section elements in components. There are only three levels of numbered section elements in a refentry.

refsection
> The refsection element is a recursive division in a refentry. It is an alternative to the numbered reference section tags (refsect1...refsect3). Like the section element, the refsection element is recursive.

glossdiv, bibliodiv, *and* indexdiv
> The glossary, bibliography, and index elements can be broken into top-level divisions, but not sections. Unlike sections, these elements do not nest.

Meta-Information

All of the elements at the section level and above, and many other elements, include a wrapper for meta-information about the content. That element is named info. In earlier versions of DocBook, there were many similarly named elements for this purpose: bookinfo, chapterinfo, etc. In DocBook V5.0, there is only one.

The meta-information wrapper is designed to contain bibliographic information about the content (author, title, publisher, and so on) as well as other meta-information such as revision histories, keyword sets, and index terms.

An `info` can contain:

title
: The text of the title of a section of a document or of a formal block-level element

titleabbrev
: The abbreviation of a title

subtitle
: The subtitle of a document

abstract
: A summary

address
: A real-world address, generally a postal address

annotation
: An annotation

artpagenums
: The page numbers of an article as published

author
: The name of an individual author

authorgroup
: A wrapper for author information when a document has multiple authors or collaborators

authorinitials
: The initials or other short identifier for an author

bibliocoverage
: The spatial or temporal coverage of a document

biblioid
: An identifier for a document

bibliomisc
: Untyped bibliographic information

bibliomset
: A cooked container for related bibliographic information

bibliorelation
: The relationship of a document to another

biblioset
: A raw container for related bibliographic information

bibliosource
: The source of a document

collab
: Identifies a collaborator

confgroup
: A wrapper for document meta-information about a conference

contractnum
: The contract number of a document

contractsponsor
: The sponsor of a contract

copyright
: Copyright information about a document

date
: The date of publication or revision of a document

edition
: The name or number of an edition of a document

editor
: The name of the editor of a document

extendedlink
: An XLink extended link

issuenum
: The number of an issue of a journal

itermset
: A set of index terms in the meta-information of a document

keywordset
: A set of keywords describing the content of a document

legalnotice
: A statement of legal obligations or requirements

mediaobject
: A displayed media object (video, audio, image, etc.)

orgname
: The name of an organization

othercredit
: A person or entity, other than an author or editor, credited in a document

pagenums
: The numbers of the pages in a book, for use in a bibliographic entry

printhistory
: The printing history of a document

productname
: The formal name of a product

productnumber
: A number assigned to a product

pubdate
: The date of publication of a document

publisher
: The publisher of a document

publishername
: The name of the publisher of a document

releaseinfo
: Information about a particular release of a document

revhistory
: A history of the revisions to a document

seriesvolnums
: Numbers of the volumes in a series of books

subjectset
: A set of terms describing the subject matter of a document

volumenum
: The volume number of a document in a set (as of books in a set or articles in a journal)

The title, titleabbrev, and subtitle elements can usually appear either immediately before or inside the info wrapper (but not both). This means you don't need the extra wrapper in the common case where all you want to specify is a title.

Block Elements

The block elements occur immediately below the component and sectioning elements. These are the (roughly) paragraph-level elements in DocBook. They can be divided into a number of categories: lists, admonitions, line-specific environments, synopses of several sorts, tables, figures, examples, and a dozen or more miscellaneous elements.

Block versus inline elements

At the paragraph level, it's convenient to divide elements into two classes, *block* and *inline*. From a structural point of view, this distinction is based loosely on their relative size, but it's easiest to describe the difference in terms of their presentation.

Block elements are usually presented with a paragraph (or larger) break before and after them. Most can contain other block elements, and many can contain character data and inline elements. Paragraphs, lists, sidebars, tables, and block quotations are all common examples of block elements.

Inline elements are generally represented without any obvious breaks. The most common distinguishing mark of inline elements is a font change, but inline elements may present no visual distinction at all. Inline elements contain character data and possibly other inline elements, but they never contain block elements. Inline elements are used to mark up data such as cross-references, filenames, commands, options, subscripts and superscripts, and glossary terms.

Lists

There are eight list elements in DocBook:

calloutlist
> A list of callouts and their descriptions. The callouts are marks, frequently numbered and typically on a graphic (imageobjectco) or verbatim environment (programlistingco or screenco), that are described in a calloutlist.

bibliolist
> A list of bibliography entries (biblioentry or bibliomixed elements).

glosslist
> A list of glossary terms and their definitions.

itemizedlist
> An unordered (bulleted) list. There are attributes to control the marks used.

orderedlist
> A numbered list. There are attributes to control the type of enumeration.

segmentedlist
> A repeating set of named items. For example, a list of states and their capitals might be represented as a segmentedlist. Segmented lists consist of segtitles, seglistitems, and segs.

simplelist
> An unadorned list of items. simplelists can be inline or arranged in columns.

variablelist
> A list of terms and definitions or descriptions. (This list of list types is a variablelist.)

Admonitions

There are five types of admonitions in DocBook: caution, important, note, tip, and warning.

All of the admonitions have the same structure: an optional title followed by paragraph-level elements. DocBook does not impose any specific semantics on the individual admonitions. For example, DocBook does not mandate that warnings be reserved for cases where bodily harm can result.

Line-specific environments

These environments preserve whitespace and line breaks in the source text. DocBook does not provide the equivalent of HTML's br tag, so there's no way to interject a line break into normal running text.

address

The address element is intended for postal addresses. In addition to being line-specific, address contains additional elements suitable for marking up names and addresses: city, country, fax, otheraddr, personname, phone, pob, postcode, state, and street.

literallayout

A literallayout does not have any semantic association beyond the preservation of whitespace and line breaks. In particular, while programlisting and screen are frequently presented in a fixed-width font, a change of fonts is not ordinarily implied by literallayout.

programlisting *and* programlistingco

The programlisting and programlistingco elements are verbatim environments, usually presented in Courier or some other fixed-width font, for program sources, code fragments, and similar listings. The two elements are the same, except that programlistingco supports markup for callouts.

screen *and* screenco

The screen and screenco elements are verbatim or literal environments for text screen captures, other fragments of an ASCII display, and similar things. screen is also a frequent catchall for any verbatim text. The two elements are the same, except that screenco supports markup for callouts.

screenshot

screenshot is actually a wrapper for a mediaobject intended for screenshots of a GUI, for example.

synopsis

A synopsis is a verbatim environment for command and function synopses.

Examples, figures, and tables

Examples, figures, and tables are supported with the block-level elements: example, informalexample, figure, informalfigure, table, and informaltable.

The distinction between formal and informal elements is that formal elements have titles while informal ones do not.

DocBook supports CALS tables (defined with tgroup, colspec, spanspec, thead, tfoot, tbody, row, entry, entrytbl, and caption) and HTML tables (defined with col, colgroup, thead, tfoot, tbody, tr, td, and caption).

Paragraphs

There are three paragraph elements: para, simpara (simple paragraphs may not contain other block-level elements), and formalpara (formal paragraphs have titles).

Equations

There are two block-equation elements, `equation` and `informalequation` (for inline equations, use `inlineequation`).

Informal equations don't have titles. For reasons of backward compatibility, `equations` are not required to have titles. However, it may be more difficult for some stylesheet languages to properly enumerate `equation`s if they lack titles.

Graphics and media

Graphics occur most frequently in `figure`s and `screenshot`s, but they can also occur outside those wrappers. DocBook considers a `mediaobject` a block element, even if it occurs in an inline context. For graphics that you want to be represented inline, use `inlinemediaobject`.

Media objects (and inline media objects) can contain five kinds of content:

`audioobject`
: A wrapper for audio data and its associated meta-information. (Which contains `audiodata`.)

`imageobject`
: A wrapper for image data and its associated meta-information. (Which contains `imagedata`.)

`imageobjectco`
: A wrapper for an image object with callouts. (Which contains `imagedata` and callout-related information).

`videoobject`
: A wrapper for video data and its associated meta-information. (Which contains `videodata`.)

`textobject`
: A wrapper for a text description of an object and its associated meta-information. (Which contains `textdata`.)

The audio, image, video, and text data in a media object are, by definition, alternatives.

Questions and answers

The `qandaset` element is suitable for FAQs (Frequently Asked Questions) and other similar collections of questions and answers. Each `qandaentry` contains a `question` and its `answer`(s). The set of questions and answers can be divided into sections with `qandadiv`.

Procedures and tasks

A `procedure` contains `steps`, which may contain `substeps` or `stepalternatives`.

The `task` element is a wrapper around the `procedure` element that provides additional, optional elements, including `tasksummary`, `taskprerequisites`, `example`, and `taskrelated`.

Synopses

DocBook provides a number of elements for describing command, function, and class synopses:

`cmdsynopsis`
> A syntax summary for a software command. A `cmdsynopsis` contains `arg`, `command`, and `group` elements. For long synopses, the `sbr` tag can be used to indicate where a break should occur. Complex synopses can be composed from `synopfragments`.

`funcsynopsis`
> The syntax summary for a function definition. A function synopsis consists of one or more `funcprototypes` and may include additional, literal information in a `funcsynopsisinfo`. Each prototype consists of `modifiers`, a `funcdef`, and a collection of `paramdef`, `varargs`, and/or `void` elements.

`classsynopsis`
> The syntax summary for a class definition. A class synopsis consists of one or more `ooclass`, `ooexception`, or `oointerface` elements followed by zero or more `constructorsynopsis`, `destructorsynopsis`, `fieldsynopsis`, and `methodsynopsis` elements Like `funcsynopsis`, it may include additional, literal information, in this case, in a `classsynopsisinfo`.

Miscellaneous block elements

The following block elements are also available:

`blockquote`
> A block quotation. Block quotations may have `attributions`.

`epigraph`
> A short introduction, typically a quotation, at the beginning of a document or component. The `epigraph` element may include an `attribution` element.

`msgset`
> A set of related error messages.

`sidebar`
> A sidebar.

Inline Elements

Users of DocBook are provided with a surfeit of inline elements. Inline elements are used to mark up running text. In published documents, inline elements often cause a font change or other small change, but they do not cause line or paragraph breaks.

In practice, writers generally settle on the tagging of inline elements that suits their time and subject matter. This may be a large number of elements or only a handful. What is important is that you choose to mark up not every possible item, but only those for which distinctive tagging will be useful in the production of the finished document for the readers who will search through it.

The following comprehensive list may be a useful tool for the process of narrowing down the elements that you will choose to mark up; it is not intended to overwhelm you by its sheer length. For convenience, we've divided the inlines into several subcategories.

The classification used here is not meant to be authoritative, only helpful in providing a feel for the nature of the inlines. Several elements appear in more than one category, and arguments could be made to support the placement of additional elements in other categories or entirely new categories.

Traditional publishing inlines

These inlines identify things that commonly occur in general writing:

abbrev
: An abbreviation, especially one followed by a period.

acronym
: An often pronounceable word made from the initial (or selected) letters of a name or phrase.

emphasis
: Emphasized text.

footnote
: A footnote. The location of the footnote element identifies the location of the first reference to the footnote. Additional references to the same footnote can be inserted with footnoteref.

phrase
: A span of text.

quote
: An inline quotation.

trademark
: A trademark.

Cross-references

The cross-reference inlines identify both explicit cross-references, such as `link`, and implicit cross-references, such as `glossterm`. You can make most of the implicit references explicit with a `linkend` attribute.

anchor
: A spot in the document

citation
: An inline bibliographic reference to another published work

citerefentry
: A citation to a reference page

citetitle
: The title of a cited work

firstterm
: The first occurrence of a term

glossterm
: A glossary term

link
: A hypertext link

olink
: A link that addresses its target indirectly

xref
: A cross-reference to another part of the document

Markup

These inlines are used to mark up text for special presentation:

foreignphrase
: A word or phrase in a language other than the primary language of the document

wordasword
: A word meant specifically as a word and not representing anything else

computeroutput
: Data, generally text, displayed or presented by a computer

literal
: Inline text that is some literal value

markup
: A string of formatting markup in text that is to be represented literally

prompt
: A character or string indicating the start of an input field in a computer display

replaceable
> Content that may or must be replaced by the user

tag
> A component of XML (or SGML) markup

userinput
> Data entered by the user

Mathematics

DocBook does not define a complete set of elements for representing equations. The *Mathematical Markup Language (MathML)* [MathML] is a standard that defines a comprehensive grammar for representing equations. MathML markup may be used in any of the equation elements (equation,informalequation, and inlineequation). For simple mathematics equations that do not require extensive markup, the mathphrase element is an alternative.

inlineequation
> A mathematical equation or expression occurring inline

mathphrase
> A mathematical phrase that can be represented with ordinary text and a small amount of markup

subscript
> A subscript (as in H_2O, the molecular formula for water)

superscript
> A superscript (as in x^2, the mathematical notation for x multiplied by itself)

User interfaces

These elements describe aspects of a user interface:

accel
> A graphical user interface (GUI) keyboard shortcut

guibutton
> The text on a button in a GUI

guiicon
> A graphic and/or text appearing as an icon in a GUI

guilabel
> The text of a label in a GUI

guimenu
> The name of a menu in a GUI

guimenuitem
> The name of a terminal menu item in a GUI

guisubmenu
: The name of a submenu in a GUI

keycap
: The text printed on a key on a keyboard

keycode
: The internal, frequently numeric, identifier for a key on a keyboard

keycombo
: A combination of input actions

keysym
: The symbolic name of a key on a keyboard

menuchoice
: A selection or series of selections from a menu

mousebutton
: The conventional name of a mouse button

shortcut
: A key combination for an action that is also accessible through a menu

Programming languages and constructs

Many of the technical inlines in DocBook are related to programming:

classname
: The name of a class, in the object-oriented programming sense

constant
: A programming or system constant

errorcode
: An error code

errorname
: An error name

errortype
: The classification of an error message

function
: The name of a function or subroutine, as in a programming language

literal
: Inline text that is some literal value

msgtext
: The actual text of a message component in a message set

parameter
: A value or a symbolic reference to a value

property
: A unit of data associated with some part of a computer system

replaceable
: Content that may or must be replaced by the user

returnvalue
: The value returned by a function

symbol
: A name that is replaced by a value before processing

token
: A unit of information

type
: The classification of a value

varname
: The name of a variable

Operating systems

These inlines identify parts of an operating system, or an operating environment:

application
: The name of a software program

command
: The name of an executable program or other software command

envar
: A software environment variable

filename
: The name of a file

msgtext
: The actual text of a message component in a message set

option
: An option for a software command

parameter
: A value or a symbolic reference to a value

prompt
: A character or string indicating the start of an input field in a computer display

systemitem
: A system-related item or term

General purpose

There are also a number of general-purpose technical inlines:

`application`
> The name of a software program

`database`
> The name of a database, or part of a database

`email`
> An email address

`filename`
> The name of a file

`hardware`
> A physical part of a computer system

`literal`
> Inline text that is some literal value

`option`
> An option for a software command

`optional`
> Optional information

`replaceable`
> Content that may or must be replaced by the user

`symbol`
> A name that is replaced by a value before processing

`token`
> A unit of information

`type`
> The classification of a value

Roots: Starting Your DocBook Document

There's one final detail of the physical and logical structures of DocBook that we've left out: where can your document begin? In other words, what are the valid "document elements" of DocBook documents? Naturally, you can start at set and book, but can you also start at chapter? What about para or personname?

If you come to DocBook from the DTD days, this question may seem odd. A DTD doesn't provide any facility to impose constraints on where a document can begin. If the element occurs in the DTD, you can start with it.

RELAX NG does give us the ability to impose such constraints. In fact, it *requires* that we do. Of course, we could make the constraint vacuous by listing every possible element as a potential document element.

But, on reflection, that's not necessarily the best choice. It's valuable to have metadata associated with documents, so only elements with an `info` element can be root elements, but not every element with an `info` element is currently included. In DocBook V5.0 the following elements are available: `acknowledgements`, `appendix`, `article`, `bibliography`, `book`, `chapter`, `colophon`, `dedication`, `glossary`, `index`, `para`, `part`, `preface`, `refentry`, `reference`, `refsect1`, `refsect2`, `refsect3`, `refsection`, `sect1`, `sect2`, `sect3`, `sect4`, `sect5`, `section`, `set`, `setindex`, and `toc`.

With the next point release of DocBook, V5.1, the technical committee may take the position that any element that can contain an `info` wrapper can be a document element. This would dramatically expand the list of valid root elements.

Making a DocBook Book

A typical `book`, in English at least, consists of some meta-information in an `info` (`title`, `author`, `copyright`, etc.), one or more `preface`s, several `chapter`s, and perhaps a few `appendix`es. A `book` may also contain `bibliography`s, `glossary`s, `index`es, and a `colophon`.

Example 2-1 shows the structure of a typical book. Additional content is required where the ellipses occur.

Example 2-1. A typical book

```
<book>
<info>
  <title>My First Book</title>
  <author><firstname>Jane</firstname><surname>Doe</surname></author>
  <copyright><year>2010</year><holder>Jane Doe</holder></copyright>
</info>
<preface><title>Foreword</title> ... </preface>
<chapter> ... </chapter>
<chapter> ... </chapter>
<chapter> ... </chapter>
<appendix> ... </appendix>
<appendix> ... </appendix>
<index> ... </index>
</book>
```

Making a Chapter

`chapter`s, `preface`s, and `appendix`es all have a similar structure. They consist of a `title`, possibly some additional meta-information, and any number of block-level elements followed by any number of top-level sections. Each section may in turn contain any number of block-level elements followed by any number from the next section level, as shown in Example 2-2.

Example 2-2. A typical chapter

```
<chapter><title>My Chapter</title>
  <para> ... </para>
  <section><title>First Section</title>
    <para> ... </para>
    <example> ... </example>
  </section>
</chapter>
```

Making an Article

For documents smaller than a book, such as journal articles, white papers, or technical notes, `article` is frequently the most logical starting point. The body of an `article` is essentially the same as the body of a `chapter` or any other component-level element, as shown in Example 2-3.

`articles` may include `appendixes`, `bibliographys`, `indexes`, and `glossarys`.

Example 2-3. A typical article

```
<article>
  <info>
    <title>My Article</title>
    <author><honorific>Dr</honorific><firstname>Emilio</firstname>
            <surname>Lizardo</surname></author>
  </info>
  <para> ... </para>
  <section><title>On the Possibility of Going Home</title>
    <para> ... </para>
  </section>
  <bibliography> ... </bibliography>
</article>
```

Making a Reference Page

The reference page or manual page in DocBook was inspired by, and in fact designed to reproduce, the common UNIX "manpage" concept. (We use the word "page" loosely here to mean a document of variable length containing reference material on a specific topic.) DocBook is rich in markup tailored for such documents, which often vary greatly in content, however well structured they may be. To reflect both the structure and the variability of such texts, DocBook specifies that reference pages have a strict sequence of parts, even though several of them are actually optional.

Of the following sequence of elements that may appear in a `refentry`, only two are obligatory: `refnamediv` and either `refsect1` or `refsection`.

info

> The `info` element contains meta-information about the reference page (which should not be confused with `refmeta`, which it precedes). It marks up information

about the author of the document, or the product to which it pertains, or the document's revision history, or other such information.

refmeta

refmeta contains a title for the reference page (which may be inferred if the refmeta element is not present) and an indication of the volume number in which this reference page occurs. The manvolnum is a very UNIX-centric concept. In traditional UNIX documentation, the subject of a reference page is typically identified by name and volume number; this allows you to distinguish between the *uname* command, "uname(1)" in volume 1 of the documentation, and the uname function, "uname(3)" in volume 3.

Additional information of this sort, such as conformance or vendor information specific to the particular environment you are working in, may be stored in refmiscinfo.

refnamediv

The first obligatory element is refnamediv, which is a wrapper for information about whatever you're documenting, rather than the document itself. It can begin with a refdescriptor if several items are being documented as a group and the group has a name. The refnamediv must contain at least one refname, that is, the name of whatever you're documenting, and a single short statement that sums up the use or function of the item(s) at a glance: its refpurpose. Also available is the refclass, intended to detail the operating system configurations that the software element in question supports.

If no refentrytitle is given in the refmeta, the title of the reference page is the refdescriptor, if present, or the first refname.

refsynopsisdiv

A refsynopsisdiv is intended to provide a quick synopsis of the topic covered by the reference page. For commands, this is generally a syntax summary of the command, and for functions, the function prototype, but other options are possible. A title is allowed, but not required, presumably because the application that processes reference pages will generate the appropriate title if it is not given. In traditional UNIX documentation, its title is always "Synopsis."

refsect1...refsect3

Within refentrys, there are only three levels of sectioning elements: refsect1, refsect2, and refsect3.

refsection

As with sect1, sect2, etc., there is a recursive version of the reference section elements: refsection.

Example 2-4 shows the beginning of a refentry that illustrates one possible reference page.

Example 2-4. A sample reference page

```
<refentry xml:id="printf">
  <refmeta>
    <refentrytitle>printf</refentrytitle>
      <manvolnum>3S</manvolnum>
  </refmeta>

  <refnamediv>
    <refname>printf</refname>
    <refname>fprintf</refname>
    <refname>sprintf</refname>
    <refpurpose>print formatted output</refpurpose>
  </refnamediv>

  <refsynopsisdiv>
    <funcsynopsis>
      <funcsynopsisinfo>
        #include <stdio.h>
      </funcsynopsisinfo>

      <funcprototype>
        <funcdef>int <function>printf</function></funcdef>
        <paramdef>const char *<parameter>format</parameter></paramdef>
        <varargs/>
      </funcprototype>

      <funcprototype>
        <funcdef>int <function>fprintf</function></funcdef>
        <paramdef>FILE *<parameter>strm</parameter></paramdef>
        <paramdef>const char *<parameter>format</parameter></paramdef>
        <varargs/>
      </funcprototype>

      <funcprototype>
        <funcdef>int <function>sprintf</function></funcdef>
        <paramdef>char *<parameter>s</parameter></paramdef>
        <paramdef>const char *<parameter>format</parameter></paramdef>
        <varargs/>
      </funcprototype>
    </funcsynopsis>

  </refsynopsisdiv>

  <refsect1><title>Description</title>
    <para><indexterm><primary>functions</primary>
                      <secondary>printf</secondary></indexterm>
          <indexterm><primary>printing function</primary></indexterm>

      <function>printf</function> places output on the standard
      output stream stdout.
    </para>
  </refsect1>
</refentry>
```

Making Front and Back Matter

DocBook contains markup for the usual variety of front and back matter necessary for books and articles: indexes, glossaries, bibliographies, and tables of contents. In many cases, these components are generated automatically, at least in part, from your document by an external processor, but you can create them by hand, and in either case, store them in DocBook.

Some forms of back matter, such as indexes and glossaries, usually require additional markup *in the document* to make generation by an application possible. Bibliographies are usually composed by hand like the rest of your text, unless you are automatically selecting bibliographic entries out of some larger database. Our principal concern here is to acquaint you with the kind of markup you need to include in your documents if you want to construct these components.

Front matter, like the table of contents, is almost always generated automatically from the text of a document by the processing application. If you need information about how to mark up a table of contents in DocBook, please consult the reference page for toc.

Making an Index

In some highly structured documents such as reference manuals, you can automate the whole process of generating an index successfully without altering or adding to the original source. You can design a processing application to select the information and compile it into an adequate index. But this is rare.

In most cases—and even in the case of some reference manuals—a useful index still requires human intervention to mark occurrences of words or concepts that will appear in the text of the index.

Marking index terms

DocBook distinguishes two kinds of index markers: those that are singular and result in a single page entry in the index itself, and those that are multiple and refer to a range of pages.

You put a singular index marker where the subject it refers to actually occurs in your text:

```
<para>
  <indexterm><primary>Big Cats</primary>
  <secondary>Tigers</secondary></indexterm>
  The tiger is a very large cat indeed.
</para>
```

This index term has two levels, primary and secondary. They correspond to an increasing amount of indented text in the resultant index. DocBook allows for three levels of index terms, with the third labeled tertiary.

There are two ways that you can index a range of text. The first is to put index marks at both the beginning and end of the discussion. The mark at the beginning asserts that it is the start of a range, and the mark at the end refers back to the beginning. In this way, the processing application can determine what range of text is indexed. Here's the previous tiger example recast as starting and ending index terms:

```
<para>
  <indexterm xml:id="tiger-desc" class="startofrange">
  <primary>Big Cats</primary>
  <secondary>Tigers</secondary></indexterm>
  The tiger is a very large cat indeed…
</para>
    ⋮
<para>
So much for tigers<indexterm startref="tiger-desc" class="endofrange"/>.
Let's talk about leopards.
</para>
```

Note that the mark at the start of the range identifies itself as the start of a range with the class attribute, and provides an xml:id. The mark at the end of the range points back to the start.

Another way to mark up a range of text is to specify that the entire content of an element, such as a chapter or section, is the complete range. In this case, all you need is for the index term to point to the xml:id of the element that contains the content in question. The zone attribute of indexterm provides this functionality.

One of the interesting features of this method is that the actual index marks do not have to occur anywhere near the text being indexed. It is possible to collect all of them together, for example, in one file, but it is not invalid to have the index marker occur near the element it indexes.

Suppose the discussion of tigers in your document comprises a whole text object (such as a sect1 or a chapter) with an xml:id value of tiger-desc. You can put the following tag anywhere in your document to index that range of text:

```
<indexterm zone="tiger-desc">
<primary>Big Cats</primary>
<secondary>Tigers</secondary></indexterm>
```

DocBook also contains markup for index hits that point to other index hits (e.g., "See Cats, big" or "See also Lions"). See the reference pages for see and seealso.

Printing an index

After you have added the appropriate markup to your document, an external application can use this information to build an index. The resultant index must have information about the page numbers on which the concepts appear. It's usually the document formatter that builds the index. In this case, it may never be instantiated in DocBook.

However, there are applications that can produce an index marked up in DocBook. The following example includes some one- and two-level `indexentry` elements (which correspond to the primary and secondary levels in the `indexterm`s themselves) that begin with the letter D:

```
<index><title>Index</title>
  <indexdiv><title>D</title>
    <indexentry>
      <primaryie>database (bibliographic), 253, 255</primaryie>
        <secondaryie>structure, 255</secondaryie>
        <secondaryie>tools, 259</secondaryie>
    </indexentry>
    <indexentry>
      <primaryie>dates (language specific), 179</primaryie>
    </indexentry>
    <indexentry>
      <primaryie>DC fonts, <emphasis>172</emphasis>, 177</primaryie>
        <secondaryie>Math fonts, 177</secondaryie>
    </indexentry>
  </indexdiv>
</index>
```

The structure of `indexentry` is parallel to the structure of `indexterm`. Where `indexterm` has `primary`, `secondary`, `tertiary`, `see`, and `seealso`, `indexentry` has `primaryie`, `secondaryie`, `tertiaryie`, `seeie`, and `seealsoie`.

Making a Glossary

A `glossary`, like a `bibliography`, is often constructed by hand. However, some applications are capable of building a skeletal index from glossary term markup in the document. If all of your terms are defined in some glossary database, it may even be possible to construct the complete glossary automatically.

To enable automatic glossary generation, or simply automatic linking from glossary terms in the text to glossary entries, you must add markup to your documents. In the text, you mark up a term for compilation later with the inline `glossterm` tag. This tag can have a `linkend` attribute whose value is the ID of the actual entry in the glossary.[*]

For instance, if you have this markup in your document:

```
<glossterm linkend="xml">Extensible Markup Language</glossterm> is a new standard…
```

---

[*] Some formatters are able to establish the link by examining the content of the terms and the glossary. In that case, the author does not need to make explicit links.

your glossary might look like this:

```
<glossary><title>Example Glossary</title>
⋮
  <glossdiv><title>E</title>

    <glossentry xml:id="xml"><glossterm>Extensible Markup Language</glossterm>
      <acronym>XML</acronym>
      <glossdef>
       <para>Some reasonable definition here.</para>
       <glossseealso otherterm="sgml">
      </glossdef>
    </glossentry>

  </glossdiv>
⋮
</glossary>
```

Note that the `glossterm` tag reappears in the glossary to mark up the term and distinguish it from its definition within the `glossentry`. The `xml:id` that the `glossentry` referenced in the text is the ID of the `glossentry` in the `glossary` itself. You can use the link between source and glossary to create a link in electronic formats, as we have done with the HTML and PDF forms of the glossary in this book.

You can use the `baseform` attribute on `glossterm` and `firstterm` when the term marked up in context is in a different form, for example, plural. Here is an example:

```
<para>
  Using <glossterm baseform="DTD">DTDs</glossterm> can
  be hazardous to your sanity.
</para>
```

Making a Bibliography

There are two ways to set up a bibliography in DocBook: you can have the data *raw* or *cooked*. When you use "raw" data, you wrap your entry in the `biblioentry` element and mark up each item individually. The processor determines the display order and supplies punctuation. When you use "cooked" data, you wrap your entry in the `bibliomixed` and provide the data in the order in which you want it displayed, and you include the punctuation.

Here's an example of a raw bibliographical item, wrapped in the `biblioentry` element:

```
<biblioentry xreflabel="Kites75">
  <authorgroup>
    <author><firstname>Andrea</firstname><surname>Bahadur</surname></author>
    <author><firstname>Mark</firstname><surname>Shwarek</surname></author>
  </authorgroup>
  <copyright><year>1974</year><year>1975</year>
    <holder>Product Development International Holding N. V.</holder>
    </copyright>
  <isbn>0-88459-021-6</isbn>
  <publisher>
```

```
  <publishername>Plenary Publications International, Inc.</publishername>
</publisher>
<title>Kites</title>
<subtitle>Ancient Craft to Modern Sport</subtitle>
<pagenums>988-999</pagenums>
<seriesinfo>
  <title>The Family Creative Workshop</title>
  <seriesvolnums>1-22</seriesvolnums>
  <editor>
    <firstname>Allen</firstname>
    <othername role=middle>Davenport</othername>
    <surname>Bragdon</surname>
    <contrib>Editor in Chief</contrib>
  </editor>
</seriesinfo>
</biblioentry>
```

The "raw" data in a `biblioentry` is comprehensive to a fault—there are enough fields to suit a host of different bibliographical styles, and that is the point. An abundance of data requires processing applications to select, punctuate, order, and format the bibliographical data, and it is unlikely that all the information provided will actually be output.

All the "cooked" data in a `bibliomixed` entry in a bibliography, on the other hand, is intended to be presented to the reader in the form and sequence in which it is provided. It even includes punctuation between the fields of data:

```
<bibliomixed>
  <bibliomset relation="article">
    <surname>Walsh</surname>, <firstname>Norman</firstname>.
    <title role="article">Introduction to Cascading Style Sheets</title>.
  </bibliomset>
  <bibliomset relation="journal">
    <title>The World Wide Web Journal</title>
    <volumenum>2</volumenum><issuenum>1</issuenum>.
    <publishername>O'Reilly & Associates, Inc.</publishername> and
    <corpname>The World Wide Web Consortium</corpname>.
    <pubdate>Winter, 1996</pubdate></bibliomset>.
</bibliomixed>
```

Clearly, these two ways of marking up bibliographical entries are suited to different circumstances. You should use one or the other for your bibliography, not both. Strictly speaking, mingling the raw and the cooked may be "kosher" as far as the schema is concerned, but it will almost certainly cause problems for most processing applications.

## CHAPTER 3

Validating DocBook Documents

A key feature of XML markup is that you *validate* it. The DocBook schema is a precise description of valid nesting: the order of elements, and their content. All DocBook documents must conform to this description or they are not DocBook documents (by definition). The validation technology that is built into XML is the Document Type Definition or DTD. A *validating parser* is a program that can read the DTD and a particular document and determine whether the exact nesting and order of elements in the document is valid according to the DTD.

DocBook is now defined by a RELAX NG grammar and Schematron rules, so it is no longer necessary to validate with the DTD. In fact, it isn't even very valuable since the DTD version doesn't enforce many DocBook constraints. Instead, an external RELAX NG and Schematron validator must be used.

Validation is performed on a document *after* it has been parsed. It is possible for parsing errors to occur as well as validation errors (if, for example, your document isn't well-formed XML). We're going to assume that your documents are well-formed and not discuss XML parsing errors.

If you are not using a structured editor that can provide guidance on the markup as you type, validation with an external tool is a particularly important step in the document creation process. You cannot expect to get rational results from subsequent processing (such as document publishing) if your documents are not valid.

There are several free validators that will handle RELAX NG and Schematron, including Jing and MSV. For more detail about available tools, see "XML Tools" on page 500.

ID/IDREF Constraints and Validation

In XML, attributes of type ID and IDREF provide a straightforward cross-referencing mechanism. In DocBook, the `xml:id` attribute contains values of type ID, and the `linkend` attribute contains values of type IDREF.

Within any document, no two attributes of type ID may have the same value. In addition, for any attribute of type IDREF, there must be one, and only one, instance of an attribute of type ID with the same value in the same document. In other words, you can't have two elements with the same ID, and every IDREF must match an ID that exists somewhere in the same document.

> Checking these constraints is not a core part of RELAX NG. If you want RELAX NG to check them, you need to enable a set of "DTD compatibility" extensions. Unfortunately, the DTD compatibility extensions do not work well with the DocBook grammar. However, because DocBook uses `xml:id` for its ID attribute, it's not necessary to enforce the constraints with RELAX NG. You can either tell your processor not to perform the DTD compatibility extension checks, or ignore the warning messages that they produce. You could also use Schematron to check ID/IDREF constraints.

Validating Your Documents

RELAX NG validation is supported natively in some editing environments, such as <oXygen/> (see Figure 3-1), XMLmind, and Emacs (with `nxml-mode`). <oXygen/> and XMLmind also support Schematron validation. There are also several standalone validators—for example, Jing and Sun's Multi-Schema Validator (MSV).

If your documents make use of several namespaces (e.g., SVG and MathML embedded in DocBook), tools that support NVDL, *Namespace-based Validation Dispatching Language* [NVDL], can greatly simplify complex validation scenarios.

Understanding Validation Errors

Every validator produces slightly different error messages, but most indicate exactly (at least technically[*]) what is wrong and where the error occurred. With a little experience, this information is all you'll need to quickly identify what's wrong.

In the rest of this section, we'll look at a number of common errors and the messages they produce in MSV. We've chosen MSV because it generally produces informative error messages.

---

[*] It is often the case that you can correct an error in the document in several ways. The validator suggests one possible fix, but this is not always the right fix. For example, the validator may suggest that you can correct out-of-context data by adding another element, when in fact it's "obvious" to human eyes that the problem is a missing end tag.

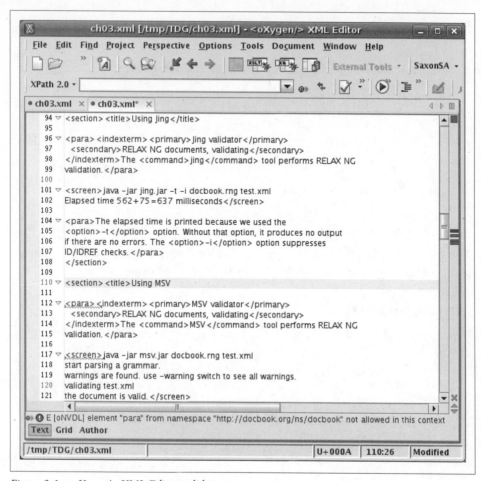

Figure 3-1. <oXygen/> XML Editor validation

Character Data Not Allowed Here

Out-of-context character data is frequently caused by a missing start tag, but sometimes it's just the result of typing in the wrong place!

```
<chapter xmlns="http://docbook.org/ns/docbook" version="5.0">
<title>Test Chapter</title>
<para>
This is a paragraph in the test chapter. It is unremarkable in
every regard. This is a paragraph in the test chapter. It is
unremarkable in every regard. This is a paragraph in the test
chapter. It is unremarkable in every regard.
</para>
You can't put character data here.
<para>
<emphasis role="bold">This</emphasis> paragraph contains
<emphasis>some <emphasis>emphasized</emphasis> text</emphasis>
```

```
and a <superscript>super</superscript>script
and a <subscript>sub</subscript>script.
</para>
<para>
This is a paragraph in the test chapter. It is unremarkable in
every regard. This is a paragraph in the test chapter. It is
unremarkable in every regard. This is a paragraph in the test
chapter. It is unremarkable in every regard.
</para>
</chapter>
```

```
java -jar msv.jar docbook.rng badpcdata.xml
start parsing a grammar.
warnings are found. use -warning switch to see all warnings.
validating badpcdata.xml
Error at line:10, column:7 of badpcdata.xml
    unexpected character literal
```

You can't put character data directly in a **chapter**. Here, a wrapper element, such as
para, is missing around the sentence between the first two paragraphs.

Misspelled Start Tag

If you spell a start tag incorrectly, or use the wrong namespace, the parser will get
confused:

```
<chapter xmlns="http://docbook.org/ns/docbook" version="5.0">
<title>Test Chapter</title>
<para>
This is a paragraph in the test chapter. It is unremarkable in
every regard. This is a paragraph in the test chapter. It is
unremarkable in every regard. This is a paragraph in the test
chapter. It is unremarkable in every regard.
</para>
<paar>
<emphasis role="bold">This</emphasis> paragraph contains
<emphasis>some <emphasis>emphasized</emphasis> text</emphasis>
and a <superscript>super</superscript>script
and a <subscript>sub</subscript>script.
</para>
<para>
This is a paragraph in the test chapter. It is unremarkable in
every regard. This is a paragraph in the test chapter. It is
unremarkable in every regard. This is a paragraph in the test
chapter. It is unremarkable in every regard.
</para>
</chapter>
```

```
java -jar msv.jar docbook.rng misspell.xml
start parsing a grammar.
warnings are found. use -warning switch to see all warnings.
validating misspell.xml
Error at line:9, column:7 of misspell.xml
```

```
        tag name "paar" is not allowed. Possible tag names are: <address>,<anchor>,
      <annotation>,<bibliography>,<bibliolist>,<blockquote>,<bridgehead>,
      <calloutlist>,<caution>,<classsynopsis>,<cmdsynopsis>,
      <constraintdef>,<constructorsynopsis>,<destructorsynopsis>,<epigraph>,
      <equation>,<example>,<fieldsynopsis>,<figure>,<formalpara>,
      <funcsynopsis>,<glossary>,<glosslist>,<important>,<index>,
      <indexterm>,<informalequation>,<informalexample>,<informalfigure>,
      <informaltable>,<itemizedlist>,<literallayout>,<mediaobject>,
      <methodsynopsis>,<msgset>,<note>,<orderedlist>,<para>,
      <procedure>,<productionset>,<programlisting>,<programlistingco>,
      <qandaset>,<refentry>,<remark>,<revhistory>,<screen>,<screenco>,
      <screenshot>,<section>,<section>,<segmentedlist>,<sidebar>,
      <simpara>,<simplelist>,<simplesect>,<synopsis>,<table>,<task>,
      <tip>,<toc>,<variablelist>,<warning>
```

Luckily, these are usually easy to spot, unless you accidentally spell the name of another element. In that case, your error might appear to be out of context.

Out-of-Context Start Tag

Sometimes the problem isn't spelling, but rather placing a tag in the wrong context. When this happens, the validator tries to figure out what it can add to your document to make it valid. Then it tries to recover by continuing as if it had seen what it just added. Of course, this may cause future errors:

```
<chapter xmlns="http://docbook.org/ns/docbook" version="5.0">
<title>Test Chapter</title>
<para>
This is a paragraph in the test chapter. It is unremarkable in
every regard. This is a paragraph in the test chapter. It is
unremarkable in every regard. This is a paragraph in the test
chapter. It is unremarkable in every regard.
</para>
<para><title>Paragraph With Inlines</title>
<emphasis role="bold">This</emphasis> paragraph contains
<emphasis>some <emphasis>emphasized</emphasis> text</emphasis>
and a <superscript>super</superscript>script
and a <subscript>sub</subscript>script.
</para>
<para>
This is a paragraph in the test chapter. It is unremarkable in
every regard. This is a paragraph in the test chapter. It is
unremarkable in every regard. This is a paragraph in the test
chapter. It is unremarkable in every regard.
</para>
</chapter>


$ java -jar msv.jar docbook.rng context.xml
start parsing a grammar.
warnings are found. use -warning switch to see all warnings.
validating context.xml
Error at line:9, column:14 of context.xml
```

```
tag name "title" is not allowed. Possible tag names are: <abbrev>,<accel>,
<acronym>,<address>,…,<varname>,<warning>,<wordasword>,<xref>
```

In this example, we probably wanted a `formalpara` so that we could have a title on the paragraph. But note that the validator didn't suggest this alternative. The validator only tries to add additional elements, rather than rename elements that it's already seen.

Publishing DocBook Documents

Creating and validating XML documents is usually only half the battle. After you've composed your document, you'll want to publish it. Publishing, for our purposes, means either print or web publishing. For XML documents, this is usually accomplished with some kind of *stylesheet*. In some environments, it is now possible to publish an XML document on the Web simply by putting it online with a stylesheet.

A Survey of Stylesheet Languages

Over the years, a number of attempts have been made to produce a standard stylesheet language and, failing that, a large number of proprietary languages have been developed. Since this book was first written, three standards have emerged as the clear frontrunners:

CSS

The W3C CSS Working Group created CSS as a style attachment language for HTML. It has also been advanced as a stylesheet language for XML. Some browsers will style arbitrary XML with CSS and some commercial products exist that will render XML+CSS either online or in print.

XSL

XSLT 1.0 is well established and is probably the most common styling technology for DocBook. XSLT 2.0 offers a number of important new features (at the expense of some complexity, naturally) and is growing in popularity.

It's worth observing that there are two, related technologies in play here. XSLT 1.0 and 2.0, the transformation languages, and XSL Formatting Objects (XSL-FO). XSL-FO is an XML vocabulary for describing constraints on page layout.

XQuery

XQuery 1.0, developed in parallel with XPath 2.0, provides a different set of features than XSL, but can be used to transform DocBook into other formats.

Stylesheet Examples

By way of comparison, here's an example of each of the standard style languages. In each case, the stylesheet fragment shown contains the rules that reasonably formatted the following paragraph:

```
<para>This is an example paragraph. It should be presented in a
reasonable body font. <emphasis>Emphasized</emphasis> words
should be printed in italics. A single level of
<emphasis>Nested <emphasis>emphasis</emphasis> should also
be supported.</emphasis>
</para>
```

CSS stylesheet

CSS stylesheets consist of selectors and formatting properties, as shown in Example 4-1.

Example 4-1. A fragment of a CSS stylesheet

```
@namespace "http://docbook.org/ns/docbook"

para                 { display: block }
emphasis             { display: inline;
                       font-style: italic; }
emphasis emphasis { display: inline;
                       font-style: normal; }
```

As this edition is being written, namespace selection in CSS, while widely supported, is still a Candidate Recommendation at W3C.

XSL stylesheet

XSL stylesheets are XML documents, as shown in Example 4-2. The element in the XSL stylesheet that controls the presentation of specific elements is the `xsl:template` element.

Example 4-2. A fragment of an XSL stylesheet

```
<?xml version='1.0'?>
<xsl:stylesheet xmlns:xsl="http://www.w3.org/1999/XSL/Transform"
                xmlns:fo="http://www.w3.org/1999/XSL/Format"
                xmlns:db="http://docbook.org/ns/docbook"
                version="1.0">

<xsl:template match="db:para">
  <fo:block>
    <xsl:apply-templates/>
  </fo:block>
</xsl:template>

<xsl:template match="db:emphasis">
  <fo:inline font-style="italic">
    <xsl:apply-templates/>
  </fo:inline>
```

```
</xsl:template>

<xsl:template match="db:emphasis/db:emphasis">
  <fo:inline font-style="normal">
    <xsl:apply-templates/>
  </fo:inline>
</xsl:template>

</xsl:stylesheet>
```

A complete stylesheet for generating an entire XSL-FO document would require additional boilerplate text not shown.

XQuery

XQuery is expressed in a mixture of text and XML fragments, as shown in Example 4-3.

Example 4-3. A fragment of XQuery

```
xquery version "1.0";

declare default function namespace "http://www.w3.org/2005/xpath-functions";

declare namespace db="http://docbook.org/ns/docbook";
declare namespace fo="http://www.w3.org/1999/XSL/Format";

declare function local:convert($node as node()) as node()* {
  if (empty($node))
  then
    ()
  else
    typeswitch ($node)
      case text() return $node
      case document-node() return local:convert($node/node())
      case element(db:para) return local:para($node)
      case element(db:emphasis) return local:emphasis($node)
      default return ("ERROR: UNEXPECTED NODE", local:convert($node/node()))
};

declare function local:param($node as element()) as element() {
  <fo:block>
    { local:convert($node/node()) }
  </fo:block>
};

declare function local:emphasis($node as element()) as element() {
  if ($node/parent::db:emphasis)
  then
    <fo:inline font-style="normal">
      { local:convert($node/node()) }
    </fo:inline>
  else
    <fo:inline font-style="italic">
      { local:convert($node/node()) }
```

```
    </fo:inline>
};
```

A complete query for generating an XSL-FO document would require additional boilerplate text not shown.

Using XSL to Publish DocBook Documents

The community of people using DocBook has created a set of open source XSL stylesheets that are maintained at Sourceforge.net (*http://sourceforge.net/projects/docbook*). These stylesheets can be used to transform DocBook XML into a wide variety of formats, including HTML, Javahelp, XSL-FO (for processing into print), ePub, and HTML help.

For a detailed discussion of using XSL to publish DocBook documents, see *DocBook XSL: The Complete Guide* [Stayton07].

Customizing DocBook

For some applications, DocBook "out of the box" may not be exactly what you need. Perhaps you need additional inline elements or perhaps you want to remove elements that you never want your authors to use. By design, DocBook makes this sort of customization easy.

It is even easier to customize DocBook 5.0 than it was to customize earlier releases. This is because DocBook 5.0 uses RELAX NG to express its schema. RELAX NG provides better support for modifications than DTDs, and the DocBook schema takes full advantage of that support.

This chapter describes the organization of the RELAX NG schema for DocBook and how to make your own *customization layer*. It contains methods and examples for adding, removing, and modifying elements and attributes, and conventions for naming and versioning DocBook customizations. It assumes some familiarity with RELAX NG. If you are unfamiliar with RELAX NG, you can find a tutorial introduction in the *RELAX NG Tutorial* [RNG-Intro].

You can use customization layers to extend DocBook or subset it. Creating a schema that is a strict subset of DocBook means that all of your instances are still completely valid DocBook instances, which may be important to your tools and stylesheets, and to other people with whom you share documents. An *extension* adds new structures, or changes the schema in a way that is not compatible with DocBook. Extensions can be very useful, but might have a great impact on your environment.

Customization layers can be as small as restricting an attribute value or as large as adding an entirely different hierarchy on top of the inline elements.

Should You Do This?

Changing a schema can have a wide-ranging impact on the tools and stylesheets that you use. It can have an impact on your authors and on your legacy documents. This is especially true if you make an extension. If you rely on your support staff to install and maintain your authoring and publishing tools, check with them before you invest a lot of time modifying the schema. There may be additional issues that are outside your immediate control. Proceed with caution.

That said, DocBook is designed to be easy to modify. This chapter assumes that you are comfortable with XML and RELAX NG grammar syntax, but the examples presented should be a good springboard to learning the syntax if it's not already familiar to you.

If You Change DocBook, It's Not DocBook Anymore!

The license agreement under which DocBook is distributed gives you complete freedom to change, modify, reuse, and generally hack the schema in any way you want, except that you must not call your alterations "DocBook."

Namespace and Version

Starting with DocBook V5.0, DocBook is identified by its namespace, *http://docbook .org/ns/docbook*. The particular version of DocBook to which an element conforms is identified by its version attribute. If the element does not specify a version, the version of the closest ancestor DocBook element that does specify a version is assumed. The version attribute is required on the root DocBook element.

Here is how these attributes would appear on the book element.

```
<book xmlns="http://docbook.org/ns/docbook"
      version="5.0">
  ...
</book>
```

If you change the DocBook schema, the namespace remains the same, but you must provide an alternate version identifier for the schema and the modules you changed. The version attribute identifies the version of DocBook the alternate is based on, specifies what type of variant it is, and names the variant and any additional modules. While the format for the version string is not part of the normative specification, the DocBook Technical Committee recommends the following format:

```
base_version-(subset|extension|variant) (name[-version])+
```

For example, version 1.0 of Acme Corporation's extension of DocBook V5.0 could be identified as "5.0-extension acme-1.0".

If your schema is a proper subset, use the subset keyword in the version. If your schema extends the markup model, use the extension keyword. If you'd rather not characterize your variant specifically as a subset or an extension, use the variant keyword.

Public Identifiers

Although not directly supported by RELAX NG, in some cases it may still be valuable to identify a DocBook V5.0 customization layer with a public identifier. A public identifier for DocBook V5.0 is:

```
-//OASIS//DTD DocBook V5.0//EN
```

If you make any changes to the structure of the schema, you must change the public identifier. You should change both the owner identifier and the description. Formal public identifiers for the base DocBook modules would have identifiers with the following syntax:

```
-//OASIS//text-class DocBook description Vversion//EN
```

Your public identifiers should use the following syntax:

```
-//Owner-ID//text-class DocBook Vversion-Based (Subset|Extension|Variant) \
Description-and-version//lang
```

For example:

```
-//O'Reilly//DTD DocBook V5.0-Based Subset V1.1//EN
```

If your schema is a proper subset, use the `Subset` keyword in the description. If your schema extends the markup model, use the `Extension` keyword. If you'd rather not characterize your variant specifically as a subset or an extension, use the `Variant` keyword.

Customization Layers

A RELAX NG grammar is a collection of patterns. These patterns can be stored in a single file or in a collection of files that import each other. Patterns can augment each other in a variety of ways. A complete grammar is the union of the specified patterns.

For convenience, the DocBook grammar is distributed in a single file.

RELAX NG Syntax

There are two standard syntaxes for RELAX NG, an XML syntax and a "compact" text syntax. The two forms have the same expressive power; it is possible to transform between them with no loss of information.

Many users find the relative terseness of the compact syntax makes it a convenient form for reading and writing RELAX NG. We will use compact syntax in our examples.

DocBook Schema Structure

The DocBook RELAX NG schema is highly modular, using named patterns extensively. Every element, attribute, attribute list, and enumeration has its own named pattern. In addition, there are named patterns for logical combinations of elements and attributes. These named patterns provide "hooks" into the schema that allow you to do a wide range of customization by simply redefining one or more of the named patterns.

The names of the patterns used in a RELAX NG grammar can be defined in any way the schema designer chooses. To make it easier to navigate, the DocBook RELAX NG grammar employs the following naming conventions:

db.*.attlist
: Defines the list of attributes associated with an element. For example, db.emphasis.attlist is the pattern that matches all of the attributes of the emphasis element.

db.*.attribute
: Defines a single attribute. For example, db.conformance.attribute is the pattern that matches the conformance attribute on all of the elements where it occurs.

db.*.attributes
: Defines a collection of attributes. For example, db.effectivity.attributes is all of the effectivity attributes (arch, audience, etc.).

db.*.blocks
: Defines a list (a choice) of a set of related block elements. For example, db.list.blocks is a pattern that matches any of the list elements.

db.*.contentmodel
: Defines a fragment of a content model shared by several elements.

db.*.enumeration
: Defines an enumeration, usually one used in an attribute value. For example, db.revisionflag.enumeration is a pattern that matches the list of values that can be used as the value of a revisionflag attribute.

db.*.info
: Defines the info element for a particular element. For example, db.example.info is the pattern that matches info on the example element.

    Almost all of the info elements are the same, but they are described with distinct patterns so that customizers can change them individually.

db.*.inlines
: Defines a list (a choice) of a set of related inline elements. For example, db.link.inlines is a pattern that matches any of the linking-related elements.

db.*.role.attribute
: Defines the role attribute for a particular element. For example, db.emphasis.role is the pattern that matches role on the emphasis element.

    All of the role attributes are the same, but they are described with distinct patterns so that customizers can change them selectively.

db.*
: Defines a particular DocBook element. For example, db.title is the pattern that matches the title element.

RELAX NG allows multiple patterns to match the same element, so sometimes these patterns come in flavors, for example, db.indexterm.singular, db.index term.startofrange, and db.indexterm.endofrange. Each of these patterns matches indexterm with varying attributes.

These are conventions, not hard and fast rules. There are patterns that don't follow these conventions.

The General Structure of Customization Layers

Creating a customized schema is similar to creating a customization layer for XSL. The schema customization layer is a new RELAX NG schema that defines your changes and includes the standard DocBook schema. You then validate using the schema customization as your schema. Although customization layers vary in complexity, most of them have the same general structure as other customization layers of similar complexity.

In the most common case, you probably want to include all of DocBook, but you want to make some small changes. These customization layers tend to look like this:

```
namespace db = "http://docbook.org/ns/docbook"
# perhaps other namespace declarations

include "docbook.rnc"                    ❶

# new patterns and augmented patterns    ❷
```

❶ Start by importing the base DocBook schema.

❷ Then you can add new patterns or augment existing patterns.

If you want to completely replace a pattern (e.g., to remove or completely change an element), the template is a little different.

```
namespace db = "http://docbook.org/ns/docbook"
# perhaps other namespace declarations

include "docbook.rnc" {
    # redefinitions of DocBook patterns    ❶
}

# new patterns and augmented patterns    ❷
```

❶ You can redefine patterns in the body of an import statement. These patterns completely replace any that appear in the imported schema.

❷ As before, patterns outside the include statement can augment existing patterns (even redefined ones).

There are other possibilities as well; these examples are illustrative, not exhaustive.

Writing, Testing, and Using a Customization Layer

The procedure for writing, testing, and using a customization layer is always about the same. In this section, we'll go through the process in some detail. The rest of the sections in this chapter describe a range of useful customization layers.

Deciding What to Change

If you're considering writing a customization layer, there must be something that you want to change. Perhaps you want to add an element or attribute, remove one, or change some other aspect of the schema.

Adding an element, particularly an inline element, is one possibility. For example, if you're writing about cryptography, you might want to add a "cleartext" element. The next section describes how to create a customization layer to do this.

Deciding How to Change a Customization Layer

Figuring out what to change may be the hardest part of the process. For the clear text example, there are several patterns that you could possibly change. The choice will depend on the exact focus of your document. Here are several candidates, all of which look plausible: technical inlines, programming inlines, and domain inlines. Let's suppose you chose the domain inlines.

As shown in Example 5-1, your customization would import the DocBook schema, extend the domain inlines, and then provide a pattern that matches the new element.

Example 5-1. Adding cleartext with a customization layer

```
namespace db = "http://docbook.org/ns/docbook"
default namespace = "http://docbook.org/ns/docbook"

include "docbook.rnc"

db.domain.inlines |= db.cleartext                      ❶

# Define a new cleartext element:                      ❷

db.cleartext.role.attribute = attribute role { text } ❸
db.cleartext.attlist =                                 ❹
   db.cleartext.role.attribute?
 & db.common.attributes
 & db.common.linking.attributes

db.cleartext =                                         ❺
   element cleartext {
      db.cleartext.attlist,
```

```
    db._text
}
```

❶ The |= operator adds a new choice to a pattern. So this line makes the db.clear text pattern a valid option anywhere that db.domain.inlines appears.

❷ Next, we create a pattern for the cleartext element. The convention in the DocBook schema is to create three patterns, one for the role attribute, one for all the attributes, and one for the element. By following this convention, we make it easier for someone to customize our customization.

❸ Defining a separate pattern for the role attribute makes it easy for customizers to change it on a per-element basis.

❹ Defining a separate pattern for the attributes makes it easy for customizers to change them on a per-element basis. This pattern includes the pattern we just created for the role attribute.

❺ The pattern for the element pulls it all together. The pattern db._text matches text plus a number of ubiquitous or nearly ubiquitous inlines. Use this pattern unless you *really* want only text.

Using Your Customization Layer

Using a customization layer is simple. Just put the customization into a file—for example, *mycustomization.rnc*—and then refer to that file instead of the DocBook schema when your tools offer the option.

Testing Your Work

Schemas, by their nature, contain many complex, interrelated patterns. Whenever you make a change to the schema, it's always wise to use a validator to check your work.

Start by validating a document that's plain, vanilla DocBook, one that you know is valid according to the DocBook standard schema. This will help you identify any errors that you've introduced to the schema. Once you are confident the schema is correct, begin testing with instances that you expect (and don't expect) to be valid against it.

The following sections contain examples for several common customizations.

Removing Elements

DocBook has a large number of elements. In some authoring environments, it may be useful or necessary to remove unneeded elements.

Removing msgset

The msgset element is a favorite target. It has a complex internal structure designed for describing interrelated error messages, especially on systems that may exhibit messages from several different components. Many technical documents can do without it, and removing it leaves one less complexity to explain to your authors.

Example 5-2 shows a customization layer that removes the msgset element.

Example 5-2. Removing msgset

```
namespace db = "http://docbook.org/ns/docbook"

include "docbook.rnc" {
    db.msgset = notAllowed
}
```

The complexity of msgset is really in its msgentry children. DocBook V4.5 introduced a simple alternative, simplemsgentry. Example 5-3 demonstrates how you could allow msgset but only support the simpler alternative.

Example 5-3. Removing msgentry

```
namespace db = "http://docbook.org/ns/docbook"

include "docbook.rnc" {
    db.msgentry = notAllowed
}
```

Closer examination of the msgentry content model will reveal that it contains a number of descendants. It isn't necessary, but it wouldn't be wrong, to define their patterns as notAllowed as well.

Removing Computer Inlines

DocBook contains a large number of computer inlines. The DocBook inlines define a domain-specific vocabulary. If you're working in another domain, many of them may be unnecessary.

They're defined in a set of patterns that ultimately roll up to the db.domain.inlines pattern. If you make that pattern notAllowed, you'll remove them all in one fell swoop. Example 5-4 is a customization that does this.

Example 5-4. Removing computer inlines

```
namespace db = "http://docbook.org/ns/docbook"

include "docbook.rnc" {
    db.domain.inlines = notAllowed
}
```

If you want to be more selective, you might consider making one or more of the following notAllowed instead:

- db.error.inlines: errors and error messages
- db.gui.inlines: GUI elements
- db.keyboard.inlines: key and keyboard elements
- db.markup.inlines: markup elements
- db.math.inlines: mathematical expressions
- db.os.inlines: operating system inlines
- db.programming.inlines: programming-related inlines

 Be aware that a customization layer that removed this many technical inlines would also remove some larger technical structures or make them unusable.

Removing Synopsis Elements

Another possibility is removing the complex synopsis elements. The customization layer in Example 5-5 removes cmdsynopsis and funcsynopsis.

Example 5-5. Removing cmdsynopsis and funcsynopsis

```
namespace db = "http://docbook.org/ns/docbook"

include "docbook.rnc" {
   db.funcsynopsis = notAllowed
   db.cmdsynopsis = notAllowed
}
```

Removing Sectioning Elements

Perhaps you want to restrict your authors to only three levels of sectioning. To do that, you could remove the sect4 and sect5 elements, as shown in Example 5-6.

Example 5-6. Removing the sect4 and sect5 elements

```
namespace db = "http://docbook.org/ns/docbook"

include "docbook.rnc" {
   db.sect4 = notAllowed

   # Strictly speaking, we don't need to remove sect5 because, having removed
   # sect4, there's no way to reach it. But it seems cleaner to do so.
   db.sect5 = notAllowed
}
```

This technique works if your authors are using numbered sections, which you could require them to do by removing the **section** element. But suppose instead you want to allow them to use recursive sections, but limit them to only three levels.

One way to do this would be to define new **section2** and **section3** patterns, as shown in Example 5-7.

Example 5-7. Limiting recursive sections to three levels

```
namespace db = "http://docbook.org/ns/docbook"
default namespace = "http://docbook.org/ns/docbook"

include "docbook.rnc" {
    db.section =
        element section {
            db.section.attlist,
            db.section.info,
            db.recursive.blocks.or.section2s,
            db.navigation.components*
        }
}

db.recursive.section2s = (db.section2+, db.simplesect*) | db.simplesect+

db.recursive.blocks.or.section2s =
  (db.all.blocks+, db.recursive.section2s?) | db.recursive.section2s

db.section2 =
    element section {
        db.section.attlist,
        db.section.info,
        db.recursive.blocks.or.section3s,
        db.navigation.components*
    }

db.recursive.section3s = (db.section3+, db.simplesect*) | db.simplesect+

db.recursive.blocks.or.section3s =
  (db.all.blocks+, db.recursive.section3s?) | db.recursive.section3s

db.section3 =
    element section {
        db.section.attlist,
        db.section.info,
        db.all.blocks+
        db.navigation.components*
    }
```

Another solution, assuming your validation environment supports Schematron, is simply to add a new rule, as shown in Example 5-8.

Example 5-8. Limiting recursive sections to three levels using Schematron

```
namespace db = "http://docbook.org/ns/docbook"
namespace s = "http://www.ascc.net/xml/schematron"
```

```
default namespace = "http://docbook.org/ns/docbook"

include "docbook.rnc" {
   db.section =
      [
         s:pattern [
            name = "Limit depth of sections"
            s:rule [
               context = "db:section"
               s:assert [
                  test = "count(ancestor::db:section) < 2"
                  "Sections can be no more than three levels deep"
               ]
            ]
         ]
      ]
      element section {
         db.section.attlist,
         db.section.info,
         db.recursive.blocks.or.sections,
         db.navigation.components*
      }
}
```

In this example, we've put the Schematron pattern inline in the RELAX NG grammar. If your validation strategy requires that they be in a separate document, it may be more convenient to simply create them separately.

Removing Admonitions from Table Entries

Sometimes what you want to do is not as simple as entirely removing an element. Instead, you may want to remove it only from some contexts. The way to do this is to redefine the patterns used to calculate the elements allowed in those contexts.

Standard DocBook allows any inline element or any block element to appear in a table cell. You might decide that it's unreasonable to allow admonitions (note, caution, warning, etc.) to appear in a table cell.

In order to remove them, you must change what is allowed in the entry element, as shown in Example 5-9.

Example 5-9. Removing admonitions from tables

```
namespace db = "http://docbook.org/ns/docbook"
default namespace = "http://docbook.org/ns/docbook"

include "docbook.rnc" {
   db.entry = element entry {
      db.entry.attlist,
      (db.all.inlines* | db.some.blocks*)
   }
}
```

```
db.some.blocks =
   db.somenopara.blocks
 | db.para.blocks
 | db.extension.blocks

db.somenopara.blocks =
   db.list.blocks
 | db.formal.blocks
 | db.informal.blocks
 | db.publishing.blocks
 | db.graphic.blocks
 | db.technical.blocks
 | db.verbatim.blocks
 | db.bridgehead
 | db.remark
 | db.revhistory
 | db.indexterm
 | db.synopsis.blocks
```

The extent to which any particular change is easy or hard depends in part on how many patterns need to be changed. The DocBook Technical Committee is generally open to the idea of adding more patterns if it improves the readability of customization layers. If you think some refactoring would make your job easier, feel free to ask.

Removing Attributes

Just as there may be more elements than you need, there may be more attributes.

Suppose your processing system doesn't support "continued" lists. You want to remove the `continuation` attribute from the `orderedlist` element. There are two ways you could accomplish this. One way would be to redefine the `db.orderedlist.continuation.attribute` pattern as not allowed; the other would be to redefine the `db.orderedlist.attlist` pattern so that it does not include the `continuation` attribute. Either will accomplish the goal. Example 5-10 uses the first method.

Example 5-10. Removing continuation from orderedlist

```
namespace db = "http://docbook.org/ns/docbook"

include "docbook.rnc" {
   db.orderedlist.continuation.attribute = empty
}
```

Subsetting the Common Attributes

DocBook defines a set of "common attributes," which appear on *every* element. Depending on how you process your documents, removing some of them can both simplify the authoring task and improve processing speed.

Some obvious candidates are:

*Effectivity attributes (*arch, os, condition...*)*
> If you're not using all of the effectivity attributes in your documents, you can get rid of up to seven attributes in one fell swoop.

xml:lang
> If you're not producing multilingual documents, you can remove xml:lang.

remap
> The remap attribute is designed to hold the name of a semantically equivalent construct from a previous markup scheme (e.g., a Microsoft Word–style template name, if you're converting from Word). If you're authoring from scratch, or not preserving previous constructs with remap, you can get rid of it.

xreflabel
> If your processing system isn't using xreflabel, it's a candidate as well.

The customization layer in Example 5-11 reduces the common attributes to just xml:id, version, and xml:lang.

Example 5-11. Removing common attributes

```
namespace db = "http://docbook.org/ns/docbook"

include "docbook.rnc" {
   db.common.base.attributes =
       db.version.attribute?
     & db.xml.lang.attribute?
}
```

Adding Elements

Adding a new inline or block element is generally a straightforward matter of creating a pattern for the new element and using |= to add it to the right pattern, as we did in Example 5-1. But if your new element is more intimately related to the existing structure of the document, it may require more surgery.

Example 5-12 extends DocBook by adding a sect6 element.

Example 5-12. Adding a sect6 element

```
namespace db = "http://docbook.org/ns/docbook"
default namespace = "http://docbook.org/ns/docbook"

include "docbook.rnc" {
   db.sect5.sections = (db.sect6+, db.simplesect*) | db.simplesect+
}

db.sect6.sections = db.simplesect+

db.sect6.status.attribute = db.status.attribute
```

```
db.sect6.role.attribute = attribute role { text }
db.sect6.attlist =
   db.sect6.role.attribute?
 & db.common.attributes
 & db.common.linking.attributes
 & db.label.attribute?
 & db.sect6.status.attribute?

db.sect6.info = db._info.title.req

db.sect6 =
   element sect6 {
      db.sect6.attlist,
      db.sect6.info,
      ((db.all.blocks+, db.sect6.sections?)
       | db.sect6.sections),
      db.navigation.components*
   }
```

Here we've redefined sect5 to include sect6 and provided a pattern for sect6.

Adding Attributes

The simplest way to add an attribute to a single element is to add it to the attlist pattern for that element. Example 5-13 adds the optional attributes born and died to the attribute list for author. The db.author.attlist pattern is redefined to interleave the two new optional attributes with the existing attributes on the list.

Example 5-13. Adding born and died attributes

```
namespace db = "http://docbook.org/ns/docbook"
default namespace = "http://docbook.org/ns/docbook"

include "docbook.rnc"

db.author.attlist &=                          ❶
  attribute born { db.date.contentmodel }?       ❷
  & attribute died { db.date.contentmodel }?
```

❶ &= interleaves the two new optional attributes with the existing attributes on the list.

❷ db.date.contentmodel is a pattern used for any attribute or element that represents a date.

Other Modifications

Changing the Contents of the role Attribute

The role attribute, found on almost all of the elements in DocBook, is a text attribute that can be used to subclass an element. In some applications, it may be useful to modify the definition of role so that authors must choose one of a specific set of possible values.

In Example 5-14, the role attribute on the procedure element is constrained to the value required or optional.

Example 5-14. Changing role on procedure

```
namespace db = "http://docbook.org/ns/docbook"

include "docbook.rnc" {
    db.procedure.role.attribute = attribute role { "required" | "optional" }
}
```

Adding a Value to an Enumerated Attribute

Example 5-15 adds the value "large" to the db.spacing.enumeration pattern. Any attribute that is defined using db.spacing.enumeration will now have large as a legal value. Note that while it is easy to add a value to an enumeration, to remove a value from an enumeration you need to redefine the entire enumeration, minus the values you don't need.

Example 5-15. Adding a value to an enumeration

```
namespace db = "http://docbook.org/ns/docbook"
default namespace = "http://docbook.org/ns/docbook"

include "docbook.rnc"

# add a value to an enumeration
db.spacing.enumeration |= "large"
```

Reference

This reference describes every element in DocBook V5.0.

Organization of Reference Pages

The description of each element in this reference is divided into the following sections:

Synopsis
> Provides a quick synopsis of the element. The content of the synopsis varies according to the nature of the element described, but may include any or all of the following sections:

> *Content Model*
>> Describes the content model of the element, the mixture of things that it can contain. See "Understanding Content Models" on page 72.

> *Attributes*
>> Provides a synopsis of the attributes on the element. For brevity, common attributes are described only once, in this introduction. Likewise, common linking attributes are described once.

> *Additional Constraints*
>> Provides a synopsis of any additional constraints on the element. These constraints are expressed using Schematron in the RELAX NG grammar.

Description
> Describes the semantics of the element.

> *Processing expectations*
>> Summarizes specific formatting expectations of the element. Many processing expectations are influenced by attribute values. Be sure to consult the description of element attributes as well.

> *Future changes*
>> Identifies changes that are scheduled for future versions of the schema. These changes are highlighted because they involve some backward

incompatibility that may make currently valid DocBook documents no longer valid under the new version.

Attributes
Describes the semantics of each attribute.

See Also
Lists similar or related elements.

Examples
Provides examples of proper usage for the element. Generally, the smallest example required to reasonably demonstrate the element is used. In many cases, a formatted version of the example is also shown.

All of the examples in the book are valid according to the RELAX NG grammar.

Formatted examples are indicated using a vertical bar.

Understanding Content Models

Each element synopsis begins with a description of its content model. Content models are the way that grammars describe the name, number, and order of other elements that may be used inside an element.

Content model notation

Presenting the content models is an editorial challenge. Presenting the RELAX NG patterns would be easy and absolutely correct, but would only be valuable to readers who understand both RELAX NG and the patterns in the schema. Presenting the RELAX NG patterns "fully expanded" to just element and attribute names would remove the requirement to understand the patterns, but the result is so verbose that it completely obscures the actual meaning.

On the Web and in other interactive media, it's possible to format the content models in a "natural language" list format with names that can be expanded to show more detail. That format is useful even without the ability to expand patterns interactively. Unfortunately, that presentation occupies significant vertical space and, were it used, this book would run to more than a thousand pages. That's not really practical.

Instead, we compromise with a compact syntax reminiscent of DTD syntax. It's not any sort of standard, but it has the dual advantages of being reasonably concise and reasonably easy to understand:

name
A name is the name of a DocBook element.

( )
Parentheses delimit groups.

*, +, ?

> Symbols appear after names and groups to indicate how many occurrences are allowed. If a "*" is present, zero or more occurrences are allowed; if a "+" is present, one or more occurrences are allowed; if a "?" is present, the symbol may occur zero or one time; if no symbol is present, exactly one occurrence is allowed.

|

> A vertical bar indicates a choice. Either the item that precedes or the item that follows the bar is allowed.

&

> An ampersand indicates an "interleave." Both the item that precedes and the item that follows the & are allowed, but they may occur in any order.

,

> A comma separates items in a sequence. Both the item that precedes and the item that follows the "," are allowed, and they must occur in that order.

Here are a few examples:

A

> Exactly one "A" element is allowed.

A | B | C

> Exactly one "A", or exactly one "B", or exactly one "C" is allowed.

A,B,C

> Exactly one "A", followed by exactly one "B", followed by exactly one "C" is allowed.

A & B & C

> Exactly one "A" and exactly one "B" and exactly one "C" is allowed *in any order*. This pattern allows `<A/><B/><C/>`, `<B/><C/><A/>`, `<C/><A/><B/>`, etc. but does not allow `<A/><A/><C/>` or `<A/><B/>`.

A+,B*,C?

> At least one, but possibly more than one "A", followed by zero or more "B"s, followed by an optional (zero or one) "C" is allowed.

A,(B|C)+,D

> Exactly one "A", followed by one or more "B" or "C" elements, followed by exactly one "D" is allowed. Because the group can be repeated, this pattern matches `<A/><B/><D/>`, `<A/><C/><D/>`, `<A/><B/><C/><D/>`, `<A/><B/><C/><C/><C/><D/>`, etc.

Some element names are defined by more than one pattern. When this is the case, the name of the pattern is explicitly shown in a superscript following the name.

In order to avoid long, repetitive lists of element names, similar items are grouped together and only the name of the group is given. For example, a **para** may contain the "Bibliography inlines," the "Error inlines," etc. The author has the choice of using any of the elements belonging to the group. Here is a summary of the elements included in each group:

Bibliography inlines
> A choice of one of the following: `citation, citerefentry, citetitle, citebiblioid, author, person, personname, org, orgname, editor,` or `jobtitle`

Computer-output inlines
> A choice of one of the following: `inlinemediaobject, remark, superscript, subscript, xref, link, olink, anchor, biblioref, alt, annotation, indexterm, prompt, envar, filename, command, computeroutput, userinput, replaceable, package, parameter, termdef, nonterminal, systemitem, option, optional, property, co, tag, markup, token, symbol, literal, code, constant, email,` or `uri`

Error inlines
> A choice of one of the following: `errorcode, errortext, errorname,` or `errortype`

Graphic inlines
> `inlinemediaobject`

GUI inlines
> A choice of one of the following: `guiicon, guibutton, guimenuitem, guimenu, guisubmenu, guilabel, menuchoice,` or `mousebutton`

Indexing inlines
> `indexterm`

Keyboard inlines
> A choice of one of the following: `keycombo, keycap, keycode, keysym, shortcut,` or `accel`

Linking inlines
> A choice of one of the following: `xref, link, olink, anchor,` or `biblioref`

Markup inlines
> A choice of one of the following: `tag, markup, token, symbol, literal, code, constant, email,` or `uri`

Math inlines
> `inlineequation`

Object-oriented programming inlines
> A choice of one of the following: `ooclass, ooexception,` or `oointerface`

Operating system inlines
> A choice of one of the following: `prompt, envar, filename, command, computerout put,` or `userinput`

Product inlines
> A choice of one of the following: `trademark, productnumber, productname, data base, application,` or `hardware`

Programming inlines

A choice of one of the following: function, parameter, varname, returnvalue, type, classname, exceptionname, interfacename, methodname, modifier, initializer, ooclass, ooexception, or oointerface

Publishing inlines

A choice of one of the following: abbrev, acronym, date, emphasis, footnote, foot noteref, foreignphrase, phrase, quote, subscript, superscript, wordasword, first term, glossterm, or coref

Technical inlines

A choice of one of the following: replaceable, package, parameter, termdef, nonter minal, systemitem, option, optional, or property

Ubiquitous inlines

A choice of one of the following: inlinemediaobject, remark, superscript, subscript, xref, link, olink, anchor, biblioref, alt, annotation, or indexterm

User-input inlines

A choice of one of the following: inlinemediaobject, remark, superscript, subscript, xref, link, olink, anchor, biblioref, alt, annotation, indexterm, prompt, envar, filename, command, computeroutput, userinput, replaceable, package, parameter, termdef, nonterminal, systemitem, option, optional, property, co, tag, markup, token, symbol, literal, code, constant, email, uri, guiicon, guibutton, guimenuitem, guimenu, guisubmenu, guilabel, menuchoice, mousebutton, keycombo, keycap, keycode, keysym, shortcut, or accel

Admonition elements

A choice of one of the following: caution, important, note, tip, or warning

Formal elements

A choice of one of the following: example, figure, table, or equation

Graphic elements

A choice of one of the following: mediaobject or screenshot

"Info" elements

A choice of one of the following: abstract, address, artpagenums, author, author group, authorinitials, bibliocoverage, biblioid, bibliosource, collab, confgroup, contractsponsor, contractnum, copyright, cover, date, edition, editor, issuenum, keywordset, legalnotice, mediaobject, org, orgname, othercredit, pagenums, prin thistory, pubdate, publisher, publishername, releaseinfo, revhistory, seriesvol nums, subjectset, volumenum, annotation, extendedlink, bibliomisc, bibliomset, bibliorelation, biblioset, itermset, productname, or productnumber

Informal elements

A choice of one of the following: informalexample, informalfigure, informalta ble, or informalequation

List elements

A choice of one of the following: `itemizedlist`, `orderedlist`, `procedure`, `simplelist`, `variablelist`, `segmentedlist`, `glosslist`, `bibliolist`, `calloutlist`, or `qandaset`

Paragraph elements

A choice of one of the following: `anchor`, `para`, `formalpara`, or `simpara`

Publishing elements

A choice of one of the following: `sidebar`, `blockquote`, `address`, or `epigraph`

Synopsis elements

A choice of one of the following: `funcsynopsis`, `classsynopsis`, `methodsynopsis`, `constructorsynopsis`, `destructorsynopsis`, `fieldsynopsis`, or `cmdsynopsis`

Technical elements

A choice of one of the following: `procedure`, `task`, `productionset`, `constraintdef`, or `msgset`

Verbatim elements

A choice of one of the following: `screen`, `literallayout`, `programlistingco`, `screenco`, `programlisting`, or `synopsis`

Content models and validity

A validator uses the content models to determine if a given document is valid. In order for a document to be valid, the content of every element in the document must "match" the content model for that element.

In practical terms, "match" means that it must be possible to expand the content model until it exactly matches the sequence of elements in the document.

For example, consider the content model of the `epigraph`:

epigraph ::= (info?$^{\text{db.titleforbidden.info}}$, attribution?,(literallayout | *Paragraph elements*)+)

Does the following example "match" that content model?

```
<epigraph>
<para>Some text</para>
</epigraph>
```

Yes, it is valid because the following expansion of the content model exactly matches the actual content: choose zero occurrences of `info`, choose zero occurrences of `attribution`, choose the alternative `para` from the "*Paragraph elements*" choice, and choose to let the "one or more" match once.

By the same token, this example is not valid because there is no expansion of the content model that can match it:

```
<epigraph>
<para>Some text</para>
<attribution>John Doe</attribution>
</epigraph>
```

Common Attributes

There are many "common attributes" that occur on every DocBook element. They are summarized here for brevity and to make the additional attributes that occur on many elements stand out.

Name	Type
annotations	*text*
dir	*Enumeration:*
	ltr
	rtl
	lro
	rlo
remap	*text*
revisionflag	*Enumeration:*
	changed
	added
	deleted
	off
role	*text*
version	*text*
xml:base	anyURI
xml:id	ID
xml:lang	*text*
xreflabel	*text*

annotations
:   Identifies one or more annotations that apply to this element

dir
:   Identifies the direction of text in an element:

    ltr
    :   Left-to-right text

    rtl
    :   Right-to-left text

    lro
    :   Left-to-right override

    rlo
    :   Right-to-left override

remap
> Provides the name or similar semantic identifier assigned to the content in some previous markup scheme

revisionflag
> Identifies the revision status of the element:
>
> changed
> > The element has been changed.
>
> added
> > The element is new (has been added to the document).
>
> deleted
> > The element has been deleted.
>
> off
> > Revision markup has been explicitly turned off for this element.

role
> Provides additional, user-specified classification for an element

version
> Specifies the DocBook version of the element and its descendants

xml:base
> Specifies the base URI of the element and its descendants

xml:id
> Identifies the unique ID value of the element

xml:lang
> Specifies the natural language of the element and its descendants

xreflabel
> Provides the text that is to be generated for a cross-reference to the element

Common Effectivity Attributes

The common attributes include a collection of "effectivity attributes." These attributes are available for authors to identify to whom a particular element applies. Effectivity attributes are often used for profiling: building documents that contain information only relevant to a particular audience.

For example, a section might be identified as available only to readers with a "top-secret" security clearance or a paragraph might be identified as affecting only users running the implementation provided by a particular vendor.

Name	Type
arch	*text*
audience	*text*
condition	*text*

Name	Type
conformance	*text*
os	*text*
revision	*text*
security	*text*
userlevel	*text*
vendor	*text*
wordsize	*text*

arch
> Designates the computer or chip architecture to which the element applies

audience
> Designates the intended audience to which the element applies; for example, system administrators, programmers, or new users

condition
> Provides a standard place for application-specific effectivity

conformance
> Indicates standards conformance characteristics of the element

os
> Indicates the operating system to which the element is applicable

revision
> Indicates the editorial revision to which the element belongs

security
> Indicates something about the security level associated with the element to which it applies

userlevel
> Indicates the level of user experience for which the element applies

vendor
> Indicates the computer vendor to which the element applies

wordsize
> Indicates the word size (width in bits) of the computer architecture to which the element applies

The names of the effectivity attributes are suggestive of several classes of common effectivity information. The semantically neutral condition attribute was added to give authors a place to put values that don't fit neatly into one of the other alternatives.

In authoring environments where many different kinds of effectivity information are required, it's not uncommon to see local extensions that add new attributes. It's also not uncommon to see attributes used without regard to the class of information suggested by the name.

Common Linking Attributes

The following attributes occur on all elements that can be the start of a link. They are summarized here once for brevity and to make the additional attributes that occur on many elements stand out.

Name	Type
linkend/linkends	IDREF/IDREFS
xlink:actuate	*Enumeration:*
	onLoad
	onRequest
	other
	none
xlink:arcrole	anyURI
xlink:href	anyURI
xlink:role	anyURI
xlink:show	*Enumeration:*
	new
	replace
	embed
	other
	none
xlink:title	*text*
xlink:type	*text*

linkend/linkends
> Points to an internal link target by identifying the value of its `xml:id` attribute

xlink:actuate
> Identifies the XLink actuate behavior of the link:
>
> onLoad
>> An application should traverse to the ending resource immediately on loading the starting resource.
>
> onRequest
>> An application should traverse from the starting resource to the ending resource only on a post-loading event triggered for the purpose of traversal.

other

> The behavior of an application traversing to the ending resource is unconstrained by this specification. The application should look for other markup present in the link to determine the appropriate behavior.

> The behavior of an application traversing to the ending resource is unconstrained by this specification. No other markup is present to help the application determine the appropriate behavior.

xlink:arcrole

> Identifies the XLink arcrole of the link

xlink:href

> Identifies a link target with a URI

xlink:role

> Identifies the XLink role of the link

xlink:show

> Identifies the XLink show behavior of the link:

new

> An application traversing to the ending resource should load the resource in a new window, frame, pane, or other relevant presentation context.

replace

> An application traversing to the ending resource should load the resource in the same window, frame, pane, or other relevant presentation context in which the starting resource was loaded.

embed

> An application traversing to the ending resource should load its presentation in place of the presentation of the starting resource.

other

> The behavior of an application traversing to the ending resource is unconstrained by XLink. The application should look for other markup present in the link to determine the appropriate behavior.

> The behavior of an application traversing to the ending resource is unconstrained by this specification. No other markup is present to help the application determine the appropriate behavior.

xlink:title

> Identifies the XLink title of the link

xlink:type

> Identifies the XLink link type

DocBook Element Reference

abbrev

Synopsis

abbrev ::= (text | phrase $^{db.\_phrase}$ | replaceable | trademark | *Graphic inlines* | *Indexing inlines* | *Linking inlines* | *Ubiquitous inlines*)*

Attributes

Common attributes and common linking attributes.

Description

An abbreviation, especially one followed by a period.

Processing expectations

Formatted inline.

See Also

acronym, emphasis, foreignphrase, phrase, quote, wordasword

Examples

```
<article xmlns='http://docbook.org/ns/docbook'>
<title>Example abbrev</title>

<para>The <abbrev>Assn.</abbrev> of Computing Machinery would probably never
abbreviate "Association" like this.
</para>

</article>
```

The Assn. of Computing Machinery would probably never abbreviate "Association" like this.

abstract
A summary

Synopsis

abstract ::= ((((title? & titleabbrev?), info? ^{db.titleforbidden.info}) | info ^{db.titleonly.info}), *Paragraph elements+*)

Attributes

Common attributes and common linking attributes.

Description

An abstract can occur in most components of DocBook. It is expected to contain some sort of summary of the content with which it is associated (by containment).

Processing expectations

Formatted as a displayed block. Sometimes suppressed. Often presented in alternate outputs.

See Also

blockquote, epigraph, sidebar

Examples

```
<article xmlns='http://docbook.org/ns/docbook'>
<info>
  <title>Example abstract</title>
  <abstract>
    <para>In brief, …
    </para>
  </abstract>
</info>

<para>…</para>

</article>
```

accel
A graphical user interface (GUI) keyboard shortcut

Synopsis

accel ::= (text | phrase ^{db._phrase} | replaceable | *Graphic inlines* | *Indexing inlines* | *Linking inlines* | *Ubiquitous inlines*)*

Attributes

Common attributes and common linking attributes.

Description

An accelerator is usually a letter used with a Meta key (such as Ctrl or Alt) to activate some element of a GUI without using the mouse to point and click at it.

Processing expectations

Formatted inline.

See Also

guibutton, guiicon, guilabel, guimenu, guimenuitem, guisubmenu, keycap, keycode, key combo, keysym, menuchoice, mousebutton, shortcut

Examples

```
<article xmlns='http://docbook.org/ns/docbook'>
<title>Example accel</title>

<para os="windows">You can exit most Windows applications by selecting
<guimenuitem><accel>Q</accel>uit</guimenuitem> or
<guimenuitem>E<accel>x</accel>it</guimenuitem> from
the <guimenu><accel>F</accel>ile</guimenu> menu.
</para>

</article>
```

You can exit most Windows applications by selecting Quit or Exit from the File menu.

---

acknowledgements

Acknowledgments of a book or other component

Synopsis

acknowledgements ::= (((((title? & titleabbrev? & subtitle?), info? ^{db.titleforbidden.info}) | info? ^{db.info}), (annotation | bridgehead | remark | revhistory | *Indexing inlines* | *Admonition elements* | *Formal elements* | *Graphic elements* | *Informal elements* | *List elements* | *Paragraph elements* | *Publishing elements* | *Synopsis elements* | *Technical elements* | *Verbatim elements*)+)

Attribute synopsis

Common attributes and common linking attributes.

Additional attributes:

- label
- status

Additional constraints

- If this element is the root element, it must have a **version** attribute.

Description

The acknowledgements section of a book or other component provides the author(s) with a place to identify individuals, organizations, and other sources of support and to acknowledge their contributions to the work.

Processing expectations

Formatted as a displayed block. In books, it usually introduces a forced page break and often starts on the next recto page. In smaller components, such as articles, it may simply appear as another section.

Attributes

Common attributes and common linking attributes.

label
> Specifies an identifying string for presentation purposes

status
> Identifies the editorial or publication status of the element on which it occurs

Examples

```
<book xmlns='http://docbook.org/ns/docbook'>
<title>An Example Book</title>
<info>
  <author><personname>
    <firstname>Norman</firstname><surname>Walsh</surname>
  </personname></author>
</info>

<acknowledgements>
<para>Many thanks to the hundreds of contributors to the
example project. In particular, I'd like to thank the following
individuals, without whose contributions, this work would
not be half as useful:</para>
<itemizedlist>
<listitem>
<para><personname><firstname>A</firstname>
<surname>Nonymous</surname></personname>, for …
</para>
</listitem>
<!-- ... -->
</itemizedlist>
</acknowledgements>

<chapter><title>A Chapter</title>
<para>The body of the book…</para>
</chapter>
</book>
```

---

acronym
An often pronounceable word made from the initial (or selected) letters of a name or phrase

Synopsis
acronym ::= (text | phrase ^{db._phrase} | replaceable | trademark | *Graphic inlines* | *Indexing inlines* | *Linking inlines* | *Ubiquitous inlines*)*

Attribute synopsis
Common attributes and common linking attributes.

Description
A pronounceable contraction of initials. An acronym is often printed in all capitals or small capitals, although this is sometimes incorrect (consider dpi or bps).

Processing expectations
Formatted inline.

See Also

abbrev, emphasis, foreignphrase, phrase, quote, wordasword

Examples

```
<article xmlns='http://docbook.org/ns/docbook'>
<title>Example acronym</title>

<para>In the United States, <acronym>NASA</acronym> stands for the
National Aeronautics and Space Administration.
</para>

</article>
```

In the United States, NASA stands for the National Aeronautics and Space Administration.

---

address
A real-world address, generally a postal address

Synopsis

address ::= (text | city | country | email | fax | otheraddr | personname | phone | phrase $^{db.\_phrase}$ | pob | postcode | replaceable | state | street | uri | *Graphic inlines* | *Indexing inlines* | *Linking inlines* | *Ubiquitous inlines*)*

Attribute synopsis

Common attributes and common linking attributes.

Additional attributes:

- continuation (enumeration) = "continues" | "restarts"
- linenumbering (enumeration) = "numbered" | "unnumbered"
- startinglinenumber (integer)
- language
- xml:space (enumeratiocan) = "preserve"

Description

An address is generally a postal address, although it does contain elements for fax and email addresses as well as the catchall otheraddr.

Processing expectations

Formatted as a displayed block. This element is displayed "verbatim"; whitespace and line breaks within this element are significant.

Attributes

Common attributes and common linking attributes.

continuation

Determines whether line numbering continues from the previous element or restarts.

Enumerated values:	
"continues"	Line numbering continues from the immediately preceding element with the same name.
"restarts"	Line numbering restarts (begins at 1, usually).

language
> Identifies the language (i.e., programming language) of the verbatim content.

linenumbering
> Determines whether lines are numbered.

Enumerated values:	
"numbered"	Lines are numbered.
"unnumbered"	Lines are not numbered.

startinglinenumber
> Specifies the initial line number.

xml:space
> Can be used to indicate explicitly that whitespace in the verbatim environment is preserved. Whitespace must always be preserved in verbatim environments whether this attribute is specified or not.

Enumerated values:	
"preserve"	Whitespace must be preserved.

See Also

city, country, email, fax, otheraddr, phone, pob, postcode, state, street

Examples

```
<article xmlns='http://docbook.org/ns/docbook'>
<title>Example address</title>

<para>An example of a postal mail address in the United States:
<address>
John and Jane Doe
<street>100 Main Street</street>
<city>Anytown</city>, <state>NY</state> <postcode>12345</postcode>
<country>USA</country>
</address>
</para>

</article>
```

An example of a postal mail address in the United States:

John and Jane Doe
100 Main Street

```
Anytown, NY 12345
USA

<article xmlns='http://docbook.org/ns/docbook'>
<title>Example address</title>

<para>An example of a post office box address in the United States:
<address>
<pob>P.O. Box 1234</pob>
<city>Anytown</city>, <state>MA</state> <postcode>12345</postcode>
<country>USA</country>
</address>
</para>

</article>
```

An example of a post office box address in the United States:

```
P.O. Box 1234
Anytown, MA 12345
USA
```

```
<article xmlns='http://docbook.org/ns/docbook'>
<title>Example address</title>

<para>Addresses can also include phone numbers:
<address>
John Smith
<street>100 Pine Blvd</street>
<city>Anytown</city>, <state>NY</state> <postcode>12345</postcode>
<country>USA</country>
<phone>914.555.1212</phone>
<fax>914.555.1212</fax>
</address>
</para>

</article>
```

Addresses can also include phone numbers:

```
John Smith
100 Pine Blvd
Anytown, NY 12345
USA
914.555.1212
914.555.1212
```

affiliation

The institutional affiliation of an individual

Synopsis

affiliation ::= (shortaffil?, jobtitle*, (org? | (orgname?, orgdiv*, address*)))

Attribute synopsis

Common attributes and common linking attributes.

Description

The institutional affiliation of an author, contributor, or other individual.

Processing expectations

May be formatted inline or as a displayed block, depending on context. Sometimes suppressed.

See Also

`firstname`, `honorific`, `jobtitle`, `lineage`, `orgdiv`, `orgname`, `othername`, `shortaffil`, `surname`

---

alt
A text-only annotation, often used for accessibility

Synopsis

alt ::= (text | *Graphic inlines*)*

Attribute synopsis

Common attributes.

Description

A text (or other nonvisual) description of a graphical element. This is intended to be an alternative to the graphical presentation.

Processing expectations

May be formatted inline or as a displayed block, depending on context. Sometimes suppressed.

---

anchor
A spot in the document

Synopsis

anchor ::= empty

Attribute synopsis

Common attributes (ID required).

Description

An anchor identifies a single spot in the content. This may serve as the target for a cross-reference, for example, from a `link`. The `anchor` element may occur almost anywhere.

Processing expectations

An anchor has no content and generally produces no output. It is a link target.

See Also

`link`, `olink`, `xref`

Examples

```
<article xmlns='http://docbook.org/ns/docbook'>
<title>Example anchor</title>
```

```
<para>The anchor element<anchor xml:id="example.anchor.1"/> is empty and contributes
nothing to the flow of the content in which it occurs.  It is only useful
as a target.
</para>

</article>
```

> The anchor element is empty and contributes nothing to the flow of the content in which it occurs. It is only useful as a target.

annotation

Synopsis

annotation ::= ((((title? & titleabbrev?), info? ^{db.titleforbidden.info}) | info ^{db.titleonly.info}), (annotation | bridgehead | remark | revhistory | *Indexing inlines* | *Admonition elements* | *Formal elements* | *Graphic elements* | *Informal elements* | *List elements* | *Paragraph elements* | *Publishing elements* | *Synopsis elements* | *Technical elements* | *Verbatim elements*)+)

Attribute synopsis

Common attributes.

Additional attributes:

* annotates

Additional constraints

* annotation must not occur among the children or descendants of annotation.

Description

The annotation element is a "block" annotation. Block annotations can be used for pop ups and other "out of line" effects.

An annotation element is associated with another element by using a reference to an xml:id value. The association can go in either direction. An annotation element can use an annotates attribute on itself to point to an xml:id on another element. Or the other element can use an annotations attribute (one of the common attributes) on itself to point to an xml:id on an annotation element. There is no assumption that an annotation element is associated with its parent or any other ancestor element.

The attribute type of annotations and annotates is plain text, not IDREF or IDREFS. That enables modular content files to form associations with elements in other files without generating validation errors.

Processing expectations

Application specific.

Attributes

Common attributes.

annotates
> Identifies one or more elements to which this annotation applies

Examples

```
<article xmlns='http://docbook.org/ns/docbook'>
<title>Example of an annotation</title>

<annotation xml:id="note-parts-list">
  <para>This list is not comprehensive.</para>
</annotation>

<para annotations="note-parts-list">
  An automobile contains an engine,
  wheels, doors, and windows.
</para>

</article>
```

---

answer
An answer to a question posed in a qandaset

Synopsis
answer ::= (label?, (annotation | bridgehead | remark | revhistory | *Indexing inlines* | *Admonition elements* | *Formal elements* | *Graphic elements* | *Informal elements* | *List elements* | *Paragraph elements* | *Publishing elements* | *Synopsis elements* | *Technical elements* | *Verbatim elements*) +)

Attribute synopsis
Common attributes and common linking attributes.

Description
Within a qandaentry, a question may have an answer. An answer is optional (some questions have no answers) and may be repeated (some questions have more than one answer).

Processing expectations
An answer is frequently introduced with a label, such as "A:". If an answer has a label child element, the content of that label is used as the label for the answer. The default label attribute on the nearest ancestor qandaset of an answer can be used to indicate that a processing application should automatically generate a label for the answer.

See Also
qandadiv, qandaentry, qandaset, question

appendix

An appendix in a book or article

Synopsis

appendix ::= ((((title & titleabbrev? & subtitle?), info? ^{db.titleforbidden.info}) | info ^{db.titlereq.info}), ((bibliography | glossary | index | toc)*, (((annotation | bridgehead | remark | revhistory | *Indexing inlines* | *Admonition elements* | *Formal elements* | *Graphic elements* | *Informal elements* | *List elements* | *Paragraph elements* | *Publishing elements* | *Synopsis elements* | *Technical elements* | *Verbatim elements*)+, ((section+, simplesect*) | simplesect+ | (sect1+, simplesect*) | refentry+)?) | (section+, simplesect*) | simplesect+ | (sect1+, simplesect*) | refentry+), (bibliography | glossary | index | toc)*))

Attribute synopsis

Common attributes and common linking attributes.

Additional attributes:

- label
- status

Additional constraints

- If this element is the root element, it must have a version attribute.

Description

Appendixes usually occur at the end of a document.

Processing expectations

Formatted as a displayed block. Usually introduces a forced page break and often starts on the next recto page. Sometimes restarts page numbering. Typically, appendixes are lettered rather than numbered, and appear in the table of contents.

Attributes

Common attributes and common linking attributes.

label
> Specifies an identifying string for presentation purposes

status
> Identifies the editorial or publication status of the element on which it occurs

See Also

article, book, chapter, colophon, dedication, part, partintro, preface, set

Examples

```
<book xmlns='http://docbook.org/ns/docbook'>
<title>Example book</title>

<chapter>
<title>Required Chapter</title>

<para>At least one chapter, reference, part, or article is required in
a book.
```

```
    </para>

    </chapter>

    <appendix>
    <title>Demonstration Appendix</title>

    <para>This appendix demonstrates an appendix in a book. It has the
    same broad content model as a chapter.
    </para>

    </appendix>
    </book>
```

application

Synopsis
application ::= (text | phrase ^{db._phrase} | replaceable | *Graphic inlines* | *Indexing inlines* | *Linking inlines* | *Ubiquitous inlines*)*

Attribute synopsis
Common attributes and common linking attributes.

Additional attributes:

- class (enumeration) = "hardware" | "software"

Description
The appellation "application" is usually reserved for larger software packages. For example, WordPerfect is an application, but *grep* is not. In some domains, application may also apply to a piece of hardware.

Processing expectations
Formatted inline.

Attributes
Common attributes and common linking attributes.

class
> Identifies the class of application

Enumerated values:	
"hardware"	A hardware application
"software"	A software application

See Also
database, filename, hardware, productname

Examples

```
<article xmlns='http://docbook.org/ns/docbook'>
<title>Example application</title>

<para><application>XMLmind</application> is one of several word
processors that support DocBook <acronym>XML</acronym>.
</para>

</article>
```

XMLmind is one of several word processors that support DocBook XML.

---

arc

An XLink arc in an extendedlink

Synopsis
arc ::= empty

Attribute synopsis
Common attributes.

Additional attributes:

- `xlink:from` (NMTOKEN)
- `xlink:to` (NMTOKEN)

Description
An arc in an extendedlink. See *XML Linking Language (XLink) Version 1.0* [XLink] for more details.

Processing expectations
Suppressed.

Attributes
Common attributes.

xlink:from
    Specifies the XLink traversal-from

xlink:to
    Specifies the XLink traversal-to

---

area (db.area.inareaset)

A region defined for a callout in a graphic or code example

Synopsis
area (db.area.inareaset) ::= alt?

Attribute synopsis
Common attributes and common linking attributes.

Additional attributes:

- **coords**
- `label`
- *Exactly one of:*
  - —`units` (enumeration) = "calspair" | "linecolumn" | "linecolumnpair" | "linerange"
  - —*Each of:*
    - —`units` (enumeration) = "other"
    - —**otherunits** (NMTOKEN)

Required attributes are shown in **bold**.

Description

An `area` in an `areaset` has an optional `xml:id`. In every other respect, it is the same as an `area` in an `areaspec`.

---

area (db.area)   A region defined for a callout in a graphic or code example

Synopsis

area (db.area) ::= alt?

Attribute synopsis

Common attributes (ID required) and common linking attributes.

Additional attributes:

- **coords**
- `label`
- *Exactly one of:*
  - —`units` (enumeration) = "calspair" | "linecolumn" | "linecolumnpair" | "linerange"
  - —*Each of:*
    - —`units` (enumeration) = "other"
    - —**otherunits** (NMTOKEN)

Required attributes are shown in **bold**.

Description

An `area` is an empty element holding information about a region in a graphic, program listing, or screen.

The region is generally decorated with a number, symbol, or other distinctive mark. The mark is usually used as the label for the `callout` in a `calloutlist`, which allows the reader to identify which callouts are associated with which regions. The marks may be generated by the processing application from the areas, or it may be added by some other process. (This is an interchange issue. See Appendix D.)

For a complete description of callouts, see callout.

Processing expectations

Suppressed. This element provides data for processing but it is not expected to be rendered directly.

The processing expectations of callouts are likely to deserve special consideration for interchange. See Appendix D.

The coords, which are required, identify the location of the region. The coordinates are CDATA; how they are interpreted depends on the units specified:

calspair

> The coordinates are expressed using the semantics of the CALS graphic attributes. The format of the coordinates is "x1,y1 x2,y2". This identifies a rectangle with the lower-left corner at (x1,y1) and the upper-right corner at (x2,y2). The x and y coordinates are integers in the range 0 to 10000; they express a percentage of the total distance from 0.00 to 100.00%. The lower-left corner is (0,0).

linecolumn

> The coordinates are expressed using lines and columns. The format of the coordinates is "line column." In a graphic context, the meaning of this unit is unspecified.

linerange

> The coordinates are expressed using lines. The format of the coordinates is "startingline endingline." In a graphic context, the meaning of this unit is unspecified.

linecolumnpair

> The coordinates are expressed as a continuous flow of characters. The format of the coordinates is "line1 col1 line2 col2". This identifies a flow of characters that begins at col1 of line1 and extends to col2 of line2. If line1 and line2 are different, then the region includes all of the intervening lines (including text that occurs before col1 and after col2). In other words, this unit does not specify a rectangle. In a graphic context, the meaning of this unit is unspecified.

otherunits

> If specified, then the otherunits attribute is expected to identify the units in some implementation-specific way.

The units attribute is not required; if it is not specified, the semantics of the coordinates must be inherited from the surrounding areaspec or areaset element or implied in some implementation-specific manner.

In processing systems in which the mark is inserted automatically, the label attribute is provided as a mechanism for specifying what the mark should be.

The author may point to any relevant information with `linkends`. DocBook does not specify a semantic for these links. One possible use would be for providing a link back to the appropriate `callout` in an online environment.

Attributes

Common attributes (ID required) and common linking attributes.

coords
> Provides the coordinates of the area. The coordinates must be interpreted using the `units` specified.

label
> Specifies an identifying number or string that may be used in presentation. The area label might be drawn on top of the figure, for example, at the position indicated by the coords attribute.

otherunits
> Identifies the units used in the `coords` attribute when the `units` attribute is "other". This attribute is forbidden otherwise.

units
> Identifies the units used in the `coords` attribute. The default units vary according to the type of callout specified: `calspair` for graphics and `linecolumn` for line-oriented elements.

Enumerated values:	
"calspair"	Coordinates expressed as a pair of CALS graphic coordinates
"linecolumn"	Coordinates expressed as a line and column
"linecolumnpair"	Coordinates expressed as a pair of lines and columns
"linerange"	Coordinates expressed as a line range

units
> Indicates that nonstandard units are used for this `area`. In this case, `otherunits` must be specified.

Enumerated values:	
"other"	Coordinates expressed in some nonstandard units

See Also

area (db.area.inareaset)

areaset

A set of related areas in a graphic or code example

Synopsis

areaset ::= area ^{db.area.inareaset}+

Attribute synopsis

Common attributes (ID required) and common linking attributes.

Additional attributes:

- `label`
- *Exactly one of:*
    - —`units` (enumeration) = "calspair" | "linecolumn" | "linecolumnpair" | "linerange"
    - —*Each of:*
        - —`units` (enumeration) = "other"
        - —**otherunits** (NMTOKEN)

Required attributes are shown in **bold**.

Description

An `areaset` contains one or more `area`s. These `area`s are bound in a set in order to associate them with a single `callout` description. See `area` for a more complete description of the areas.

For a complete description of callouts, see `callout`.

Processing expectations

Suppressed.

Attributes

Common attributes (ID required) and common linking attributes.

label

Specifies an identifying string for presentation purposes.

otherunits

Identifies the units used in the `coords` attribute when the `units` attribute is "other". This attribute is forbidden otherwise.

units

Identifies the units used in the `coords` attribute. The default units vary according to the type of callout specified: `calspair` for graphics and `linecolumn` for line-oriented elements.

Enumerated values:	
"calspair"	Coordinates expressed as a pair of CALS graphic coordinates
"linecolumn"	Coordinates expressed as a line and column
"linecolumnpair"	Coordinates expressed as a pair of lines and columns

Enumerated values:	
"linerange"	Coordinates expressed as a line range

units

    Indicates that nonstandard units are used for this `area`. In this case, `otherunits` must be specified.

Enumerated values:	
"other"	Coordinates expressed in some nonstandard units

areaspec

A collection of regions in a graphic or code example

Synopsis
areaspec ::= (area $^{db.area}$ | areaset)+

Attribute synopsis
Common attributes and common linking attributes.

Additional attributes:

- *Exactly one of:*
  - —units (enumeration) = "calspair" | "linecolumn" | "linecolumnpair" | "linerange"
  - —*Each of:*
    - —units (enumeration) = "other"
    - —**otherunits** (NMTOKEN)

Required attributes are shown in **bold**.

Description
An `areaspec` holds a collection of regions and/or region sets in a graphic, program listing, or screen that are associated with `callout` descriptions. See `area` for a description of the attributes.

Processing expectations
Suppressed. This element provides data for processing but it is not expected to be rendered directly.

Attributes
Common attributes and common linking attributes.

otherunits

    Identifies the units used in the `coords` attribute when the `units` attribute is "other". This attribute is forbidden otherwise.

units

> Identifies the units used in the `coords` attribute. The default units vary according to the type of callout specified: `calspair` for graphics and `linecolumn` for line-oriented elements.

Enumerated values:	
"calspair"	Coordinates expressed as a pair of CALS graphic coordinates
"linecolumn"	Coordinates expressed as a line and column
"linecolumnpair"	Coordinates expressed as a pair of lines and columns
"linerange"	Coordinates expressed as a line range

units

> Indicates that nonstandard units are used for this `area`. In this case, `otherunits` must be specified.

Enumerated values:	
"other"	Coordinates expressed in some nonstandard units

See Also

`calloutlist, co, coref, imageobjectco, programlistingco, screenco`

---

arg

An argument in a cmdsynopsis

Synopsis

arg ::= (text | arg | group | option | phrase ^{db._phrase} | replaceable | sbr | synopfragmentref | *Graphic inlines* | *Indexing inlines* | *Linking inlines* | *Ubiquitous inlines*)*

Attribute synopsis

Common attributes and common linking attributes.

Additional attributes:

- `choice` (enumeration) = "opt" | "plain" | "req" [default="opt"]
- `rep` (enumeration) = "norepeat" | "repeat" [default="norepeat"]

Description

Used in `cmdsynopsis` for command arguments. See `cmdsynopsis` for more information and examples.

Processing expectations

May be formatted inline or as a displayed block, depending on context.

Attributes

Common attributes and common linking attributes.

choice
> Indicates optionality

Enumerated values:	
"opt"	Formatted to indicate that it is optional
"plain"	Formatted without indication
"req"	Formatted to indicate that it is required

rep
> Indicates whether or not repetition is possible

Enumerated values:	
"norepeat"	Cannot be repeated
"repeat"	Can be repeated

See Also
cmdsynopsis, group, refsynopsisdiv, sbr, synopfragment, synopfragmentref

---

article

An article

Synopsis
article ::= ((((title & titleabbrev? & subtitle?), info? ^{db.titleforbidden.info}) | info ^{db.titlereq.info}), (acknowledgements | appendix | bibliography | colophon | glossary | index | toc)*, (((annotation | bridgehead | remark | revhistory | *Indexing inlines* | *Admonition elements* | *Formal elements* | *Graphic elements* | *Informal elements* | *List elements* | *Paragraph elements* | *Publishing elements* | *Synopsis elements* | *Technical elements* | *Verbatim elements*)+, ((section+, simplesect*) | simplesect + | (sect1+, simplesect*) | refentry+)?) | (section+, simplesect*) | simplesect+ | (sect1+, simple sect*) | refentry+), (acknowledgements | appendix | bibliography | colophon | glossary | index | toc)*)

Attribute synopsis
Common attributes and common linking attributes.

Additional attributes:

- class (enumeration) = "faq" | "journalarticle" | "productsheet" | "specification" | "techreport" | "whitepaper"
- label
- status

Additional constraints

- If this element is the root element, it must have a **version** attribute.

Description

The `article` element is a general-purpose container for articles. The content model is both quite complex and rather loose in order to accommodate the wide range of possible `article` structures. Although changes to the `article` element have been discussed on several occasions, no better model has been presented.

An `article` may include a table of contents and multiple lists of tables, figures, and so on before the main text of the article. It may also include a number of common back matter components at the end.

Processing expectations

Formatted as a displayed block. Frequently causes a forced page break in print media. May be numbered separately and presented in the table of contents.

Attributes

Common attributes and common linking attributes.

class

> Identifies the nature of the article

Enumerated values:	
"faq"	A collection of frequently asked questions
"journalarticle"	An article in a journal or other periodical
"productsheet"	A description of a product
"specification"	A specification
"techreport"	A technical report
"whitepaper"	A white paper

label

> Specifies an identifying string for presentation purposes

status

> Identifies the editorial or publication status of the element on which it occurs

See Also

appendix, book, chapter, colophon, dedication, part, partintro, preface, set

Examples

```
<article xmlns='http://docbook.org/ns/docbook'>
<info>
  <title>A World Wide Web Interface to CTAN</title>
  <titleabbrev>CTAN-Web</titleabbrev>
  <author><personname>
    <firstname>Norman</firstname><surname>Walsh</surname>
  </personname></author>
  <authorinitials>ndw</authorinitials>
  <artpagenums>339-343</artpagenums>
  <volumenum>15</volumenum>
```

```
        <issuenum>3</issuenum>
        <publisher><publishername>The TeX User's Group</publishername></publisher>
        <pubdate>1994</pubdate>
        <revhistory>
            <revision>
                <revnumber>1.0</revnumber>
                <date>1994-03-28</date>
                <revremark>Submitted.</revremark>
            </revision>
            <revision>
                <revnumber>0.5</revnumber>
                <date>1994-02-15</date>
                <revremark>First draft for review.</revremark>
            </revision>
        </revhistory>
    </info>

    <para>The body of the article …</para>

</article>
```

artpagenums

The page numbers of an article as published

Synopsis
artpagenums ::= (text | phrase ^{db.–phrase} | replaceable | *Graphic inlines* | *Indexing inlines* | *Linking inlines* | *Ubiquitous inlines*)*

Attribute synopsis
Common attributes and common linking attributes.

Description
This element holds the page numbers of an article as published. Its content is not intended to influence the page numbers used by a presentation system formatting the parent article.

Processing expectations
Formatted inline. Sometimes suppressed.

Examples

See biblioset for an example using the artpagenums element.

attribution

The source of a block quote or epigraph

Synopsis
attribution ::= (text | citation | citetitle | person | personname | phrase ^{db.–phrase} | replaceable | *Graphic inlines* | *Indexing inlines* | *Linking inlines* | *Ubiquitous inlines*)*

Attribute synopsis
Common attributes and common linking attributes.

Description

An `attribution` identifies the source to whom a `blockquote` or `epigraph` is ascribed.

Processing expectations

May be formatted inline or as a displayed block, depending on context. Sometimes suppressed. Although it appears at the beginning of the content model for `blockquote` and `epigraph`, it is often output at the end.

See Also

blockquote, epigraph

Examples

```
<article xmlns='http://docbook.org/ns/docbook'>
<title>Example attribution</title>

<blockquote>
<attribution>William Shakespeare</attribution>
<literallayout>
What say you?  Will you yield, and this avoid?
Or, guilty in defense, be thus destroyed?
</literallayout>
</blockquote>

</article>
```

What say you? Will you yield, and this avoid?
Or, guilty in defense, be thus destroyed?

—William Shakespeare

audiodata

Pointer to external audio data

Synopsis

audiodata ::= info? ^{db.titleforbidden.info}

Attribute synopsis

Common attributes.

Additional attributes:

- *Each of:*
  - —format
  - —*Exactly one of:*
    - —**fileref** (anyURI)
    - —**entityref** (ENTITY)

Required attributes are shown in **bold**.

Description

This empty element points to external audio data.

Processing expectations

There are two ways to provide content for `audiodata`: `entityref` or `fileref`. It is best to use only one of these methods. However, if multiple sources are provided, `entityref` will be used in favor of `fileref`.

Attributes

Common attributes.

entityref
> Identifies the location of the data by external identifier (entity name)

fileref
> Identifies the location of the data by URI

format
> Specifies the format of the data

Examples

See `audioobject` for an example.

---

audioobject

A wrapper for audio data and its associated meta-information

Synopsis

audioobject ::= (info? ^{db.titleforbidden.info}, audiodata)

Attribute synopsis

Common attributes and common linking attributes.

Description

An `audioobject` is a wrapper for `audiodata`.

Processing expectations

Its content is rendered aurally or not at all. It might not be rendered, depending on its placement within a `mediaobject` or `inlinemediaobject` and the constraints on the publishing system. For a more detailed description of the semantics involved, see `mediaobject`.

See Also

`caption`, `imageobject`, `inlinemediaobject`, `mediaobject`, `textobject`, `videoobject`

Examples

```
<article xmlns='http://docbook.org/ns/docbook'>
<title>Example audioobject</title>

<mediaobject>
  <audioobject>
```

```
      <audiodata fileref="phaser.wav"/>
    </audioobject>
    <textobject>
      <phrase>A <trademark>Star Trek</trademark> phaser sound effect</phrase>
    </textobject>
  </mediaobject>

</article>
```

author

Synopsis

author ::= ((personname, (address | affiliation | contrib | email | personblurb | uri)*)) | (orgname, (address | affiliation | contrib | email | orgdiv | uri)*))

Attribute synopsis

Common attributes and common linking attributes.

Description

The author element holds information about the author of a document. When inside one of the bibliographic elements, author refers to the author of the document described by that element. Otherwise, it refers to the author of the current document or document section.

Processing expectations

May be formatted inline or as a displayed block, depending on context. Sometimes suppressed.

See Also

authorgroup, collab, contrib, editor, othercredit, personblurb, personname

Examples

```
<article xmlns='http://docbook.org/ns/docbook'>
<info>
  <title>Example author</title>

  <author>
    <personname>
      <honorific>Mr</honorific>
      <firstname>Norman</firstname>
      <surname>Walsh</surname>
      <othername role='mi'>D</othername>
    </personname>
    <affiliation>
      <shortaffil>ATI</shortaffil>
      <jobtitle>Senior Application Analyst</jobtitle>
      <orgname>ArborText, Inc.</orgname>
      <orgdiv>Application Development</orgdiv>
    </affiliation>
  </author>
</info>
```

```
<para>…</para>

</article>
```

authorgroup

Wrapper for author information when a document has multiple authors or collaborators

Synopsis

authorgroup ::= (author | editor | othercredit)+

Attribute synopsis

Common attributes and common linking attributes.

Description

The authorgroup element is a wrapper around multiple authors or other collaborators.

Processing expectations

May be formatted inline or as a displayed block, depending on context. Sometimes given very special treatment, especially on title pages or other displayed areas. Sometimes suppressed.

See Also

author, collab, contrib, editor, othercredit, personblurb, personname

Examples

```
<article xmlns='http://docbook.org/ns/docbook'>
<info>
  <title>Example authorgroup</title>

  <authorgroup>
    <author>
      <personname>
    <honorific>Dr.</honorific>
    <firstname>Lois</firstname>
    <surname>Common-Denominator</surname>
      </personname>
      <affiliation>
    <shortaffil>Director, M. Behn School of Coop. Eng.</shortaffil>
    <jobtitle>Director of Cooperative Efforts</jobtitle>
    <orgname>The Marguerite Behn International School of
    Cooperative Engineering</orgname>
      </affiliation>
    </author>

    <editor>
      <personname>
    <firstname>Peter</firstname>
    <surname>Parker</surname>
    <lineage>Sr.</lineage>
    <othername>Spiderman</othername>
      </personname>
      <personblurb>
```

```
    <para>Peter's a super hero in his spare time.</para>
      </personblurb>
    </editor>
  </authorgroup>
</info>

<para>…</para>

</article>
```

authorinitials

Synopsis

authorinitials ::= (text | phrase ^{db._phrase} | replaceable | *Graphic inlines* | *Indexing inlines* | *Linking inlines* | *Ubiquitous inlines*)*

Attribute synopsis

Common attributes and common linking attributes.

Description

Author initials occur most frequently in a `revision` or `remark`.

Processing expectations

Formatted inline. Sometimes suppressed.

bibliocoverage

Synopsis

bibliocoverage ::= (text | phrase ^{db._phrase} | replaceable | *Graphic inlines* | *Indexing inlines* | *Linking inlines* | *Ubiquitous inlines*)*

Attribute synopsis

Common attributes and common linking attributes.

Additional attributes:

- *All of:*
  - —*Exactly one of:*
    - — spatial (enumeration) = "dcmipoint" | "iso3166" | "dcmibox" | "tgn"
    - —*Each of:*
      - — spatial (enumeration) = "otherspatial"
      - —**otherspatial** (NMTOKEN)
  - —*Exactly one of:*
    - — temporal (enumeration) = "dcmiperiod" | "w3c-dtf"
    - —*Each of:*

— `temporal` (enumeration) = "othertemporal"

—**othertemporal** (NMTOKEN)

Required attributes are shown in **bold**.

Description

The `bibliocoverage` element is equivalent to the coverage element of the *Dublin Core Metadata Element Set* [DCMI].

The Dublin Core defines coverage as "the extent or scope of the content of the resource." It goes on to say:

> Spatial topic and spatial applicability may be a named place or a location specified by its geographic coordinates. Temporal topic may be a named period, date, or date range. A jurisdiction may be a named administrative entity or a geographic place to which the resource applies.

> Recommended best practice is to use a controlled vocabulary such as the *Thesaurus of Geographic Names Online* [TGN]. Where appropriate, named places or time periods can be used in preference to numeric identifiers such as sets of coordinates or date ranges.

DocBook V4.2 added `bibliocoverage`, `bibliorelation`, and `bibliosource` to make the DocBook meta-information wrappers a superset of the Dublin Core.

Processing expectations

Formatted inline. Sometimes suppressed.

This element is used for both spatial and temporal coverage, but only one should be specified at a time. In other words, on any given instance of the `bibliocoverage` element, specify either the `spatial` attribute or the `temporal` attribute, but not both.

Attributes

Common attributes and common linking attributes.

otherspatial
    A keyword that identifies the type of nonstandard coverage

othertemporal
    A keyword that identifies the type of nonstandard coverage

spatial
    Specifies the type of spatial coverage

Enumerated values:	
"dcmipoint"	The DCMI Point identifies a point in space using its geographic coordinates.
"iso3166"	ISO 3166 codes are used to represent names of countries.
"dcmibox"	The DCMI Box identifies a region of space using its geographic limits.
"tgn"	This value is taken from the Getty *Thesaurus of Geographic Names Online*.

spatial
: Specifies the type of spatial coverage

Enumerated values:	
"otherspatial"	Identifies a nonstandard type of coverage

temporal
: Specifies the type of temporal coverage

Enumerated values:	
"dcmiperiod"	A specification of the limits of a time interval
"w3c-dtf"	W3C encoding rules for dates and times—a profile based on ISO 8601

temporal
: Specifies the type of temporal coverage

Enumerated values:	
"othertemporal"	Specifies a nonstandard type of coverage

bibliodiv

A section of a bibliography

Synopsis

bibliodiv ::= ((((title & titleabbrev? & subtitle?), info? $^{db.titleforbidden.info}$) | info $^{db.titlereq.info}$), (annotation | bridgehead | remark | revhistory | *Indexing inlines* | *Admonition elements* | *Formal elements* | *Graphic elements* | *Informal elements* | *List elements* | *Paragraph elements* | *Publishing elements* | *Synopsis elements* | *Technical elements* | *Verbatim elements*)*, (biblioentry | bibliomixed)+)

Attribute synopsis

Common attributes and common linking attributes.

Additional attributes:

- label
- status

Description

A bibliodiv is a section of a bibliography. A bibliography might be divided into sections in order to group different types of sources together, such as books, journal articles, websites, and so on.

A bibliography may contain any number of biblioentry or bibliomixed elements or any number of bibliodivs, but it cannot contain a mixture of both at the same level.

Processing expectations

Formatted as a displayed block. Some systems may display only those entries within a `bibliodiv` that are cited in the containing document. This may be an interchange issue. See Appendix D.

Attributes

Common attributes and common linking attributes.

label
> Specifies an identifying string for presentation purposes

status
> Identifies the editorial or publication status of the element on which it occurs

---

biblioentry
A raw entry in a bibliography

Synopsis

biblioentry ::= (citebiblioid | citerefentry | citetitle | person | personblurb | personname | subtitle | title | titleabbrev | *Publishing inlines* | *"Info" elements*)+

Attribute synopsis

Common attributes and common linking attributes.

Description

A `biblioentry` is an entry in a `bibliography`. The contents of `biblioentry` are a "database" of named fields. Presentation systems frequently suppress some elements in a `biblioentry`.

Processing expectations

Formatted as a displayed block.

A `biblioentry` is "raw." It contains a database-like collection of named fields. It is the responsibility of the processing system to select elements from within a `biblioentry`, present them in the correct order, and add all punctuation.

There is no expectation that a system will present all of the fields in a `biblioentry` or that they will be displayed in the order in which they occur.

Correct formatting of `biblioentry`s is an interchange issue. See Appendix D.

See Also

bibliomisc, bibliomixed, bibliomset, biblioset

bibliography

A bibliography

Synopsis

bibliography ::= ((((title? & titleabbrev? & subtitle?), info? ^{db.titleforbidden.info}) | info? ^{db.info}), (annotation | bridgehead | remark | revhistory | *Indexing inlines* | *Admonition elements* | *Formal elements* | *Graphic elements* | *Informal elements* | *List elements* | *Paragraph elements* | *Publishing elements* | *Synopsis elements* | *Technical elements* | *Verbatim elements*)*, (bibliodiv+ | (bibliioentry | bibliomixed)+))

Attribute synopsis

Common attributes and common linking attributes.

Additional attributes:

- label
- status

Additional constraints

- If this element is the root element, it must have a version attribute.

Description

A bibliography. A DocBook bibliography may contain some introductory information, but its main content is a set of bibliography entries (either biblioentry or biblio mixed). These may occur directly inside the bibliography element or inside bibliodiv elements.

Processing expectations

Formatted as a displayed block. A bibliography in a book frequently causes a forced page break in print media.

Some systems may display only those entries within a bibliography that are cited in the containing document. This may be an interchange issue. See Appendix D.

The two styles of bibliography entry have quite different processing expectations. A biblioentry is "raw"; it contains a database-like collection of named fields. A biblio mixed entry is "cooked"; the fields occur in the order in which they will be presented and additional punctuation may be sprinkled between the fields.

See biblioentry and bibliomixed for further discussion.

Attributes

Common attributes and common linking attributes.

label
> Specifies an identifying string for presentation purposes

status
> Identifies the editorial or publication status of the element on which it occurs

Examples

The entries in a **bibliography** come in two general forms, "raw" and "cooked." A raw entry is a database-like collection of named fields:

```
<bibliography xmlns='http://docbook.org/ns/docbook'>
<title>A Test Bibliography</title>

<bibliodiv><title>Books</title>

<biblioentry>
  <abbrev>AhoSethiUllman96</abbrev>
  <authorgroup>
    <author><personname>
      <firstname>Alfred V.</firstname><surname>Aho</surname>
    </personname></author>
    <author><personname>
      <firstname>Ravi</firstname><surname>Sethi</surname>
    </personname></author>
    <author><personname>
      <firstname>Jeffrey D.</firstname><surname>Ullman</surname>
    </personname></author>
  </authorgroup>
  <copyright><year>1996</year>
            <holder>Bell Telephone Laboratories, Inc.</holder></copyright>
  <editor><personname>
    <firstname>James T.</firstname><surname>DeWolf</surname>
</personname></editor>
  <biblioid class="isbn">0-201-10088-6</biblioid>
  <publisher>
    <publishername>Addison-Wesley Publishing Company</publishername>
  </publisher>
  <title>Compilers, Principles, Techniques, and Tools</title>
</biblioentry>

<biblioentry xreflabel="Kites75">
  <authorgroup>
    <author><personname>
      <firstname>Andrea</firstname><surname>Bahadur</surname>
    </personname></author>
    <author><personname>
      <firstname>Mark</firstname><surname>Shwarek</surname>
    </personname></author>
  </authorgroup>
  <copyright><year>1974</year><year>1975</year>
    <holder>Product Development International Holding N. V.</holder>
    </copyright>
  <biblioid class="isbn">0-88459-021-6</biblioid>
  <publisher>
    <publishername>Plenary Publications International, Inc.</publishername>
  </publisher>
  <title>Kites</title>
  <subtitle>Ancient Craft to Modern Sport</subtitle>
  <pagenums>988-999</pagenums>
</biblioentry>
```

```
</bibliodiv>
<bibliodiv><title>Periodicals</title>

<biblioentry>
  <abbrev>Walsh97</abbrev>
  <biblioset relation='journal'>
    <title>XML: Principles, Tools, and Techniques</title>
    <publisher>
      <publishername>O'Reilly &amp; Associates, Inc.</publishername>
    </publisher>
    <biblioid class='issn'>1085-2301</biblioid>
    <editor><personname>
      <firstname>Dan</firstname><surname>Connolly</surname>
    </personname></editor>
  </biblioset>
  <biblioset relation='article'>
    <title>A Guide to XML</title>
    <author><personname>
      <surname>Walsh</surname><firstname>Norman</firstname>
    </personname></author>
    <copyright><year>1997</year><holder>ArborText, Inc.</holder></copyright>
    <pagenums>97-108</pagenums>
  </biblioset>
</biblioentry>

</bibliodiv>

</bibliography>
```

A cooked entry is formatted, including additional text, so that it is easy to render.

```
<bibliography xmlns='http://docbook.org/ns/docbook'>
<title>References</title>

<bibliomixed>
  <bibliomset relation='article'>Walsh, Norman.
    <title role='article'>Introduction to Cascading Style Sheets</title>.
  </bibliomset>
  <bibliomset relation='journal'>
    <title>The World Wide Web Journal</title>
    <volumenum>2</volumenum><issuenum>1</issuenum>.
    <publishername>O'Reilly &amp; Associates, Inc.</publishername> and
    The World Wide Web Consortium. Winter, 1996</bibliomset>.
</bibliomixed>

</bibliography>
```

biblioid
An identifier for a document

Synopsis

biblioid ::= (text | phrase ^{db.–phrase} | replaceable | *Graphic inlines* | *Indexing inlines* | *Linking inlines* | *Ubiquitous inlines*)*

Attribute synopsis

Common attributes and common linking attributes.

Additional attributes:

- *Exactly one of:*
  - —class (enumeration) = "doi" | "isbn" | "isrn" | "issn" | "libraryofcongress" | "pubsnumber" | "uri"
  - —*All of:*
    - —**class** (enumeration) = "other"
    - —**otherclass** (NMTOKEN)

Required attributes are shown in **bold**.

Description

A bibliographic identifier, such as an ISBN number, Library of Congress identifier, or URI.

This element supersedes the isbn, issn, and pubsnumber elements.

Processing expectations

Formatted inline. Sometimes suppressed.

Attributes

Common attributes and common linking attributes.

class
> Identifies the kind of bibliographic identifier

Enumerated values:	
"doi"	A digital object identifier
"isbn"	An international standard book number
"isrn"	An international standard technical report number (ISO 10444)
"issn"	An international standard serial number
"libraryofcongress"	A Library of Congress reference number
"pubsnumber"	A publication number (an internal number or possibly an organizational standard)
"uri"	A Uniform Resource Identifier

class
> Identifies the kind of bibliographic identifier

Enumerated values:	
"other"	Indicates that the identifier is some "other" kind

otherclass
  Identifies the nature of the nonstandard bibliographic identifier

See Also
issuenum, productnumber, seriesvolnums, volumenum

bibliolist

A wrapper for a list of bibliography entries

Synopsis
bibliolist ::= ((((title? & titleabbrev?), info? ^{db.titleforbidden.info}) | info ^{db.titleonly.info})?, (annotation | bridgehead | remark | revhistory | *Indexing inlines* | *Admonition elements* | *Formal elements* | *Graphic elements* | *Informal elements* | *List elements* | *Paragraph elements* | *Publishing elements* | *Synopsis elements* | *Technical elements* | *Verbatim elements*)*, (biblioentry | bibliomixed)+)

Attribute synopsis
Common attributes and common linking attributes.

Description
While bibliographys are usually limited to component or section boundaries, appearing at the end of a book or chapter, for instance, bibliolists can appear anywhere that the other list types are allowed.

Using a bibliolist in running text, instead of a variablelist, for example, maintains the semantic distinction of a bibliography.

Processing expectations
Formatted as a displayed block.

bibliomisc

Untyped bibliographic information

Synopsis
bibliomisc ::= (text | phrase ^{db.-phrase} | replaceable | *Graphic inlines* | *Indexing inlines* | *Linking inlines* | *Ubiquitous inlines*)*

Attribute synopsis
Common attributes and common linking attributes.

Description
The bibliomisc element is a wrapper for bibliographic information that does not fit neatly into the other bibliographic fields (such as author and publisher).

Processing expectations
Formatted inline. It is recommended that the role attribute be used to identify the kind of information that this element contains.

See Also
biblioentry, bibliomixed, bibliomset, biblioset

---

bibliomixed
A cooked entry in a bibliography

Synopsis
bibliomixed ::= (text | citebiblioid | citerefentry | citetitle | person | personblurb | person name | subtitle | title | titleabbrev | *Publishing inlines* | *"Info" elements*)*

Attribute synopsis
Common attributes and common linking attributes.

Description
A bibliomixed is an entry in a bibliography. The contents of bibliomixed include all necessary punctuation for formatting. Presentation systems usually display all of the elements in a bibliomixed.

Processing expectations
Formatted as a displayed block.

A bibliomixed entry is "cooked." In addition to named fields, it can contain interspersed text to provide punctuation and other formatting information.

The processing system is generally expected to present each and every element in the entry, and all interspersed #PCDATA, in the order in which it occurs.

See Also
biblioentry, bibliomisc, bibliomset, biblioset

---

bibliomset
A cooked container for related bibliographic information

Synopsis
bibliomset ::= (text | citebiblioid | citerefentry | citetitle | person | personblurb | personname | phrase ^db._phrase | replaceable | subtitle | title | titleabbrev | *Graphic inlines* | *Indexing inlines* | *Linking inlines* | *Publishing inlines* | *Ubiquitous inlines* | *"Info" elements*)*

Attribute synopsis
Common attributes and common linking attributes.

Additional attributes:

- relation

Description
A bibliomset is a "cooked" wrapper for a collection of bibliographic information.

The purpose of this wrapper is to assert the relationship that binds the collection. For example, in a bibliomixed entry for an article in a journal, you might use two bibliom sets to wrap the fields related to the article and the fields related to the journal.

Processing expectations

Formatted as a displayed block.

A `bibliomset` is "cooked." In addition to named fields, it can contain interspersed text to provide punctuation and other formatting information.

The processing system is generally expected to present each and every element in the set, all interspersed `#PCDATA`, in the order in which it occurs.

Attributes

Common attributes and common linking attributes.

relation
> Identifies the relationship between the bibliographic elements

See Also

`biblioentry, bibliomisc, bibliomixed, biblioset`

Examples

```
<bibliography xmlns='http://docbook.org/ns/docbook'>
<title>Example bibliomset</title>

<bibliomixed>
  <bibliomset relation='article'>Walsh, Norman.
    <title role='article'>Introduction to Cascading Style Sheets</title>.
  </bibliomset>
  <bibliomset relation='journal'>
    <title>The World Wide Web Journal</title>
    <volumenum>2</volumenum><issuenum>1</issuenum>.
    <publishername>O'Reilly &amp; Associates, Inc.</publishername> and
    The World Wide Web Consortium. Winter, 1996.
  </bibliomset>
</bibliomixed>

</bibliography>
```

biblioref

A cross-reference to a bibliographic entry

Synopsis

biblioref ::= empty

Attribute synopsis

Common attributes and common linking attributes.

Additional attributes:

- `begin` (token)
- `end` (token)
- `endterm` (IDREF)
- `units` (token)

- `xrefstyle`

Description

A `biblioref` is a special-purpose cross-reference element. It is used for references to bibliography entries where additional formatting is necessary.

Processing expectations

Formatted inline.

Attributes

Common attributes and common linking attributes.

begin
> Identifies the beginning of a reference; the location within the work that is being referenced

end
> Identifies the end of a reference

endterm
> Points to the element whose content is to be used as the text of the link

units
> The units (e.g., pages) used to identify the beginning and ending of a reference

xrefstyle
> Specifies a keyword or keywords identifying additional style information

---

bibliorelation   The relationship of a document to another

Synopsis

bibliorelation ::= (text | phrase ^{db.—phrase} | replaceable | *Graphic inlines* | *Indexing inlines* | *Linking inlines* | *Ubiquitous inlines*)*

Attribute synopsis

Common attributes and common linking attributes.

Additional attributes:

- *Exactly one of:*
  - —class (enumeration) = "doi" | "isbn" | "isrn" | "issn" | "libraryofcongress" | "pubsnumber" | "uri"
  - —*All of:*
    - —**class** (enumeration) = "other"
    - —**otherclass** (NMTOKEN)
- *Exactly one of:*

— type (enumeration) = "hasformat" | "haspart" | "hasversion" | "isformatof" | "ispartof" | "isreferencedby" | "isreplacedby" | "isrequiredby" | "isversionof" | "references" | "replaces" | "requires"

— *Each of:*

    — type (enumeration) = "othertype"

    — **othertype** (NMTOKEN)

Required attributes are shown in **bold**.

Description

The bibliorelation element satisfies the relation element of the Dublin Core Metadata Initiative (*http://dublincore.org/*).

The Dublin Core defines relation as "a reference to a related resource." It goes on to note that "recommended best practice is to reference the resource by means of a string or number conforming to a formal identification system."

DocBook V4.2 added bibliocoverage, bibliorelation, and bibliosource to make the DocBook meta-information wrappers a complete superset of the Dublin Core.

Processing expectations

Formatted inline. Sometimes suppressed.

Attributes

Common attributes and common linking attributes.

class

    Identifies the kind of bibliographic identifier

Enumerated values:	
"doi"	A digital object identifier
"isbn"	An international standard book number
"isrn"	An international standard technical report number (ISO 10444)
"issn"	An international standard serial number
"libraryofcongress"	A Library of Congress reference number
"pubsnumber"	A publication number (an internal number or possibly an organizational standard)
"uri"	A Uniform Resource Identifier

class

    Identifies the kind of bibliographic identifier

Enumerated values:	
"other"	Indicates that the identifier is some "other" kind

otherclass
Identifies the nature of the nonstandard bibliographic identifier

othertype
A keyword that identifies the type of the nonstandard relationship

type
Identifies the type of relationship

Enumerated values:	
"hasformat"	The described resource pre-existed the referenced resource, which is essentially the same intellectual content presented in another format.
"haspart"	The described resource includes the referenced resource either physically or logically.
"hasversion"	The described resource has a version, edition, or adaptation, namely, the referenced resource.
"isformatof"	The described resource is the same intellectual content of the referenced resource, but presented in another format.
"ispartof"	The described resource is a physical or logical part of the referenced resource.
"isreferencedby"	The described resource is referenced, cited, or otherwise pointed to by the referenced resource.
"isreplacedby"	The described resource is supplanted, displaced, or superseded by the referenced resource.
"isrequiredby"	The described resource is required by the referenced resource, either physically or logically.
"isversionof"	The described resource is a version, edition, or adaptation of the referenced resource; changes in version imply substantive changes in content rather than differences in format.
"references"	The described resource references, cites, or otherwise points to the referenced resource.
"replaces"	The described resource supplants, displaces, or supersedes the referenced resource.
"requires"	The described resource requires the referenced resource to support its function, delivery, or coherence of content.

type
Identifies the type of relationship

Enumerated values:	
"othertype"	The described resource has a nonstandard relationship with the referenced resource.

biblioset

Synopsis

biblioset ::= (citebiblioid | citerefentry | citetitle | person | personblurb | personname | subtitle | title | titleabbrev | *Publishing inlines* | *"Info" elements*)+

Attribute synopsis

Common attributes and common linking attributes.

Additional attributes:

- relation

Description

A biblioset is a "raw" wrapper for a collection of bibliographic information.

The purpose of this wrapper is to assert the relationship that binds the collection. For example, in a biblioentry for an article in a journal, you might use two bibliosets to wrap the fields related to the article and the fields related to the journal.

Processing expectations

Formatted as a displayed block.

A biblioset is "raw." It contains a database-like collection of named fields. It is the responsibility of the processing system to select elements from within a biblioset, present them in the correct order, and add all punctuation.

There is no expectation that a system will present all of the fields in a biblioset or that they will be displayed in the order in which they occur.

Correct formatting of bibliosets is an interchange issue. See Appendix D.

Attributes

Common attributes and common linking attributes.

relation
> Identifies the relationship between the bibliographic elements

See Also

biblioentry, bibliomisc, bibliomixed, bibliomset

Examples

```
<bibliography xmlns='http://docbook.org/ns/docbook'>
<title>Example biblioset</title>

<biblioentry>
  <abbrev>Walsh97</abbrev>
  <biblioset relation='journal'>
    <title>XML: Principles, Tools, and Techniques</title>
    <publisher>
      <publishername>O'Reilly &amp; Associates, Inc.</publishername>
    </publisher>
    <biblioid class='issn'>1085-2301</biblioid>
```

```
    <editor><personname>
      <firstname>Dan</firstname><surname>Connolly</surname>
    </personname></editor>
  </biblioset>
  <biblioset relation='article'>
    <title>A Guide to XML</title>
    <author><personname>
      <surname>Walsh</surname><firstname>Norman</firstname>
    </personname></author>
    <copyright><year>1997</year><holder>ArborText, Inc.</holder></copyright>
    <artpagenums>97-108</artpagenums>
  </biblioset>
</biblioentry>

</bibliography>
```

bibliosource

The source of a document

Synopsis

bibliosource ::= (text | phrase ^{db.–phrase} | replaceable | *Graphic inlines* | *Indexing inlines* | *Linking inlines* | *Ubiquitous inlines*)*

Attribute synopsis

Common attributes and common linking attributes.

Additional attributes:

- *Exactly one of:*
  - class (enumeration) = "doi" | "isbn" | "isrn" | "issn" | "libraryofcongress" | "pubsnumber" | "uri"
  - *All of:*
    - **class** (enumeration) = "other"
    - **otherclass** (NMTOKEN)

Required attributes are shown in **bold**.

Description

The bibliosource element satisfies the source element of the Dublin Core Metadata Initiative (*http://dublincore.org/*).

The Dublin Core defines source as "a reference to a resource from which the present resource is derived." It goes on to note that "the present resource may be derived from the source resource in whole or in part. Recommended best practice is to reference the resource by means of a string or number conforming to a formal identification system."

DocBook V4.2 added bibliocoverage, bibliorelation, and bibliosource to make the DocBook meta-information wrappers a complete superset of the Dublin Core.

Processing expectations

Formatted inline. Sometimes suppressed.

Attributes

Common attributes and common linking attributes.

class

Identifies the kind of bibliographic identifier

Enumerated values:	
"doi"	A digital object identifier
"isbn"	An international standard book number
"isrn"	An international standard technical report number (ISO 10444)
"issn"	An international standard serial number
"libraryofcongress"	A Library of Congress reference number
"pubsnumber"	A publication number (an internal number or possibly an organizational standard)
"uri"	A Uniform Resource Identifier

class

Identifies the kind of bibliographic identifier

Enumerated values:	
"other"	Indicates that the identifier is some "other" kind

otherclass

Identifies the nature of the nonstandard bibliographic identifier

---

blockquote

A quotation set off from the main text

Synopsis

blockquote ::= (((((title? & titleabbrev?), info? ^{db.titleforbidden.info}) | info ^{db.titleonly.info}), attribu tion?, (annotation | bridgehead | remark | revhistory | *Indexing inlines* | *Admonition elements* | *Formal elements* | *Graphic elements* | *Informal elements* | *List elements* | *Paragraph elements* | *Publishing elements* | *Synopsis elements* | *Technical elements* | *Verbatim elements*)+)

Attribute synopsis

Common attributes and common linking attributes.

Description

Block quotations are set off from the main text, as opposed to occurring inline.

Processing expectations

Formatted as a displayed block.

See Also

abstract, attribution, epigraph, sidebar

Examples

```
<article xmlns='http://docbook.org/ns/docbook'>
<title>Example blockquote</title>

<blockquote><attribution>Richard Dawkins</attribution>
<para>The universe that we observe has precisely the properties we should
expect if there is, at bottom, no design, no purpose, no evil and
no good, nothing but pitiless indifference.
</para>
</blockquote>

</article>
```

> The universe that we observe has precisely the properties we should expect if there
> is, at bottom, no design, no purpose, no evil and no good, nothing but pitiless
> indifference.
>
> —Richard Dawkins

book

Synopsis

book ::= ((((title? & titleabbrev? & subtitle?), info? [db.titleforbidden.info]) | info? [db.info]), (acknowl edgements | appendix | article | bibliography | chapter | colophon | dedication | glossary | index | part | preface | reference | toc)*)

Attribute synopsis

Common attributes and common linking attributes.

Additional attributes:

- label
- status

Additional constraints

- If this element is the root element, it must have a **version** attribute.

Description

A complete book. This is probably the most common document starting point in Doc-Book documents. The content model of **book** was made dramatically less restrictive in DocBook V3.1.

Processing expectations

Formatted as a displayed block. Generally causes a forced page break, restarts page numbering, and may generate additional front and back matter (e.g., tables of contents and indexes) automatically. In a **set**, **book** almost always begins on the next available recto page.

The input order of major components is taken to be the desired output order.

Attributes
Common attributes and common linking attributes.

label
> Specifies an identifying string for presentation purposes

status
> Identifies the editorial or publication status of the element on which it occurs

See Also
appendix, article, chapter, colophon, dedication, part, partintro, preface, set

Examples

```
<book xmlns='http://docbook.org/ns/docbook'>
<title>An Example Book</title>
<titleabbrev>Example</titleabbrev>
<info>
  <legalnotice><para>No notice is required.</para></legalnotice>
  <author><personname>
    <firstname>Norman</firstname><surname>Walsh</surname>
  </personname></author>
</info>
<dedication>
<para>This book is dedicated to you.
</para>
</dedication>
<preface><title>Foreword</title>
<para>Some content is always required.
</para>
</preface>
<chapter><title>A Chapter</title>
<para>Content is required in chapters too.
</para>
</chapter>
<appendix><title>Optional Appendix</title>
<para>Appendixes are optional.
</para>
</appendix>
</book>
```

bridgehead
A free-floating heading

Synopsis
bridgehead ::= (text | *Bibliography inlines* | *Error inlines* | *Graphic inlines* | *GUI inlines* | *Indexing inlines* | *Keyboard inlines* | *Linking inlines* | *Markup inlines* | *Math inlines* | *Object-oriented programming inlines* | *Operating system inlines* | *Product inlines* | *Programming inlines* | *Publishing inlines* | *Technical inlines* | *Ubiquitous inlines*)*

Attribute synopsis
Common attributes and common linking attributes.

Additional attributes:

- *At most one of:*
  —renderas (enumeration) = "sect1" | "sect2" | "sect3" | "sect4" | "sect5"
  —*All or none of:*
    —renderas (enumeration) = "other"
    —otherrenderas (NMTOKEN)

Description
Some documents, usually legacy documents, use headings that are not tied to the normal sectional hierarchy. These headings may be represented in DocBook with the bridgehead element.

A bridgehead may also be useful in fiction or journalistic works that don't have a nested hierarchy.

Processing expectations
A bridgehead is formatted as a block, using the same display properties as the section heading which it masquerades as. The renderas attribute controls which heading it mimics.

Attributes
Common attributes and common linking attributes.

otherrenderas
> Identifies the nature of the nonstandard rendering

renderas
> Indicates how the bridge head should be rendered

Enumerated values:	
"sect1"	Render as a first-level section.
"sect2"	Render as a second-level section.
"sect3"	Render as a third-level section.
"sect4"	Render as a fourth-level section.
"sect5"	Render as a fifth-level section.

renderas
> Indicates how the bridge head should be rendered

Enumerated values:	
"other"	Identifies a nonstandard rendering

See Also
sect1, sect2, sect3, sect4, sect5, section, simplesect

callout
A "called out" description of a marked area

Synopsis
callout ::= (annotation | bridgehead | remark | revhistory | *Indexing inlines* | *Admonition elements* | *Formal elements* | *Graphic elements* | *Informal elements* | *List elements* | *Paragraph elements* | *Publishing elements* | *Synopsis elements* | *Technical elements* | *Verbatim elements*)+

Attribute synopsis
Common attributes.

Additional attributes:

- **arearefs** (IDREFS)

Required attributes are shown in **bold**.

Description
A "callout" is a visual device for associating annotations with an image, program listing, or similar figure. Each location is identified with a mark, and the annotation is identified with the same mark. This is somewhat analogous to the notion of footnotes in print.

An example will help illustrate the concept. In the following example, the synopsis for the *mv* command is annotated with two marks. Note the location of the old and new filenames.

```
mv ❶oldfile ❷newfile
```

Somewhere else in the document, usually close by, a `calloutlist` provides a description for each of the callouts:

❶ The old filename. The *mv* command renames the file currently called *oldfile*, which must exist when *mv* is executed.

❷ The new filename. The *mv* command changes the name of the old file to *newfile*. If *newfile* exists when *mv* is executed, it will be replaced by the old file.

Each `callout` contains an annotation for an individual callout or a group of callouts. The `callout` points to the areas that it annotates with ID references. The areas are identified by coordinates in an **area** or **areaset**, or by an explicit **co** element.

Processing expectations
Formatted as a displayed block.

A `callout` usually generates text that points the reader to the appropriate area on the object being augmented. Often, these are numbered bullets or other distinct visual icons. The same icons should be used in both places. In other words, whatever identifies the callouts on the object should generate the same icons on the respective callouts.

In online environments, it may also be possible to establish a linking relationship between the two elements.

The processing expectations of `callouts` are likely to deserve special consideration for interchange. See Appendix D. This is especially true if your interchange partners are producing documentation in a medium that has restricted visual presentation features, such as aural media or Braille.

Attributes
Common attributes.

arearefs
> Identifies the areas described by this callout.

calloutlist
A list of callouts

Synopsis
calloutlist ::= ((((title? & titleabbrev?), info? ^{db.titleforbidden.info}) | info ^{db.titleonly.info}), (annotation | bridgehead | remark | revhistory | *Indexing inlines* | *Admonition elements* | *Formal elements* | *Graphic elements* | *Informal elements* | *List elements* | *Paragraph elements* | *Publishing elements* | *Synopsis elements* | *Technical elements* | *Verbatim elements*)*, callout+)

Attribute synopsis
Common attributes and common linking attributes.

Description
A `calloutlist` is a list of annotations or descriptions. Each `callout` points to the area on a `mediaobject`, `programlisting`, or `screen` that it augments.

The areas are identified by coordinates in an `area` or `areaset`, or by an explicit `co` element.

Processing expectations
Formatted as a displayed block.

See Also
areaspec, co, coref, imageobjectco, itemizedlist, listitem, orderedlist, programlistingco, screenco, segmentedlist, simplelist, variablelist

caption (db.caption)
A caption

Synopsis
caption (db.caption) ::= (info? ^{db.titleforbidden.info}, (annotation | bridgehead | remark | revhistory | *Indexing inlines* | *Admonition elements* | *Formal elements* | *Graphic elements* | *Informal elements* | *List elements* | *Paragraph elements* | *Publishing elements* | *Synopsis elements* | *Technical elements* | *Verbatim elements*)+)

Attribute synopsis
Common attributes and common linking attributes.

Additional constraints

- example must not occur among the children or descendants of caption.
- figure must not occur among the children or descendants of caption.
- table must not occur among the children or descendants of caption.
- equation must not occur among the children or descendants of caption.
- sidebar must not occur among the children or descendants of caption.
- task must not occur among the children or descendants of caption.
- caution must not occur among the children or descendants of caption.
- important must not occur among the children or descendants of caption.
- note must not occur among the children or descendants of caption.
- tip must not occur among the children or descendants of caption.
- warning must not occur among the children or descendants of caption.

Description

A caption is an extended description of a mediaobject or figure or other formal or informal element. Unlike a textobject, which is an alternative to the other elements in the mediaobject, the caption augments the object.

Processing expectations

Formatted as a displayed block.

See Also

audioobject, caption (db.html.caption), imageobject, inlinemediaobject, mediaobject, textobject, videoobject

Examples

See informalfigure for an example that uses caption.

caption (db.html.caption)

An HTML table caption

Synopsis

caption (db.html.caption) ::= (text | *Bibliography inlines* | *Error inlines* | *Graphic inlines* | *GUI inlines* | *Indexing inlines* | *Keyboard inlines* | *Linking inlines* | *Markup inlines* | *Math inlines* | *Object-oriented programming inlines* | *Operating system inlines* | *Product inlines* | *Programming inlines* | *Publishing inlines* | *Technical inlines* | *Ubiquitous inlines*)*

Attribute synopsis

Attributes:

- class
- style
- title

- lang
- onclick
- ondblclick
- onmousedown
- onmouseup
- onmouseover
- onmousemove
- onmouseout
- onkeypress
- onkeydown
- onkeyup

Additional constraints

- example must not occur among the children or descendants of caption.
- figure must not occur among the children or descendants of caption.
- table must not occur among the children or descendants of caption.
- equation must not occur among the children or descendants of caption.
- sidebar must not occur among the children or descendants of caption.
- task must not occur among the children or descendants of caption.
- caution must not occur among the children or descendants of caption.
- important must not occur among the children or descendants of caption.
- note must not occur among the children or descendants of caption.
- tip must not occur among the children or descendants of caption.
- warning must not occur among the children or descendants of caption.

Description
In an HTML table, a caption is a short text description for the table it is associated with.

Processing expectations
Formatted as a displayed block.

Attributes

class
> Assigns a class name or set of class names to an element. Any number of elements may be assigned the same class name or names. Multiple class names must be separated by whitespace characters.

lang
> Specifies the base language of an element's attribute values and text content. The default value of this attribute is unknown.

onclick
> Occurs when the pointing device button is clicked over an element.

ondblclick
> Occurs when the pointing device button is double-clicked over an element.

onkeydown
> Occurs when a key is pressed down over an element.

onkeypress
> Occurs when a key is pressed and released over an element.

onkeyup
> Occurs when a key is released over an element.

onmousedown
> Occurs when the pointing device button is pressed over an element.

onmousemove
> Occurs when the pointing device is moved while it is over an element.

onmouseout
> Occurs when the pointing device is moved away from an element.

onmouseover
> Occurs when the pointing device is moved onto an element.

onmouseup
> Occurs when the pointing device button is released over an element.

style
> Specifies style information for the current element.

title
> Offers advisory information about the element for which it is set.

See Also

`audioobject`, `caption` (db.caption), `imageobject`, `inlinemediaobject`, `mediaobject`, `tex tobject`, `videoobject`

Examples

See `table` (db.html.table) for an example that uses `caption`.

---

caution

Synopsis

caution ::= ((((`title`? & `titleabbrev`?), `info`? ^{db.titleforbidden.info}) | `info` ^{db.titleonly.info}), (`annotation` | `bridgehead` | `remark` | `revhistory` | *Indexing inlines* | *Admonition elements* | *Formal elements* | *Graphic elements* | *Informal elements* | *List elements* | *Paragraph elements* | *Publishing elements* | *Synopsis elements* | *Technical elements* | *Verbatim elements*)+)

Attribute synopsis

Common attributes and common linking attributes.

Additional constraints

- caution must not occur among the children or descendants of caution.
- important must not occur among the children or descendants of caution.
- note must not occur among the children or descendants of caution.
- tip must not occur among the children or descendants of caution.
- warning must not occur among the children or descendants of caution.

Description

A caution is an admonition, usually set off from the main text.

In some types of documentation, the semantics of admonitions are clearly defined (a caution might imply the possibility of harm to equipment whereas a warning might imply harm to a person). However, DocBook makes no such assertions.

Processing expectations

Formatted as a displayed block. Often outputs the generated text "Caution" or some other visible indication of the type of admonition, especially if a title is not present. Sometimes outputs a graphical icon or other symbol as well.

See Also

important, note, tip, warning

Examples

```
<article xmlns='http://docbook.org/ns/docbook'>
<title>Example caution</title>

<caution><title>No User-Serviceable Parts Inside</title>
<para>Breaking this seal voids all warranties.
</para>
</caution>

</article>
```

No User-Serviceable Parts Inside

Breaking this seal voids all warranties.

chapter

A chapter, as of a book

Synopsis

chapter ::= (((((title & titleabbrev? & subtitle?), info? $^{db.titleforbidden.info}$) | info $^{db.titlereq.info}$), ((bibliography | glossary | index | toc)*, (((annotation | bridgehead | remark | revhistory | *Indexing inlines* | *Admonition elements* | *Formal elements* | *Graphic elements* | *Informal elements* | *List elements* | *Paragraph elements* | *Publishing elements* | *Synopsis elements* | *Technical elements* | *Verbatim elements*)+, ((section+, simplesect*) | simplesect+ | (sect1+, simplesect*) | refentry+)?) | (section+, simplesect*) | simplesect+ | (sect1+, simplesect*) | refentry+), (bibliography | glossary | index | toc)*))

Attribute synopsis

Common attributes and common linking attributes.

Additional attributes:

- label
- status

Additional constraints

- If this element is the root element, it must have a version attribute.

Description

A chapter is a chapter of a book.

Processing expectations

Formatted as a displayed block. Usually introduces a forced page break and often starts on the next recto page. The first chapter of a document usually restarts page numbering. Typically, chapters are numbered and presented in the table of contents.

Attributes

Common attributes and common linking attributes.

label

> Specifies an identifying string for presentation purposes

status

> Identifies the editorial or publication status of the element on which it occurs

See Also

appendix, article, book, colophon, dedication, part, partintro, preface, set

Examples

```
<chapter xmlns='http://docbook.org/ns/docbook'
    label="6" xml:id="figures" version="5.0">
<info>
  <title>Pictures and Figures</title>
  <keywordset>
    <keyword>images</keyword>
    <keyword>illustrations</keyword>
  </keywordset>
```

```
  <itermset>
    <indexterm zone="figures"><primary>Figures</primary></indexterm>
    <indexterm zone="figures"><primary>Pictures</primary></indexterm>
    <indexterm zone="notreal">
       <primary>Sections</primary><secondary>Not Real</secondary>
    </indexterm>
  </itermset>
</info>
<epigraph>
<attribution>William Safire</attribution>
<para>Knowing how things work is the basis for appreciation, and is
thus a source of civilized delight.
</para>
</epigraph>
<para>Pictures and figures …
</para>
<sect1><title>Top Level Section</title>
<para>…
</para>
<bridgehead xml:id="notreal" renderas='sect3'>Not a Real Section</bridgehead>
<para>This paragraph appears to be under a Sect3 heading, but it's really
in the same Sect1 as the preceding paragraph.
</para>
</sect1>
</chapter>
```

---

citation

An inline bibliographic reference to another published work

Synopsis

citation ::= (text | *Bibliography inlines* | *Error inlines* | *Graphic inlines* | *GUI inlines* | *Indexing inlines* | *Keyboard inlines* | *Linking inlines* | *Markup inlines* | *Math inlines* | *Object-oriented programming inlines* | *Operating system inlines* | *Product inlines* | *Programming inlines* | *Publishing inlines* | *Technical inlines* | *Ubiquitous inlines*)*

Attribute synopsis

Common attributes and common linking attributes.

Description

The content of a citation is assumed to be a reference string, perhaps identical to an abbreviation in an entry in a bibliography.

Processing expectations

Formatted inline.

See Also

citebiblioid, citerefentry, citetitle

Examples

```
<article xmlns='http://docbook.org/ns/docbook' version='5.0'>
<title>Example citation</title>

<para>Consult <citation>AhoSethiUllman96</citation> for more details on
```

```
abstract syntax tree construction.
</para>

<para>…</para>

<bibliolist>
<title>Bibliography</title>

<biblioentry>
  <abbrev>AhoSethiUllman96</abbrev>
  <authorgroup>
    <author><personname>
      <firstname>Alfred V.</firstname><surname>Aho</surname>
    </personname></author>
    <author><personname>
      <firstname>Ravi</firstname><surname>Sethi</surname>
    </personname></author>
    <author><personname>
      <firstname>Jeffrey D.</firstname><surname>Ullman</surname>
    </personname></author>
  </authorgroup>
  <copyright><year>1996</year>
            <holder>Bell Telephone Laboratories, Inc.</holder></copyright>
  <editor>
    <personname>
      <firstname>James T.</firstname><surname>DeWolf</surname>
    </personname>
  </editor>
  <biblioid class="isbn">0-201-10088-6</biblioid>
  <publisher>
    <publishername>Addison-Wesley Publishing Company</publishername>
  </publisher>
  <citetitle>Compilers, Principles, Techniques, and Tools</citetitle>
</biblioentry>
</bibliolist>

</article>
```

Consult [AhoSethiUllman96] for more details on abstract syntax tree construction.

…

Bibliography

[AhoSethiUllman96] Alfred V. Aho, Ravi Sethi, and Jeffrey D. Ullman. Copyright ©
    1996 Bell Telephone Laboratories, Inc.. James T. DeWolf. 0-201-10088-6. Addison-
    Wesley Publishing Company. *Compilers, Principles, Techniques, and Tools*.

citebiblioid
A citation of a bibliographic identifier

Synopsis

citebiblioid ::= (text | phrase ^{db._phrase} | replaceable | *Graphic inlines* | *Indexing inlines* | *Linking inlines* | *Ubiquitous inlines*)*

Attribute synopsis

Common attributes and common linking attributes.

Additional attributes:

* *Exactly one of:*
  —class (enumeration) = "doi" | "isbn" | "isrn" | "issn" | "libraryofcongress" | "pubsnumber" | "uri"
  —*All of:*
    —**class** (enumeration) = "other"
    —**otherclass** (NMTOKEN)

Required attributes are shown in **bold**.

Description

A citebiblioid identifies a citation to another work by bibliographic identifier.

Processing expectations

Formatted inline.

Attributes

Common attributes and common linking attributes.

class
> Identifies the kind of bibliographic identifier

Enumerated values:	
"doi"	A digital object identifier
"isbn"	An international standard book number
"isrn"	An international standard technical report number (ISO 10444)
"issn"	An international standard serial number
"libraryofcongress"	A Library of Congress reference number
"pubsnumber"	A publication number (an internal number or possibly an organizational standard)
"uri"	A Uniform Resource Identifier

class
> Identifies the kind of bibliographic identifier

Enumerated values:	
"other"	Indicates that the identifier is some "other" kind

otherclass
> Identifies the nature of the nonstandard bibliographic identifier

See Also

citation, citerefentry, citetitle

---

citerefentry

Synopsis

citerefentry ::= (refentrytitle, manvolnum?)

Attribute synopsis

Common attributes and common linking attributes.

Description

This element is a citation to a refentry. It must include a refentrytitle that should exactly match the title of a refentry.

Processing expectations

This element implicitly links to the refentry with the same refentrytitle (in the same volume, as defined by manvolnum).

Formatted inline. Usually the manvolnum is put in parentheses.

See Also

citation, citebiblioid, citetitle

Examples

```
<article xmlns='http://docbook.org/ns/docbook'>
<title>Example citerefentry</title>

<para>For a further description of print formats, consult the
<citerefentry><refentrytitle>printf</refentrytitle>
<manvolnum>3S</manvolnum></citerefentry> manual page.
</para>

</article>
```

> For a further description of print formats, consult the printf manual page.

---

citetitle

Synopsis

citetitle ::= (text | *Bibliography inlines* | *Error inlines* | *Graphic inlines* | *GUI inlines* | *Indexing inlines* | *Keyboard inlines* | *Linking inlines* | *Markup inlines* | *Math inlines* | *Object-oriented programming inlines* | *Operating system inlines* | *Product inlines* | *Programming inlines* | *Publishing inlines* | *Technical inlines* | *Ubiquitous inlines*)*

Attribute synopsis

Common attributes and common linking attributes.

Additional attributes:

- pubwork (enumeration) = "article" | "bbs" | "book" | "cdrom" | "chapter" | "dvd" | "emailmessage" | "gopher" | "journal" | "manuscript" | "newsposting" | "part" | "refentry" | "section" | "series" | "set" | "webpage" | "wiki"

Description

A citetitle provides inline markup for the title of a cited work.

Processing expectations

Formatted inline. Often italicized for books and quoted for articles.

Attributes

Common attributes and common linking attributes.

pubwork
> Identifies the nature of the publication being cited

Enumerated values:	
"article"	An article
"bbs"	A bulletin board system
"book"	A book
"cdrom"	A CD-ROM
"chapter"	A chapter (as of a book)
"dvd"	A DVD
"emailmessage"	An email message
"gopher"	A gopher page
"journal"	A journal
"manuscript"	A manuscript
"newsposting"	A posting to a newsgroup
"part"	A part (as of a book)
"refentry"	A reference entry
"section"	A section (as of a book or article)
"series"	A series
"set"	A set (as of books)
"webpage"	A web page
"wiki"	A wiki page

See Also

citation, citebiblioid, citerefentry

Examples

```
<article xmlns='http://docbook.org/ns/docbook'>
<title>Example citetitle</title>

<para>For a complete methodology for DTD creation, see
<citetitle pubwork="book">Developing SGML DTDs: From Text to Model
to Markup</citetitle> by Eve Maler and Jeanne El Andaloussi.
</para>

</article>
```

> For a complete methodology for DTD creation, see *Developing SGML DTDs: From Text to Model to Markup* by Eve Maler and Jeanne El Andaloussi.

---

city
The name of a city in an address

Synopsis
city ::= (text | phrase ^{db.–phrase} | replaceable | *Graphic inlines* | *Indexing inlines* | *Linking inlines* | *Ubiquitous inlines*)*

Attribute synopsis
Common attributes and common linking attributes.

Description
The name of a city in an address.

Processing expectations
Formatted inline. In an address, this element may inherit the verbatim qualities of an address.

See Also
address, country, email, fax, otheraddr, phone, pob, postcode, state, street

---

classname
The name of a class, in the object-oriented programming sense

Synopsis
classname ::= (text | phrase ^{db.–phrase} | replaceable | *Graphic inlines* | *Indexing inlines* | *Linking inlines* | *Ubiquitous inlines*)*

Attribute synopsis
Common attributes and common linking attributes.

Description
The classname tag is used to identify the name of a class. This is likely to occur only in documentation about object-oriented programming systems, languages, and architectures.

DocBook does not contain a complete set of inlines appropriate for describing object-oriented programming environments. (While it has `classname`, for example, it has nothing suitable for methods.) This will be addressed in a future version of DocBook.

Processing expectations
Formatted inline.

See Also
property, symbol, token, type

Examples

```
<article xmlns='http://docbook.org/ns/docbook'>
<title>Example classname</title>

<para>All user-interface components must be descendants of the
<classname>Widget</classname> class.
</para>

</article>
```

All user-interface components must be descendants of the `Widget` class.

---

classsynopsis

The syntax summary for a class definition

Synopsis
classsynopsis ::= (*Object-oriented programming inlines*+, (classsynopsisinfo | constructorsynopsis | destructorsynopsis | fieldsynopsis | methodsynopsis)*)

Attribute synopsis
Common attributes and common linking attributes.

Additional attributes:

- `class` (enumeration) = "class" | "interface"
- `language`

Description
A `classsynopsis` contains the syntax summary of a class (generally speaking, a class in the object-oriented programming language sense).

This is one of the few places where DocBook attempts to model as well as describe. Unlike `funcsynopsis`, which was designed with C language function prototypes in mind, the content model of `classsynopsis` was designed to capture a wide range of object-oriented language semantics.

Processing expectations
For the most part, the processing application is expected to generate all of the parentheses, semicolons, commas, and so on required in the rendered synopsis. The

exception to this rule is that the spacing and other punctuation inside a parameter that is a pointer to a function must be provided in the source markup.

Attributes

Common attributes and common linking attributes.

class

> Specifies the nature of the synopsis

Enumerated values:	
"class"	This is the synopsis of a class.
"interface"	This is the synopsis of an interface.

language

> Identifies the language (i.e., programming language) of the content

---

classsynopsisinfo

Information supplementing the contents of a classsynopsis

Synopsis

classsynopsisinfo ::= (info? [db.titleforbidden.info], ((text | lineannotation | *Bibliography inlines* | *Computer-output inlines* | *Error inlines* | *Graphic inlines* | *GUI inlines* | *Indexing inlines* | *Keyboard inlines* | *Linking inlines* | *Markup inlines* | *Math inlines* | *Object-oriented programming inlines* | *Operating system inlines* | *Product inlines* | *Programming inlines* | *Publishing inlines* | *Technical inlines* | *Ubiquitous inlines* | *User-input inlines*)* | textobject))

Attribute synopsis

Common attributes and common linking attributes.

Additional attributes:

- continuation (enumeration) = "continues" | "restarts"
- linenumbering (enumeration) = "numbered" | "unnumbered"
- startinglinenumber (integer)
- language
- xml:space (enumeration) = "preserve"

Description

Supplementary information in a classsynopsis. See classsynopsis.

Unlike the other info elements, classsynopsisinfo is not a container for meta-information. Instead, classsynopsisinfo is a verbatim environment for adding additional information to a class synopsis.

Processing expectations

This element is displayed "verbatim"; whitespace and line breaks within this element are significant.

Attributes

Common attributes and common linking attributes.

continuation

Determines whether line numbering continues from the previous element or restarts.

Enumerated values:	
"continues"	Line numbering continues from the immediately preceding element with the same name.
"restarts"	Line numbering restarts (begins at 1, usually).

language

Identifies the language (i.e., programming language) of the verbatim content.

linenumbering

Determines whether lines are numbered.

Enumerated values:	
"numbered"	Lines are numbered.
"unnumbered"	Lines are not numbered.

startinglinenumber

Specifies the initial line number.

xml:space

Can be used to indicate explicitly that whitespace in the verbatim environment is preserved. Whitespace must always be preserved in verbatim environments whether this attribute is specified or not.

Enumerated values:	
"preserve"	Whitespace must be preserved.

cmdsynopsis   A syntax summary for a software command

Synopsis

cmdsynopsis ::= (info? [db.titleforbidden.info], (arg | command | group | sbr)+, synopfragment*)

Attribute synopsis

Common attributes and common linking attributes.

Additional attributes:

- cmdlength
- label

- sepchar

Description

A cmdsynopsis summarizes the options and parameters of a command started from a text prompt. This is usually a program started from the DOS, Windows, or UNIX shell prompt.

A cmdsynopsis operates under the following general model: commands have arguments that may be grouped; arguments and groups may be required or optional and may be repeated.

Processing expectations

The processing expectations of cmdsynopsis are fairly complex:

- Arguments are generally identified with a prefix character.

   In the UNIX world, this character is almost universally the dash or hyphen, although plus signs and double dashes have become more common in recent years.

   In the DOS/Windows world, forward slashes are somewhat more common than dashes.

   The DocBook processing expectations on this point are intentionally vague. In some environments it may be most convenient to generate these characters automatically; in other environments it may be more convenient to insert them literally in the content.

   Whichever processing model you choose, note that this will be an interchange issue if you share documents with other users (see Appendix D).

- Brackets are used to distinguish between optional, required, or plain arguments. Usually square brackets are placed around optional arguments, [-g], and curly brackets are placed around required arguments, {-g}. Plain arguments are required, but are not decorated with brackets.

- Repeatable arguments are followed by an ellipsis.

- Multiple arguments within a group are considered exclusive and are separated by vertical bars.

- Groups, like arguments, may be optional, required, or plain and may or may not repeat. The same brackets and ellipses that are used to indicate these characteristics on arguments are used on groups.

- Arguments and groups may nest more or less arbitrarily.

- The element is formatted as a displayed block. The processing system is free to introduce line breaks where required, but the sbr element may be introduced by the author to provide an explicit break location.

Attributes

Common attributes and common linking attributes.

cmdlength
> Indicates the displayed length of the command; this information may be used to intelligently indent command synopses that extend beyond one line

label
> Specifies an identifying string for presentation purposes

sepchar
> Specifies the character that should separate the command and its top-level arguments

See Also

arg, funcsynopsis, group, refsynopsisdiv, sbr, synopfragment, synopfragmentref, synopsis

Examples

```
<article xmlns='http://docbook.org/ns/docbook'>
<title>Example cmdsynopsis</title>

<cmdsynopsis>
  <command>cd</command>
  <arg choice='req'><replaceable>directory</replaceable></arg>
</cmdsynopsis>

</article>
```

> cd {*directory*}

```
<article xmlns='http://docbook.org/ns/docbook'>
<title>Example cmdsynopsis</title>

<cmdsynopsis>
  <command>cal</command>
  <arg>-j</arg>
  <arg>-y</arg>
  <arg>month <arg>year</arg></arg>
</cmdsynopsis>

</article>
```

> cal [-j] [-y] [month [year]]

```
<article xmlns='http://docbook.org/ns/docbook'>
<title>Example cmdsynopsis</title>

<cmdsynopsis>
  <command>chgrp</command>
  <arg>-R
    <group>
      <arg>-H</arg>
      <arg>-L</arg>
      <arg>-P</arg>
    </group>
  </arg>
  <arg>-f</arg>
```

```
    <arg choice='plain'><replaceable>group</replaceable></arg>
    <arg rep='repeat' choice='plain'><replaceable>file</replaceable></arg>
  </cmdsynopsis>

</article>
```

chgrp [-R [[-H] | [-L] | [-P]]] [-f] *group file*...

```
  <article xmlns='http://docbook.org/ns/docbook'>
  <title>Example cmdsynopsis</title>

  <cmdsynopsis>
    <command>emacs</command>
    <arg>-t <replaceable>file</replaceable></arg>
    <arg>-q</arg>
    <arg>-u <replaceable>user</replaceable></arg>
    <arg>+<replaceable>number</replaceable></arg>
    <arg rep='repeat'>-f <replaceable>function</replaceable></arg>
    <sbr/>
    <arg rep='repeat'>-l <replaceable>file</replaceable></arg>
    <arg rep='repeat' choice='plain'><replaceable>file</replaceable></arg>
  </cmdsynopsis>

</article>
```

emacs [-t *file*] [-q] [-u *user*] [+*number*] [-f *function*...]
[-l *file*...] *file*...

CO

Synopsis
co ::= empty

Attribute synopsis
Common attributes (ID required).

Additional attributes:

- `label`

Description
A co identifies (by its location) a point of reference for a callout. See `callout`.

Processing expectations
Formatted inline.

Attributes
Common attributes (ID required).

label
> Specifies an identifying string for presentation purposes

See Also
`areaspec`, `calloutlist`, `coref`, `imageobjectco`, `programlistingco`, `screenco`

Examples

```
<article xmlns='http://docbook.org/ns/docbook' version="5.0">
<title>Example co</title>

<informalexample>
<screen> Volume in drive C is SYSTEM          Serial number is 2350:717C
 Directory of  C:\


10/17/97   9:04        &lt;DIR>     bin
10/16/97  14:11        &lt;DIR>     DOS               <co xml:id="co.dos"/>
10/16/97  14:40        &lt;DIR>     Program Files
10/16/97  14:46        &lt;DIR>     TEMP
10/17/97   9:04        &lt;DIR>     tmp
10/16/97  14:37        &lt;DIR>     WINNT
10/16/97  14:25            119     AUTOEXEC.BAT   <co xml:id="co.autoexec.bat"/>
 2/13/94   6:21         54,619     COMMAND.COM    <co xml:id="co.command.com"/>
10/16/97  14:25            115     CONFIG.SYS     <co xml:id="co.config.sys"/>
11/16/97  17:17     61,865,984     pagefile.sys
 2/13/94   6:21          9,349     WINA20.386     <co xml:id="co.wina20.386"/></screen>
<calloutlist>
<callout arearefs="co.dos">
<para>This directory holds <trademark>MS-DOS</trademark>, the
operating system that was installed before <trademark>Windows
NT</trademark>.
</para>
</callout>

<callout arearefs="co.autoexec.bat co.command.com co.config.sys">
<para>System startup code for DOS.
</para>
</callout>

<callout arearefs="co.wina20.386">
<para>Some sort of <trademark>Windows 3.1</trademark> hack for some
386 processors, as I recall.
</para>
</callout>
</calloutlist>
</informalexample>

</article>
```

```
    Volume in drive C is SYSTEM          Serial number is 2350:717C
    Directory of  C:\

  10/17/97   9:04        <DIR>     bin
  10/16/97  14:11        <DIR>     DOS             ❶
  10/16/97  14:40        <DIR>     Program Files
  10/16/97  14:46        <DIR>     TEMP
  10/17/97   9:04        <DIR>     tmp
  10/16/97  14:37        <DIR>     WINNT
  10/16/97  14:25            119   AUTOEXEC.BAT    ❷
   2/13/94   6:21         54,619   COMMAND.COM     ❸
  10/16/97  14:25            115   CONFIG.SYS      ❹
```

```
    11/16/97  17:17     61,865,984  pagefile.sys
     2/13/94   6:21          9,349  WINA20.386      ❺
```

❶   This directory holds MS-DOS™, the operating system that was installed before Windows NT™.

❷❸❹ System startup code for DOS.

❺   Some sort of Windows 3.1™ hack for some 386 processors, as I recall.

Compare this example with the example for `screenco`.

---

code
An inline code fragment

Synopsis
code ::= (text | phrase ^{db.–phrase} | replaceable | *Graphic inlines* | *Indexing inlines* | *Linking inlines* | *Object-oriented programming inlines* | *Programming inlines* | *Ubiquitous inlines*)*

Attribute synopsis
Common attributes and common linking attributes.

Additional attributes:

- language

Description
The `code` element is an inline element for identifying small fragments of programming language code.

Processing expectations
Formatted inline.

Attributes
Common attributes and common linking attributes.

language
> Identifies the (computer) language of the code fragment

---

col
Specifications for a column in an HTML table

Synopsis
col ::= empty

Attribute synopsis
Attributes:

- align (enumeration) = "left" | "center" | "right" | "justify" | "char"
- char
- charoff (enumeration) = xsd:integer | xsd:string (Pattern: "[0–9]+%")

- span (nonNegativeInteger)
- valign (enumeration) = "top" | "middle" | "bottom" | "baseline"
- width

Description
Identifies a column specification in an HTML table.

Processing expectations
Processed like an HTML col.

Attributes

align
> Specifies the alignment of data and the justification of text in a cell.

Enumerated values:	
"left"	Left-flush data/Left-justify text. This is the default value for table data.
"center"	Center data/Center-justify text. This is the default value for table headers.
"right"	Right-flush data/Right-justify text.
"justify"	Double-justify text.
"char"	Align text around a specific character. If a user agent doesn't support character alignment, behavior in the presence of this value is unspecified.

char
> Specifies a single character within a text fragment to act as an axis for alignment. The default value for this attribute is the decimal point character for the current language as set by the lang attribute (e.g., the period in English and the comma in French). User agents are not required to support this attribute.

charoff
> When present, specifies the offset to the first occurrence of the alignment character on each line. If a line doesn't include the alignment character, it should be horizontally shifted to end at the alignment position. When charoff is used to set the offset of an alignment character, the direction of offset is determined by the current text direction (set by the dir attribute). In left-to-right texts (the default), offset is from the left margin. In right-to-left texts, offset is from the right margin. User agents are not required to support this attribute.

Enumerated values:	
xsd:integer	An explicit offset
xsd:string (Pattern: "[0–9]+%")	A percentage offset

class
> Assigns a class name or set of class names to an element. Any number of elements may be assigned the same class name or names. Multiple class names must be separated by whitespace characters.

lang
> Specifies the base language of an element's attribute values and text content. The default value of this attribute is unknown.

onclick
> Occurs when the pointing device button is clicked over an element.

ondblclick
> Occurs when the pointing device button is double-clicked over an element.

onkeydown
> Occurs when a key is pressed down over an element.

onkeypress
> Occurs when a key is pressed and released over an element.

onkeyup
> Occurs when a key is released over an element.

onmousedown
> Occurs when the pointing device button is pressed over an element.

onmousemove
> Occurs when the pointing device is moved while it is over an element.

onmouseout
> Occurs when the pointing device is moved away from an element.

onmouseover
> Occurs when the pointing device is moved onto an element.

onmouseup
> Occurs when the pointing device button is released over an element.

span
> An attribute whose value must be an integer > 0, and that specifies the number of columns "spanned" by the col element; the col element shares its attributes with all the columns it spans. The default value for this attribute is 1 (i.e., a single column). If the span attribute is set to N > 1, the current col element shares its attributes with the next N-1 columns.

style
> Specifies style information for the current element.

title
> Offers advisory information about the element for which it is set.

valign
> Specifies the vertical position of data within a cell.

Enumerated values:	
"top"	Cell data is flush with the top of the cell.
"middle"	Cell data is centered vertically within the cell. This is the default value.
"bottom"	Cell data is flush with the bottom of the cell.
"baseline"	All cells in the same row as a cell whose valign attribute has this value should have their textual data positioned so that the first text line occurs on a baseline common to all cells in the row. This constraint does not apply to subsequent text lines in these cells.

width
> Specifies a default width for each column spanned by the current col element. It has the same meaning as the width attribute for the colgroup element and overrides it.

colgroup
A group of columns in an HTML table

Synopsis
colgroup ::= col*

Attribute synopsis
Attributes:

- align (enumeration) = "left" | "center" | "right" | "justify" | "char"
- char
- charoff (enumeration) = xsd:integer | xsd:string (Pattern: "[0–9]+%")
- span (nonNegativeInteger)
- valign (enumeration) = "top" | "middle" | "bottom" | "baseline"
- width

Description
Identifies a column group in an HTML table.

Processing expectations
Processed like an HTML colgroup.

Attributes

align
> Specifies the alignment of data and the justification of text in a cell.

Enumerated values:	
"left"	Left-flush data/Left-justify text. This is the default value for table data.
"center"	Center data/Center-justify text. This is the default value for table headers.
"right"	Right-flush data/Right-justify text.

Enumerated values:	
"justify"	Double-justify text.
"char"	Align text around a specific character. If a user agent doesn't support character alignment, behavior in the presence of this value is unspecified.

char
> Specifies a single character within a text fragment to act as an axis for alignment. The default value for this attribute is the decimal point character for the current language as set by the `lang` attribute (e.g., the period in English and the comma in French). User agents are not required to support this attribute.

charoff
> When present, specifies the offset to the first occurrence of the alignment character on each line. If a line doesn't include the alignment character, it should be horizontally shifted to end at the alignment position. When `charoff` is used to set the offset of an alignment character, the direction of offset is determined by the current text direction (set by the `dir` attribute). In left-to-right texts (the default), offset is from the left margin. In right-to-left texts, offset is from the right margin. User agents are not required to support this attribute.

Enumerated values:	
`xsd:integer`	An explicit offset
`xsd:string` (Pattern: "[0–9]+%")	A percentage offset

class
> Assigns a class name or set of class names to an element. Any number of elements may be assigned the same class name or names. Multiple class names must be separated by whitespace characters.

lang
> Specifies the base language of an element's attribute values and text content. The default value of this attribute is unknown.

onclick
> Occurs when the pointing device button is clicked over an element.

ondblclick
> Occurs when the pointing device button is double-clicked over an element.

onkeydown
> Occurs when a key is pressed down over an element.

onkeypress
> Occurs when a key is pressed and released over an element.

onkeyup
> Occurs when a key is released over an element.

onmousedown
> Occurs when the pointing device button is pressed over an element.

onmousemove
> Occurs when the pointing device is moved while it is over an element.

onmouseout
> Occurs when the pointing device is moved away from an element.

onmouseover
> Occurs when the pointing device is moved onto an element.

onmouseup
> Occurs when the pointing device button is released over an element.

span
> An attribute that must be an integer > 0, and that specifies the number of columns in a column group. In the absence of a `span` attribute, each `colgroup` defines a column group containing one column. If the `span` attribute is set to N > 0, the current `colgroup` element defines a column group containing N columns. User agents must ignore this attribute if the `colgroup` element contains one or more `col` elements.

style
> Specifies style information for the current element.

title
> Offers advisory information about the element for which it is set.

valign
> Specifies the vertical position of data within a cell.

Enumerated values:	
"top"	Cell data is flush with the top of the cell.
"middle"	Cell data is centered vertically within the cell. This is the default value.
"bottom"	Cell data is flush with the bottom of the cell.
"baseline"	All cells in the same row as a cell whose `valign` attribute has this value should have their textual data positioned so that the first text line occurs on a baseline common to all cells in the row. This constraint does not apply to subsequent text lines in these cells.

width
> Specifies a default width for each column in the current column group. In addition to the standard pixel, percentage, and relative values, this attribute allows the special form "0*" (zero asterisk), which means that the width of each column in the group should be the minimum width necessary to hold the column's contents. This implies that a column's entire contents must be known before its width may be correctly computed. Authors should be aware that specifying "0*" will prevent visual user agents from rendering a table incrementally. This attribute is overridden for any column in the column group whose width is specified via a `col` element.

collab

Synopsis

collab ::= ((org | orgname | person | personname)+, affiliation*)

Attribute synopsis

Common attributes and common linking attributes.

Description

This element identifies a collaborative partner in a document. It associates the name of a collaborator with his or her affiliation.

Processing expectations

May be formatted inline or as a displayed block, depending on context. Sometimes suppressed.

See Also

author, authorgroup, contrib, editor, othercredit, personblurb, personname

Examples

```
<book xmlns='http://docbook.org/ns/docbook'>
<info>
  <title>DocBook: The Definitive Guide</title>
  <collab>
    <personname><firstname>Lenny</firstname>
    <surname>Muellner</surname></personname>
  </collab>
  <collab>
    <personname><firstname>Norman</firstname>
    <surname>Walsh</surname></personname>
  </collab>
</info>

<chapter><title>Just an Example</title>
<para>This is just an example, in real life, Lenny and Norm are both
<tag>author</tag>s.
</para>
</chapter>
</book>
```

colophon

Synopsis

colophon ::= ((((title? & titleabbrev? & subtitle?), info? db.titleforbidden.info) | info? db.info),
(annotation | bridgehead | remark | revhistory | *Indexing inlines* | *Admonition elements* | *Formal elements* | *Graphic elements* | *Informal elements* | *List elements* | *Paragraph elements* | *Publishing elements* | *Synopsis elements* | *Technical elements* | *Verbatim elements*)+)

Attribute synopsis

Common attributes and common linking attributes.

Additional attributes:

- `label`
- `status`

Additional constraints

- If this element is the root element, it must have a **version** attribute.

Description

A `colophon`, if present, almost always occurs at the very end of a book. It contains factual information about the book, especially about its production, and includes details about typographic style, the fonts used, the paper used, and perhaps the binding method of the book.

Font geeks like Norm think every book should have one.

Processing expectations

Formatted as a displayed block.

Attributes

Common attributes and common linking attributes.

label
> Specifies an identifying string for presentation purposes

status
> Identifies the editorial or publication status of the element on which it occurs

See Also

appendix, article, book, chapter, dedication, part, partintro, preface, set

Examples

```
<book xmlns='http://docbook.org/ns/docbook'>
<title>Example colophon</title>

<colophon>
<para>Draft versions of the first edition of this book were produced
with the DocBook DSSSL Stylesheets. Final production was performed
with Troff.</para>
<para>XSLT and XSL were used to produce the second edition.</para>
</colophon>

</book>
```

colspec

Synopsis

colspec ::= empty

Attribute synopsis

Common attributes and common linking attributes.

Additional attributes:

- `align` (enumeration) = "center" | "char" | "justify" | "left" | "right"
- `char`
- `charoff` (decimal)
- `colname`
- `colnum` (positiveInteger)
- `colsep` (enumeration) = "0" | "1"
- `colwidth`
- `rowsep` (enumeration) = "0" | "1"

Description

The attributes of this empty element specify the presentation characteristics of entries in a column of a table.

Each `colspec` refers to a single column. Columns are numbered sequentially from left to right in the table. If the `colnum` attribute is not specified, the `colspec` is for the next column after the preceding `colspec` or column 1 if it is the first `colspec`.

Processing expectations

Suppressed. This element is expected to obey the semantics of the *CALS Table Model Document Type Definition* [calsdtd].

Attributes

Common attributes and common linking attributes.

align

Specifies the horizontal alignment of text in an entry.

Enumerated values:	
"center"	Centered
"char"	Aligned on a particular character
"justify"	Left and right justified
"left"	Left justified
"right"	Right justified

char

Specifies the alignment character when `align` is set to "char".

charoff
> Specifies the percentage of the column's total width that should appear to the left of the first occurrence of the character identified in `char` when `align` is set to "char".

colname
> Provides a name for a column specification.

colnum
> The number of the column to which this specification applies. Must be greater than any preceding column number. Defaults to one more than the number of the preceding column, if there is one, or one.

colsep
> Specifies the presence or absence of the column separator.

Enumerated values:	
"0"	No column separator rule.
"1"	Provide a column separator rule on the right.

colwidth
> Specifies the width of the column.

rowsep
> Specifies the presence or absence of the row separator.

Enumerated values:	
"0"	No row separator rule.
"1"	Provide a row separator rule below.

See Also
entry, entrytbl, informaltable, row, spanspec, table, tbody, tfoot, tgroup, thead

---

command
The name of an executable program or other software command

Synopsis
command ::= (text | phrase $^{db.\_phrase}$ | replaceable | *Graphic inlines* | *Indexing inlines* | *Linking inlines* | *Ubiquitous inlines*)*

Attribute synopsis
Common attributes and common linking attributes.

Description
This element holds the name of an executable program or the text of a command that a user enters to execute a program.

A command is an integral part of the cmdsynopsis environment as well as being a common inline.

Processing expectations

Formatted inline.

See Also

constant, literal, replaceable, varname

Examples

```
<article xmlns='http://docbook.org/ns/docbook'>
<title>Example command</title>

<para>In <acronym>UNIX</acronym>,
<command>ls</command> is used to get a directory listing.
</para>

</article>
```

In UNIX, *ls* is used to get a directory listing.

---

computeroutput

Synopsis

computeroutput ::= (text | *Computer-output inlines* | *Graphic inlines* | *Indexing inlines* | *Linking inlines* | *Markup inlines* | *Operating system inlines* | *Technical inlines* | *Ubiquitous inlines*)*

Attribute synopsis

Common attributes and common linking attributes.

Description

A computeroutput identifies lines of text generated by a computer program (messages, results, or other output).

Note that computeroutput is not a verbatim environment, but an inline.

Processing expectations

Formatted inline. It's often presented in a fixed-width font.

See Also

constant, envar, filename, lineannotation, literal, literallayout, markup, option, optional, parameter, programlisting, prompt, replaceable, screen, screenshot, synopsis, systemitem, tag, userinput, varname

Examples

```
<article xmlns='http://docbook.org/ns/docbook'>
<title>Example computeroutput</title>

<para>The output from the date command,
<computeroutput>Sun  Nov 16, 1997  21:03:29</computeroutput>,
```

```
    uses fixed-width fields so that it can easily be parsed.
    </para>

    </article>
```

The output from the *date* command, Sun Nov 16, 1997 21:03:29, uses fixed-width fields so that it can easily be parsed.

---

confdates
The dates of a conference for which a document was written

Synopsis
confdates ::= (text | phrase ^{db.–phrase} | replaceable | *Graphic inlines* | *Indexing inlines* | *Linking inlines* | *Ubiquitous inlines*)*

Attribute synopsis
Common attributes and common linking attributes.

Description
A confdates element holds the dates of a conference for which a document was written or at which it was presented.

Processing expectations
May be formatted inline or as a displayed block, depending on context. Sometimes suppressed.

See Also
confgroup, confnum, confsponsor, conftitle, contractnum, contractsponsor

---

confgroup
A wrapper for document meta-information about a conference

Synopsis
confgroup ::= (address | confdates | confnum | confsponsor | conftitle)*

Attribute synopsis
Common attributes and common linking attributes.

Description
If a document—for example, an article—is written in connection with a conference, the elements in this wrapper are used to hold information about the conference: titles, sponsors, addresses, dates, etc.

Processing expectations
May be formatted inline or as a displayed block, depending on context. Sometimes suppressed.

See Also
confdates, confnum, confsponsor, conftitle, contractnum, contractsponsor

Examples

```
<article xmlns='http://docbook.org/ns/docbook'>
<info>
  <title>Example confgroup</title>
  <confgroup>
    <confdates>April, 1998</confdates>
    <conftitle>The World Wide Web Conference</conftitle>
    <confnum>7</confnum>
    <address>Brisbane, Australia</address>
    <confsponsor>World Wide Web Conference Committee (W3C3)</confsponsor>
  </confgroup>
</info>

<para>…</para>

</article>
```

---

confnum
An identifier, frequently numerical, associated with a conference for which a document was written

Synopsis
confnum ::= (text | phrase db._phrase | replaceable | *Graphic inlines* | *Indexing inlines* | *Linking inlines* | *Ubiquitous inlines*)*

Attribute synopsis
Common attributes and common linking attributes.

Description
See confgroup.

Processing expectations
May be formatted inline or as a displayed block, depending on context. Sometimes suppressed.

See Also
confdates, confgroup, confsponsor, conftitle, contractnum, contractsponsor

---

confsponsor
The sponsor of a conference for which a document was written

Synopsis
confsponsor ::= (text | phrase db._phrase | replaceable | *Graphic inlines* | *Indexing inlines* | *Linking inlines* | *Ubiquitous inlines*)*

Attribute synopsis
Common attributes and common linking attributes.

Description
See confgroup.

Processing expectations

May be formatted inline or as a displayed block, depending on context. Sometimes suppressed.

See Also

confdates, confgroup, confnum, conftitle, contractnum, contractsponsor

---

conftitle

The title of a conference for which a document was written

Synopsis

conftitle ::= (text | phrase ^{db.–phrase} | replaceable | *Graphic inlines* | *Indexing inlines* | *Linking inlines* | *Ubiquitous inlines*)*

Attribute synopsis

Common attributes and common linking attributes.

Description

See confgroup.

Processing expectations

May be formatted inline or as a displayed block, depending on context. Sometimes suppressed.

See Also

confdates, confgroup, confnum, confsponsor, contractnum, contractsponsor

---

constant

A programming or system constant

Synopsis

constant ::= (text | phrase ^{db.–phrase} | replaceable | *Graphic inlines* | *Indexing inlines* | *Linking inlines* | *Ubiquitous inlines*)*

Attribute synopsis

Common attributes and common linking attributes.

Additional attributes:

- class (enumeration) = "limit"

Description

A constant identifies a value as immutable. It is most often used to identify system limitations or other defined constants.

Processing expectations

Formatted inline.

Attributes

Common attributes and common linking attributes.

class
Identifies the class of constant

Enumerated values:	
"limit"	The value is a limit of some kind.

See Also
command, computeroutput, literal, markup, option, optional, parameter, prompt, replaceable, tag, userinput, varname

Examples

```
<article xmlns='http://docbook.org/ns/docbook'>
<title>Example constant</title>

<para>In ACL, <constant>main::PCS</constant> contains the path component
separator character.
</para>

</article>
```

In ACL, main::PCS contains the path component separator character.

```
<article xmlns='http://docbook.org/ns/docbook'>
<title>Example constant</title>

<para>The maximum legal length for a pathname is
<constant class='limit'>PATH_MAX</constant>, defined in
<filename class='headerfile'>limits.h</filename>.
</para>

</article>
```

The maximum legal length for a pathname is PATH_MAX, defined in *limits.h*.

---

constraint

A constraint in an EBNF production

Synopsis
constraint ::= empty

Attribute synopsis
Common attributes and common linking attributes.

Description
A constraint is a cross-reference to a description of a constraint that cannot be expressed in the grammar (generally logical rather than syntactic constraints).

See Also
lhs, production, productionrecap, productionset, rhs

constraintdef

Synopsis

constraintdef ::= ((((title? & titleabbrev?), info? ^{db.titleforbidden.info}) | info ^{db.titleonly.info}), (annotation | bridgehead | remark | revhistory | *Indexing inlines* | *Admonition elements* | *Formal elements* | *Graphic elements* | *Informal elements* | *List elements* | *Paragraph elements* | *Publishing elements* | *Synopsis elements* | *Technical elements* | *Verbatim elements*)+)

Attribute synopsis

Common attributes and common linking attributes.

Description

A constraintdef contains a description of a constraint that cannot be expressed in the grammar (generally logical rather than syntactic constraints).

Processing expectations

Formatted as a displayed block.

constructorsynopsis

Synopsis

constructorsynopsis ::= (modifier*, methodname?, (methodparam+ | void?), exceptionname*)

Attribute synopsis

Common attributes and common linking attributes.

Additional attributes:

- language

Description

A constructorsynopsis contains the syntax summary of a constructor in an object-oriented programming language. Unlike a methodsynopsis, which it closely resembles, it may not identify a return type and the methodname is optional (in some languages, constructor names can be generated automatically).

Processing expectations

For the most part, the processing application is expected to generate all of the parentheses, semicolons, commas, and so on required in the rendered synopsis.

Attributes

Common attributes and common linking attributes.

language
> Identifies the language (i.e., programming language) of the content

contractnum

Synopsis

contractnum ::= (text | phrase ^{db._phrase} | replaceable | *Graphic inlines* | *Indexing inlines* | *Linking inlines* | *Ubiquitous inlines*)*

Attribute synopsis

Common attributes and common linking attributes.

Description

The contractnum element that occurs in bibliographic metadata contains information about the contract number of a contract under which a document was written.

Processing expectations

May be formatted inline or as a displayed block, depending on context. Sometimes suppressed.

See Also

confdates, confgroup, confnum, confsponsor, conftitle, contractsponsor

contractsponsor

Synopsis

contractsponsor ::= (text | phrase ^{db._phrase} | replaceable | *Graphic inlines* | *Indexing inlines* | *Linking inlines* | *Ubiquitous inlines*)*

Attribute synopsis

Common attributes and common linking attributes.

Description

The contractsponsor element that occurs in bibliographic metadata contains information about the sponser of a contract under which a document was written.

Processing expectations

May be formatted inline or as a displayed block, depending on context. Sometimes suppressed.

See Also

confdates, confgroup, confnum, confsponsor, conftitle, contractnum

Examples

```
<article xmlns='http://docbook.org/ns/docbook'>
<info>
  <title>Retrofitting Class A Widgets</title>
  <contractsponsor>Xyzzy Engineering Resources</contractsponsor>
  <contractnum>314-592-7</contractnum>
  <biblioid>XER-314-7A</biblioid>
  <author>
    <orgname>Technical Documentation Consultants, Inc.</orgname>
  </author>
```

```
    <collab>
      <personname>
        <firstname>John</firstname>
        <surname>Whorfin</surname>
      </personname>
      <affiliation><orgname>Yoyodyne Propulsion Systems</orgname></affiliation>
    </collab>
  </info>

  <para>…</para>

  </article>
```

contrib

Synopsis
contrib ::= (text | phrase [db._phrase] | replaceable | *Graphic inlines* | *Indexing inlines* | *Linking inlines* | *Ubiquitous inlines*)*

Attribute synopsis
Common attributes and common linking attributes.

Description
The contrib element contains a summary or description of the contributions made by an author, editor, or other credited source.

Processing expectations
May be formatted inline or as a displayed block, depending on context. Sometimes suppressed.

See Also
author, authorgroup, collab, editor, othercredit, personblurb, personname

copyright

Synopsis
copyright ::= (year+, holder*)

Attribute synopsis
Common attributes and common linking attributes.

Description
The copyright element holds information about the date(s) and holder(s) of a document copyright. If an extended block of text describing the copyright or other legal status is required, use legalnotice.

The copyright element is confined to meta-information. For copyright statements in running text, see trademark.

Processing expectations

May be formatted inline or as a displayed block, depending on context. Sometimes suppressed.

A displayed copyright notice usually includes the copyright symbol, ©, as generated text and is formatted with commas separating multiple years. Additional generated text, such as the legend "All rights reserved," may also be generated.

See Also

legalnotice, productname, trademark

Examples

```
<article xmlns='http://docbook.org/ns/docbook'>
<info>
  <title>Example copyright</title>
  <copyright>
    <year>2009</year>
    <year>2010</year>
    <holder>O'Reilly Media, Inc.</holder>
  </copyright>
</info>

<para>…</para>

</article>
```

coref

A cross-reference to a co

Synopsis

coref ::= empty

Attribute synopsis

Common attributes.

Additional attributes:

- label

Description

The coref element plays a role for callouts that is analogous to the role of footnoteref for footnotes.

Use one co and one or more coref elements when you want to indicate that the same callout should appear in several places.

 A coref is not a cross-reference to a callout (use xref for that); rather, it is an indication that the callout appears semantically in more than one place.

Processing expectations

Formatted inline.

Attributes

Common attributes.

label

> Specifies an identifying string for presentation purposes

See Also

`areaspec`, `calloutlist`, `co`, `imageobjectco`, `programlistingco`, `screenco`

---

country

The name of a country

Synopsis

country ::= (text | phrase ^{db._phrase} | `replaceable` | *Graphic inlines* | *Indexing inlines* | *Linking inlines* | *Ubiquitous inlines*)*

Attribute synopsis

Common attributes and common linking attributes.

Description

The name of a country, typically in an address.

Processing expectations

Formatted inline. In an `address`, this element may inherit the verbatim qualities of an address.

See Also

`address`, `city`, `email`, `fax`, `otheraddr`, `phone`, `pob`, `postcode`, `state`, `street`

---

cover

Additional content for the cover of a publication

Synopsis

cover ::= (`bridgehead` | `remark` | `revhistory` | *Graphic elements* | *Informal elements* | *List elements* | *Paragraph elements* | *Publishing elements* | *Synopsis elements* | *Technical elements* | *Verbatim elements*)+

Attribute synopsis

Common attributes and common linking attributes.

Description

The `cover` element contains additional material to be printed on the cover of a publication. Multiple `cover` elements may be used to hold material for the inside and outside front and back covers, the spine, dust jackets, etc.

Because there is likely to be great variation in the number of covers, and the means by which the **cover** elements are processed, DocBook does not attempt to define semantics for their order or relationship to one another.

The title, authors, and other bibliographic metadata that appears in the `info` element should not be repeated inside the **cover**. The intent is merely that **cover** can contain any additional material required.

Processing expectations

Formatted as a displayed block. Sometimes suppressed.

Examples

The following example shows a **cover** tag as it might have appeared in the source for the first edition of this book.

```
<book xmlns='http://docbook.org/ns/docbook'>
<info>
  <title>DocBook</title>
  <subtitle>The Definitive Guide</subtitle>
  <biblioid class="isbn">978-0-596-8050-2-9</biblioid>
  <authorgroup>
    <author>
      <personname>
      <firstname>Norman</firstname>
      <surname>Walsh</surname>
      </personname>
    </author>
  </authorgroup>
  <publisher>
    <publishername>O'Reilly Media, Inc.</publishername>
    <address><city>Beijing</city></address>
    <address><city>Cambridge</city></address>
    <address><city>Farnham</city></address>
    <address><city>Köln</city></address>
    <address><city>Paris</city></address>
    <address><city>Sebastopol</city></address>
    <address><city>Taipei</city></address>
    <address><city>Tokyo</city></address>
  </publisher>
  <copyright>
    <year>2010</year>
    <holder>Norman Walsh, All rights reserved.</holder>
  </copyright>
  <releaseinfo>Published by O'Reilly Media, Inc.,
101 Morris Street, Sebastopol, CA 95472.</releaseinfo>
  <editor>
    <personname>
      <firstname>Richard L.</firstname>
      <surname>Hamilton</surname>
    </personname>
  </editor>
  <revhistory>
    <revision>
      <date>March 2010</date>
```

```
        <revremark>Second Edition.</revremark>
      </revision>
      <revision>
        <date>October 1999</date>
        <revremark>First Edition.</revremark>
      </revision>
    </revhistory>
    <legalnotice>
      <para>Nutshell Handbook, the Nutshell Handbook logo, and the…</para>
      <para>Many of the designations used by manufacturers…</para>
      <para>While every precaution has been taken in the preparation…</para>
    </legalnotice>
    <cover>
      <para role="tagline">The Official Documentation for DocBook</para>
      <mediaobject>
        <imageobject>
        <imagedata fileref="graphics/duck-cover.png">
          <info>
            <othercredit>
              <orgname>O'Reilly Media</orgname>
            </othercredit>
            <othercredit>
              <orgname>Dover Archives</orgname>
            </othercredit>
          </info>
        </imagedata>
        </imageobject>
      </mediaobject>
    </cover>
    <cover>
      <mediaobject>
        <imageobject>
        <imagedata fileref="graphics/duck-backcover.png"/>
        </imageobject>
      </mediaobject>
      <para>DocBook is a system for writing structured documents using…</para>
      <para><citetitle>DocBook: The Definitive Guide</citetitle> is the…</para>
      <itemizedlist>
        <listitem>
        <para>A brief introduction to  …</para>
        </listitem>
        <listitem>
        <para>A guide to creating documents with the DocBook schema…</para>
        </listitem>
        <listitem>
        <para>…</para>
        </listitem>
      </itemizedlist>
      <para>In an era of collaborative creation of technology, …</para>
      <formalpara>
        <title>Norman Walsh</title>
        <para>is a …</para>
      </formalpara>
    </cover>
  </info>
```

```
<preface>
<title>Preface</title>

<para>DocBook provides a system …</para>
</preface>

<!-- … -->

</book>
```

In this example, we assume that the first **cover** element contains additional material for the front cover and the second **cover** element contains additional material for the back cover.

---

database

Synopsis
database ::= (text | phrase ^{db._phrase} | replaceable | *Graphic inlines* | *Indexing inlines* | *Linking inlines* | *Ubiquitous inlines*)*

Attribute synopsis
Common attributes and common linking attributes.

Additional attributes:

- class (enumeration) = "altkey" | "constraint" | "datatype" | "field" | "foreignkey" | "group" | "index" | "key1" | "key2" | "name" | "primarykey" | "procedure" | "record" | "rule" | "secondarykey" | "table" | "user" | "view"

Description
The name of a database, or part of a database.

Processing expectations
Formatted inline.

Attributes
Common attributes and common linking attributes.

class
> Identifies the class of database artifact

Enumerated values:	
"altkey"	An alternate or secondary key
"constraint"	A constraint
"datatype"	A data type
"field"	A field
"foreignkey"	A foreign key

Enumerated values:	
"group"	A group
"index"	An index
"key1"	The first or primary key
"key2"	An alternate or secondary key
"name"	A name
"primarykey"	The primary key
"procedure"	A (stored) procedure
"record"	A record
"rule"	A rule
"secondarykey"	The secondary key
"table"	A table
"user"	A user
"view"	A view

See Also
application, filename, hardware, productname

Examples

```
<article xmlns='http://docbook.org/ns/docbook'>
<title>Example database</title>

<para>The <database>ProjectStatus</database> database has been updated.
Please note that <database class='field'>Year</database> has been
extended to four digits.
</para>

</article>
```

The ProjectStatus database has been updated. Please note that Year has been extended to four digits.

---

date

The date of publication or revision of a document

Synopsis
date ::= (A date value. | A dateTime value. | A gYearMonth value. | A gYear value. | text)

Attribute synopsis
Common attributes and common linking attributes.

Description
The date element identifies a date.

Processing expectations

Formatted inline.

DocBook does not specify the format of the date.

See Also

`edition`, `printhistory`, `pubdate`, `releaseinfo`, `revhistory`

---

dedication

The dedication of a book or other component

Synopsis

dedication ::= ((((title? & titleabbrev? & subtitle?), info? ^{db.titleforbidden.info}) | info? ^{db.info}), (annotation | bridgehead | remark | revhistory | *Indexing inlines* | *Admonition elements* | *Formal elements* | *Graphic elements* | *Informal elements* | *List elements* | *Paragraph elements* | *Publishing elements* | *Synopsis elements* | *Technical elements* | *Verbatim elements*)+)

Attribute synopsis

Common attributes and common linking attributes.

Additional attributes:

- `label`
- `status`

Additional constraints

- If this element is the root element, it must have a **version** attribute.

Description

A `dedication` is a page or section, most often at the very beginning of a book (before any other body matter), containing a tribute to something (frequently someone) in connection with the writing or publication of the **book**.

Processing expectations

Formatted as a displayed block. Frequently appears on a page by itself at the beginning of a book.

Attributes

Common attributes and common linking attributes.

label

  Specifies an identifying string for presentation purposes

status

  Identifies the editorial or publication status of the element on which it occurs

See Also

`appendix`, `article`, `book`, `chapter`, `colophon`, `part`, `partintro`, `preface`, `set`

Examples

```
<book xmlns='http://docbook.org/ns/docbook'>
<title>The Best XML Jokes</title>
<info>
  <author><personname>
    <firstname>A</firstname><surname>Nonymous</surname>
  </personname></author>
</info>

<dedication>
<para>To my mother and father, for teaching me to laugh.
</para>
</dedication>

<chapter><title>Parsing Jokes</title>
<para>What did the lexer say to the angle bracket? …
</para>
</chapter>
<!-- ... -->
</book>
```

destructorsynopsis

A syntax summary for a destructor

Synopsis
destructorsynopsis ::= (modifier*, methodname?, (methodparam+ | void?), exceptionname*)

Attribute synopsis
Common attributes and common linking attributes.

Additional attributes:

• language

Description
A destructorsynopsis contains the syntax summary of a destructor in an object-oriented programming language. Unlike a methodsynopsis, which it closely resembles, it may not identify a return type and the methodname is optional (in some languages, destructors have an immutable name which may be generated automatically).

Processing expectations
For the most part, the processing application is expected to generate all of the parentheses, semicolons, commas, and so on required in the rendered synopsis.

Attributes
Common attributes and common linking attributes.

language
> Identifies the language (i.e., programming language) of the content

edition

The name or number of an edition of a document

Synopsis

edition ::= (text | phrase ^{db._phrase} | replaceable | *Graphic inlines* | *Indexing inlines* | *Linking inlines* | *Ubiquitous inlines*)*

Attribute synopsis

Common attributes and common linking attributes.

Description

The edition contains the name or number of the edition of the document.

Processing expectations

May be formatted inline or as a displayed block, depending on context. Sometimes suppressed.

See Also

date, printhistory, pubdate, releaseinfo, revhistory

editor

The name of the editor of a document

Synopsis

editor ::= ((personname, (address | affiliation | contrib | email | personblurb | uri)*) | (orgname, (address | affiliation | contrib | email | orgdiv | uri)*))

Attribute synopsis

Common attributes and common linking attributes.

Description

The name of the editor of a document.

Processing expectations

May be formatted inline or as a displayed block, depending on context. Sometimes suppressed.

See Also

author, authorgroup, collab, contrib, othercredit, personblurb, personname

email

An email address

Synopsis

email ::= (text | phrase ^{db._phrase} | replaceable | *Graphic inlines* | *Indexing inlines* | *Linking inlines* | *Ubiquitous inlines*)*

Attribute synopsis

Common attributes and common linking attributes.

Description

Inline markup identifying an email address.

Processing expectations

Formatted inline. An `email` may generate surrounding punctuation, such as angle brackets. This is an interchange issue. See Appendix D.

In some processing environments, `email` may automatically generate a hypertext link (a `mailto:` URL).

In an `address`, this element may inherit the verbatim qualities of an address.

See Also

address, city, country, fax, otheraddr, phone, pob, postcode, state, street

---

emphasis (db._emphasis)   A limited span of emphasized text

Synopsis

emphasis (db._emphasis) ::= (text | emphasis ^{db._emphasis} | phrase ^{db._phrase} | replaceable | *Graphic inlines* | *Indexing inlines* | *Linking inlines* | *Ubiquitous inlines*)*

Attribute synopsis

Common attributes and common linking attributes.

Description

An `emphasis` element indicates that certain text should be stressed in some way. This pattern defines the `emphasis` element with a very limited content model.

Processing expectations

Formatted inline. Emphasized text is traditionally presented in italics or boldface. A `role` attribute of `bold` or `strong` is often used to generate boldface, if italics is the default presentation.

An `emphasis` is often used wherever its typographic presentation is desired, even when other markup might theoretically be more appropriate.

See Also

abbrev, acronym, emphasis (db.emphasis), foreignphrase, phrase, quote, wordasword

---

emphasis (db.emphasis)   Emphasized text

Synopsis

emphasis (db.emphasis) ::= (text | *Bibliography inlines* | *Error inlines* | *Graphic inlines* | *GUI inlines* | *Indexing inlines* | *Keyboard inlines* | *Linking inlines* | *Markup inlines* | *Math inlines* | *Object-oriented programming inlines* | *Operating system inlines* | *Product inlines* | *Programming inlines* | *Publishing inlines* | *Technical inlines* | *Ubiquitous inlines*)*

Attribute synopsis

Common attributes and common linking attributes.

Description

An emphasis element indicates that certain text should be stressed in some way. This pattern defines the emphasis element with a very limited content model.

Processing expectations

Formatted inline. Emphasized text is traditionally presented in italics or boldface. A role attribute of bold or strong is often used to generate boldface, if italics is the default presentation.

An emphasis is often used wherever its typographic presentation is desired, even when other markup might theoretically be more appropriate.

See Also

abbrev, acronym, emphasis (db._emphasis), foreignphrase, phrase, quote, wordasword

Examples

```
<article xmlns='http://docbook.org/ns/docbook'>
<title>Example emphasis</title>

<para>The <emphasis>most</emphasis> important example of this
phenomenon occurs in A. Nonymous's book
<citetitle>Power Snacking</citetitle>.
</para>

</article>
```

The *most* important example of this phenomenon occurs in A. Nonymous's book *Power Snacking*.

entry

A cell in a table

Synopsis

entry ::= ((text | *Bibliography inlines* | *Error inlines* | *Graphic inlines* | *GUI inlines* | *Indexing inlines* | *Keyboard inlines* | *Linking inlines* | *Markup inlines* | *Math inlines* | *Object-oriented programming inlines* | *Operating system inlines* | *Product inlines* | *Programming inlines* | *Publishing inlines* | *Technical inlines* | *Ubiquitous inlines*)* | (annotation | bridgehead | remark | revhistory | *Indexing inlines* | *Admonition elements* | *Formal elements* | *Graphic elements* | *Informal elements* | *List elements* | *Paragraph elements* | *Publishing elements* | *Synopsis elements* | *Technical elements* | *Verbatim elements*)*)

Attribute synopsis

Common attributes and common linking attributes.

Additional attributes:

- align (enumeration) = "center" | "char" | "justify" | "left" | "right"
- char
- charoff (decimal)
- *At most one of:*

—colname

—namest

—spanname

—*All or none of:*

   —namest

   —nameend

- colsep (enumeration) = "0" | "1"
- morerows (integer)
- rotate (enumeration) = "0" | "1"
- rowsep (enumeration) = "0" | "1"
- valign (enumeration) = "bottom" | "middle" | "top"

Description

An entry is a cell in a table.

Each entry may specify its starting column. Entries that do not explicitly specify a starting column begin implicitly in the column that is immediately adjacent to the preceding cell. Note that entrys with the morerows attribute from preceding rows implicitly occupy cells in the succeeding rows.

A row is not required to be full. It is legal for some entries to be completely absent (at the beginning, middle, or end of a row).

Processing expectations

This element is expected to obey the semantics of the *CALS Table Model Document Type Definition* [calsdtd].

The content of entry is formatted to fit within the table cell that it occupies. Horizontal and vertical spanning may allow the content of an entry to occupy several physical cells.

Attributes

Common attributes and common linking attributes.

align

   Specifies the horizontal alignment of text in an entry.

Enumerated values:	
"center"	Centered
"char"	Aligned on a particular character
"justify"	Left and right justified
"left"	Left justified
"right"	Right justified

char
> Specifies the alignment character when `align` is set to "char".

charoff
> Specifies the percentage of the column's total width that should appear to the left of the first occurrence of the character identified in `char` when `align` is set to "char".

colname
> Specifies a column specification by name.

colsep
> Specifies the presence or absence of the column separator.

Enumerated values:	
"0"	No column separator rule.
"1"	Provide a column separator rule on the right.

morerows
> Specifies the number of additional rows which this entry occupies. Defaults to zero.

nameend
> Specifies an ending column by name.

namest
> Specifies a starting column by name.

rotate
> Specifies the rotation of this entry. A value of 1 (true) rotates the cell 90 degrees counter-clockwise. A value of 0 (false) leaves the cell unrotated.

Enumerated values:	
"0"	Do not rotate the cell.
"1"	Rotate the cell 90 degrees counterclockwise.

rowsep
> Specifies the presence or absence of the row separator.

Enumerated values:	
"0"	No row separator rule.
"1"	Provide a row separator rule below.

spanname
> Specifies a span by name.

valign
> Specifies the vertical alignment of text in an entry.

Enumerated values:	
"bottom"	Aligned on the bottom of the entry
"middle"	Aligned in the middle
"top"	Aligned at the top of the entry

See Also

colspec, entrytbl, informaltable, row, spanspec, table, tbody, tfoot, tgroup, thead

---

entrytbl
A subtable appearing in place of an entry in a table

Synopsis
entrytbl ::= (colspec*, spanspec*, thead? ^{db.cals.entrytbl.thead}, tbody ^{db.cals.entrytbl.tbody})

Attribute synopsis
Common attributes and common linking attributes.

Additional attributes:

- align (enumeration) = "center" | "char" | "justify" | "left" | "right"
- char
- charoff (decimal)
- *At most one of:*
  - —colname
  - —namest
  - —spanname
  - —*All or none of:*
    - —namest
    - —nameend
- cols (positiveInteger)
- colsep (enumeration) = "0" | "1"
- rowsep (enumeration) = "0" | "1"
- tgroupstyle

Description
The entrytbl element allows for a single level of nesting within CALS tables.

An entry table may occur in a row instead of an **entry**. An **entrytbl** has most of the elements of a table but may not include itself, thus limiting nesting to a single level.

An entrytbl can span horizontally (across columns), but it cannot span across rows. Whether this is by accident or by design is unclear, but it has always been that way in CALS.

Processing expectations

This element is expected to obey the semantics of the *CALS Table Model Document Type Definition* [calsdtd].

The content of entrytbl is formatted, *as a table*, to fit within the table cell that it occupies. Horizontal and vertical spanning may allow an entrytbl to occupy several physical cells in the table that contains it.

If multiple entrytbls occur in a single row, formatters that support entrytbl are not required to ensure that subrows within the various tables are vertically aligned.

Many formatters are incapable of supporting entrytbls. This is an interchange issue. See Appendix D.

Attributes

Common attributes and common linking attributes.

align

Specifies the horizontal alignment of text in an entry.

Enumerated values:	
"center"	Centered
"char"	Aligned on a particular character
"justify"	Left and right justified
"left"	Left justified
"right"	Right justified

char

Specifies the alignment character when align is set to "char".

charoff

Specifies the percentage of the column's total width that should appear to the left of the first occurrence of the character identified in char when align is set to "char".

colname

Specifies a column specification by name.

cols

The number of columns in the entry table. Must be an integer greater than zero.

colsep

Specifies the presence or absence of the column separator.

Enumerated values:	
"0"	No column separator rule.
"1"	Provide a column separator rule on the right.

nameend
> Specifies an ending column by name.

namest
> Specifies a starting column by name.

rowsep
> Specifies the presence or absence of the row separator.

Enumerated values:	
"0"	No row separator rule.
"1"	Provide a row separator rule below.

spanname
> Specifies a span by name.

tgroupstyle
> Additional style information for downstream processing; typically the name of a style.

See Also

colspec, entry, informaltable, row, spanspec, table, tbody, tfoot, tgroup, thead

Examples

```
<article xmlns='http://docbook.org/ns/docbook'>
<title>Example entrytbl</title>

<informaltable frame='all' rowsep='1' colsep='1'>
<tgroup cols='3'>
<tbody>
<row>
  <entry>a1</entry>
  <entry>b1</entry>
  <entry>c1</entry>
</row>
<row>
  <entry>a2</entry>
  <entrytbl cols='3' rowsep='1' colsep='1'>
    <tbody>
      <row>
        <entry>b2a1</entry>
        <entry>b2b1</entry>
        <entry>b2c1</entry>
      </row>
      <row>
```

```
      <entry>b2a2</entry>
      <entry>b2b2</entry>
      <entry>b2c2</entry>
    </row>
    <row>
      <entry>b2a3</entry>
      <entry>b2b3</entry>
      <entry>b2c3</entry>
    </row>
  </tbody>
</entrytbl>
<entry>c2</entry>
</row>
<row>
  <entry>a3</entry>
  <entry>b3</entry>
  <entry>c3</entry>
</row>
</tbody>
</tgroup>
</informaltable>

</article>
```

a1	b1			c1
a2	b2a1	b2b1	b2c1	c2
	b2a2	b2b2	b2c2	
	b2a3	b2b3	b2c3	
a3	b3			c3

envar

A software environment variable

Synopsis

envar ::= (text | phrase ^{db._phrase} | replaceable | *Graphic inlines* | *Indexing inlines* | *Linking inlines* | *Ubiquitous inlines*)*

Attribute synopsis

Common attributes and common linking attributes.

Description

An envar is an "environment variable." Environment variables are used most often in the UNIX, DOS, and Windows environments.

Processing expectations

Formatted inline.

See Also

computeroutput, filename, prompt, systemitem, userinput

Examples

```
<article xmlns='http://docbook.org/ns/docbook'>
<title>Example envar</title>

<para>In order to translate public identifiers into local system identifiers,
<application>Jade</application> and <application>SP</application> read the catalog files
pointed to by <envar>SGML_CATALOG_FILES</envar>.
</para>

</article>
```

In order to translate public identifiers into local system identifiers, Jade and SP read the catalog files pointed to by `SGML_CATALOG_FILES`.

---

epigraph
A short inscription at the beginning of a document or component

Synopsis
epigraph ::= (info? $^{\text{db.titleforbidden.info}}$, attribution?, (literallayout | *Paragraph elements*)+)

Attribute synopsis
Common attributes and common linking attributes.

Description
An epigraph is a short inscription, often a quotation or poem, set at the beginning of a document or component. Epigraphs are usually related somehow to the content that follows them and may help set the tone for the component.

Processing expectations
Formatted as a displayed block.

See Also
abstract, attribution, blockquote, sidebar

---

equation
A displayed mathematical equation

Synopsis
equation ::= (((((title? & titleabbrev?), info? $^{\text{db.titleforbidden.info}}$) | info $^{\text{db.titleonly.info}}$), alt?, (mediaobject+ | mathphrase+ | mml:*+), caption? $^{\text{db.caption}}$)

Attribute synopsis
Common attributes and common linking attributes.

Additional attributes:

- floatstyle
- label
- pgwide (enumeration) = "0" | "1"

Additional constraints

- example must not occur among the children or descendants of equation.
- figure must not occur among the children or descendants of equation.
- table must not occur among the children or descendants of equation.
- equation must not occur among the children or descendants of equation.
- caution must not occur among the children or descendants of equation.
- important must not occur among the children or descendants of equation.
- note must not occur among the children or descendants of equation.
- tip must not occur among the children or descendants of equation.
- warning must not occur among the children or descendants of equation.

Description

An equation is a formal mathematical equation (with an optional rather than a required title).

If the MathML Module is used, equation can also contain the mml:math element.

Processing expectations

Formatted as a displayed block. For an inline equation, use inlineequation.

Processing systems that number equations or build a table of equations at the beginning of a document may have difficulty correctly formatting documents that contain both equations with titles and equations without titles. You are advised to use informalequation for equations without titles.

Attributes

Common attributes and common linking attributes.

floatstyle
> Specifies style information to be used when rendering the float

label
> Specifies an identifying string for presentation purposes

pgwide
> Indicates if the element is rendered across the column or the page

Enumerated values:	
"0"	The element should be rendered in the current text flow (with the flow column width).
"1"	The element should be rendered across the full text page.

See Also

example, figure, informalequation, informalexample, informalfigure, informaltable, inlineequation, subscript, superscript, table

Examples

```
<article xmlns='http://docbook.org/ns/docbook'>
<title>Example equation</title>

<equation xml:id="eq.fermat">
<title>Fermat's Last Theorem</title>
  <alt>x^n + y^n ≠ z^n ∀ n ≠ 2</alt>
  <mediaobject>
    <imageobject>
      <imagedata fileref="figures/fermat.png"/>
    </imageobject>
    <textobject>
      <phrase>x^n + y^n ≠ z^n ∀ n ≠ 2</phrase>
    </textobject>
  </mediaobject>
</equation>

</article>
```

Equation 1. Fermat's Last Theorem

$$x^n + y^n \neq z^n \, \forall n > 2$$

Alternatively, for relatively simple equations such as Fermat's Last Theorem, mathphrase is often sufficient:

```
<article xmlns='http://docbook.org/ns/docbook'>
<title>Example equation</title>

<equation xml:id="eq.fermat.mathphrase">
<title>Fermat's Last Theorem</title>
  <alt>x^n + y^n ≠ z^n ∀ n ≠ 2</alt>
  <mathphrase>x<superscript>n</superscript>
+ y<superscript>n</superscript>
≠ z<superscript>n</superscript>
∀ n ≠ 2</mathphrase>
</equation>

</article>
```

Equation 2. Fermat's Last Theorem

$$x^n + y^n \neq z^n \, \forall n \neq 2$$

errorcode

Synopsis

errorcode ::= (text | phrase ^{db.-phrase} | replaceable | *Graphic inlines* | *Indexing inlines* | *Linking inlines* | *Ubiquitous inlines*)*

Attribute synopsis

Common attributes and common linking attributes.

Description

An error code. Error codes are often numeric, but in some environments they may be symbolic constants.

DocBook provides four elements for identifying the parts of an error message: error code, for the alphanumeric error code (e.g., "–2"); errorname, for the symbolic name of the error (e.g., "ENOENT"); errortext, for the text of the error message (e.g., "file not found"); and errortype, for the error type (e.g., "recoverable").

Processing expectations

Formatted inline.

See Also

errorname, errortext, errortype, msgset

Examples

```
<article xmlns='http://docbook.org/ns/docbook'>
<title>Example errorcode</title>

<para>On most DOS-derived systems, functions signal a <errortext>File
Not Found</errortext> error by returning
<errorcode>2</errorcode> (<errorname>ENOENT</errorname>).  This is usually a
<errortype>recoverable</errortype> (nonfatal) error.
</para>

</article>
```

On most DOS-derived systems, functions signal a File Not Found error by returning 2 (ENOENT). This is usually a recoverable (nonfatal) error.

```
<article xmlns='http://docbook.org/ns/docbook'>
<title>Example errorcode</title>

<para>On most UNIX systems, functions signal a <errorname>File
Not Found</errorname> error by returning
<errorcode>ENOENT</errorcode>, defined in
<filename>errno.h</filename>.  This is usually a
<errortype>recoverable</errortype> (nonfatal) error.
</para>

</article>
```

On most UNIX systems, functions signal a File Not Found error by returning ENOENT, defined in *errno.h*. This is usually a recoverable (nonfatal) error.

errorname

An error name

Synopsis

errorname ::= (text | phrase ^{db._phrase} | replaceable | *Graphic inlines* | *Indexing inlines* | *Linking inlines* | *Ubiquitous inlines*)*

Attribute synopsis

Common attributes and common linking attributes.

Description

An errorname holds the symbolic name of an error.

DocBook provides four elements for identifying the parts of an error message: error code, for the alphanumeric error code (e.g., "–2"); errorname, for the symbolic name of the error (e.g., "ENOENT"); errortext, for the text of the error message (e.g., "file not found"); and errortype, for the error type (e.g., "recoverable").

Prior to DocBook V4.2, the errorname element was the recommended element for error *messages*. However, this left no element for symbolic names, so the errortext element was added and the semantics of the error elements adjusted slightly.

Processing expectations

Formatted inline.

See Also

errorcode, errortext, errortype, msgset

errortext

An error message

Synopsis

errortext ::= (text | phrase ^{db._phrase} | replaceable | *Graphic inlines* | *Indexing inlines* | *Linking inlines* | *Ubiquitous inlines*)*

Attribute synopsis

Common attributes and common linking attributes.

Description

An errortext holds the text of an error message.

DocBook provides four elements for identifying the parts of an error message: error code, for the alphanumeric error code (e.g., "–2"); errorname, for the symbolic name of the error (e.g., "ENOENT"); errortext, for the text of the error message (e.g., "file not found"); and errortype, for the error type (e.g., "recoverable").

Prior to DocBook V4.2, the errorname element was the recommended element for error *messages*. However, this left no element for symbolic names, so the errortext element was added and the semantics of the error elements adjusted slightly.

Processing expectations

Formatted inline.

See Also

errorcode, errorname, errortype, msgset

---

errortype

The classification of an error message

Synopsis

errortype ::= (text | phrase ^{db._phrase} | replaceable | *Graphic inlines* | *Indexing inlines* | *Linking inlines* | *Ubiquitous inlines*)*

Attribute synopsis

Common attributes and common linking attributes.

Description

The errortype element identifies a class of error. The exact classifications are naturally going to vary by system, but "recoverable" and "fatal" are two possibilities.

DocBook provides four elements for identifying the parts of an error message: errorcode, for the alphanumeric error code (e.g., "–2"); errorname, for the symbolic name of the error (e.g., "ENOENT"); errortext, for the text of the error message (e.g., "file not found"); and errortype, for the error type (e.g., "recoverable").

Processing expectations

Formatted inline.

See Also

errorcode, errorname, errortext, msgset

---

example

A formal example, with a title

Synopsis

example ::= ((((title & titleabbrev?), info? ^{db.titleforbidden.info}) | info ^{db.titleonlyreq.info}), (annotation | bridgehead | remark | revhistory | *Indexing inlines* | *Admonition elements* | *Formal elements* | *Graphic elements* | *Informal elements* | *List elements* | *Paragraph elements* | *Publishing elements* | *Synopsis elements* | *Technical elements* | *Verbatim elements*)+, caption? ^{db.caption})

Attribute synopsis

Common attributes and common linking attributes.

Additional attributes:

- floatstyle
- label
- *At most one of*:
    - width (nonNegativeInteger)
    - pgwide (enumeration) = "0" | "1"

Additional constraints

- `example` must not occur among the children or descendants of `example`.
- `figure` must not occur among the children or descendants of `example`.
- `table` must not occur among the children or descendants of `example`.
- `equation` must not occur among the children or descendants of `example`.
- `caution` must not occur among the children or descendants of `example`.
- `important` must not occur among the children or descendants of `example`.
- `note` must not occur among the children or descendants of `example`.
- `tip` must not occur among the children or descendants of `example`.
- `warning` must not occur among the children or descendants of `example`.

Description

An `example` is a formal example with a title. Examples often contain `programlistings` or other large block elements. Frequently, they are given `xml:ids` and referenced from the text with `xref` or `link`.

Processing expectations

Formatted as a displayed block.

DocBook does not specify the location of the example within the final displayed flow of text; it may float or remain where it is located.

A list of examples may be generated at the beginning of a document.

If a `label` is specified, that label will be used for identifying the example and in generated cross-references. If unspecified, `examples` are often, but not always, numbered.

If a `width` is specified, formatters may use this value to determine scaling or rotation.

Attributes

Common attributes and common linking attributes.

floatstyle
> Specifies style information to be used when rendering the float

label
> Specifies an identifying string for presentation purposes

pgwide
> Indicates if the element is rendered across the column or the page

Enumerated values:	
"0"	The element should be rendered in the current text flow (with the flow column width).
"1"	The element should be rendered across the full text page.

width
> Specifies the width (in characters) of the element

See Also

equation, figure, informalequation, informalexample, informalfigure, informaltable, table

Examples

```
<article xmlns='http://docbook.org/ns/docbook'>
<title>Example example</title>

<example xml:id="ex.dssslfunction">
<title>A DSSSL Function</title>
<programlisting>
(define (node-list-filter-by-gi nodelist gilist)
  ;; Returns the node-list that contains every element of the original
  ;; nodelist whose gi is in gilist
  (let loop ((result (empty-node-list)) (nl nodelist))
    (if (node-list-empty? nl)
    result
    (if (member (gi (node-list-first nl)) gilist)
        (loop (node-list result (node-list-first nl))
          (node-list-rest nl))
        (loop result (node-list-rest nl))))))
</programlisting>
</example>

</article>
```

Example 25. A DSSSL Function

```
(define (node-list-filter-by-gi nodelist gilist)
  ;; Returns the node-list that contains every element of the original
  ;; nodelist whose gi is in gilist
  (let loop ((result (empty-node-list)) (nl nodelist))
    (if (node-list-empty? nl)
    result
    (if (member (gi (node-list-first nl)) gilist)
        (loop (node-list result (node-list-first nl))
          (node-list-rest nl))
        (loop result (node-list-rest nl))))))
```

exceptionname

The name of an exception

Synopsis

exceptionname ::= (text | phrase ^{db._phrase} | replaceable | *Graphic inlines* | *Indexing inlines* | *Linking inlines* | *Ubiquitous inlines*)*

Attribute synopsis

Common attributes and common linking attributes.

Description

The exceptionname element is used to identify the name of an exception. This is likely to occur only in documentation about object-oriented programming systems, languages, and architectures.

Processing expectations

Formatted inline.

---

extendedlink

An XLink extended link

Synopsis

extendedlink ::= (arc | locator)+

Attribute synopsis

Common attributes.

Description

An XLink extended link. See XLink (*http://www.w3.org/TR/xlink/*) for more details.

Processing expectations

Suppressed.

---

fax

A fax number

Synopsis

fax ::= (text | phrase ^{db._phrase} | replaceable | *Graphic inlines* | *Indexing inlines* | *Linking inlines* | *Ubiquitous inlines*)*

Attribute synopsis

Common attributes and common linking attributes.

Description

A fax is a fax number in an address.

Processing expectations

Formatted inline. Sometimes suppressed. In an address, this element may inherit the verbatim qualities of an address.

See Also

address, city, country, email, otheraddr, phone, pob, postcode, state, street

---

fieldsynopsis

The name of a field in a class definition

Synopsis

fieldsynopsis ::= (modifier*, type?, varname, initializer?)

Attribute synopsis

Common attributes and common linking attributes.

Additional attributes:

- `language`

Description

A `fieldsynopsis` contains the syntax summary of a field (generally speaking, fields in the object-oriented programming language sense).

Processing expectations

For the most part, the processing application is expected to generate all of the parentheses, semicolons, commas, and so on required in the rendered synopsis.

Attributes

Common attributes and common linking attributes.

language
> Identifies the language (i.e., programming language) of the content

---

figure

A formal figure, generally an illustration, with a title

Synopsis

figure ::= ((((title & titleabbrev?), info? ^{db.titleforbidden.info}) | info ^{db.titleonlyreq.info}), (annotation | bridgehead | remark | revhistory | *Indexing inlines* | *Admonition elements* | *Formal elements* | *Graphic elements* | *Informal elements* | *List elements* | *Paragraph elements* | *Publishing elements* | *Synopsis elements* | *Technical elements* | *Verbatim elements*)+, caption? ^{db.caption})

Attribute synopsis

Common attributes and common linking attributes.

Additional attributes:

- `floatstyle`
- `label`
- `pgwide` (enumeration) = "0" | "1"

Additional constraints

- `example` must not occur among the children or descendants of `figure`.
- `figure` must not occur among the children or descendants of `figure`.
- `table` must not occur among the children or descendants of `figure`.
- `equation` must not occur among the children or descendants of `figure`.
- `caution` must not occur among the children or descendants of `figure`.
- `important` must not occur among the children or descendants of `figure`.
- `note` must not occur among the children or descendants of `figure`.

- `tip` must not occur among the children or descendants of `figure`.

- `warning` must not occur among the children or descendants of `figure`.

Description

A `figure` is a formal example with a title. Figures often contain `mediaobject`s, or other large display elements. Frequently, they are given IDs and referenced from the text with `xref` or `link`.

Processing expectations

Formatted as a displayed block.

A `figure` may contain multiple display elements. DocBook does not specify how these elements are to be presented with respect to one another.

DocBook does not specify the location of the figure within the final displayed flow of text; it may float or remain where it is located.

A list of figures may be generated at the beginning of a document.

Attributes

Common attributes and common linking attributes.

floatstyle
> Specifies style information to be used when rendering the float

label
> Specifies an identifying string for presentation purposes

pgwide
> Indicates if the element is rendered across the column or the page

Enumerated values:	
"0"	The element should be rendered in the current text flow (with the flow column width).
"1"	The element should be rendered across the full text page.

See Also

equation, example, informalequation, informalexample, informalfigure, informalta
ble, table

Examples

```
<article xmlns='http://docbook.org/ns/docbook'>
<title>Example figure</title>

<figure xml:id="ex.pythagorean">
<title>The Pythagorean Theorem Illustrated</title>
<mediaobject>
  <imageobject>
    <imagedata fileref="figures/pythag.png"/>
  </imageobject>
  <textobject><phrase>An illustration of the Pythagorean Theorem</phrase>
```

```
    </textobject>
  </mediaobject>
 </figure>

</article>
```

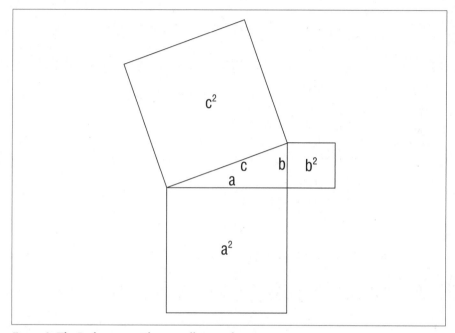

Figure 2. The Pythagorean Theorem Illustrated

filename

Synopsis

filename ::= (text | phrase ^{db._phrase} | replaceable | *Graphic inlines* | *Indexing inlines* | *Linking inlines* | *Ubiquitous inlines*)*

Attribute synopsis

Common attributes and common linking attributes.

Additional attributes:

- class (enumeration) = "devicefile" | "directory" | "extension" | "headerfile" | "libraryfile" | "partition" | "symlink"
- path

Description

A filename is the name of a file on a local or network disk. It may be a simple name or may include a path or other elements specific to the operating system.

Processing expectations
Formatted inline.

Attributes
Common attributes and common linking attributes.

class
>   Identifies the class of filename

Enumerated values:	
"devicefile"	A device
"directory"	A directory
"extension"	A filename extension
"headerfile"	A header file (as for a programming language)
"libraryfile"	A library file
"partition"	A partition (as of a hard disk)
"symlink"	A symbolic link

path
>   Specifies the path of the filename

See Also
application, computeroutput, database, envar, hardware, productname, prompt, systemitem, userinput

Examples

```
<article xmlns='http://docbook.org/ns/docbook'>
<title>Example filename</title>

<para>The symbolic constants for error numbers are defined in
<filename class='headerfile'>errno.h</filename> in
<filename class='directory'>/usr/include/sys</filename>.
</para>

</article>
```

The symbolic constants for error numbers are defined in *errno.h* in */usr/include/sys*.

---

firstname

A given name of a person

Synopsis
firstname ::= (text | phrase ^{db.-phrase} | replaceable | *Graphic inlines* | *Indexing inlines* | *Linking inlines* | *Ubiquitous inlines*)*

Attribute synopsis
Common attributes and common linking attributes.

Description

Use `firstname` for any given name or chosen name of a person. This is also used for forenames and sometimes nicknames.

A `firstname` is *an alternative* to `givenname`.

Processing expectations

Formatted inline. In an `address`, this element may inherit the verbatim qualities of an address.

See Also

`affiliation`, `honorific`, `lineage`, `othername`, `surname`

---

firstterm
The first occurrence of a term

Synopsis

firstterm ::= (text | *Bibliography inlines* | *Error inlines* | *Graphic inlines* | *GUI inlines* | *Indexing inlines* | *Keyboard inlines* | *Linking inlines* | *Markup inlines* | *Math inlines* | *Object-oriented programming inlines* | *Operating system inlines* | *Product inlines* | *Programming inlines* | *Publishing inlines* | *Technical inlines* | *Ubiquitous inlines*)*

Attribute synopsis

Common attributes and common linking attributes.

Additional attributes:

* `baseform`

Additional constraints

* `@linkend` on `firstterm` must point to a `glossentry`.

Description

This element marks the first occurrence of a word or term in a given context.

Processing expectations

Formatted inline. A `firstterm` is often given special typographic treatment, such as italics.

Attributes

Common attributes and common linking attributes.

baseform
> Specifies the base form of the term, the one that appears in the glossary. This allows adjectival, plural, and other variations of the term to appear in the element. The element content is the default base form.

See Also

`glossterm`

Examples

```
<article xmlns='http://docbook.org/ns/docbook'>
<title>Example firstterm</title>

<para>In an <firstterm>object-oriented</firstterm> programming language,
data and procedures (called <glossterm>methods</glossterm>) are
bound together.
</para>

</article>
```

In an *object-oriented* programming language, data and procedures (called *methods*) are bound together.

---

footnote

Synopsis

footnote ::= (annotation | bridgehead | remark | revhistory | *Indexing inlines* | *Admonition elements* | *Formal elements* | *Graphic elements* | *Informal elements* | *List elements* | *Paragraph elements* | *Publishing elements* | *Synopsis elements* | *Technical elements* | *Verbatim elements*)+

Attribute synopsis

Common attributes and common linking attributes.

Additional attributes:

- label (NMTOKEN)

Additional constraints

- footnote must not occur among the children or descendants of footnote.
- example must not occur among the children or descendants of footnote.
- figure must not occur among the children or descendants of footnote.
- table must not occur among the children or descendants of footnote.
- equation must not occur among the children or descendants of footnote.
- indexterm must not occur among the children or descendants of footnote.
- sidebar must not occur among the children or descendants of footnote.
- task must not occur among the children or descendants of footnote.
- epigraph must not occur among the children or descendants of footnote.
- caution must not occur among the children or descendants of footnote.
- important must not occur among the children or descendants of footnote.
- note must not occur among the children or descendants of footnote.
- tip must not occur among the children or descendants of footnote.
- warning must not occur among the children or descendants of footnote.

Description

This element is a wrapper around the contents of a footnote.

Additional references to the same footnote may be generated with `footnoteref`.

Processing expectations

The `footnote` element usually generates a mark (a superscript symbol or number) at the place in the flow of the document in which it occurs. The body of the footnote is then presented elsewhere, typically at the bottom of the page.

Alternative presentations are also possible. In print environments that do not support footnotes at the bottom of the page, they may be presented as endnotes occurring at the end of the component that contains the `footnote`. Online systems may choose to present them inline or as "pop ups," or links, or any combination thereof.

Attributes

Common attributes and common linking attributes.

label
> Identifies the desired footnote mark

Examples

```
<article xmlns='http://docbook.org/ns/docbook'>
<title>Example footnote</title>

<para>An annual percentage rate (<abbrev>APR</abbrev>) of 13.9%<footnote>
<para>The prime rate, as published in the <citetitle>Wall Street
Journal</citetitle> on the first business day of the month,
plus 7.0%.
</para>
</footnote>
will be charged on all balances carried forward.
</para>

</article>
```

An annual percentage rate (APR) of 13.9%* will be charged on all balances carried forward.

---

footnoteref

A cross-reference to a footnote (a footnote mark)

Synopsis

footnoteref ::= empty

Attribute synopsis

Common attributes.

---

* The prime rate, as published in the *Wall Street Journal* on the first business day of the month, plus 7.0%.

Additional attributes:

- `label`

Additional constraints

- `@linkend` on `footnoteref` must point to a `footnote`.

Description

This element forms an IDREF link to a `footnote`. It generates the same mark or link as the `footnote` to which it points.

In technical documentation, `footnoteref` occurs most frequently in tables.

Processing expectations

The `footnoteref` element usually generates the same mark as the `footnote` to which it points, although its mark can be influenced by the `label` attribute.

Attributes

Common attributes.

label
> Specifies an identifying string for presentation purposes

Examples

```
<article xmlns='http://docbook.org/ns/docbook'>
<title>Example footnoteref</title>

<informaltable>
<tgroup cols='2'>
<tbody>
<row>
<entry>foo<footnote xml:id='fnrex1a'><para>A meaningless
word</para></footnote></entry>
<entry>3<footnote xml:id='fnrex1b'><para>A meaningless
number</para></footnote></entry>
</row>
<row>
<entry>bar<footnoteref linkend='fnrex1a'/></entry>
<entry>5<footnoteref linkend='fnrex1b'/></entry>
</row>
</tbody>
</tgroup>
</informaltable>

</article>
```

foo[a]	3[b]
bar[a]	5[b]

a A meaningless word
b A meaningless number

foreignphrase

A word or phrase in a language other than the primary language of the document

Synopsis

foreignphrase ::= (text | *Bibliography inlines* | *Graphic inlines* | *Indexing inlines* | *Linking inlines* | *Product inlines* | *Publishing inlines*)*

Attribute synopsis

Common attributes and common linking attributes.

Description

The foreignphrase element can be used to mark up the text of a foreign word or phrase. "Foreign" in this context means that it is a language other than the primary language of the document and is not intended to be pejorative in any way.

Processing expectations

A foreignphrase is often given special typographic treatment, such as italics.

See Also

abbrev, acronym, emphasis, phrase, quote, wordasword

Examples

```
<article xmlns='http://docbook.org/ns/docbook'>
<title>Example foreignphrase</title>

<para>Like so many others, it became a <foreignphrase>de facto</foreignphrase>
standard.
</para>

</article>
```

Like so many others, it became a *de facto* standard.

formalpara

A paragraph with a title

Synopsis

formalpara ::= (((((title & titleabbrev?), info? ^{db.titleforbidden.info}) | info ^{db.titleonlyreq.info}), *Indexing inlines**, para)

Attribute synopsis

Common attributes and common linking attributes.

Description

Formal paragraphs have a title.

Processing expectations

Formatted as a displayed block. The title of a formalpara is often rendered as a run-in head.

See Also

para, simpara

Examples

```
<article xmlns='http://docbook.org/ns/docbook'>
<title>Example formalpara</title>

<formalpara><title>This Paragraph Has a Title</title>
<para>This is a test.  This is only a test.  Had this been a real
example, it would have made more sense.  Or less.
</para>
</formalpara>

</article>
```

This Paragraph Has a Title.
This is a test. This is only a test. Had this been a real example, it would have made more
sense. Or less.

---

funcdef   A function (subroutine) name and its return type

Synopsis
funcdef ::= (text | function | phrase ^{db._phrase} | replaceable | type | *Graphic inlines* | *Indexing in-lines* | *Linking inlines* | *Ubiquitous inlines*)*

Attribute synopsis
Common attributes and common linking attributes.

Description
A funcdef contains the name of a programming language function and its return type.

Within the funcdef, the function name is identified with function, and the rest of the content is assumed to be the return type.

In the following definition, max is the name of the function and int is the return type:

```
<funcdef>int <function>max</function></funcdef>
```

Processing expectations
Formatted inline. For a complete description of the processing expectations, see funcsynopsis.

See Also
funcparams, funcprototype, funcsynopsisinfo, function, paramdef, parameter, return value, varargs, void

Examples

```
<article xmlns='http://docbook.org/ns/docbook'>
<title>Example funcdef</title>

<funcsynopsis>
<funcprototype>
<funcdef>int <function>rand</function></funcdef>
  <void/>
```

```
    </funcprototype>
    </funcsynopsis>

    </article>

    int rand();
```

---

funcparams

Synopsis

funcparams ::= (text | phrase ^{db._phrase} | replaceable | *Graphic inlines* | *Indexing inlines* | *Linking inlines* | *Ubiquitous inlines*)*

Attribute synopsis

Common attributes and common linking attributes.

Description

In some programming languages (such as C), it is possible for a function to have a pointer to another function as one of its parameters. In the syntax summary for such a function, the funcparams element provides a wrapper for the function pointer.

For example, the following prototype describes the function sort, which takes two parameters. The first parameter, arr, is an array of integers. The second parameter is a pointer to a function, comp, that returns an int. The comp function takes two parameters, both of type int *:

```
<funcprototype>
  <funcdef>void <function>sort</function></funcdef>
    <paramdef>int *<parameter>arr</parameter>[]</paramdef>
    <paramdef>int <parameter>(* comp)</parameter>
      <funcparams>int *, int *</funcparams></paramdef>
</funcprototype>
```

Processing expectations

Formatted inline. For a complete description of the processing expectations, see funcsynopsis.

See Also

funcdef, funcprototype, funcsynopsisinfo, function, paramdef, parameter, return value, varargs, void

Examples

```
<article xmlns='http://docbook.org/ns/docbook'>
<title>Example funcparams</title>

<funcsynopsis>
<funcprototype>
  <funcdef>void <function>qsort</function></funcdef>
    <paramdef>void *<parameter>dataptr</parameter>[]</paramdef>
```

```
            <paramdef>int <parameter>left</parameter></paramdef>
            <paramdef>int <parameter>right</parameter></paramdef>
            <paramdef>int (*<parameter>comp</parameter>)
               <funcparams>void *, void *</funcparams></paramdef>
        </funcprototype>
        </funcsynopsis>

        </article>

    void qsort(dataptr, left, right, comp);

    void *dataptr[];
    int left;
    int right;
    int (*comp) (void *, void *);
```

funcprototype

The prototype of a function

Synopsis

funcprototype ::= (modifier*, funcdef, ((paramdef+, varargs?) | varargs | void), modifier*)

Attribute synopsis

Common attributes and common linking attributes.

Description

A wrapper for a function prototype in a funcsynopsis.

Processing expectations

See funcsynopsis.

See Also

funcdef, funcparams, funcsynopsisinfo, function, paramdef, parameter, returnvalue, varargs, void

funcsynopsis

The syntax summary for a function definition

Synopsis

funcsynopsis ::= (info? db.titleforbidden.info, (funcprototype | funcsynopsisinfo)+)

Attribute synopsis

Common attributes and common linking attributes.

Additional attributes:

- language

Description

A `funcsynopsis` contains the syntax summary of a function prototype or a set of function prototypes. The content model of this element was designed specifically to capture the semantics of most C-language function prototypes (for use in UNIX reference pages).

This is one of the few places where DocBook attempts to model as well as describe. Using `funcsynopsis` for languages that are unrelated to C may prove difficult.

Processing expectations

For the most part, the processing application is expected to generate all of the parentheses, semicolons, commas, and so on required in the rendered synopsis. The exception to this rule is that the spacing and other punctuation inside a parameter that is a pointer to a function must be provided in the source markup.

With sufficient author cooperation, it should be possible to mark up a function synopsis with enough clarity so that a processing system can generate either K&R-style or ANSI-style renderings.

Attributes

Common attributes and common linking attributes.

language
> Identifies the language (i.e., programming language) of the content

See Also

cmdsynopsis, synopsis

Examples

There are two common presentation styles for function synopses, "K&R" style and "ANSI" style.

K&R examples

```
<article xmlns='http://docbook.org/ns/docbook'>
<title>Example funcsynopsis</title>

<funcsynopsis>
<funcprototype>
  <?dbhtml funcsynopsis-style='kr'?>
  <funcdef>int <function>max</function></funcdef>
  <paramdef>int <parameter>int1</parameter></paramdef>
  <paramdef>int <parameter>int2</parameter></paramdef>
</funcprototype>
</funcsynopsis>

</article>
```

```
int max(int1, int2);

int int1;
int int2;
```

```
<article xmlns='http://docbook.org/ns/docbook'>
<title>Example funcsynopsis</title>

<funcsynopsis>
<funcsynopsisinfo>
#include &lt;varargs.h&gt;
</funcsynopsisinfo>
<funcprototype>
  <?dbhtml funcsynopsis-style='kr'?>
  <funcdef>int <function>max</function></funcdef>
  <varargs/>
</funcprototype>
</funcsynopsis>

</article>
```

#include <varargs.h>

int max(...);

```
<article xmlns='http://docbook.org/ns/docbook'>
<title>Example funcsynopsis</title>

<funcsynopsis>
<funcprototype>
<?dbhtml funcsynopsis-style='kr'?>
<funcdef>int <function>rand</function></funcdef>
  <void/>
</funcprototype>
</funcsynopsis>

</article>
```

int rand();

```
<article xmlns='http://docbook.org/ns/docbook'>
<title>Example funcsynopsis</title>

<funcsynopsis>
<funcprototype>
  <?dbhtml funcsynopsis-style='kr'?>
  <funcdef>void <function>qsort</function></funcdef>
    <paramdef>void *<parameter>dataptr</parameter>[]</paramdef>
    <paramdef>int <parameter>left</parameter></paramdef>
    <paramdef>int <parameter>right</parameter></paramdef>
    <paramdef>int <parameter>(* comp)</parameter>
      <funcparams>void *, void *</funcparams></paramdef>
</funcprototype>
</funcsynopsis>

</article>
```

void qsort(dataptr, left, right, (* comp));

```
void *dataptr[];
int left;
int right;
int (* comp) (void *, void *);
```

ANSI examples

```
<article xmlns='http://docbook.org/ns/docbook'>
<title>Example funcsynopsis</title>

<funcsynopsis>
<funcprototype>
  <?dbhtml funcsynopsis-style='ansi'?>
  <funcdef>int <function>max</function></funcdef>
  <paramdef>int <parameter>int1</parameter></paramdef>
  <paramdef>int <parameter>int2</parameter></paramdef>
</funcprototype>
</funcsynopsis>

</article>
```

```
int max(int1, int2);

int int1;
int int2;
```

```
<article xmlns='http://docbook.org/ns/docbook'>
<title>Example funcsynopsis</title>

<funcsynopsis>
<funcsynopsisinfo>
#include &lt;varargs.h&gt;
</funcsynopsisinfo>
<funcprototype>
  <?dbhtml funcsynopsis-style='ansi'?>
  <funcdef>int <function>max</function></funcdef>
  <varargs/>
</funcprototype>
</funcsynopsis>

</article>
```

```
#include <varargs.h>

int max(...);
```

```
<article xmlns='http://docbook.org/ns/docbook'>
<title>Example funcsynopsis</title>

<funcsynopsis>
<funcprototype>
<?dbhtml funcsynopsis-style='ansi'?>
<funcdef>int <function>rand</function></funcdef>
  <void/>
```

```
    </funcprototype>
    </funcsynopsis>

  </article>
```

```
int rand();
```

```
  <article xmlns='http://docbook.org/ns/docbook'>
  <title>Example funcsynopsis</title>

  <funcsynopsis>
  <funcprototype>
    <?dbhtml funcsynopsis-style='ansi'?>
    <funcdef>void <function>qsort</function></funcdef>
      <paramdef>void *<parameter>dataptr</parameter>[]</paramdef>
      <paramdef>int <parameter>left</parameter></paramdef>
      <paramdef>int <parameter>right</parameter></paramdef>
      <paramdef>int <parameter>(* comp)</parameter>
        <funcparams>void *, void *</funcparams></paramdef>
  </funcprototype>
  </funcsynopsis>

  </article>
```

```
void qsort(dataptr, left, right, (* comp));

void *dataptr[];
int left;
int right;
int (* comp) (void *, void *);
```

funcsynopsisinfo

Information supplementing the funcdefs of a funcsynopsis

Synopsis

funcsynopsisinfo ::= (info? $^{\text{db.titleforbidden.info}}$, ((text | lineannotation | *Bibliography inlines* | *Computer-output inlines* | *Error inlines* | *Graphic inlines* | *GUI inlines* | *Indexing inlines* | *Keyboard inlines* | *Linking inlines* | *Markup inlines* | *Math inlines* | *Object-oriented programming inlines* | *Operating system inlines* | *Product inlines* | *Programming inlines* | *Publishing inlines* | *Technical inlines* | *Ubiquitous inlines* | *User-input inlines*)* | textobject))

Attribute synopsis

Common attributes and common linking attributes.

Additional attributes:

- continuation (enumeration) = "continues" | "restarts"
- linenumbering (enumeration) = "numbered" | "unnumbered"
- startinglinenumber (integer)
- language

- `xml:space` (enumeration) = "preserve"

Description

Supplementary information in a `funcsynopsis`. See `funcsynopsis`.

Unlike the other info elements, `funcsynopsisinfo` is not a container for meta-information. Instead, `funcsynopsisinfo` is a verbatim environment for adding additional information to a function synopsis.

Processing expectations

This element is displayed "verbatim"; whitespace and line breaks within this element are significant.

Attributes

Common attributes and common linking attributes.

continuation

> Determines whether line numbering continues from the previous element or restarts.

Enumerated values:	
"continues"	Line numbering continues from the immediately preceding element with the same name.
"restarts"	Line numbering restarts (begins at 1, usually).

language

> Identifies the language (i.e., programming language) of the verbatim content.

linenumbering

> Determines whether lines are numbered.

Enumerated values:	
"numbered"	Lines are numbered.
"unnumbered"	Lines are not numbered.

startinglinenumber

> Specifies the initial line number.

xml:space

> Can be used to indicate explicitly that whitespace in the verbatim environment is preserved. Whitespace must always be preserved in verbatim environments whether this attribute is specified or not.

Enumerated values:	
"preserve"	Whitespace must be preserved.

See Also

funcdef, funcparams, funcprototype, function, paramdef, parameter, returnvalue, varargs, void

Examples

```
<article xmlns='http://docbook.org/ns/docbook'>
<title>Example funcsynopsis</title>

<funcsynopsis>
<funcsynopsisinfo>
#include &lt;varargs.h&gt;
</funcsynopsisinfo>
<funcprototype>
  <funcdef>int <function>max</function></funcdef>
  <varargs/>
</funcprototype>
</funcsynopsis>

</article>
```

#include <varargs.h>

int max(...);

---

function

The name of a function or subroutine, as in a programming language

Synopsis

function ::= (text | phrase ^{db._phrase} | replaceable | *Graphic inlines* | *Indexing inlines* | *Linking inlines* | *Ubiquitous inlines*)*

Attribute synopsis

Common attributes and common linking attributes.

Description

This element marks up the name of a function. To mark up the parts of a function definition, see funcsynopsis.

Processing expectations

Formatted inline.

In some environments, the function element generates additional punctuation, such as a set of trailing parentheses.

See Also

funcdef, funcparams, funcprototype, funcsynopsisinfo, paramdef, parameter, return value, varargs, void

glossary

A glossary

Synopsis

glossary ::= ((((title? & titleabbrev? & subtitle?), info? ^{db.titleforbidden.info}) | info? ^{db.info}), (anno tation | bridgehead | remark | revhistory | *Indexing inlines* | *Admonition elements* | *Formal elements* | *Graphic elements* | *Informal elements* | *List elements* | *Paragraph elements* | *Publishing elements* | *Synopsis elements* | *Technical elements* | *Verbatim elements*)*, (glossdiv* | glossentry*), bibliography?)

Attribute synopsis

Common attributes and common linking attributes.

Additional attributes:

- label
- status

Additional constraints

- If this element is the root element, it must have a **version** attribute.

Description

A glossary contains a collection of terms and brief descriptions or definitions of those terms.

Processing expectations

Formatted as a displayed block. A glossary in a book frequently causes a forced page break in print media.

Attributes

Common attributes and common linking attributes.

label
> Specifies an identifying string for presentation purposes

status
> Identifies the editorial or publication status of the element on which it occurs

Examples

```
<glossary xmlns='http://docbook.org/ns/docbook'>
<title>Example Glossary</title>

<para>This is not a real glossary, it's just an example.
</para>

<!-- ... -->

<glossdiv><title>E</title>

<glossentry xml:id="xml"><glossterm>Extensible Markup Language</glossterm>
  <acronym>XML</acronym>
<glossdef>
  <para>Some reasonable definition here.</para>
```

```
        <glossseealso otherterm="sgml">SGML</glossseealso>
    </glossdef>
    </glossentry>

    </glossdiv>

    <!-- ... -->

    <glossdiv><title>S</title>

    <glossentry><glossterm>SGML</glossterm>
    <glosssee otherterm="sgml"/>
    </glossentry>

    <glossentry xml:id="sgml"><glossterm>Standard Generalized
      Markup Language</glossterm><acronym>SGML</acronym>
      <abbrev>ISO 8879:1986</abbrev>
    <glossdef>
      <para>Some reasonable definition here.</para>
      <glossseealso otherterm="xml">XML</glossseealso>
    </glossdef>
    </glossentry>

    </glossdiv>
    </glossary>
```

This is not a real glossary, it's just an example.

glossdef

A definition in a glossentry

Synopsis
glossdef ::= ((annotation | bridgehead | remark | revhistory | *Indexing inlines* | *Admonition elements* | *Formal elements* | *Graphic elements* | *Informal elements* | *List elements* | *Paragraph elements* | *Publishing elements* | *Synopsis elements* | *Technical elements* | *Verbatim elements*)+, gloss seealso*)

Attribute synopsis
Common attributes and common linking attributes.

Additional attributes:

* subject

Description
A glossdef contains the description or definition of a glossterm.

Processing expectations
Formatted as a displayed block.

Attributes
Common attributes and common linking attributes.

---

subject
> Specifies a list of keywords for the definition

See Also
glosssee, glossseealso

glossdiv

Synopsis
glossdiv ::= ((((title & titleabbrev? & subtitle?), info? ^{db.titleforbidden.info}) | info ^{db.titlereq.info}),
(annotation | bridgehead | remark | revhistory | *Indexing inlines* | *Admonition elements* | *Formal elements* | *Graphic elements* | *Informal elements* | *List elements* | *Paragraph elements* | *Publishing elements* | *Synopsis elements* | *Technical elements* | *Verbatim elements*)*, glossentry+)

Attribute synopsis
Common attributes and common linking attributes.

Additional attributes:

- label
- status

Description
A glossdiv is a section of a glossary. A glossary might be divided into sections in order to group terms, perhaps alphabetically.

A glossary may contain any number of glossentry or glossdiv elements, but it cannot contain a mixture of both at the same level.

Processing expectations
Formatted as a displayed block.

Attributes
Common attributes and common linking attributes.

label
> Specifies an identifying string for presentation purposes

status
> Identifies the editorial or publication status of the element on which it occurs

glossentry

Synopsis
glossentry ::= (glossterm, acronym?, abbrev?, *Indexing inlines**, (glossdef+ | glosssee))

Attribute synopsis
Common attributes and common linking attributes.

Additional attributes:

- `sortas`

Description

A `glossentry` is a wrapper around a glossary term and its definition.

Processing expectations

Formatted as a displayed block. Glossary entries are usually formatted to highlight the terms and definitions, frequently in a style similar to `varlistentry`s.

Attributes

Common attributes and common linking attributes.

sortas
> Specifies the string by which the element's content is to be sorted; if unspecified, the content is used

---

glosslist

A wrapper for a list of glossary entries

Synopsis

glosslist ::= ((((title? & titleabbrev?), info? $^{\text{db.titleforbidden.info}}$) | info $^{\text{db.titleonly.info}}$)?, (annotation | bridgehead | remark | revhistory | *Indexing inlines* | *Admonition elements* | *Formal elements* | *Graphic elements* | *Informal elements* | *List elements* | *Paragraph elements* | *Publishing elements* | *Synopsis elements* | *Technical elements* | *Verbatim elements*)*, glossentry+)

Attribute synopsis

Common attributes and common linking attributes.

Description

While `glossary`s are usually limited to component or section boundaries, appearing at the end of a `book` or `chapter`, for instance, `glosslist`s can appear anywhere that the other list types are allowed.

Using a `glosslist` in running text, instead of a `variablelist`, for example, maintains the semantic distinction of a glossary. This distinction may be necessary if you want to automatically point to the members of the list with `glossterm`s in the body of the text.

Processing expectations

Formatted as a displayed block.

Examples

```
<article xmlns='http://docbook.org/ns/docbook'>
<title>Example glosslist</title>

<glosslist>
<glossentry><glossterm>C</glossterm>
<glossdef>
<para>A programming language invented by K&amp;R.
</para>
```

```
</glossdef>
</glossentry>
<glossentry><glossterm>Pascal</glossterm>
<glossdef>
<para>A programming language invented by Niklaus Wirth.
</para>
</glossdef>
</glossentry>
</glosslist>

</article>
```

C   A programming language invented by K&R.

Pascal   A programming language invented by Niklaus
                                     Wirth.

glosssee
A cross-reference from one glossentry to another

Synopsis

glosssee ::= (text | *Bibliography inlines* | *Error inlines* | *Graphic inlines* | *GUI inlines* | *Indexing inlines* | *Keyboard inlines* | *Linking inlines* | *Markup inlines* | *Math inlines* | *Object-oriented programming inlines* | *Operating system inlines* | *Product inlines* | *Programming inlines* | *Publishing inlines* | *Technical inlines* | *Ubiquitous inlines*)*

Attribute synopsis

Common attributes and common linking attributes.

Additional attributes:

- otherterm (IDREF)

Additional constraints

- @otherterm on glosssee must point to a glossentry.

Description

A glosssee directs the reader to another glossentry instead of this one. A "See" cross-reference occurs in place of the definition.

Processing expectations

Formatted as a displayed block, in the same style as a glossdef.

The glosssee elements are expected to generate the necessary cross-reference text, usually "See" in English, as well as any necessary punctuation.

Attributes

Common attributes and common linking attributes.

otherterm
   Identifies the other term

See Also
glossdef, glossseealso

---

glossseealso

A cross-reference from one glossentry to another

Synopsis
glossseealso ::= (text | *Bibliography inlines* | *Error inlines* | *Graphic inlines* | *GUI inlines* | *Indexing inlines* | *Keyboard inlines* | *Linking inlines* | *Markup inlines* | *Math inlines* | *Object-oriented programming inlines* | *Operating system inlines* | *Product inlines* | *Programming inlines* | *Publishing inlines* | *Technical inlines* | *Ubiquitous inlines*)*

Attribute synopsis
Common attributes and common linking attributes.

Additional attributes:

- otherterm (IDREF)

Additional constraints

- @otherterm on glossseealso must point to a glossentry.

Description
A glossseealso directs the reader to another glossentry for additional information. It is presented in addition to the glossdef.

Processing expectations
Formatted as a displayed block, in the same style as the glossdef.

The glossseealso elements are expected to generate the necessary cross-reference text, usually "See also" in English, as well as any necessary punctuation.

Attributes
Common attributes and common linking attributes.

otherterm
    Identifies the other term

See Also
glossdef, glosssee

---

glossterm

A glossary term

Synopsis
glossterm ::= (text | *Bibliography inlines* | *Error inlines* | *Graphic inlines* | *GUI inlines* | *Indexing inlines* | *Keyboard inlines* | *Linking inlines* | *Markup inlines* | *Math inlines* | *Object-oriented programming inlines* | *Operating system inlines* | *Product inlines* | *Programming inlines* | *Publishing inlines* | *Technical inlines* | *Ubiquitous inlines*)*

Attribute synopsis

Common attributes and common linking attributes.

Additional attributes:

- `baseform`

Additional constraints

- `@linkend` on `glossterm` must point to a `glossentry`.

Description

A `glossterm` identifies a term that appears in a `glossary` or `glosslist`. This element occurs in two very different places: it is both an inline, and a structure element of a `glossentry`. As an inline, it identifies a term defined in a glossary, and may point to it. Within a `glossentry`, it identifies the term defined by that particular entry.

Processing expectations

As an inline, `glossterm`s frequently get special typographic treatment, such as italics. In an online environment, they may also form a link (explicitly or implicitly) to the corresponding definition in a glossary.

The `glossterm`s must not be nested within other `glossterm`s. The processing of nested `glossterm`s is undefined.

As part of a `glossentry`, `glossterm`s are usually set as a block and separated from the definition.

Attributes

Common attributes and common linking attributes.

baseform
> Specifies the base form of the term, the one that appears in the glossary. This allows adjectival, plural, and other variations of the term to appear in the element. The element content is the default base form.

See Also

`firstterm`

Examples

See `glossary` for an example using this element.

---

group

A group of elements in a cmdsynopsis

Synopsis

group ::= (arg | group | option | replaceable | sbr | synopfragmentref)+

Attribute synopsis

Common attributes and common linking attributes.

Additional attributes:

- `choice` (enumeration) = "opt" | "plain" | "req" [default="opt"]
- `rep` (enumeration) = "norepeat" | "repeat" [default="norepeat"]

Description

A `group` surrounds several related items. Usually, they are grouped because they are mutually exclusive. The user is expected to select one of the items.

Processing expectations

Formatted inline. The additional processing expectations of a `group` are significant. For a complete discussion, see `cmdsynopsis`.

- Multiple arguments within a group are considered exclusive and are separated by vertical bars.
- Brackets are used to distinguish between optional, required, or plain arguments. Usually square brackets are placed around optional arguments, `[-f | -g]`, and curly brackets are placed around required arguments, `{-f | -g}`. Plain arguments are required, but are not decorated with brackets.
- Repeatable arguments are followed by an ellipsis.

Attributes

Common attributes and common linking attributes.

choice
> Indicates optionality

Enumerated values:	
"opt"	Formatted to indicate that it is optional
"plain"	Formatted without indication
"req"	Formatted to indicate that it is required

rep
> Indicates whether or not repetition is possible

Enumerated values:	
"norepeat"	Cannot be repeated
"repeat"	Can be repeated

See Also

arg, cmdsynopsis, refsynopsisdiv, sbr, synopfragment, synopfragmentref

Examples

```
<article xmlns='http://docbook.org/ns/docbook'>
<title>Example group in cmdsynopsis</title>
```

```
<cmdsynopsis>
  <command>mycmd</command>
  <group>
  <arg>-r <replaceable>revision</replaceable></arg>
    <group>
      <arg choice="plain">-h</arg>
      <arg choice="plain">-l</arg>
      <arg choice="plain">-p</arg>
    </group>
  </group>
  <group choice="req">
    <arg choice="plain">URL</arg>
    <arg choice="plain">filename</arg>
  </group>
  <arg rep="repeat">parameters</arg>
</cmdsynopsis>

</article>
```

mycmd [[-r *revision*] [-h | -l | -p]] { URL | filename } [parameters...]

guibutton

The text on a button in a GUI

Synopsis
guibutton ::= (text | accel | phrase ^{db.–phrase} | replaceable | *Graphic inlines* | *Indexing inlines* | *Linking inlines* | *Ubiquitous inlines*)*

Attribute synopsis
Common attributes and common linking attributes.

Description
A guibutton identifies the text that appears on a button in a graphical user interface.

Processing expectations
Formatted inline.

See Also
accel, guiicon, guilabel, guimenu, guimenuitem, guisubmenu, keycap, keycode, key combo, keysym, menuchoice, mousebutton, shortcut

Examples

```
<article xmlns='http://docbook.org/ns/docbook'>
<title>Example guibutton</title>

<para>The exact text of the <guilabel>Legend</guilabel> and other labels on the
graph is dependent upon the language of the current locale.  Likewise,
the text of the <guibutton>OK</guibutton> button and other buttons may vary.
The <guiicon><inlinemediaobject>
<imageobject>
<imagedata fileref="figures/legend.png"/>
</imageobject>
```

```
</inlinemediaobject></guiicon>
icon and the other icons on the left side of the display may be
configured by the local administrator, but they are not
generally expected to vary from locale to locale.
</para>

</article>
```

The exact text of the Legend and other labels on the graph is dependent upon the language of the current locale. Likewise, the text of the OK button and other buttons may vary. The ▣ icon and the other icons on the left side of the display may be configured by the local administrator, but they are not generally expected to vary from locale to locale.

guiicon
Graphic and/or text appearing as an icon in a GUI

Synopsis
guiicon ::= (text | accel | phrase ^{db.–phrase} | replaceable | *Graphic inlines* | *Indexing inlines* | *Linking inlines* | *Ubiquitous inlines*)*

Attribute synopsis
Common attributes and common linking attributes.

Description
A guiicon identifies a graphic or text icon that appears in a graphical user interface.

Processing expectations
Formatted inline.

See Also
accel, guibutton, guilabel, guimenu, guimenuitem, guisubmenu, keycap, keycode, keycombo, keysym, menuchoice, mousebutton, shortcut

Examples

```
<article xmlns='http://docbook.org/ns/docbook'>
<title>Example guiicon</title>

<para>The exact text of the <guilabel>Legend</guilabel> and other labels on the
graph is dependent upon the language of the current locale.  Likewise,
the text of the <guibutton>OK</guibutton> button and other buttons may vary.
The <guiicon><inlinemediaobject>
<imageobject>
<imagedata fileref="figures/legend.png"/>
</imageobject>
</inlinemediaobject></guiicon>
icon and the other icons on the left side of the display may be
configured by the local administrator, but they are not
generally expected to vary from locale to locale.
</para>

</article>
```

The exact text of the Legend and other labels on the graph is dependent upon the language of the current locale. Likewise, the text of the OK button and other buttons may vary. The ⊞ icon and the other icons on the left side of the display may be configured by the local administrator, but they are not generally expected to vary from locale to locale.

guilabel

Synopsis
guilabel ::= (text | accel | phrase ^{db._phrase} | replaceable | *Graphic inlines* | *Indexing inlines* | *Linking inlines* | *Ubiquitous inlines*)*

Attribute synopsis
Common attributes and common linking attributes.

Description
A guilabel identifies text that appears as a label in a graphical user interface.

What constitutes a label may vary from application to application. In general, any text that appears in a GUI may be considered a label—for example, a message in a dialog box or a window title.

Processing expectations
Formatted inline.

See Also
accel, guibutton, guiicon, guimenu, guimenuitem, guisubmenu, keycap, keycode, key combo, keysym, menuchoice, mousebutton, shortcut

Examples

```
<article xmlns='http://docbook.org/ns/docbook'>
<title>Example guilabel</title>

<para>The exact text of the <guilabel>Legend</guilabel> and other labels on the
graph is dependent upon the language of the current locale.  Likewise,
the text of the <guibutton>OK</guibutton> button and other buttons may vary.
The <guiicon><inlinemediaobject>
<imageobject>
<imagedata fileref="figures/legend.png"/>
</imageobject>
</inlinemediaobject></guiicon>
icon and the other icons on the left side of the display may be
configured by the local administrator, but they are not
generally expected to vary from locale to locale.
</para>

</article>
```

The exact text of the Legend and other labels on the graph is dependent upon the language of the current locale. Likewise, the text of the OK button and other buttons may vary. The ▣ icon and the other icons on the left side of the display may be configured by the local administrator, but they are not generally expected to vary from locale to locale.

guimenu
The name of a menu in a GUI

Synopsis
guimenu ::= (text | accel | phrase ^{db.–phrase} | replaceable | *Graphic inlines* | *Indexing inlines* | *Linking inlines* | *Ubiquitous inlines*)*

Attribute synopsis
Common attributes and common linking attributes.

Description
A guimenu identifies a menu name in a graphical user interface. In particular, this is distinct from a menu item (guimenuitem), which is terminal, and a submenu (guisubmenu), which occurs as a selection from a menu.

Processing expectations
Formatted inline.

See Also
accel, guibutton, guiicon, guilabel, guimenuitem, guisubmenu, keycap, keycode, keycombo, keysym, menuchoice, mousebutton, shortcut

Examples

```
<article xmlns='http://docbook.org/ns/docbook'>
<title>Example guimenu</title>

<para>You can exit from GNU Emacs with the keyboard shortcut
<keycombo><keysym>C-c</keysym><keysym>C-x</keysym></keycombo>
or by selecting <guimenuitem>Exit Emacs</guimenuitem> from
the <guimenu>Files</guimenu> menu.
</para>

</article>
```

You can exit from GNU Emacs with the keyboard shortcut C-c+C-x or by selecting Exit Emacs from the Files menu.

guimenuitem
The name of a terminal menu item in a GUI

Synopsis
guimenuitem ::= (text | accel | phrase ^{db.–phrase} | replaceable | *Graphic inlines* | *Indexing inlines* | *Linking inlines* | *Ubiquitous inlines*)*

Attribute synopsis
Common attributes and common linking attributes.

Description

A guimenuitem identifies a terminal selection from a menu in a graphical user interface. In particular, this is distinct from a menu (guimenu) and a submenu (guisubmenu). The distinction between a guimenuitem and a guisubmenu is simply whether or not the selection is terminal or leads to an additional submenu.

Processing expectations

Formatted inline.

See Also

accel, guibutton, guiicon, guilabel, guimenu, guisubmenu, keycap, keycode, keycombo, keysym, menuchoice, mousebutton, shortcut

Examples

```
<article xmlns='http://docbook.org/ns/docbook'>
<title>Example guimenuitem</title>

<para>You can exit from GNU Emacs with the keyboard shortcut
<keycombo><keysym>C-c</keysym><keysym>C-x</keysym></keycombo>
or by selecting <guimenuitem>Exit Emacs</guimenuitem> from
the <guimenu>Files</guimenu> menu.
</para>

</article>
```

You can exit from GNU Emacs with the keyboard shortcut C-c+C-x or by selecting Exit Emacs from the Files menu.

guisubmenu

The name of a submenu in a GUI

Synopsis

guisubmenu ::= (text | accel | phrase ^{db._phrase} | replaceable | *Graphic inlines* | *Indexing inlines* | *Linking inlines* | *Ubiquitous inlines*)*

Attribute synopsis

Common attributes and common linking attributes.

Description

The name of a submenu in a graphical user interface is identified by the guisubmenu element. A submenu is a menu invoked from another menu that leads either to terminal items (guimenuitems) or to additional submenus.

Processing expectations

Formatted inline.

See Also

accel, guibutton, guiicon, guilabel, guimenu, guimenuitem, keycap, keycode, keycombo, keysym, menuchoice, mousebutton, shortcut

Examples

```
<article xmlns='http://docbook.org/ns/docbook'>
<title>Example guisubmenu</title>

<para>In GNU Emacs, the <guimenuitem>Print Buffer</guimenuitem> command is
located off of the <guisubmenu>Print</guisubmenu> submenu of the
<guimenu>Tools</guimenu> menu.
</para>

</article>
```

In GNU Emacs, the Print Buffer command is located off of the Print submenu of the Tools menu.

---

hardware
A physical part of a computer system

Synopsis

hardware ::= (text | phrase ^{db.–phrase} | replaceable | *Graphic inlines* | *Indexing inlines* | *Linking inlines* | *Ubiquitous inlines*)*

Attribute synopsis

Common attributes and common linking attributes.

Description

A hardware element identifies some physical component of a computer system. Even though DocBook provides a broad range of inlines for describing the various software components of a system, it provides relatively few for describing hardware.

If you need to identify a number of different hardware components, you may wish to consider extending DocBook, or at least using the role attribute to further classify hardware.

Processing expectations

Formatted inline.

See Also

application, database, filename, productname

Examples

```
<article xmlns='http://docbook.org/ns/docbook'>
<title>Example hardware</title>

<para>The <acronym>IRQ</acronym> of the <hardware>SCSI Controller</hardware>
can be set to 7, 11, or 15.  The factory default setting is 7.
</para>

</article>
```

The IRQ of the SCSI Controller can be set to 7, 11, or 15. The factory default setting is 7.

---

holder

The name of the individual or organization that holds a copyright

Synopsis

holder ::= (text | phrase ^{db._phrase} | replaceable | *Graphic inlines* | *Indexing inlines* | *Linking inlines* | *Ubiquitous inlines*)*

Attribute synopsis

Common attributes and common linking attributes.

Description

A holder in copyright identifies an individual or organization that asserts a copyright on the document.

Processing expectations

The formatting of holder depends on the formatting of its parent copyright. In the case of a copyright with multiple holders, additional punctuation may need to be generated when holder is processed.

Examples

See copyright for an example that uses this element.

honorific

The title of a person

Synopsis

honorific ::= (text | phrase ^{db._phrase} | replaceable | *Graphic inlines* | *Indexing inlines* | *Linking inlines* | *Ubiquitous inlines*)*

Attribute synopsis

Common attributes and common linking attributes.

Description

An honorific occurs in the name of an individual. It is the honorific title of the individual, such as "Dr.," "Mr.," or "Ms."

Processing expectations

Formatted inline. In an address, this element may inherit the verbatim qualities of an address.

On some systems, honorific may generate the trailing period automatically.

See Also

affiliation, firstname, lineage, othername, surname

imagedata (db.imagedata.mathml)

A MathML expression in a media object

Synopsis

imagedata (db.imagedata.mathml) ::= (info? ^{db.titleforbidden.info}, mml:*+)

Attribute synopsis
Common attributes.

Additional attributes:

- align (enumeration) = "center" | "char" | "justify" | "left" | "right"
- contentdepth
- contentwidth
- depth
- format (enumeration) = "mathml"
- scale (positiveInteger)
- scalefit (enumeration) = "0" | "1"
- valign (enumeration) = "bottom" | "middle" | "top"
- width

Description
This element contains one or more MathML elements.

Processing expectations
Render the image. May be formatted inline or as a displayed block, depending on context.

See imagedata for more details about the processing expectations.

Attributes
Common attributes.

align
> Specifies the (horizontal) alignment of the image data

Enumerated values:	
"center"	Centered horizontally
"char"	Aligned horizontally on the specified character
"justify"	Fully justified (left and right margins or edges)
"left"	Left aligned
"right"	Right aligned

contentdepth
> Specifies the depth of the content rectangle
contentwidth
> Specifies the width of the content rectangle
depth
> Specifies the depth of the element

format
> Specifies that the format of the data is MathML

Enumerated values:	
"mathml"	Specifies MathML

scale
> Specifies the scaling factor

scalefit
> Determines if anamorphic scaling is forbidden

Enumerated values:	
"0"	False (do not scale to fit; anamorphic scaling may occur)
"1"	True (scale to fit; anamorphic scaling is forbidden)

valign
> Specifies the vertical alignment of the image data

Enumerated values:	
"bottom"	Aligned on the bottom of the region
"middle"	Centered vertically
"top"	Aligned on the top of the region

width
> Specifies the width of the element

See Also
imagedata (db.imagedata)

---

imagedata (db.imagedata.svg)

An SVG drawing in a media object

Synopsis
imagedata (db.imagedata.svg) ::= (info? db.titleforbidden.info, svg:*+)

Attribute synopsis
Common attributes.

Additional attributes:

- align (enumeration) = "center" | "char" | "justify" | "left" | "right"
- contentdepth
- contentwidth

- depth
- format (enumeration) = "svg"
- scale (positiveInteger)
- scalefit (enumeration) = "0" | "1"
- valign (enumeration) = "bottom" | "middle" | "top"
- width

Description
This element contains one or more SVG elements.

Processing expectations
Render the image. May be formatted inline or as a displayed block, depending on context.

See imagedata for more details about the processing expectations.

Attributes
Common attributes.

align

Specifies the (horizontal) alignment of the image data

Enumerated values:	
"center"	Centered horizontally
"char"	Aligned horizontally on the specified character
"justify"	Fully justified (left and right margins or edges)
"left"	Left aligned
"right"	Right aligned

contentdepth

Specifies the depth of the content rectangle

contentwidth

Specifies the width of the content rectangle

depth

Specifies the depth of the element

format

Specifies that the format of the data is SVG

Enumerated values:	
"svg"	Specifies SVG

scale

Specifies the scaling factor

scalefit
> Determines if anamorphic scaling is forbidden

Enumerated values:	
"0"	False (do not scale to fit; anamorphic scaling may occur)
"1"	True (scale to fit; anamorphic scaling is forbidden)

valign
> Specifies the vertical alignment of the image data

Enumerated values:	
"bottom"	Aligned on the bottom of the region
"middle"	Centered vertically
"top"	Aligned on the top of the region

width
> Specifies the width of the element

See Also
imagedata (db.imagedata)

imagedata (db.imagedata)

Pointer to external image data

Synopsis
imagedata (db.imagedata) ::= info? db.titleforbidden.info

Attribute synopsis
Common attributes.

Additional attributes:

- align (enumeration) = "center" | "char" | "justify" | "left" | "right"
- contentdepth
- contentwidth
- depth
- *Each of:*
  - —format
  - —*Exactly one of:*
    - —**fileref** (anyURI)
    - —**entityref** (ENTITY)
- scale (positiveInteger)

- `scalefit` (enumeration) = "0" | "1"
- `valign` (enumeration) = "bottom" | "middle" | "top"
- `width`

Required attributes are shown in **bold**.

Description
This element points to an external entity containing graphical image data.

Processing expectations
Render the image. May be formatted inline or as a displayed block, depending on context.

There are two ways to provide content for `imagedata`: `entityref` or `fileref`. It is best to use only one of these methods; however, if multiple sources are provided, `entityref` will be used in favor of `fileref`.

The `imagedata` provides a selection of attributes that can be used to control how the image is rendered. These attributes define two rectangles, the *viewport area* and the *content area*, and how these rectangles are related to each other. The *intrinsic size* of the image is a third rectangle that sometimes influences the way an image is rendered.

It is important to understand the distinction between these three areas. When rendering an image, the viewport area defines the space reserved in the flow of content for the image. If a 6in × 4in viewport area is specified, that's how much space will be reserved for the image, independent of the actual size of the rendered image. The content area defines the actual size of the rendered image, independent of the intrinsic size of the image. The intrinsic size of the image is its actual, real size.

DocBook provides three mutually exclusive mechanisms for specifying the content area of an image: it can be specified directly, it can be specified by selecting a scale factor, or it can be specified to be the same size as the viewport area.

Finally, DocBook provides two attributes, `align` and `valign`, to specify the alignment of the content area within the viewport area.

DocBook provides no mechanism for specifying how an image should be rendered if the content area exceeds the viewport area in either or both dimensions. Implementations are free to perform clipping, allow the image to overflow, and/or generate errors.

Units of measure. The sizes of the viewport area and the content area are defined in terms of lengths (width and depth).

Lengths must be expressed as a decimal value followed immediately by an optional unit of measure or a percentage. Six and one eighth inches, for example, must be expressed as "6.125in". It is an error to put a space or other punctuation between the decimal value and the unit of measure.

Examples of common units of measure include:

pt	Points (1/72 of an inch)
cm	Centimeters
mm	Millimeters
in	Inches
pc	Picas (1/6 of an inch)
px	Pixels
em	Ems

If no unit of measure is provided, px is assumed. Note that pixels have no universally accepted absolute size and ems are relative units of measure. Implementations may define pixel sizes differently and stylesheets may or may not be able to determine the current font size in order to correctly calculate the absolute size of an em. It is best to avoid these units of measure.

Percentages are expressed as a decimal value followed immediately by a % sign.

Specifying the viewport area. The viewport area is specified by the width and depth attributes.

If neither width nor depth is specified, an implementation is free to choose defaults. These defaults may be influenced by context. For example, when rendering an inline graphic, the viewport area often defaults to the size of the content area. For block graphics, the width often defaults to the column width while the depth defaults to the depth of the content area.

If only one of width or depth is specified, an implementation is free to choose a default for the other dimension.

Viewport area dimensions expressed as a percentage are a percentage of the available area. For example, a width of 50% when an implementation is rendering in a column 6in wide is equivalent to specifying a width of 3in.

Percentages must be used with care. Some media are unbounded in one or more directions (e.g., web pages are generally unbounded in depth). Specifying a percentage of an unbounded dimension is undefined. Implementations may choose arbitrary defaults or may generate errors.

Specifying the content area. The content area is specified by the contentwidth and content depth attributes.

If neither content width nor content depth is specified, an implementation is expected to render the image at its intrinsic size (unless scaling or scaling to fit is requested). If only one of content width or content depth is specified, an implementation is expected to choose a default for the other dimension such that the image is scaled proportionally. For example, if an image has an intrinsic size of one square inch and the content width is specified as 2in, the content depth must default to 2in.

Content area dimensions expressed as a percentage are a percentage of the intrinsic size of the image.

Percentages must be used with care. Some implementations may be unable to determine the intrinsic size of an image and will therefore be forced to make compromises. Implementations may choose arbitrary values or may generate errors if the intrinsic size cannot be obtained.

Scaling. Scaling can be specified in two ways: with the `scale` attribute or with the `scalefit` attribute.

If `scale` is specified, it must be a positive integer. It is always interpreted to be a percentage value, where `100` represents 100%.

The legal values of `scalefit` are `0` (false) or `1` (true). If scaling to fit is requested, the content area is scaled until *either* the content width is the same as the viewport width (and the content depth is less than or equal to the viewport depth) *or* the content depth is the same as the viewport depth (and the content width is less than or equal to the viewport width), whichever comes first. In other words, scaling to fit never causes anamorphic scaling; it simply scales the image as large as possible without overflowing the bounds of the viewport area.

Specification of content area, scaling, and scaling to fit are mutually exclusive. If a content area (`contentwidth`, `contentdepth`, or both) is specified, *both* scaling and scaling to fit are ignored. If the content area is not specified and both scaling and scaling to fit are specified, `scalefit` is ignored.

In order to achieve a level of backward compatibility with previous versions of DocBook (which did not have attributes for specifying a content area) while maintaining coherent semantics, the default value of `scalefit` depends on other attributes.

Viewport area	Content area	scalefit default
Unspecified	Unspecified	Irrelevant
Specified	Unspecified	1
Unspecified	Specified	0
Specified	Specified	0

If a viewport area is specified (and neither a content area nor scaling is specified) and `scalefit` is explicitly `0`, the viewport area specification must be ignored, and the image must not be resized.

Alignment. Two alignment attributes are provided: `align` and `valign`.

If specified, `align` indicates how the content area should be aligned horizontally within the viewport area. If not specified, implementations are free to choose any default value.

If specified, `valign` indicates how the content area should be aligned vertically within the viewport area. If not specified, implementations are free to choose any default value.

Examples. If nothing is specified about the size of an image, it is rendered in a content area that is the same as its intrinsic size in a viewport area that is implementation defined:

```
<imagedata fileref="image.png"/>
```

If a viewport area is specified, the image is rendered in a content area that is the same as its intrinsic size in the specified viewport area:

```
<imagedata fileref="image.png" width="6in" depth="5.5in" scalefit="0"/>
```

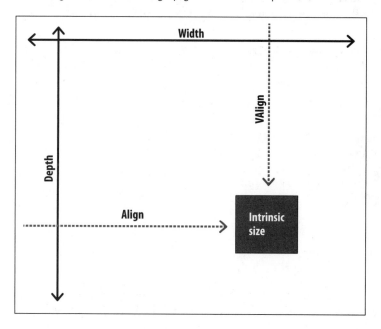

If a content area is specified, the image is scaled (possibly anamorphically) to that size and rendered in a viewport area that is implementation defined:

```
<imagedata fileref="image.png" contentwidth="4in" contentdepth="3in"/>
```

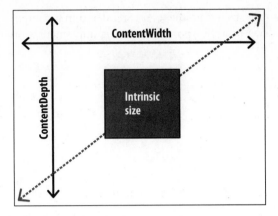

If a scaling factor is specified, the intrinsic size is scaled uniformly by that amount to obtain the content area which is rendered in a viewport area that is implementation defined:

```
<imagedata fileref="image.png" scale="300"/>
```

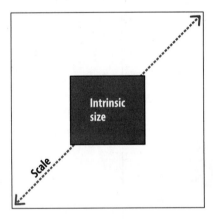

If a viewport area is specified and scaling to fit is requested, the intrinsic size is scaled (uniformly) as large as possible without extending beyond the bounds of the viewport area which is rendered as specified:

```
<imagedata fileref="image.png" width="6in" depth="5.5in"/>
<!-- note that scalefit="1" is the default in this case -->
```

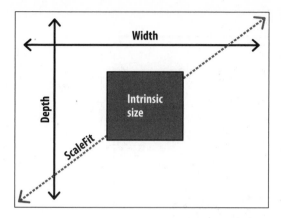

If the viewport area and content area are specified, the image is scaled (possibly ana-morphically) to the content area size and rendered in the specified viewport area:

```
<imagedata fileref="image.png" width="6in" depth="5.5in"
           contentwidth="4in" contentdepth="3in"/>
```

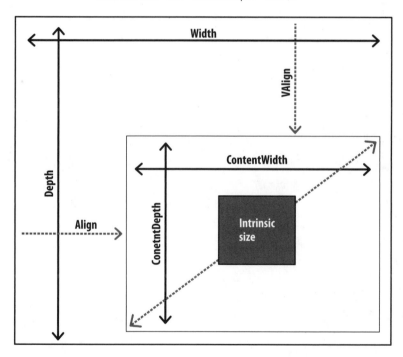

If the viewport area and a scaling factor are specified, the intrinsic size is scaled uni-formly by the scaling factor amount to obtain the content area which is rendered in the specified viewport area:

```
<imagedata fileref="image.png" width="6in" depth="5.5in" scale="300"/>
```

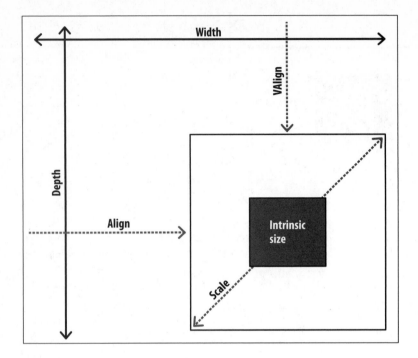

Attributes

Common attributes.

align

Specifies the (horizontal) alignment of the image data

Enumerated values:	
"center"	Centered horizontally
"char"	Aligned horizontally on the specified character
"justify"	Fully justified (left and right margins or edges)
"left"	Left aligned
"right"	Right aligned

contentdepth

Specifies the depth of the content rectangle

contentwidth

Specifies the width of the content rectangle

depth

Specifies the depth of the element

entityref

Identifies the location of the data by external identifier (entity name)

fileref
> Identifies the location of the data by URI

format
> Specifies the format of the data

scale
> Specifies the scaling factor

scalefit
> Determines if anamorphic scaling is forbidden

Enumerated values:	
"0"	False (do not scale to fit; anamorphic scaling may occur)
"1"	True (scale to fit; anamorphic scaling is forbidden)

valign
> Specifies the vertical alignment of the image data

Enumerated values:	
"bottom"	Aligned on the bottom of the region
"middle"	Centered vertically
"top"	Aligned on the top of the region

width
> Specifies the width of the element

See Also
imagedata (db.imagedata.mathml)

imageobject
A wrapper for image data and its associated meta-information

Synopsis
imageobject ::= (info? [db.titleforbidden.info], (imagedata [db.imagedata] | imagedata [db.imagedata.mathml] | image data [db.imagedata.svg]))

Attribute synopsis
Common attributes and common linking attributes.

Description
An imageobject is a wrapper containing imagedata and its associated meta-information.

If the SVG Module is used, imageobject can also contain the svg:svg element.

Processing expectations

May be formatted inline or as a displayed block, depending on context. It might not be rendered at all, depending on its placement within a `mediaobject` or `inlinemediaob ject` and the constraints on the publishing system. For a more detailed description of the semantics involved, see `mediaobject`.

See Also

audioobject, caption, inlinemediaobject, mediaobject, textobject, videoobject

Examples

```
<article xmlns='http://docbook.org/ns/docbook'>
<title>Example imageobject</title>

<mediaobject>
  <imageobject>
    <imagedata fileref="figures/eiffeltower.png" format="PNG" scale="70"/>
  </imageobject>
  <imageobject>
    <imagedata fileref="figures/eiffeltower.eps" format="EPS"/>
  </imageobject>
  <textobject>
    <phrase>The Eiffel Tower</phrase>
  </textobject>
  <caption>
    <para>Designed by Gustave Eiffel in 1889, The Eiffel Tower is one
          of the most widely recognized buildings in the world.
    </para>
  </caption>
</mediaobject>

</article>
```

Designed by Gustave Eiffel in 1889, The Eiffel Tower is one of the most widely recognized buildings in the world.

imageobjectco
A wrapper for an image object with callouts

Synopsis
imageobjectco ::= (info? ^{db.titleforbidden.info}, areaspec, imageobject+, calloutlist*)

Attribute synopsis
Common attributes and common linking attributes.

Description
The use of callouts, such as numbered bullets, provides an annotation mechanism. In an online system, these bullets are frequently "hot" and clicking on them navigates to the corresponding annotation.

An imageobjectco is a wrapper around an areaspec and a set of alternative imageobjects. More than one imageobject may be provided (just as more than one media object may occur inside mediaobject), but they must share exactly the same callout coordinates and exactly one must be selected by the processing system. (Use multiple imageobjectco elements inside a mediaobject to provide alternatives with different callout coordinates.)

An areaspec identifies the locations (coordinates) on the image where the callouts occur. The imageobjectco may also contain the list of annotations in a calloutlist, although the calloutlist may also occur outside the wrapper, elsewhere in the document.

Processing expectations

Formatted as a displayed block. It may not be rendered at all, depending on its placement within the mediaobject that contains it and the constraints on the publishing system. For a more detailed description of the semantics involved, see mediaobject.

The mandatory processing expectations of an imageobjectco are minimal: a processor is expected to render the image, if possible, and the calloutlist, if present. If more than one imageobject is present, exactly one must be selected. A processor should select the first object that it can, although it is free to choose any of the objects according to implementation-dependent mechanisms.

In online environments, the processing system may be able to instantiate the linking relationships between the callout marks on the image and the annotations. For example, an HTML presentation system might use the coordinate information to construct a client-side image map. Some processing systems may even be able to go a step further and generate the callout marks automatically from the coordinate information. But this level of sophistication is not mandatory.

See Also

areaspec, calloutlist, co, coref, programlistingco, screenco

Examples

```
<article xmlns='http://docbook.org/ns/docbook'
    xmlns:xlink="http://www.w3.org/1999/xlink">
<title>Example mediaobject</title>

<para>The Sun Microsystems offices in Burlington, MA are located
on Network Drive, just off Route 3.</para>

<mediaobject>
<imageobjectco>
<areaspec units="calspair">
  <area xml:id="sunoffice" coords="5500,5627 5940,4984"
    xlink:href="http://www.sun.com/"/>
  <areaset xml:id="rt3"
      xlink:href="http://www.smartraveler.com/scripts/bostraffic.asp\
?index=5&amp;city=bos&amp;cityname=Boston">
    <area coords="1880,9968 2560,8875"/>
    <area coords="2134,9421 2814,8328"/>
    <area coords="2388,8875 3068,7781"/>
    <area coords="2642,8328 3322,7235"/>
    <area coords="2897,7781 3577,6688"/>
    <area coords="3151,7235 3831,6141"/>
```

```
        <area coords="3405,6688 4085,5595"/>
        <area coords="3659,6141 4339,5048"/>
        <area coords="3913,5595 4593,4502"/>
        <area coords="4167,5048 4847,3955"/>
        <area coords="4421,4502 5101,3408"/>
        <area coords="4676,3955 5356,2862"/>
        <area coords="4930,3408 5610,2315"/>
        <area coords="5184,2862 5864,1768"/>
        <area coords="5438,2315 6118,1222"/>
        <area coords="5692,1768 6372, 675"/>
        <area coords="5946,1222 6626, 129"/>
      </areaset>
    </areaspec>
    <imageobject>
    <imagedata fileref="figures/officemap.png"/>
    </imageobject>
    </imageobjectco>
    </mediaobject>

    </article>
```

important

An admonition set off from the text

Synopsis

important ::= ((((title? & titleabbrev?), info? ^{db.titleforbidden.info}) | info ^{db.titleonly.info}), (annotation | bridgehead | remark | revhistory | *Indexing inlines* | *Admonition elements* | *Formal elements* | *Graphic elements* | *Informal elements* | *List elements* | *Paragraph elements* | *Publishing elements* | *Synopsis elements* | *Technical elements* | *Verbatim elements*)+)

Attribute synopsis

Common attributes and common linking attributes.

Additional constraints

- caution must not occur among the children or descendants of important.
- important must not occur among the children or descendants of important.
- note must not occur among the children or descendants of important.
- tip must not occur among the children or descendants of important.
- warning must not occur among the children or descendants of important.

Description

An important element is an admonition set off from the main text.

In some types of documentation, the semantics of admonitions are clearly defined (caution might imply the possibility of harm to equipment whereas warning might imply harm to a person), but DocBook makes no such assertions.

Processing expectations

Formatted as a displayed block. It often outputs the generated text "Important" or some other visible indication of the type of admonition, especially if a `title` is not present. Sometimes outputs a graphical icon or other symbol as well.

See Also

caution, note, tip, warning

Examples

```
<article xmlns='http://docbook.org/ns/docbook'>
<title>Example important</title>

<important>
<para>No user-serviceable parts inside. Breaking this seal voids all warranties.
</para>
</important>

</article>
```

 No user-serviceable parts inside. Breaking this seal voids all warranties.

---

index

An index to a book or part of a book

Synopsis

index ::= (((((title? & titleabbrev? & subtitle?), info? ^{db.titleforbidden.info}) | info? ^{db.info}), (annotation | bridgehead | remark | revhistory | *Indexing inlines* | *Admonition elements* | *Formal elements* | *Graphic elements* | *Informal elements* | *List elements* | *Paragraph elements* | *Publishing elements* | *Synopsis elements* | *Technical elements* | *Verbatim elements*)*, (indexdiv* | indexentry* | segmentedlist))

Attribute synopsis

Common attributes and common linking attributes.

Additional attributes:

- label
- status
- type

Additional constraints

- If this element is the root element, it must have a **version** attribute.

Description

An index contains the formatted index of a document.

Processing expectations

Formatted as a displayed block. An `index` in a `book` frequently causes a forced page break in print media.

In many processing systems, indexes are generated automatically or semiautomatically and never appear instantiated as DocBook markup.

Often an empty `index` is used to indicate where the automatically generated index should be rendered.

Authors can choose to have several types of indexes: for example, function, command, and concept indexes. This can be achieved in DocBook with the `type` attribute. All of the `indexterms` with a particular `type` will be collected together in the `index` with the same `type`.

All `indexterms`, irrespective of their `type`, appear in an `index` that has no `type` attribute.

Attributes

Common attributes and common linking attributes.

label
> Specifies an identifying string for presentation purposes

status
> Identifies the editorial or publication status of the element on which it occurs

type
> Specifies the target index for this term

Examples

An `index` with a `title` and `indexdiv`s:

```
<index xmlns='http://docbook.org/ns/docbook'>
<title>Index</title>

<indexdiv><title>D</title>
<indexentry>
  <primaryie>database (bibliographic), 253, 255</primaryie>
  <secondaryie>structure, 255</secondaryie>
  <secondaryie>tools, 259</secondaryie>
</indexentry>
<indexentry>
  <primaryie>dates (language specific), 179</primaryie>
</indexentry>
<indexentry>
  <primaryie>DC fonts, <emphasis>172</emphasis>, 177</primaryie>
  <secondaryie>Math fonts, 177</secondaryie>
</indexentry>
</indexdiv>
</index>
```

An index without a `title` or divisions:

```
<index xmlns='http://docbook.org/ns/docbook'>
<indexentry>
  <primaryie>Example</primaryie>
  <secondaryie>Chapter</secondaryie>
  <seeie>Example Chapter</seeie>
</indexentry>

<indexentry>
  <primaryie>Example Chapter, 35-48</primaryie>
  <seealsoie>Examples</seealsoie>
</indexentry>

<indexentry>
  <primaryie>Examples, 18, 36, 72-133</primaryie>
</indexentry>

</index>
```

indexdiv

A division in an index

Synopsis

indexdiv ::= ((((title & titleabbrev? & subtitle?), info? ^{db.titleforbidden.info}) | info ^{db.titlereq.info}), (annotation | bridgehead | remark | revhistory | *Indexing inlines* | *Admonition elements* | *Formal elements* | *Graphic elements* | *Informal elements* | *List elements* | *Paragraph elements* | *Publishing elements* | *Synopsis elements* | *Technical elements* | *Verbatim elements*)*, (indexentry+ | segmented list))

Attribute synopsis

Common attributes and common linking attributes.

Additional attributes:

- label
- status

Description

An `indexdiv` identifies a section of an `index`. An index might be divided into sections in order to group entries, usually alphabetically.

An index may contain any number of `indexentry` or `indexdiv` elements, but it cannot contain a mixture of both at the same level.

Processing expectations

Formatted as a displayed block.

Attributes

Common attributes and common linking attributes.

label

Specifies an identifying string for presentation purposes

status
> Identifies the editorial or publication status of the element on which it occurs

indexentry

Synopsis
indexentry ::= (primaryie, (seealsoie | seeie)*, (secondaryie, (seealsoie | seeie | tertiaryie)*)*)

Attribute synopsis
Common attributes and common linking attributes.

Description
An indexentry is a wrapper for index terms as they appear in an index. It's the markup used for creating a back-of-the-book index. To identify index terms in the flow of the text, use indexterm.

The content of an indexentry is the collated, formatted list of terms and cross-references.

Processing expectations
Formatted as a displayed block. A rendered index usually places secondary items under primary items and tertiary items under secondary items.

It is very uncommon to construct an index explicitly with indexentry markup. Indexes are almost always generated automatically from embedded indexterm markup in the document.

See Also
indexterm, primary, primaryie, secondary, secondaryie, see, seealso, seealsoie, seeie, tertiary, tertiaryie

Examples

Here's how the example indexes from the indexterm description might be represented using indexentry markup:

```
<index xmlns="http://docbook.org/ns/docbook">

<indexdiv>
<title>E</title>

<indexentry>
<primaryie>Entering markup, 14, 18, 22-33</primaryie>
</indexentry>

<indexentry>
<primaryie>eSATA, 56, 58-61</primaryie>
<seealsoie>Serial ATA</seealsoie>
</indexentry>

<indexentry>
```

```
    <primaryie>evaluating expressions, 44</primaryie>
    </indexentry>
    </indexdiv>

    <indexdiv>
    <title>U</title>

    <indexentry>
    <primaryie>Ubiquitous networking, 34, 44, 173-199</primaryie>
    </indexentry>

    <indexentry>
    <primaryie>Universal Serial Bus, 50-55</primaryie>
    </indexentry>

    <indexentry>
    <primaryie>Up time, 2, 5</primaryie>
    </indexentry>

    <indexentry>
    <primaryie>USB</primaryie>
    <seeie>Universal Serial Bus</seeie>
    </indexentry>
    </indexdiv>
    </index>
```

indexterm (db.indexterm.endofrange)   Identifies the end of a range associated with an indexed term

Synopsis
indexterm (db.indexterm.endofrange) ::= empty

Attribute synopsis
Common attributes and common linking attributes.

Additional attributes:

- **class** (enumeration) = "endofrange"
- **startref** (IDREF)

Required attributes are shown in **bold**.

Description
An "end of range" indexterm marks the end of a range. It must have an associated "start of range" indexterm. The resultant index entry applies to the entire range. See indexterm (db.indexterm.singular) on page 247.

Processing expectations
See indexterm (db.indexterm.singular) on page 247.

Attributes
Common attributes and common linking attributes.

class
> Identifies the class of index term

> | **Enumerated values:** | |
> | --- | --- |
> | "endofrange" | The end of a range |

startref
> Points to the start of the range

See Also
indexentry, indexterm (db.indexterm.singular), primary, primaryie, secondary, secondaryie, see, seealso, seealsoie, seeie, tertiary, tertiaryie

---

indexterm (db.indexterm.singular)
A wrapper for an indexed term

Synopsis
indexterm (db.indexterm.singular) ::= (primary?, ((secondary, ((tertiary, (seealso+ | see)?) | seealso+ | see)?) | seealso+ | see)?)

Attribute synopsis
Common attributes and common linking attributes.

Additional attributes:

- class (enumeration) = "singular"
- pagenum
- scope (enumeration) = "all" | "global" | "local"
- significance (enumeration) = "normal" | "preferred"
- type
- zone (IDREFS)

Description
An indexterm identifies text that is to be placed in the index. In the simplest case, the placement of the indexterm in the document identifies the location of the term in the text. In other words, the indexterm is placed in the flow of the document where the indexentry in the index should point. In other cases, attributes on indexterm are used to identify the location of the term in the text.

An indexterm marks either a single point in the document or a range. A single point is marked with an indexterm placed in the text at the point of reference. There are two ways to identify a range of text:

- Place an indexterm at the beginning of the range with class set to startofrange and give this term an xml:id. Place another indexterm at the end of the range with startref pointing to the `xml:id` of the starting `indexterm`. This second `indexterm` must be empty.

The advantage of this method is that the range can span unbalanced element boundaries. (For example, a range could span from the middle of one paragraph to the middle of the next.)

- Place the `indexterm` anywhere you like and point to the element that contains the range of text you wish to index with the `zone` attribute on the `indexterm`. Note that `zone` is defined as `IDREFS`, so a single `indexterm` can point to multiple ranges.

  The advantage of this method is that `indexterm`s can be collected together or even stored totally outside the flow of the document (e.g., in the `info`).

Processing expectations

The `indexterm`s are suppressed in the primary text flow, although they contribute to the population of an index and serve as anchors for cross-references. Under no circumstances is the actual content of `indexterm` rendered in the primary flow. For example, consider:

Example 26. Example index terms

```
<para>USB<indexterm>
<primary>USB</primary><see>Universal Serial Bus</see>
</indexterm><indexterm>
<primary>Universal Serial Bus</primary></indexterm>
and Firewire<indexterm><primary>Firewire</primary></indexterm> are
common interface technologies for external hard drives, although
eSATA<indexterm><primary>eSATA</primary><seealso>Serial ATA</seealso>
</indexterm> is also used.</para>
```

When rendered, either on paper or in online form, this paragraph always appears without any of the content of the index terms:

> USB and Firewire are common interface technologies for external hard drives, although eSATA is also used.

For most elements, the processing expectations of an `indexterm` are straightforward: the location of the term serves as an anchor for the cross-reference from the index. If the word "Firewire" appears on page 75 of the document, then page 75 appears in the index entry for "Firewire". In an online presentation, there's an anchor for "Fireware" immediately after that word in the paragraph.

Several aspects of index markup require special attention: whitespace around index terms, "See" and "See also" entries, index markup in repeating and floating elements, and multiple indexes.

Whitespace around index terms. Special care should be taken when entering `indexterm`s into text, especially when one of the final output formats for your document is paginated. Most processing systems are forgiving about the amount of whitespace that you use. Outside of "line-specific" environments such as `literallayout` and `programlisting`, you can indent lines, insert tabs or spaces at will, and otherwise rely on the processor to coalesce multiple spaces into a single space.

However, when the processor is determining where a line or page break will occur in a long block of text, it's an almost universal convention that such breaks occur where whitespace occurs in the markup. Sometimes words have to be hyphenated, of course, but usually it's sufficient to break a line at a space and break a page between lines.

This means that you want to *avoid extraneous spaces* between index terms and the words with which they are associated. Consider this example:

```
<para>…long, rambling paragraph about wood ducks
<indexterm><primary>ducks</primary><secondary>wood</secondary>
</indexterm> and the habitat that they occupy, etc., etc., etc.
</para>
```

At first glance this seems fine, but consider what happens if the processor needs to break this paragraph across two pages. There is a small, but nonzero, chance that the page break will occur at the space (introduced by the line break) following the word "ducks". If this happens, the anchor associated with the entry "ducks, wood" will appear on the page *following* the relevant words. To avoid this situation, never insert whitespace between the term and the `indexterm`:

```
<para>…long, rambling paragraph about wood
ducks<indexterm><primary>ducks</primary><secondary>wood</secondary>
</indexterm> and the habitat that they occupy, etc., etc., etc.
</para>
```

The whitespace *after* the `indexterm` is necessary, of course. Without it, when the `index term` is removed for presentation, the words "ducks" and "and" will appear to run together.

Index terms between block and floating elements. Just as extraneous whitespace can lead to indexing errors, placing index terms between block elements may lead to indexing errors.

If an index term occurs between two paragraphs, and a page break occurs between those two paragraphs, the processing system may associate the index entry with either page.

This problem can be exacerbated by floating elements. Suppose an index term appears between two figures, both of which float to subsequent pages. There is no reliable way to predict what page the processing system will associate with that index term.

If the index term in question marks the beginning or end of a range, the resulting range may contain too few, too many, or perhaps even only the wrong pages!

As a general rule, it's best to avoid placing index terms between block elements that may be broken across multiple pages.

Index terms in repeating and floating elements. When an `indexterm` appears in an element whose content may be repeated in more than one place, the anchor is *only* associated with what would be considered the "primary" presentation (or presentations) of the element in the flow of the text. For example, in a traditional printed book, the `title` of a `chapter` might appear in the table of contents, in the running header, and in the body of the book on the first page of the chapter. If an `indexterm` is placed in the `title`, it serves as an anchor to *only* the first page of the chapter.

If the processing expectations of an element are that it may be repeated several times and that each of these occurrences is equally "primary,"[†] then any `indexterm` occurring in that element should generate an anchor at each location where the content is repeated.

If an `indexterm` appears in an element whose content may float, the anchor is to the location where the term occurs in the floated text. For example, if an `indexterm` occurs in a `figure` that floats to the top of some following page, the anchor is on the page where the figure actually occurs.

"See" and "See also" entries. The use of `see` and `seealso` elements in an `indexterm` also has special semantics.

A `see` entry directs the reader to another location in the index. In Example 26, the entry for USB:

```
<indexterm>
<primary>USB</primary><see>Universal Serial Bus</see>
</indexterm><indexterm>
```

directs the reader to the entry for Universal Serial Bus. The resulting index will look something like this:

```
...
Ubiquitous networking, 34, 44, 173-199
Universal Serial Bus, 50-55
Up time, 2, 5
USB, see Universal Serial Bus
Useless bits, 304, 411
...
```

There are no page numbers associated with a `see` entry. In most environments, if there is at least one `see` entry for a particular term, it is an error to have any other kind of entry for that term.

A `seealso` entry, on the other hand, directs the reader to other, possibly related terms in the index. We expect the index for "eSATA" to look something like this:

```
...
Entering markup, 14, 18, 22-33
eSATA, 56, 58-61
  (see also Serial ATA)
evaluating expressions, 44
...
```

It's entirely possible for a term to have several `seealso` entries.

---

† No elements in DocBook V5.0 have these semantics.

Multiple indexes. Authors can choose to have several types of indexes: for example, function, command, and concept indexes. This can be achieved in DocBook with the `type` attribute. All of the `indexterm`s with a particular `type` will be collected together in the `index` with the same `type`.

Attributes

Common attributes and common linking attributes.

class
> Identifies the class of index term

Enumerated values:	
"singular"	A singular index term

pagenum
> Indicates the page on which this index term occurs in some version of the printed document

scope
> Specifies the scope of the index term

Enumerated values:	
"all"	All indexes
"global"	The global index (as for a combined index of a set of books)
"local"	The local index (the index for this document only)

significance
> Specifies the significance of the term

Enumerated values:	
"normal"	Normal
"preferred"	Preferred

type
> Specifies the target index for this term

zone
> Specifies the IDs of the elements to which this term applies

See Also

indexentry, indexterm (db.indexterm.startofrange), primary, primaryie, secondary, secondaryie, see, seealso, seealsoie, seeie, tertiary, tertiaryie

Examples

```
<article xmlns='http://docbook.org/ns/docbook'>
<title>Example indexterm</title>

<para>The Tiger<indexterm>
<primary>Big Cats</primary>
<secondary>Tigers</secondary></indexterm>
is a very large cat indeed.
</para>

</article>
```

An example of a zone.

```
<chapter xmlns='http://docbook.org/ns/docbook'>
<title>Example Chapter</title>

<indexterm zone="a1"><primary>Network Configuration</primary></indexterm>

<!-- other content here -->

<section xml:id="a1"><title>Configuring Your Network</title>
<para>…</para>
</section>

</chapter>
```

indexterm (db.indexterm.startofrange)   A wrapper for an indexed term that covers a range

Synopsis
indexterm (db.indexterm.startofrange) ::= (primary?, ((secondary, ((tertiary, (seealso+ | see)?) | seealso+ | see)?) | seealso+ | see)?)

Attribute synopsis
Common attributes and common linking attributes.

Additional attributes:

- **class** (enumeration) = "startofrange"
- pagenum
- scope (enumeration) = "all" | "global" | "local"
- significance (enumeration) = "normal" | "preferred"
- type
- zone (IDREFS)

Required attributes are shown in **bold**.

Description

A "start of range" `indexterm` marks the start of a range. It must have an associated "end of range" `indexterm`. The resulting index entry applies to the entire range. See `indexterm` (`db.indexterm.singular`) on page 247.

Processing expectations

See `indexterm` (`db.indexterm.singular`) on page 247.

It is possible to construct index terms that are difficult to parse at best and totally illogical at worst. Consider the following:

```
<indexterm class='startofrange' zone="id1 id2">...</indexterm>
```

There is no way that this can fit into the semantics of an `indexterm`. Although it claims to be the start of a range, it does not have an `xml:id` for the end-of-range `indexterm` to point back to. In addition, it includes zoned terms, and mixing the two different methods for indicating a range in the same `indexterm` is probably a bad idea.

Attributes

Common attributes and common linking attributes.

class
> Identifies the class of index term

Enumerated values:	
"startofrange"	The start of a range

pagenum
> Indicates the page on which this index term occurs in some version of the printed document

scope
> Specifies the scope of the index term

Enumerated values:	
"all"	All indexes
"global"	The global index (as for a combined index of a set of books)
"local"	The local index (the index for this document only)

significance
> Specifies the significance of the term

Enumerated values:	
"normal"	Normal
"preferred"	Preferred

type

> Specifies the target index for this term

zone

> Specifies the IDs of the elements to which this term applies

See Also

indexentry, indexterm (db.indexterm.singular), primary, primaryie, secondary, secondaryie, see, seealso, seealsoie, seeie, tertiary, tertiaryie

Examples

```
<chapter xmlns='http://docbook.org/ns/docbook'>
<title>Example Chapter</title>

<!-- index term for "Example Chapter" is a span -->
<indexterm xml:id="idxexchap" class='startofrange'>
  <primary>Example Chapter</primary></indexterm>

<!-- index term for "Example Chapter" also cross-references the
     "Examples" entry in the index -->
<indexterm><primary>Example Chapter</primary>
  <seealso>Examples</seealso></indexterm>

<!-- index term for "Chapter, Example" refers the reader to the entry
     under which the index term is actually listed, "Example Chapter" -->
<indexterm><primary>Chapter</primary><secondary>Example</secondary>
  <see>Example Chapter</see></indexterm>

<!-- other content -->

<!-- index term, end of "Example Chapter" span -->
<indexterm startref="idxexchap" class="endofrange"/>

<para>some content</para>
</chapter>
```

info (db.info)

A wrapper for information about a component or other block

Synopsis

info (db.info) ::= ((title? & titleabbrev? & subtitle?) & *"Info" elements**)

Attribute synopsis

Common attributes.

Description

The info element contains meta-information about the element that contains it.

Processing expectations

Suppressed. Many of the elements in this wrapper may be used in presentation, but they are not generally printed as part of the formatting of the wrapper. The wrapper merely serves to identify where they occur.

See Also
info (db.titlereq.info)

---

info (db.titleforbidden.info)   A wrapper for information about a component or other block without a title

Synopsis
info (db.titleforbidden.info) ::= *"Info" elements**

Attribute synopsis
Common attributes.

Description
The info element contains meta-information about the element that contains it.

Processing expectations
Suppressed. Many of the elements in this wrapper may be used in presentation, but they are not generally printed as part of the formatting of the wrapper. The wrapper merely serves to identify where they occur.

See Also
info (db.info)

---

info (db.titleonly.info)   A wrapper for information about a component or other block with only a title

Synopsis
info (db.titleonly.info) ::= ((title? & titleabbrev?) & *"Info" elements**)

Attribute synopsis
Common attributes.

Description
The info element contains meta-information about the element that contains it.

Processing expectations
Suppressed. Many of the elements in this wrapper may be used in presentation, but they are not generally printed as part of the formatting of the wrapper. The wrapper merely serves to identify where they occur.

See Also
info (db.info)

---

info (db.titleonlyreq.info)   A wrapper for information about a component or other block with only a required title

Synopsis
info (db.titleonlyreq.info) ::= ((title & titleabbrev?) & *"Info" elements**)

Attribute synopsis
Common attributes.

Description
The info element contains meta-information about the element that contains it.

Processing expectations
Suppressed. Many of the elements in this wrapper may be used in presentation, but they are not generally printed as part of the formatting of the wrapper. The wrapper merely serves to identify where they occur.

See Also
info (db.info)

info (db.titlereq.info)   A wrapper for information about a component or other block with a required title

Synopsis
info (db.titlereq.info) ::= ((title & titleabbrev? & subtitle?) & *"Info" elements**)

Attribute synopsis
Common attributes.

Description
The info element contains meta-information about the element that contains it.

Processing expectations
Suppressed. Many of the elements in this wrapper may be used in presentation, but they are not generally printed as part of the formatting of the wrapper. The wrapper merely serves to identify where they occur.

See Also
info (db.info)

informalequation   A displayed mathematical equation without a title

Synopsis
informalequation ::= (info? ^{db.titleforbidden.info}, alt?, (mediaobject+ | mathphrase+ | mml:*+), caption? ^{db.caption})

Attribute synopsis
Common attributes and common linking attributes.

Description
An informalequation is usually a mathematical equation or a group of related mathematical equations.

Processing expectations
Formatted as a displayed block.

See Also

equation, example, figure, informalexample, informalfigure, informaltable, inlineeq uation, subscript, superscript, table

Examples

```
<article xmlns='http://docbook.org/ns/docbook'>
<title>Example informalequation</title>

<para>The equation
<informalequation>
  <!-- <alt>e^(pi*i) + 1 = 0</alt> -->
  <mediaobject>
    <imageobject>
      <imagedata fileref="figures/epi10.png"/>
    </imageobject>
  </mediaobject>
</informalequation>
is delightful because it joins together five of the most
important mathematical constants.
</para>

</article>
```

The equation:

$$e^{\pi i} + 1 = 0$$

is delightful because it joins together five of the most important mathematical constants.

---

informalexample

A displayed example without a title

Synopsis

informalexample ::= (info? $^{\text{db.titleforbidden.info}}$, (annotation | bridgehead | remark | revhistory | *Indexing inlines* | *Admonition elements* | *Formal elements* | *Graphic elements* | *Informal elements* | *List elements* | *Paragraph elements* | *Publishing elements* | *Synopsis elements* | *Technical elements* | *Verbatim elements*)+, caption? $^{\text{db.caption}}$)

Attribute synopsis

Common attributes and common linking attributes.

Additional attributes:

- floatstyle
- width (nonNegativeInteger)

Description

An informalexample is a wrapper for an example without a title. Examples often contain programlistings or other large block elements.

Processing expectations

Formatted as a displayed block.

Attributes

Common attributes and common linking attributes.

floatstyle

Specifies style information to be used when rendering the float

width

Specifies the width (in characters) of the element

See Also

equation, example, figure, informalequation, informalfigure, informaltable, table

Examples

```
<article xmlns='http://docbook.org/ns/docbook'>
<title>Example informalexample</title>

<informalexample>
<programlisting>
sub print_content_model {
    my($self) = shift;
    local($_) = shift;
    local(*FILE) = shift;

    my(@cm) = $self->format_content_model2($_);
    foreach $_ (@cm) {
        print FILE $self->make_links($_, 1, 1), "\n";
    }
}
</programlisting>
</informalexample>

</article>
```

```
    sub print_content_model {
        my($self) = shift;
        local($_) = shift;
        local(*FILE) = shift;

        my(@cm) = $self->format_content_model2($_);
        foreach $_ (@cm) {
            print FILE $self->make_links($_, 1, 1), "\n";
        }
    }
```

informalfigure

Synopsis

informalfigure ::= (info? ^{db.titleforbidden.info}, (annotation | bridgehead | remark | revhistory | *Indexing inlines* | *Admonition elements* | *Formal elements* | *Graphic elements* | *Informal elements* | *List elements* | *Paragraph elements* | *Publishing elements* | *Synopsis elements* | *Technical elements* | *Verbatim elements*)+, caption? ^{db.caption})

Attribute synopsis

Common attributes and common linking attributes.

Additional attributes:

- floatstyle
- label
- pgwide (enumeration) = "0" | "1"

Description

An informalfigure is a figure without a title. Figures often contain mediaobjects, or other large display elements.

Processing expectations

Formatted as a displayed block.

Attributes

Common attributes and common linking attributes.

floatstyle
> Specifies style information to be used when rendering the float

label
> Specifies an identifying string for presentation purposes

pgwide
> Indicates if the element is rendered across the column or the page

Enumerated values:	
"0"	The element should be rendered in the current text flow (with the flow column width).
"1"	The element should be rendered across the full text page.

See Also

equation, example, figure, informalequation, informalexample, informaltable, table

Examples

```
<article xmlns='http://docbook.org/ns/docbook'>
<title>Example informalfigure</title>

<informalfigure>
<mediaobject>
<imageobject>
```

```
<info>
  <author>
    <personname>
      <firstname>Norman</firstname>
      <surname>Walsh</surname>
    </personname>
  </author>
  <pubdate>1998</pubdate>
</info>
<imagedata fileref="figures/watarun.png" format="PNG" scale="70"/>
</imageobject>
<textobject><phrase>Wat Arun</phrase></textobject>
<caption><para>Wat Arun, Temple of the Dawn, on the Chao Phraya River
in Bangkok, Thailand. In April 1998, Wat Arun was in the midst of
renovation.</para>
</caption>
</mediaobject>
</informalfigure>

</article>
```

Wat Arun, Temple of the Dawn, on the Chao Phraya River in Bangkok, Thailand. In April 1998, Wat Arun was in the midst of renovation.

informaltable (db.cals.informaltable)

A table without a title

Synopsis

informaltable (db.cals.informaltable) ::= (info? db.titleforbidden.info, (alt? & *Indexing inlines** & tex tobject*), (mediaobject+ | tgroup+), caption? db.caption)

Attribute synopsis

Common attributes and common linking attributes.

Additional attributes:

- colsep (enumeration) = "0" | "1"
- floatstyle
- frame (enumeration) = "all" | "bottom" | "none" | "sides" | "top" | "topbot"
- orient (enumeration) = "land" | "port"
- pgwide (enumeration) = "0" | "1"
- rowheader (enumeration) = "firstcol" | "norowheader"
- rowsep (enumeration) = "0" | "1"
- tabstyle

Description

This informaltable element identifies an informal CALS table (one without a title). DocBook allows either CALS or HTML tables, both of which describe tables geometrically using rows, columns, and cells.

Tables may include column headers and footers with thead and tfoot, respectively. Use the rowheader attribute to identify row headers.

Processing expectations

Formatted as a displayed block.

This element is expected to obey the semantics of the *CALS Table Model Document Type Definition* [calsdtd].

Attributes

Common attributes and common linking attributes.

colsep

Specifies the presence or absence of the column separator.

Enumerated values:	
"0"	No column separator rule.
"1"	Provide a column separator rule on the right.

floatstyle

Specifies style information to be used when rendering the float.

frame

Specifies how the table is to be framed. Note that there is no way to obtain a border on only the starting edge (left, in left-to-right writing systems) of the table.

Enumerated values:	
"all"	Frame all four sides of the table. In some environments with limited control over table border formatting, such as HTML, this may imply additional borders.
"bottom"	Frame only the bottom of the table.
"none"	Place no border on the table. In some environments with limited control over table border formatting, such as HTML, this may disable other borders as well.
"sides"	Frame the left and right sides of the table.
"top"	Frame the top of the table.
"topbot"	Frame the top and bottom of the table.

orient

Specifies the orientation of the table.

Enumerated values:	
"land"	90 degrees counterclockwise from the rest of the text flow.
"port"	The same orientation as the rest of the text flow.

pgwide

Indicates if the element is rendered across the column or the page.

Enumerated values:	
"0"	The element should be rendered in the current text flow (with the flow column width).
"1"	The element should be rendered across the full text page.

rowheader

Indicates whether or not the entries in the first column should be considered row headers.

Enumerated values:	
"firstcol"	Indicates that entries in the first column of the table are functionally row headers (analogous to the way that a thead provides column headers).
"norowheader"	Indicates that entries in the first column have no special significance with respect to column headers.

rowsep

Specifies the presence or absence of the row separator.

Enumerated values:	
"0"	No row separator rule.
"1"	Provide a row separator rule below.

tabstyle
Specifies the table style.

See Also

colspec, entry, entrytbl, equation, example, figure, informalequation, informalexam ple, informalfigure, informaltable (db.html.informaltable), row, spanspec, table, tbody, tfoot, tgroup, thead

---

informaltable (db.html.informaltable)

An HTML table without a title

Synopsis

informaltable (db.html.informaltable) ::= (info? ^{db.titleforbidden.info}, (col* | colgroup*), thead? ^{db.html.thead}, tfoot? ^{db.html.tfoot}, (tbody ^{db.html.tbody}+ | tr+))

Attribute synopsis

Attributes:

* summary
* width (enumeration) = xsd:integer | xsd:string (Pattern: "[0–9]+%")
* border (nonNegativeInteger)
* frame (enumeration) = "void" | "above" | "below" | "hsides" | "lhs" | "rhs" | "vsides" | "box" | "border"
* rules (enumeration) = "none" | "groups" | "rows" | "cols" | "all"
* cellspacing (enumeration) = xsd:integer | xsd:string (Pattern: "[0–9]+%")
* cellpadding (enumeration) = xsd:integer | xsd:string (Pattern: "[0–9]+%")

Description

This informaltable element identifies an informal HTML table (one without a caption). DocBook allows either CALS or HTML tables, both of which describe tables geometrically using rows, columns, and cells.

HTML tables may include column headers and footers. To identify a row header, use a th in the row.

Why aren't HTML tables in the HTML namespace?

HTML tables were introduced in DocBook V4.3, which was not in a namespace and was defined normatively with a DTD. DTDs do not support namespaces very well. The Technical Committee decided to simply add the HTML element names to DocBook. This solution simplified specification, avoided issues of namespace support in DTDs, and solved the most compelling use case: cut-and-paste of simple, text-only HTML tables into DocBook.

Strictly speaking, it would be incorrect to put these elements in the XHTML namespace because the DocBook common attributes are allowed on all of them and the td and th elements have very different content models than their HTML counterparts.

Processing expectations

Formatted as a displayed block. This element is expected to obey the semantics described in *Tables (http://www.w3.org/TR/html401/struct/tables.html)*, as specified in *XHTML 1.0* [XHTML].

Attributes

border

Specifies the width (in pixels only) of the frame around a table.

cellpadding

Specifies the amount of space between the border of the cell and its contents. If the value of this attribute is a pixel length, all four margins should be this distance from the contents. If the value of the attribute is a percentage length, the top and bottom margins should be equally separated from the content based on a percentage of the available vertical space, and the left and right margins should be equally separated from the content based on a percentage of the available horizontal space.

Enumerated values:	
xsd:integer	An explicit padding
xsd:string (Pattern: "[0–9]+%")	A percentage padding

cellspacing

Specifies how much space the user agent should leave between the left side of the table and the lefthand side of the leftmost column, the top of the table and the top side of the topmost row, and so on for the right and bottom of the table. The attribute also specifies the amount of space to leave between cells.

Enumerated values:	
xsd:integer	An explicit spacing

Enumerated values:	
xsd:string (Pattern: "[0–9]+%")	A percentage spacing

class

Assigns a class name or set of class names to an element. Any number of elements may be assigned the same class name or names. Multiple class names must be separated by whitespace characters.

frame

Specifies which sides of the frame surrounding a table will be visible.

Enumerated values:	
"void"	No sides; this is the default value
"above"	The top side only
"below"	The bottom side only
"hsides"	The top and bottom sides only
"lhs"	The lefthand side only
"rhs"	The righthand side only
"vsides"	The right and left sides only
"box"	All four sides
"border"	All four sides

lang

Specifies the base language of an element's attribute values and text content. The default value of this attribute is unknown.

onclick

Occurs when the pointing device button is clicked over an element.

ondblclick

Occurs when the pointing device button is double-clicked over an element.

onkeydown

Occurs when a key is pressed down over an element.

onkeypress

Occurs when a key is pressed and released over an element.

onkeyup

Occurs when a key is released over an element.

onmousedown

Occurs when the pointing device button is pressed over an element.

onmousemove

Occurs when the pointing device is moved while it is over an element.

onmouseout
> Occurs when the pointing device is moved away from an element.

onmouseover
> Occurs when the pointing device is moved onto an element.

onmouseup
> Occurs when the pointing device button is released over an element.

rules
> Specifies which rules will appear between cells within a table. The rendering of rules is user agent dependent.

Enumerated values:	
"none"	No rules. This is the default value.
"groups"	Rules will appear between row groups (see thead, tfoot, and tbody) and column groups (see colgroup and col) only.
"rows"	Rules will appear between rows only.
"cols"	Rules will appear between columns only.
"all"	Rules will appear between all rows and columns.

style
> Specifies style information for the current element.

summary
> Provides a summary of the table's purpose and structure for user agents rendering to nonvisual media such as speech and Braille.

title
> Offers advisory information about the element for which it is set.

width
> Specifies the desired width of the entire table and is intended for visual user agents. When the value is a percentage value, the value is relative to the user agent's available horizontal space. In the absence of any width specification, table width is determined by the user agent.

Enumerated values:	
xsd:integer	An explicit width
xsd:string (Pattern: "[0–9]+%")	A percentage width

See Also

colspec, entry, entrytbl, equation, example, figure, informalequation, informalexample, informalfigure, informaltable (db.cals.informaltable), row, spanspec, table, tbody, tfoot, tgroup, thead

initializer

Synopsis

initializer ::= (text | phrase ^db._phrase | replaceable | *Graphic inlines* | *Indexing inlines* | *Linking inlines* | *Ubiquitous inlines*)*

Attribute synopsis

Common attributes and common linking attributes.

Description

An initializer identifies the initial or default value for a field (fieldsynopsis) or method parameter (methodparam).

Processing expectations

Formatted inline. May be suppressed in some contexts.

inlineequation

Synopsis

inlineequation ::= (alt?, (*Graphic inlines+* | mathphrase+ | mml:*+))

Attribute synopsis

Common attributes and common linking attributes.

Description

An inlineequations is an expression (usually mathematical) that occurs in the text flow.

Processing expectations

Formatted inline.

See Also

equation, informalequation, subscript, superscript

Examples

```
<article xmlns='http://docbook.org/ns/docbook'>
<title>Example inlineequation</title>

<para>Einstein's theory of relativity includes one of the most
widely recognized formulas in the world:
<inlineequation>
  <alt>e=mc^2</alt>
  <inlinemediaobject>
    <imageobject>
      <imagedata fileref="figures/emc2.png"/>
    </imageobject>
  </inlinemediaobject>
</inlineequation>
</para>

</article>
```

Einstein's theory of relativity includes one of the most widely recognized formulas in the world: $e = mc^2$

---

inlinemediaobject
An inline media object (video, audio, image, etc.)

Synopsis
inlinemediaobject ::= (info? [db.titleforbidden.info], alt?, (audioobject | imageobject | imageobjectco | textobject | videoobject)+)

Attribute synopsis
Common attributes and common linking attributes.

Description
The inlinemediaobject element contains a set of alternative "graphical objects": video object, audioobject, and imageobject. Additional textual descriptions may be provided with textobjects.

An inlinemediaobject provides a wrapper for a set of alternative presentations for some, usually graphical, information. It is the "inline" equivalent of mediaobject.

In almost all contexts where text is allowed, inlinemediaobject is also allowed. This allows an author to provide a graphic for a character or glyph—for example, one that is not available in the publisher's fonts or perhaps is not available in Unicode. Authors should exercise care when using inlinemediaobject for this purpose as graphics may be difficult or impossible to display in some contexts on some presentation systems.

Processing expectations
Formatted inline.

If possible, the processing system should use the content of the first object within the inlinemediaobject. If the first object cannot be used, the remaining objects should be considered in the order that they occur. A processor should use the first object that it can, although it is free to choose any of the remaining objects if the primary one cannot be used.

Under no circumstances may more than one object in an inlinemediaobject be used or presented at the same time.

For example, an inlinemediaobject might contain a high-resolution image, a low-resolution image, and a text description. For print publishing, the high-resolution image is used; for online systems, either the high- or low-resolution image is used, possibly including the text description as an online alternative. In a text-only environment, the text description is used.

See Also
audioobject, caption, imageobject, mediaobject, textobject, videoobject

Examples

```
<?xml version="1.0" encoding="UTF-8"?>
<article xmlns="http://docbook.org/ns/docbook">

  <title>Example inlinemediaobject</title>

  <para>Einstein's most famous equation,
    <inlineequation>
      <inlinemediaobject>
        <imageobject>
          <imagedata fileref="figures/emc2.png"/>
        </imageobject>
        <textobject>
          <phrase>E=mc<superscript>2</superscript></phrase>
        </textobject>
      </inlinemediaobject>
    </inlineequation>, expresses the relationship between matter and energy.
  </para>

</article>
```

Einstein's most famous equation, $e = mc^2$, expresses the relationship between matter and energy.

---

interfacename

The name of an interface

Synopsis

interfacename ::= (text | phrase $^{db.\_phrase}$ | replaceable | Graphic inlines | Indexing inlines | Linking inlines | Ubiquitous inlines)*

Attribute synopsis

Common attributes and common linking attributes.

Description

The interfacename element is used to identify the name of an interface. This is likely to occur only in documentation about object-oriented programming systems, languages, and architectures.

Processing expectations

Formatted inline.

---

issuenum

The number of an issue of a journal

Synopsis

issuenum ::= (text | phrase $^{db.\_phrase}$ | replaceable | Graphic inlines | Indexing inlines | Linking inlines | Ubiquitous inlines)*

Attribute synopsis

Common attributes and common linking attributes.

Description

The `issuenum` contains the issue number of a periodical.

Processing expectations

May be formatted inline or as a displayed block, depending on context. Sometimes suppressed.

See Also

`biblioid`, `productnumber`, `seriesvolnums`, `volumenum`

Examples

See `article`, `bibliography`, and `bibliomset` for examples that use this element.

---

itemizedlist
A list in which each entry is marked with a bullet or other dingbat

Synopsis

itemizedlist ::= (((((title? & titleabbrev?), info? ^{db.titleforbidden.info}) | info ^{db.titleonly.info}), (annotation | bridgehead | remark | revhistory | *Indexing inlines* | *Admonition elements* | *Formal elements* | *Graphic elements* | *Informal elements* | *List elements* | *Paragraph elements* | *Publishing elements* | *Synopsis elements* | *Technical elements* | *Verbatim elements*)*, listitem+)

Attribute synopsis

Common attributes and common linking attributes.

Additional attributes:

- `mark` (NMTOKEN)
- `spacing` (enumeration) = "compact" | "normal"

Description

In an `itemizedlist`, each member of the list is marked with a bullet, dash, or other symbol.

Processing expectations

Formatted as a displayed block.

DocBook specifies neither the initial mark nor the sequence of marks to be used in nested lists. If explicit control is desired, the `mark` attribute should be used. The values of the `mark` attribute are expected to be keywords, not representations (numerical character references, entities, etc.) of the actual mark.

DocBook does not specify a set of appropriate keywords.

In order to enforce a standard set of marks at your organization, it may be useful to construct a customization layer that limits the values of the `mark` attribute to an enumerated list. See Chapter 5.

Attributes

Common attributes and common linking attributes.

mark

> Identifies the type of mark to be used on items in this list

spacing

> Specifies (a hint about) the spacing of the content

Enumerated values:	
"compact"	The spacing should be "compact".
"normal"	The spacing should be "normal".

See Also

calloutlist, listitem, orderedlist, segmentedlist, simplelist, variablelist

Examples

```
<article xmlns='http://docbook.org/ns/docbook'>
<title>Example itemizedlist</title>

<itemizedlist mark='opencircle'>
  <listitem>
    <para>TeX and LaTeX
    </para>
  </listitem>
  <listitem override='bullet'>
    <para>Troff
    </para>
  </listitem>
  <listitem>
    <para>Lout
    </para>
  </listitem>
</itemizedlist>

</article>
```

○ TeX and LaTeX

• Troff

○ Lout

itermset
A set of index terms in the meta-information of a document

Synopsis

itermset ::= indexterm $^{db.indexterm.singular}+$

Attribute synopsis

Common attributes and common linking attributes.

Description

When `indexterms` use the `zone` attribute to point to index ranges, it may be handy to hoist them out of the flow and put them in the document meta-information.

The `itermset` element, which occurs in the DocBook containers for meta-information, is one place to put them. An `itermset` is simply a wrapper around a group of `indexterms`.

Processing expectations
Suppressed.

Although more than one `itermset` may appear in the meta-information for a document, neither a relationship nor a specific facility for constructing a relationship is defined.

---

jobtitle
The title of an individual in an organization

Synopsis
jobtitle ::= (text | phrase ^{db.–phrase} | replaceable | *Graphic inlines* | *Indexing inlines* | *Linking inlines* | *Ubiquitous inlines*)*

Attribute synopsis
Common attributes and common linking attributes.

Description

A `jobtitle` describes the position of an individual within an organization. This tag is generally reserved for the name of the title for which an individual is paid.

Processing expectations
May be formatted inline or as a displayed block, depending on context. Sometimes suppressed.

See Also
`affiliation`, `orgdiv`, `orgname`, `shortaffil`

---

keycap
The text printed on a key on a keyboard

Synopsis
keycap ::= (text | phrase ^{db.–phrase} | replaceable | *Graphic inlines* | *Indexing inlines* | *Linking inlines* | *Ubiquitous inlines*)*

Attribute synopsis
Common attributes and common linking attributes.

Additional attributes:

- *Exactly one of:*
  - `function` (enumeration) = "alt" | "backspace" | "command" | "control" | "delete" | "down" | "end" | "enter" | "escape" | "home" | "insert" | "left" | "meta" | "option" | "pagedown" | "pageup" | "right" | "shift" | "space" | "tab" | "up"

—*Each of:*

—function (enumeration) = "other"

—**otherfunction**

Required attributes are shown in **bold**.

Description

The keycap identifies the text printed on a physical key on a computer keyboard. This is distinct from any scan code that it may generate (keycode), or any symbolic name (keysym) that might exist for the key.

Processing expectations

Formatted inline.

Attributes

Common attributes and common linking attributes.

function

Identifies the function key

Enumerated values:	
"alt"	The Alt key
"backspace"	The Backspace key
"command"	The Command key
"control"	The Ctrl key
"delete"	The Delete key
"down"	The down arrow
"end"	The End key
"enter"	The Enter or Return key
"escape"	The Escape key
"home"	The Home key
"insert"	The Insert key
"left"	The left arrow
"meta"	The Meta key
"option"	The Option key
"pagedown"	The page down key
"pageup"	The page up key
"right"	The right arrow
"shift"	The Shift key
"space"	The space bar
"tab"	The Tab key

Enumerated values:	
"up"	The up arrow

function
> Identifies the function key

Enumerated values:	
"other"	Indicates a nonstandard function key

otherfunction
> Specifies a keyword that identifies the nonstandard key

See Also

accel, guibutton, guiicon, guilabel, guimenu, guimenuitem, guisubmenu, keycode, key combo, keysym, menuchoice, mousebutton, shortcut

Examples

```
<article xmlns='http://docbook.org/ns/docbook'>
<title>Example keycap</title>

<para>The <keycap>F1</keycap> key on an IBM PC keyboard generates the
scan code <keycode>0x3B</keycode> when pressed.  This value
is defined as <keysym>KEY_F1</keysym> in
<filename class="headerfile">keyboard.h</filename>.
</para>

</article>
```

> The F1 key on an IBM PC keyboard generates the scan code 0x3B when pressed. This value is defined as KEY_F1 in *keyboard.h.*

---

keycode

The internal, frequently numeric, identifier for a key on a keyboard

Synopsis

keycode ::= (text | phrase ^{db._phrase} | replaceable | *Graphic inlines* | *Indexing inlines* | *Linking inlines* | *Ubiquitous inlines*)*

Attribute synopsis

Common attributes and common linking attributes.

Description

The keycode identifies the numeric value associated with a key on a computer keyboard. This is distinct from any scan code that it may generate (keycode), or any symbolic name (keysym) that might exist for the key.

Processing expectations

Formatted inline.

See Also

accel, guibutton, guiicon, guilabel, guimenu, guimenuitem, guisubmenu, keycap, key
combo, keysym, menuchoice, mousebutton, shortcut

Examples

```
<article xmlns='http://docbook.org/ns/docbook'>
<title>Example keycode</title>

<para>The <keycap>F1</keycap> key on an IBM PC keyboard generates the
scan code <keycode>0x3B</keycode> when pressed.  This value
is defined as <keysym>KEY_F1</keysym> in
<filename class="headerfile">keyboard.h</filename>.
</para>

</article>
```

The F1 key on an IBM PC keyboard generates the scan code 0x3B when pressed. This
value is defined as KEY_F1 in *keyboard.h*.

---

keycombo

A combination of input actions

Synopsis

keycombo ::= (keycap | keycombo | keysym | mousebutton)+

Attribute synopsis

Common attributes and common linking attributes.

Additional attributes:

- *Exactly one of:*
  —action (enumeration) = "click" | "double-click" | "press" | "seq" | "simul"
  —*Each of:*
    —action (enumeration) = "other"
  —**otheraction**

Required attributes are shown in **bold**.

Description

For actions that require multiple keystrokes, mouse actions, or other physical input
selections, the keycombo element provides a wrapper for the entire set of events.

Processing expectations

Formatted inline.

Attributes

Common attributes and common linking attributes.

action

Identifies the nature of the action taken. If `keycombo` contains more than one element, `simul` is the default; otherwise, there is no default.

Enumerated values:	
"click"	A (single) mouse click
"double-click"	A double mouse click
"press"	A mouse or key press
"seq"	Sequential clicks or presses
"simul"	Simultaneous clicks or presses

action

Identifies the nature of the action taken.

Enumerated values:	
"other"	Indicates a nonstandard action

otheraction

Identifies the nonstandard action in some unspecified way.

See Also

accel, guibutton, guiicon, guilabel, guimenu, guimenuitem, guisubmenu, keycap, key
code, keysym, menuchoice, mousebutton, shortcut

Examples

```
<article xmlns='http://docbook.org/ns/docbook'>
<title>Example keycombo</title>

<para>To move a highlighted region, use
<keycombo action='simul'>
  <keycap>Shift</keycap>
  <mousebutton>Button1</mousebutton>
</keycombo>
and drag the text to the new location.
</para>

</article>
```

To move a highlighted region, use Shift+Button1 and drag the text to the new location.

---

keysym

The symbolic name of a key on a keyboard

Synopsis

keysym ::= (text | phrase ^{db._phrase} | replaceable | *Graphic inlines* | *Indexing inlines* | *Linking inlines* | *Ubiquitous inlines*)*

Attribute synopsis

Common attributes and common linking attributes.

Description

The keysym identifies the symbolic name of a key on a computer keyboard. This is distinct from any scan code that it may generate (keycode), or any symbolic name (keysym) that might exist for the key.

Processing expectations

Formatted inline.

See Also

accel, guibutton, guiicon, guilabel, guimenu, guimenuitem, guisubmenu, keycap, key code, keycombo, menuchoice, mousebutton, shortcut

Examples

```
<article xmlns='http://docbook.org/ns/docbook'>
<title>Example keysym</title>

<para>The <keycap>F1</keycap> key on an IBM PC keyboard generates the
scan code <keycode>0x3B</keycode> when pressed.  This value
is defined as <keysym>KEY_F1</keysym> in
<filename class="headerfile">keyboard.h</filename>.
</para>

</article>
```

The F1 key on an IBM PC keyboard generates the scan code 0x3B when pressed. This value is defined as KEY_F1 in *keyboard.h*.

---

keyword

One of a set of keywords describing the content of a document

Synopsis

keyword ::= text

Attribute synopsis

Common attributes and common linking attributes.

Description

A keyword is a term describing the content of a document. The keyword applies to the document component that contains it.

Processing expectations

Keywords are rarely displayed to a reader. Usually, they are reserved for searching and retrieval purposes. If they are displayed, they may be displayed either inline or as a displayed block, depending on context.

Unlike subjectterms, which should be drawn from a controlled vocabulary, keywords may be chosen freely.

See Also
keywordset, subject, subjectset, subjectterm

Examples

See keywordset for an example that uses this element.

---

keywordset
A set of keywords describing the content of a document

Synopsis
keywordset ::= keyword+

Attribute synopsis
Common attributes and common linking attributes.

Description
A set of keywords, provided by the author, editor, publisher, and so on, can be stored in the document meta-information in a keywordset.

Keywords can form an important part of an automated indexing or searching strategy for a collection of documents.

Processing expectations
May be formatted inline or as a displayed block, depending on context. Keywords are rarely displayed to a reader. Usually, they are reserved for searching and retrieval purposes.

Unlike subjectterms, which should be drawn from a controlled vocabulary, keywords may be chosen freely.

Although more than one keywordset may appear in the meta-information for a document, neither a relationship nor a specific facility for constructing a relationship is defined by DocBook.

Additionally, no relationship is defined between the keywordsets of a document component and the keywordsets of its parents or children.

See Also
keyword, subject, subjectset, subjectterm

Examples

```
<article xmlns='http://docbook.org/ns/docbook'>
<title>Example keywordset</title>
<info>
  <keywordset>
    <keyword>DocBook</keyword>
    <keyword>standard</keyword>
    <keyword>OASIS</keyword>
  </keywordset>
</info>
```

```
<para>...</para>

</article>
```

---

label

Synopsis

label ::= (text | phrase ^{db._phrase} | replaceable | *Graphic inlines* | *Indexing inlines* | *Linking inlines* | *Ubiquitous inlines*)*

Attribute synopsis

Common attributes and common linking attributes.

Description

The label of a question or answer identifies the label that is to be used when formatting the question or answer.

Processing expectations

The label element is used as the label for the question or answer. A processing application might, for example, format the label as a heading preceding the question or answer contents, or it might format it as a run-in heading in the first paragraph of the question or answer.

Examples

See qandaset for an example that uses this element.

---

legalnotice

Synopsis

legalnotice ::= ((((title? & titleabbrev?), info? ^{db.titleforbidden.info}) | info ^{db.titleonly.info}), (annotation | bridgehead | remark | revhistory | *Indexing inlines* | *Admonition elements* | *Formal elements* | *Graphic elements* | *Informal elements* | *List elements* | *Paragraph elements* | *Publishing elements* | *Synopsis elements* | *Technical elements* | *Verbatim elements*)+)

Attribute synopsis

Common attributes and common linking attributes.

Description

A legalnotice identifies a statement of legal obligation, requirement, or warranty. It occurs in the meta-information for a document in which it frequently explains copyright, trademark, and other legal formalities of a document.

Processing expectations

Formatted as a displayed block.

A `legalnotice` may be presented in a number of ways. In printed documents, it often occurs on the verso of the title page, sometimes in a reduced font size. Online, it may occur on the title page or in a separate document behind a hypertext link.

See Also
copyright, trademark

---

lhs
The lefthand side of an EBNF production

Synopsis
lhs ::= text

Attribute synopsis
Common attributes and common linking attributes.

Description
The lefthand side (`lhs`) of a production is a nonterminal defined in terms of the right-hand side (rhs) of the `production`.

See Also
constraint, production, productionrecap, productionset, rhs

---

lineage
The portion of a person's name indicating a relationship to ancestors

Synopsis
lineage ::= (text | phrase ^{db._phrase} | replaceable | *Graphic inlines* | *Indexing inlines* | *Linking inlines* | *Ubiquitous inlines*)*

Attribute synopsis
Common attributes and common linking attributes.

Description
A `lineage` is a portion of a person's name, typically "Jr." or "Sr."

Processing expectations
Formatted inline. In an `address`, this element may inherit the verbatim qualities of an address.

See Also
affiliation, firstname, honorific, othername, surname

---

lineannotation
A comment on a line in a verbatim listing

Synopsis
lineannotation ::= (text | phrase ^{db._phrase} | replaceable | *Graphic inlines* | *Indexing inlines* | *Linking inlines* | *Ubiquitous inlines*)*

Attribute synopsis

Common attributes and common linking attributes.

Description

A lineannotation is an author's or editor's comment on a line in one of the verbatim environments. These are annotations added by the documentor; they are not part of the original listing.

Processing expectations

Formatted inline. In verbatim environments like programlisting, which are often presented in a fixed-width font, they may get special typographic treatment, such as italics.

If several lineannotations occur in the same listing, they may be aligned horizontally.

See Also

computeroutput, literallayout, programlisting, screen, screenshot, synopsis, userinput

Examples

```
<article xmlns='http://docbook.org/ns/docbook'>
<title>Example lineannotation</title>

<screen>
&lt;entry>  <lineannotation>Error: No line break before block element</lineannotation>
&lt;para>
A paragraph of text.
&lt;/para>&lt;/entry>
</screen>

</article>
```

```
<entry>    Error: No line break before block element
<para>
A paragraph of text.
</para></entry>
```

link

Synopsis

link ::= (text | *Bibliography inlines* | *Error inlines* | *Graphic inlines* | *GUI inlines* | *Indexing inlines* | *Keyboard inlines* | *Linking inlines* | *Markup inlines* | *Math inlines* | *Object-oriented programming inlines* | *Operating system inlines* | *Product inlines* | *Programming inlines* | *Publishing inlines* | *Technical inlines* | *Ubiquitous inlines*)*

Attribute synopsis

Common attributes and common linking attributes.

Additional attributes:

- endterm (IDREF)
- xrefstyle

Description

The link is a general-purpose hypertext element. Usually, link surrounds the text that should be made "hot" (unlike xref which must generate the text), but the endterm attribute can be used to copy text from another element.

The link can have *either* a linkend attribute *or* an xlink:href attribute. If it has an xlink:href attribute, link is the equivalent of an HTML anchor (<html:a href="...">) for cross-reference with a Uniform Resource Identifier (URI).

Processing expectations with linkend

Formatted inline.

If the link element has content, then that content is processed for output as the "hot" text. If the link element has content and an endterm attribute, then the content is used and the endterm is ignored. If the link element has an endterm attribute and no content, then the content of the element pointed to by endterm should be repeated at the location of the link and used as the "hot" text.

Processing expectations with xlink:href

Formatted inline.

When rendered online, it is natural to make the content of the link element an active link. When rendered in print media, the URI might be ignored, printed after the text of the link, or printed as a footnote.

When the content of the link element is empty, the content of the xlink:href attribute should be rendered as the text of the link.

Attributes

Common attributes and common linking attributes.

endterm
> Points to the element whose content is to be used as the text of the link

xrefstyle
> Specifies a keyword or keywords identifying additional style information

See Also

anchor, olink, xref

Examples

```
<article xmlns='http://docbook.org/ns/docbook'>
<title>Example link</title>

<section>
  <title>Examples of <tag>link</tag></title>
```

```
<para>
  In this sentence <link linkend='nextsect'>this</link>
  word is hot and points to the following section.
</para>
<section xml:id='nextsect'>
  <title xml:id='nextsect.title'>A Subsection</title>
  <para>
    This section only exists to be the target of a couple
    of links.
  </para>
</section>
</section>

</article>
```

---

listitem
A wrapper for the elements of a list item

Synopsis

listitem ::= (annotation | bridgehead | remark | revhistory | *Indexing inlines* | *Admonition elements* | *Formal elements* | *Graphic elements* | *Informal elements* | *List elements* | *Paragraph elements* | *Publishing elements* | *Synopsis elements* | *Technical elements* | *Verbatim elements*)+

Attribute synopsis

Common attributes and common linking attributes.

Additional attributes:

*   override (NMTOKEN)

Description

The listitem element is a wrapper around an item in a list. In an itemizedlist or an orderedlist, the listitem surrounds the entire list item. In a variablelist, listitem surrounds the "definition" part of the list item.

Processing expectations

Formatted as a displayed block. List items usually generate the appropriate mark (a number or bullet) and appear indented, next to the mark. In a variablelist, the presentation may be influenced by the length of the term or terms that precede the list item and by attributes on the list itself.

Attributes

Common attributes and common linking attributes.

override

Specifies the keyword for the type of mark that should be used on *this* item, instead of the mark that would be used by default

See Also

calloutlist, itemizedlist, orderedlist, segmentedlist, simplelist, variablelist

literal

Inline text that is some literal value

Synopsis

literal ::= (text | phrase ^{db._phrase} | replaceable | *Graphic inlines* | *Indexing inlines* | *Linking inlines* | *Ubiquitous inlines*)*

Attribute synopsis

Common attributes and common linking attributes.

Description

A literal is some specific piece of data, taken literally, from a computer system. It is similar in some ways to userinput and computeroutput, but is somewhat more of a general classification. The sorts of things that constitute literals vary by domain.

Processing expectations

Formatted inline. A literal is frequently distinguished typographically and literal is often used wherever that typographic presentation is desired.

See Also

command, computeroutput, constant, markup, option, optional, parameter, prompt, replaceable, tag, userinput, varname

Examples

```
<article xmlns='http://docbook.org/ns/docbook'>
<title>Example literal</title>

<para>There are several undocumented settings for <varname>debug</varname>,
among them <literal>3.27</literal> to enable a complete trace and
<literal>3.8</literal> to debug the spellchecker. For a complete
list of the possible settings,
see <filename class="headerfile">edit/debug.h</filename>.</para>

</article>
```

There are several undocumented settings for **debug**, among them **3.27** to enable a complete trace and **3.8** to debug the spellchecker. For a complete list of the possible settings, see *edit/debug.h*.

literallayout

A block of text in which line breaks and whitespace are to be reproduced faithfully

Synopsis

literallayout ::= (info? ^{db.titleforbidden.info}, ((text | lineannotation | *Bibliography inlines* | *Computeroutput inlines* | *Error inlines* | *Graphic inlines* | *GUI inlines* | *Indexing inlines* | *Keyboard inlines* | *Linking inlines* | *Markup inlines* | *Math inlines* | *Object-oriented programming inlines* | *Operating system inlines* | *Product inlines* | *Programming inlines* | *Publishing inlines* | *Technical inlines* | *Ubiquitous inlines* | *User-input inlines*)* | textobject))

Attribute synopsis

Common attributes and common linking attributes.

Additional attributes:

- `class` (enumeration) = "monospaced" | "normal"
- `continuation` (enumeration) = "continues" | "restarts"
- `linenumbering` (enumeration) = "numbered" | "unnumbered"
- `startinglinenumber` (integer)
- `language`
- `xml:space` (enumeration) = "preserve"

Description

A `literallayout` is a verbatim environment. Unlike the other verbatim environments, it does not have strong semantic overtones and may not imply a font change.

Processing expectations

This element is displayed "verbatim"; whitespace and line breaks within this element are significant.

Unlike `programlisting` and `screen`, which usually imply a font change, `literallayout` does not. How spaces are to be represented faithfully in a proportional font is not addressed by DocBook.

In DocBook V3.1, the `class` attribute was added to give users control over the font used in `literallayouts`. If the `class` attribute is specified and its value is `monospaced`, then the `literallayout` will be presented in a monospaced font, probably the same one used for other verbatim environments. The default value for `class` is `normal`, meaning that no font change will occur.

Attributes

Common attributes and common linking attributes.

class

Specifies the class of literal layout.

Enumerated values:	
"monospaced"	The literal layout should be formatted with a monospaced font.
"normal"	The literal layout should be formatted with the current font.

continuation

Determines whether line numbering continues from the previous element or restarts.

Enumerated values:	
"continues"	Line numbering continues from the immediately preceding element with the same name.
"restarts"	Line numbering restarts (begins at 1, usually).

language
> Identifies the language (i.e., programming language) of the verbatim content.

linenumbering
> Determines whether lines are numbered.

Enumerated values:	
"numbered"	Lines are numbered.
"unnumbered"	Lines are not numbered.

startinglinenumber
> Specifies the initial line number.

xml:space
> Can be used to indicate explicitly that whitespace in the verbatim environment is preserved. Whitespace must always be preserved in verbatim environments whether this attribute is specified or not.

Enumerated values:	
"preserve"	Whitespace must be preserved.

See Also

computeroutput, lineannotation, programlisting, screen, screenshot, synopsis, userinput

Examples

```
<article xmlns='http://docbook.org/ns/docbook'>
<title>Example literallayout</title>

<blockquote>
<attribution>William Shakespeare, <citetitle>Henry V</citetitle></attribution>
<literallayout>  O, for a muse of fire, that would ascend
The brightest heaven of invention!
A kingdom for a stage, princes to act,
And monarchs to behold the swelling scene!</literallayout>
</blockquote>

</article>
```

> O, for a muse of fire, that would ascend
> The brightest heaven of invention!
> A kingdom for a stage, princes to act,
> And monarchs to behold the swelling scene!
>
> —William Shakespeare, *Henry V*

locator

Synopsis

locator ::= empty

Attribute synopsis

Common attributes.

Additional attributes:

- xlink:label (NMTOKEN)

Description

A locator in an extendedlink. See *XML Linking Language (XLink) Version 1.0* [XLink] for more details.

Processing expectations

Suppressed.

Attributes

Common attributes.

xlink:label
    Specifies the XLink label

manvolnum

Synopsis

manvolnum ::= (text | phrase ^{db._phrase} | replaceable | *Graphic inlines* | *Indexing inlines* | *Linking inlines* | *Ubiquitous inlines*)*

Attribute synopsis

Common attributes and common linking attributes.

Description

In a DocBook reference page, the manvolnum holds the number of the volume in which the refentry belongs.

The notion of a volume number is historical. UNIX manual pages ("man pages"), for which refentry was devised, were typically stored in three-ring binders. Each bound manual was a volume in a set and contained information about a particular class of things. For example, volume 1 was for user commands, and volume 8 was for administrator commands.

Volume numbers need not be strictly numerical; volume "l" frequently held manual pages for local additions to the system, and the X Window System manual pages had an "x" in the volume number: for example, 1x.

Processing expectations

The content of `manvolnum` is usually printed in parentheses after the element title or citation.

Examples

```
<article xmlns='http://docbook.org/ns/docbook'>
<title>Example manvolnum</title>

<para>For a further description of print formats, consult the
<citerefentry><refentrytitle>printf</refentrytitle>
<manvolnum>3S</manvolnum></citerefentry> manual page.
</para>

</article>
```

For a further description of print formats, consult the printf manual page.

---

markup   A string of formatting markup in text that is to be represented literally

Synopsis

markup ::= (text | phrase $^{db.\_phrase}$ | replaceable | *Graphic inlines* | *Indexing inlines* | *Linking inlines* | *Ubiquitous inlines*)*

Attribute synopsis

Common attributes and common linking attributes.

Description

A markup element contains a string of formatting markup that is to be represented literally in the text. The utility of this element is almost wholly constrained to books about document formatting tools.

Processing expectations

Formatted inline.

See Also

computeroutput, constant, literal, option, optional, parameter, prompt, replaceable, tag, userinput, varname

Examples

```
<article xmlns='http://docbook.org/ns/docbook'>
<title>Example markup</title>

<para>A presentation system using TeX as a backend might allow you
to insert inline markup, such as <markup role="tex">$x^2$</markup>,
using TeX syntax directly.
</para>

</article>
```

> A presentation system using TeX as a backend might allow you to insert inline markup, such as x^2, using TeX syntax directly.

---

mathphrase
A mathematical phrase that can be represented with ordinary text and a small amount of markup

Synopsis
mathphrase ::= (text | emphasis ^{db._emphasis} | phrase ^{db._phrase} | replaceable | *Graphic inlines* | *Indexing inlines* | *Linking inlines* | *Ubiquitous inlines*)*

Attribute synopsis
Common attributes and common linking attributes.

Description
A mathphrase is a simple, inline equation, one that can be represented using ordinary text, symbols, subscripts, and superscripts. A good example is: $E=mc^2$.

Processing expectations
Formatted inline.

Examples

```
<article xmlns='http://docbook.org/ns/docbook'>
<title>Example equation</title>

<equation xml:id="eq.fermatphrase">
  <title>Fermat's Last Theorem</title>
  <mathphrase>x<superscript>n</superscript>
+ y<superscript>n</superscript>
≠ z<superscript>n</superscript>
∀ n ≠ 2</mathphrase>
</equation>

</article>
```

---

mediaobject
A displayed media object (video, audio, image, etc.)

Synopsis
mediaobject ::= (info? ^{db.titleforbidden.info}, alt?, (audioobject | imageobject | imageobjectco | textobject | videoobject)+, caption? ^{db.caption})

Attribute synopsis
Common attributes and common linking attributes.

Description
This element contains a set of alternative "media objects." Exactly one object will be selected and rendered.

Processing expectations

Formatted as a displayed block. The primary purpose of the mediaobject is to provide a wrapper around a set of alternative presentations of the same information.

If possible, the processing system should use the content of the first object within the mediaobject. If the first object cannot be used, the remaining objects should be considered in the order that they occur. A processor should use the first object that it can, although it is free to choose any of the remaining objects if the primary one cannot be used.

Under no circumstances should more than one object in a mediaobject be used or presented at the same time.

For example, a mediaobject might contain a video, a high-resolution image, a low-resolution image, a long text description, and a short text description. In a "high-end" online system, the video is used. For print publishing, the high-resolution image is used. For other online systems, either the high- or the low-resolution image is used, possibly including the short text description as the online alternative. In a text-only environment, either the long or the short text description is used.

See Also

audioobject, caption, imageobject, inlinemediaobject, textobject, videoobject

Examples

```
<article xmlns='http://docbook.org/ns/docbook'
    xmlns:xlink="http://www.w3.org/1999/xlink">
<title>Example mediaobject</title>

<mediaobject>
  <info>
    <othercredit>
      <orgname>O'Reilly Media</orgname>
    </othercredit>
    <othercredit>
      <orgname>Dover Archives</orgname>
    </othercredit>
  </info>
  <alt>The DocBook: TDG Duck</alt>
  <imageobject>
    <imagedata align="right" width="6in" format="PNG"
        fileref="figures/duck-small.png"/>
  </imageobject>
  <imageobject>
    <imagedata align="right" width="6in" format="GIF"
        fileref="figures/duck-small.gif"/>
  </imageobject>
  <textobject>
    <para>The bird on the cover of <citetitle>DocBook: The Definitive
Guide</citetitle> is a wood duck.  Often considered one of the most
beautiful ducks in North America, the male wood duck has a metallic
purple and green head with white streaks extending from its bill
around the eyes and down to its blue and green, gold-flecked
```

```
wings. It has a white neck, chestnut-colored chest, white or red
bill, and yellow-orange legs and feet. Females have more brown, gray,
and subdued hues.</para>

    </textobject>
</mediaobject>

</article>
```

member

Synopsis

member ::= (text | *Bibliography inlines* | *Error inlines* | *Graphic inlines* | *GUI inlines* | *Indexing inlines* | *Keyboard inlines* | *Linking inlines* | *Markup inlines* | *Math inlines* | *Object-oriented programming inlines* | *Operating system inlines* | *Product inlines* | *Programming inlines* | *Publishing inlines* | *Technical inlines* | *Ubiquitous inlines*)*

Attribute synopsis

Common attributes and common linking attributes.

Description

A member is an element of a simplelist. Unlike the other lists, items in a simplelist are constrained to character data and inline elements.

Processing expectations

Formatted inline. How the inline members are formatted with respect to each other is controlled by the containing simplelist.

Examples

See simplelist for an example that uses this element.

menuchoice

Synopsis

menuchoice ::= (shortcut?, (guibutton | guiicon | guilabel | guimenu | guimenuitem | guisubmenu)+)

Attribute synopsis

Common attributes and common linking attributes.

Description

In applications that present graphical user interfaces, it is often necessary to select an item, or a series of items, from a menu in order to accomplish some action. The menu choice element provides a wrapper to contain the complete combination of selections.

Processing expectations

Formatted inline.

A menuchoice may generate arrows or other punctuation between multiple GUI elements. The shortcut may be suppressed, or sometimes it is presented in parentheses after the rest of the items.

See Also

accel, guibutton, guiicon, guilabel, guimenu, guimenuitem, guisubmenu, keycap, key code, keycombo, keysym, mousebutton, shortcut

Examples

```
<article xmlns='http://docbook.org/ns/docbook'>
<title>Example menuchoice</title>

<para>You can exit from GNU Emacs with
<menuchoice>
  <shortcut>
    <keycombo><keysym>C-x</keysym><keysym>C-c</keysym></keycombo>
  </shortcut>
  <guimenu>Files</guimenu>
  <guimenuitem>Exit Emacs</guimenuitem>
</menuchoice>.
</para>

</article>
```

You can exit from GNU Emacs with Files → Exit Emacs (**C-x+C-c**).

---

methodname

The name of a method

Synopsis

methodname ::= (text | phrase ^{db._phrase} | replaceable | *Graphic inlines* | *Indexing inlines* | *Linking inlines* | *Ubiquitous inlines*)*

Attribute synopsis

Common attributes and common linking attributes.

Description

The methodname element is used to identify the name of a method. This is likely to occur only in documentation about object-oriented programming systems, languages, and architectures.

Processing expectations

Formatted inline.

---

methodparam

Parameters to a method

Synopsis

methodparam ::= (modifier*, type?, ((modifier*, parameter, initializer?) | funcparams), modifier*)

Attribute synopsis

Common attributes and common linking attributes.

Additional attributes:

- `choice` (enumeration) = "opt" | "plain" | "req" [default="req"]
- `rep` (enumeration) = "norepeat" | "repeat" [default="norepeat"]

Description

In the syntax summary of a `constructorsynopsis`, `destructorsynopsis`, or `methodsynopsis`, `methodparam` provides the description of a parameter to the method. Typically, this includes the data type of the parameter and its name, but may also include an initial value and other modifiers.

Processing expectations

Formatted inline. For a complete description of the processing expectations, see `class synopsis`.

Attributes

Common attributes and common linking attributes.

choice

    Indicates optionality

Enumerated values:	
"opt"	Formatted to indicate that it is optional
"plain"	Formatted without indication
"req"	Formatted to indicate that it is required

rep

    Indicates whether or not repetition is possible

Enumerated values:	
"norepeat"	Cannot be repeated
"repeat"	Can be repeated

methodsynopsis

A syntax summary for a method

Synopsis

methodsynopsis ::= (`modifier`*, (`type` | `void`)?, `methodname`, (`methodparam`+ | `void`), `exceptionname`*, `modifier`*)

Attribute synopsis

Common attributes and common linking attributes.

Additional attributes:

- language

Description

A methodsynopsis contains the syntax summary of a method (generally speaking, methods in the object-oriented programming language sense).

This is one of the few places where DocBook attempts to model as well as describe. Unlike funcsynopsis which was designed with C language function prototypes in mind, the content model of methodsynopsis was designed to capture a wide range of semantics.

Processing expectations

For the most part, the processing application is expected to generate all of the parentheses, semicolons, commas, and so on required in the rendered synopsis.

Attributes

Common attributes and common linking attributes.

language
> Identifies the language (i.e., programming language) of the content

modifier

Synopsis

modifier ::= (text | phrase ^{db.–phrase} | replaceable | *Graphic inlines* | *Indexing inlines* | *Linking inlines* | *Ubiquitous inlines*)*

Attribute synopsis

Common attributes and common linking attributes.

Additional attributes:

- xml:space (enumeration) = "preserve"

Description

A modifier identifies additional information about some identifier—for example, the public or private nature of an ooclass name, or information about a static or synchronized nature of a methodsynopsis.

Processing expectations

Formatted inline.

Attributes

Common attributes and common linking attributes.

xml:space
> Can be used to indicate that whitespace in the modifier should be preserved (e.g., for multiline annotations)

Enumerated values:	
"preserve"	Extra whitespace and line breaks must be preserved.

---

mousebutton
The conventional name of a mouse button

Synopsis
mousebutton ::= (text | phrase ^{db._phrase} | replaceable | *Graphic inlines* | *Indexing inlines* | *Linking inlines* | *Ubiquitous inlines*)*

Attribute synopsis
Common attributes and common linking attributes.

Description
The mousebutton element identifies the conventional name of a mouse button. Because mouse buttons are not physically labeled, the name is just that, a convention. Adding explicit markup for the naming of mouse buttons allows easier translation from one convention to another and might allow an online system to adapt to right- or lefthanded usage.

Processing expectations
Formatted inline.

See Also
accel, guibutton, guiicon, guilabel, guimenu, guimenuitem, guisubmenu, keycap, keycode, keycombo, keysym, menuchoice, shortcut

Examples

```
<article xmlns='http://docbook.org/ns/docbook'>
<title>Example mousebutton</title>

<para>Select a region of text by dragging the mouse pointer with the
<mousebutton>left</mousebutton> mouse button depressed.  Copy the
selected text to a new location by placing the mouse pointer at the
desired position and pressing the <mousebutton>middle</mousebutton>
button.
</para>

</article>
```

Select a region of text by dragging the mouse pointer with the left mouse button depressed. Copy the selected text to a new location by placing the mouse pointer at the desired position and pressing the middle button.

msg

Synopsis

msg ::= ((((title? & titleabbrev?), info? ^{db.titleforbidden.info}) | info ^{db.titleonly.info}), msgmain, (msgrel | msgsub)*)

Attribute synopsis

Common attributes and common linking attributes.

Description

In a msgset, each msgentry contains at least one msg. A msg consists of a main message (msgmain), and optionally one or more submessages (msgsub) or related messages (msgrel).

Additional information or explanation for the message is contained in the siblings of msg within the msgentry.

See msgset.

Processing expectations

Formatted as a displayed block. Sometimes suppressed.

On the whole, the semantics of msgset are not clearly defined.

msgaud

Synopsis

msgaud ::= (text | phrase ^{db._phrase} | replaceable | *Graphic inlines* | *Indexing inlines* | *Linking inlines* | *Ubiquitous inlines*)*

Attribute synopsis

Common attributes and common linking attributes.

Description

A msgaud is part of the additional information associated with a message in a msgset. It identifies the audience to which a particular msg is relevant.

Processing expectations

May be formatted inline or as a displayed block, depending on context. Sometimes suppressed.

DocBook doesn't specify anything about how a particular audience might be identified, or how different audiences are distinguished.

On the whole, the semantics of msgset are not clearly defined.

msgentry

Synopsis

msgentry ::= (msg+, msginfo?, msgexplan*)

Attribute synopsis

Common attributes and common linking attributes.

Description

In a msgset, each msgentry contains some number of messages (msgs) and additional informative and explanatory material about them.

Processing expectations

Formatted as a displayed block.

On the whole, the semantics of msgset are not clearly defined.

msgexplan

Synopsis

msgexplan ::= ((((title? & titleabbrev?), info? db.titleforbidden.info) | info db.titleonly.info), (annotation | bridgehead | remark | revhistory | *Indexing inlines* | *Admonition elements* | *Formal elements* | *Graphic elements* | *Informal elements* | *List elements* | *Paragraph elements* | *Publishing elements* | *Synopsis elements* | *Technical elements* | *Verbatim elements*)+)

Attribute synopsis

Common attributes and common linking attributes.

Description

A msgexplan contains some sort of explanatory information about a msg or a set of msgs in a msgentry.

Processing expectations

Formatted as a displayed block. Sometimes suppressed.

If a msgentry contains multiple msgs and multiple msgexplans, DocBook makes no assertions about how they are related.

On the whole, the semantics of msgset are not clearly defined.

msginfo

Synopsis

msginfo ::= (msgaud | msglevel | msgorig)*

Attribute synopsis

Common attributes and common linking attributes.

Description

The msginfo element provides additional information about a msg in a msgentry.

Processing expectations

May be formatted inline or as a displayed block, depending on context. Sometimes suppressed.

On the whole, the semantics of msgset are not clearly defined.

---

msglevel

Synopsis

msglevel ::= (text | phrase ^{db._phrase} | replaceable | *Graphic inlines* | *Indexing inlines* | *Linking inlines* | *Ubiquitous inlines*)*

Attribute synopsis

Common attributes and common linking attributes.

Description

A msglevel is part of the additional information associated with a message in a msgset. It identifies the relative importance or severity of a message.

Processing expectations

May be formatted inline or as a displayed block, depending on context. Sometimes suppressed.

On the whole, the semantics of msgset are not clearly defined.

---

msgmain

Synopsis

msgmain ::= (((((title? & titleabbrev?), info? ^{db.titleforbidden.info}) | info ^{db.titleonly.info}), msgtext)

Attribute synopsis

Common attributes and common linking attributes.

Description

Every msg must have one primary message. This is stored in the msgmain. The primary message is distinguished from any number of submessages (msgsub) or related messages (msgrel) that a msg might have.

Processing expectations

Formatted as a displayed block.

On the whole, the semantics of msgset are not clearly defined.

msgorig

Synopsis

msgorig ::= (text | phrase ^{db._phrase} | replaceable | *Graphic inlines* | *Indexing inlines* | *Linking inlines* | *Ubiquitous inlines*)*

Attribute synopsis

Common attributes and common linking attributes.

Description

A msgorig is part of the additional information associated with a message in a msgset. It identifies the origin or source of a particular msg—for example, a piece of hardware, the operating system, or an application.

Processing expectations

May be formatted inline or as a displayed block, depending on context. Sometimes suppressed.

On the whole, the semantics of msgset are not clearly defined.

msgrel

Synopsis

msgrel ::= ((((title? & titleabbrev?), info? ^{db.titleforbidden.info}) | info ^{db.titleonly.info}), msgtext)

Attribute synopsis

Common attributes and common linking attributes.

Description

Every msg has one primary message (msgmain). It may also have any number of related messages, stored in msgrel elements within the same msg.

Related messages are usually messages that appear elsewhere in response to the same event (or set of events) that triggered the main message. For example, if a network client produces a failure or warning message, a related message might appear on the server console.

Processing expectations

May be formatted inline or as a displayed block, depending on context. Sometimes suppressed.

On the whole, the semantics of msgset are not clearly defined.

msgset

Synopsis

msgset ::= ((((title? & titleabbrev?), info? ^{db.titleforbidden.info}) | info ^{db.titleonly.info}), (msgentry+ | simplemsgentry+))

Attribute synopsis

Common attributes and common linking attributes.

Description

A msgset is a complex structure designed to hold a detailed set of messages, usually error messages. In addition to the actual text of each message, it can contain additional information about each message and the messages related to it.

Processing expectations

Formatted as a displayed block.

On the whole, the semantics of msgset are not clearly defined.

See Also

errorcode, errorname, errortext, errortype

Examples

```
<article xmlns='http://docbook.org/ns/docbook'>
<title>Example msgset</title>

<msgset>
  <msgentry>
    <msg>
      <msgmain>
        <msgtext><para>Record failed CRC</para></msgtext>
      </msgmain>
      <msgsub>
        <msgtext><para>Record <replaceable>n</replaceable>
                 in <replaceable>database</replaceable></para></msgtext>
      </msgsub>
      <msgrel>
        <msgtext><para>File read error on
                <replaceable>database</replaceable></para></msgtext>
      </msgrel>
      <msgrel>
        <msgtext><para>Panic! Corrupt record!</para></msgtext>
      </msgrel>
    </msg>
    <msginfo>
      <msglevel>severe</msglevel>
      <msgorig>server</msgorig>
      <msgaud>all</msgaud>
    </msginfo>
    <msgexplan>
      <para>Indicates that some sort of error occurred while
      attempting to load a record from the database.  Retry.
      If failure persists,contact the database administrator.
      </para>
    </msgexplan>
  </msgentry>
  <!-- more entries -->
</msgset>

</article>
```

msgsub

Synopsis

msgsub ::= ((((title? & titleabbrev?), info? ^{db.titleforbidden.info}) | info ^{db.titleonly.info}), msgtext)

Attribute synopsis

Common attributes and common linking attributes.

Description

A msgsub represents some subpart of a message. Different msgsubs might arise in different contexts.

Processing expectations

May be formatted inline or as a displayed block, depending on context. Sometimes suppressed.

On the whole, the semantics of msgset are not clearly defined.

msgtext

Synopsis

msgtext ::= (annotation | bridgehead | remark | revhistory | *Indexing inlines* | *Admonition elements* | *Formal elements* | *Graphic elements* | *Informal elements* | *List elements* | *Paragraph elements* | *Publishing elements* | *Synopsis elements* | *Technical elements* | *Verbatim elements*)+

Attribute synopsis

Common attributes and common linking attributes.

Description

The msgtext is the actual content of the message in a msgmain, msgsub, or msgrel.

Processing expectations

May be formatted inline or as a displayed block, depending on context.

On the whole, the semantics of msgset are not clearly defined.

nonterminal

Synopsis

nonterminal ::= text

Attribute synopsis

Common attributes and common linking attributes.

Additional attributes:

- **def** (anyURI)

Required attributes are shown in **bold**.

Description

A `nonterminal` is a symbol in an EBNF `production` that represents a portion of the grammar.

Processing expectations

Formatted inline.

Notice that the `def` attribute *is not* an IDREF, it is a URI. References to nonterminals often cross document boundaries, making ID/IDREF linking impossible.

Attributes

Common attributes and common linking attributes.

def

> Specifies a URI that points to a `production` where the `nonterminal` is defined

Examples

See `productionset`.

---

note

Synopsis

note ::= ((((title? & titleabbrev?), info? db.titleforbidden.info) | info db.titleonly.info), (annotation | bridgehead | remark | revhistory | *Indexing inlines* | *Admonition elements* | *Formal elements* | *Graphic elements* | *Informal elements* | *List elements* | *Paragraph elements* | *Publishing elements* | *Synopsis elements* | *Technical elements* | *Verbatim elements*)+)

Attribute synopsis

Common attributes and common linking attributes.

Additional constraints

- caution must not occur among the children or descendants of note.
- important must not occur among the children or descendants of note.
- note must not occur among the children or descendants of note.
- tip must not occur among the children or descendants of note.
- warning must not occur among the children or descendants of note.

Description

A note is an admonition set off from the main text.

In some types of documentation, the semantics of admonitions are clearly defined (caution might imply the possibility of harm to equipment whereas warning might imply harm to a person), but DocBook makes no such assertions.

Processing expectations

Formatted as a displayed block. Often outputs the generated text "Note" or some other visible indication of the type of admonition, especially if a `title` is not present. Sometimes outputs a graphical icon or another symbol as well.

See Also

caution, important, tip, warning

Examples

```
<article xmlns='http://docbook.org/ns/docbook'>
<title>Example note</title>

<note><title>Upcoming changes</title>
<para>Future versions of this feature may not be backward compatible.
Consider implementing the revised interface now.
</para>
</note>

</article>
```

Upcoming changes

Future versions of this feature may not be backward compatible. Consider implementing the revised interface now.

---

olink

A link that addresses its target indirectly

Synopsis

olink ::= (text | *Bibliography inlines* | *Error inlines* | *Graphic inlines* | *GUI inlines* | *Indexing inlines* | *Keyboard inlines* | *Linking inlines* | *Markup inlines* | *Math inlines* | *Object-oriented programming inlines* | *Operating system inlines* | *Product inlines* | *Programming inlines* | *Publishing inlines* | *Technical inlines* | *Ubiquitous inlines*)*

Attribute synopsis

Common attributes.

Additional attributes:

- `localinfo`
- `targetdoc` (anyURI)
- `targetptr`
- `type`
- `xrefstyle`

Description

Unlike link, the semantics of olink are application specific. The olink element provides a mechanism for establishing links across documents, where ID/IDREF linking is not possible and URI-based linking may be inappropriate.

In general terms, the strategy employed by olink is to point to the target document by URI, and point into that document in some application-specific way.

Other elements can also behave like olink by using the common linking attributes xlink:href and xlink:role. When an element has an xlink:role="http://docbook.org/ xlink/role/olink" attribute, then its xlink:href attribute is interpreted using olink semantics. That is, the part of xlink:href before the fragment identifier (#) is interpreted as equivalent to an olink targetdoc attribute value instead of a URI, and the part after the fragment identifier as an olink targetptr attribute value.

Processing expectations
Formatted inline.

An olink points to its target primarily with the targetdoc attribute. The targetdoc is a URI that identifies a target document.

The semantics of the link are controlled by three other attributes: targetptr, local info, and type.

The targetptr attribute (possibly in conjunction with localinfo) points into the document in some fashion. The type may provide some additional, application-specific information about the link. DocBook does not provide any semantics for the values of these attributes.

The targetptr and localinfo attributes were developed somewhat independently and arguably have somewhat overlapping semantics. While almost all applications can certainly get by with one or the other, the Technical Committee has decided that removing localinfo simply for semantic cleanliness isn't worth the effort.

Linking elements must not be nested within other linking elements (including themselves). The processing of nested linking elements is undefined.

Attributes
Common attributes.

localinfo
> Holds additional information that may be used by the application when resolving the link

targetdoc
> Specifies the URI of the document in which the link target appears

targetptr
> Specifies the location of the link target in the document

type
> Identifies application-specific customization of the link behavior

xrefstyle
> Specifies a keyword or keywords identifying additional style information

See Also

anchor, link, xref

ooclass

A class in an object-oriented programming language

Synopsis

ooclass ::= ((modifier | package)*, classname)

Attribute synopsis

Common attributes and common linking attributes.

Description

The ooclass element identifies programming language classes, generally from object-oriented programming languages. The ooclass is a wrapper for the classname plus some modifiers.

Processing expectations

Formatted inline.

ooexception

An exception in an object-oriented programming language

Synopsis

ooexception ::= ((modifier | package)*, exceptionname)

Attribute synopsis

Common attributes and common linking attributes.

Description

The ooexception element identifies programming language exceptions, generally from object-oriented programming languages. The ooexception is a wrapper for the exceptionname plus some modifiers.

Processing expectations

Formatted inline.

oointerface

Synopsis

oointerface ::= ((modifier | package)*, interfacename)

Attribute synopsis

Common attributes and common linking attributes.

Description

The oointerface element identifies programming language interfaces, generally from object-oriented programming languages. The oointerface is a wrapper for the interfacename plus some modifiers.

Processing expectations

Formatted inline.

option

Synopsis

option ::= (text | phrase ^{db._phrase} | replaceable | *Graphic inlines* | *Indexing inlines* | *Linking inlines* | *Ubiquitous inlines*)*

Attribute synopsis

Common attributes and common linking attributes.

Description

An option identifies an argument to a software command or instruction. Options may or may not be required. The optional element can be used to explicitly identify options that are not required.

Processing expectations

Formatted inline.

DocBook does not specify whether or not a symbol (such as - or /) is generated before the content of option, or what that symbol might be. Generating the text may or may not be desirable, but in either case, it is an interchange issue. See Appendix D.

See Also

computeroutput, constant, literal, markup, optional, parameter, prompt, replaceable, tag, userinput, varname

Examples

```
<article xmlns='http://docbook.org/ns/docbook'>
<title>Example option</title>

<para>The <option>-a</option> option on the <acronym>UNIX</acronym>
<command>ls</command> command or the <option>/r</option> option on the
<acronym>DOS</acronym> <command>attrib</command>
command, for example.
</para>
```

```
</article>
```

The -a option on the UNIX *ls* command or the /r option on the DOS *attrib* command, for example.

optional

Synopsis

optional ::= (text | phrase ^{db._phrase} | replaceable | *Graphic inlines* | *Indexing inlines* | *Linking inlines* | *Ubiquitous inlines*)*

Attribute synopsis

Common attributes and common linking attributes.

Description

The optional element indicates that a specified argument, option, or other text is optional. The precise meaning of "optional" varies according to the application or process being documented.

Processing expectations

Formatted inline.

Optional arguments in a synopsis are usually given special typographic treatment, and often they are surrounded by square brackets. The optional tag is expected to *generate* the brackets.

Outside a synopsis, the typographic treatment of optional is application specific.

See Also

computeroutput, constant, literal, markup, option, parameter, prompt, replaceable, tag, userinput, varname

Examples

```
<article xmlns='http://docbook.org/ns/docbook'>
<title>Example optional</title>

<synopsis>
ls <option>-abcCdfFgilLmnopqrRstux1</option>
   <optional>names</optional>
</synopsis>

</article>


    ls -abcCdfFgilLmnopqrRstux1
       [names]
```

orderedlist

A list in which each entry is marked with a sequentially incremented label

Synopsis

orderedlist ::= (((((title? & titleabbrev?), info? ^{db.titleforbidden.info}) | info ^{db.titleonly.info}), (annotation | bridgehead | remark | revhistory | *Indexing inlines* | *Admonition elements* | *Formal elements* | *Graphic elements* | *Informal elements* | *List elements* | *Paragraph elements* | *Publishing elements* | *Synopsis elements* | *Technical elements* | *Verbatim elements*)*, listitem+)

Attribute synopsis

Common attributes and common linking attributes.

Additional attributes:

- *At most one of:*
  - — continuation (enumeration) = "continues" | "restarts"
  - — startingnumber (integer)
- inheritnum (enumeration) = "ignore" | "inherit"
- numeration (enumeration) = "arabic" | "upperalpha" | "loweralpha" | "upperroman" | "lowerroman"
- spacing (enumeration) = "compact" | "normal"

Description

In an orderedlist, each member of the list is marked with a numeral, letter, or other sequential symbol (such as Roman numerals).

Processing expectations

Formatted as a displayed block.

The numeration attribute indicates the desired numeration. If it is not specified, Arabic numerals (1, 2, 3, …) are to be used.

The actual characters used in alphabetic numeration may be locale sensitive. Where the sequence "a", "b", "c" might be selected in an English locale, "ア", "イ", "ウ" might be selected if Katakana was implied by the current locale.

The continuation attribute indicates how numbering should begin relative to the immediately preceding list. If it is not specified, numbering is to be restarted at 1.

The preceding list is not required to be in the same parent. That is, a list in one chapter may be continued in the next, or indeed arbitrarily later in the document, provided no other list intervenes.

The `inheritnum` attribute indicates how items in nested lists should be numbered. If it is not specified, numbering is to ignore list nesting. Inherited numeration creates compound list item numbers.

If `inheritnum` is "inherit", then the third item of a list inside the second item of a list inside the fourth item of a list might be enumerated as "4.2.3". If `inheritnum` is "ignore", then it would be simply "3" (with the `numeration` attribute handling the actual format of the numbers).

In nested lists, some publishers prefer to use Arabic numbers throughout (4.3.2) while others prefer to step through a sequence of numerations (4.b.iii). DocBook does not specify the sequence of numerations.

Attributes
Common attributes and common linking attributes.

continuation
> Indicates how list numbering should begin relative to the immediately preceding list

Enumerated values:	
"continues"	Specifies that numbering should begin where the preceding list left off
"restarts"	Specifies that numbering should begin again at 1

inheritnum
> Indicates whether or not item numbering should be influenced by list nesting

Enumerated values:	
"ignore"	Specifies that numbering should ignore list nesting
"inherit"	Specifies that numbering should inherit from outer-level lists

numeration
> Indicates the desired numeration

Enumerated values:	
"arabic"	Specifies Arabic numeration (1, 2, 3, …)
"upperalpha"	Specifies uppercase alphabetic numeration (A, B, C, …)
"loweralpha"	Specifies lowercase alphabetic numeration (a, b, c, …)
"upperroman"	Specifies uppercase Roman numeration (I, II, III, …)
"lowerroman"	Specifies lowercase Roman numeration (i, ii, iii …)

spacing
> Specifies (a hint about) the spacing of the content

Enumerated values:	
"compact"	The spacing should be "compact".
"normal"	The spacing should be "normal".

startingnumber
Specifies the initial line number

See Also

calloutlist, itemizedlist, listitem, segmentedlist, simplelist, variablelist

Examples

```
<article xmlns='http://docbook.org/ns/docbook'>
<title>Example orderedlist</title>

<orderedlist numeration="lowerroman">
  <listitem>
    <para>One</para>
  </listitem>
  <listitem>
    <para>Two</para>
  </listitem>
  <listitem>
    <para>Three</para>
  </listitem>
  <listitem>
    <para>Four</para>
  </listitem>
</orderedlist>

</article>
```

   i. One

   ii. Two

  iii. Three

  iv. Four

org

An organization and associated metadata

Synopsis

org ::= (orgname, (address | affiliation | email | orgdiv | uri)*)

Attribute synopsis

Common attributes and common linking attributes.

Description

An org associates an organization name with other information about the organization.

Processing expectations

May be formatted inline or as a displayed block, depending on context.

Examples

```
<article xmlns='http://docbook.org/ns/docbook' version='5.0'>
<title>Example org</title>

<para>This book was edited by <org><orgname>XML Press</orgname>
  <address><city>Fort Collins</city>,
  <state>CO</state></address></org> and published by
  <org><orgname>O'Reilly Media, Inc.</orgname>
  <address><city>Sebastopol</city>, <state>CA</state>
  </address></org>.
</para>

</article>
```

---

orgdiv

A division of an organization

Synopsis

orgdiv ::= (text | *Bibliography inlines* | *Error inlines* | *Graphic inlines* | *GUI inlines* | *Indexing inlines* | *Keyboard inlines* | *Linking inlines* | *Markup inlines* | *Math inlines* | *Object-oriented programming inlines* | *Operating system inlines* | *Product inlines* | *Programming inlines* | *Publishing inlines* | *Technical inlines* | *Ubiquitous inlines*)*

Attribute synopsis

Common attributes and common linking attributes.

Description

An `orgdiv` identifies a division in an organization, such as "Chevrolet" in "General Motors."

Processing expectations

Formatted inline. Sometimes suppressed.

See Also

affiliation, jobtitle, orgname, shortaffil

---

orgname

The name of an organization

Synopsis

orgname ::= (text | phrase ^{db.—phrase} | replaceable | *Graphic inlines* | *Indexing inlines* | *Linking inlines* | *Ubiquitous inlines*)*

Attribute synopsis

Common attributes and common linking attributes.

Additional attributes:

- *At most one of:*
    —class (enumeration) = "consortium" | "corporation" | "informal" | "nonprofit"
    —*Each of:*
        —**class** (enumeration) = "other"
        —**otherclass**

Required attributes are shown in **bold**.

Description
An orgname identifies the name of an organization or corporation.

Processing expectations
Formatted inline. Sometimes suppressed.

Attributes
Common attributes and common linking attributes.

class
>   Specifies the nature of the organization

Enumerated values:	
"consortium"	A consortium
"corporation"	A corporation
"informal"	An informal organization
"nonprofit"	A nonprofit organization

class
>   Specifies the nature of the organization

Enumerated values:	
"other"	Indicates a nonstandard organization class

otherclass
>   Identifies the nonstandard nature of the organization

See Also
affiliation, jobtitle, orgdiv, publishername, shortaffil

otheraddr

Synopsis

otheraddr ::= (text | phrase ^{db.–phrase} | replaceable | *Graphic inlines* | *Indexing inlines* | *Linking inlines* | *Ubiquitous inlines*)*

Attribute synopsis

Common attributes and common linking attributes.

Description

Within an `address`, `otheraddr` is a wrapper for parts of an address other than `street`, `pob`, `postcode`, `city`, `state`, `country`, `phone`, `fax`, and `email`, all of which have elements specific to their content.

In early versions of DocBook, `address` was not allowed to contain character data (it was a database-like collection of fields). In that context, a wrapper was necessary for any random pieces of information that might be required for an address. With the introduction of character data directly in the `address` element, `otheraddr` may have lost most of its *raison d'être*.

Processing expectations

Formatted inline. This element may inherit the verbatim qualities of an `address`.

See Also

address, city, country, email, fax, phone, pob, postcode, state, street

Examples

```
<article xmlns='http://docbook.org/ns/docbook'>
<title>Example otheraddr</title>

<para>Please deliver to:
<address>The Law Offices of Dewey, Cheatem, and Howe
<street>100 Main Street</street>
<otheraddr>Third Floor</otheraddr>
<city>Anytown</city>, <state>NY</state> <postcode>12345</postcode>
<country>USA</country>
</address>
</para>

</article>
```

Please deliver to:
> The Law Offices of Dewey, Cheatem, and Howe
> 100 Main Street
> Third Floor
> Anytown, NY 12345
> USA

othercredit

A person or entity, other than an author or editor, credited in a document

Synopsis

othercredit ::= ((personname, (address | affiliation | contrib | email | personblurb | uri)*) | (orgname, (address | affiliation | contrib | email | orgdiv | uri)*))

Attribute synopsis

Common attributes and common linking attributes.

Additional attributes:

- *Exactly one of:*
  - —class (enumeration) = "copyeditor" | "graphicdesigner" | "other" | "production editor" | "technicaleditor" | "translator"
  - —*All of:*
    - —**class** (enumeration) = "other"
    - —**otherclass** (NMTOKEN)

Required attributes are shown in **bold**.

Description

DocBook allows you to directly identify authors and editors. The othercredit element provides a mechanism for identifying other individuals—for example, contributors or production editors—in a similar context.

Processing expectations

May be formatted inline or as a displayed block, depending on context. Sometimes suppressed.

Attributes

Common attributes and common linking attributes.

class

   Identifies the nature of the contributor

Enumerated values:	
"copyeditor"	A copyeditor
"graphicdesigner"	A graphic designer
"other"	Some other contributor
"productioneditor"	A production editor
"technicaleditor"	A technical editor
"translator"	A translator

class

   Identifies the nature of the contributor

otherclass
   Identifies the nature of the nonstandard contribution

See Also

author, authorgroup, collab, contrib, editor, personblurb, personname

Examples

```
<article xmlns='http://docbook.org/ns/docbook'>
<info>
  <title>Example othercredit</title>
  <author>
    <personname>
      <firstname>Norman</firstname>
      <surname>Walsh</surname>
    </personname>
  </author>
  <othercredit>
    <personname>
      <firstname>John</firstname>
      <surname>Doe</surname>
    </personname>
    <contrib>Extensive review and rough drafts of Section 1.3, 1.4, and 1.5
    </contrib>
  </othercredit>
  <biblioid>5</biblioid>
</info>

<para>…</para>

</article>
```

othername   A component of a person's name that is not a first name, surname, or lineage

Synopsis

othername ::= (text | phrase ^{db.–phrase} | replaceable | *Graphic inlines* | *Indexing inlines* | *Linking in-lines* | *Ubiquitous inlines*)*

Attribute synopsis

Common attributes and common linking attributes.

Description

An othername element is a generic wrapper for parts of an individual's name other than honorific, firstname, surname, and lineage. One common use is to identify an individual's middle name or initial. Use role to classify the type of other name.

Processing expectations
Formatted inline. In an `address`, this element may inherit the verbatim qualities of an address.

See Also
`affiliation`, `firstname`, `honorific`, `lineage`, `surname`

---

package
A software or application package

Synopsis
package ::= (text | phrase ^{db._phrase} | replaceable | *Graphic inlines* | *Indexing inlines* | *Linking inlines* | *Ubiquitous inlines*)*

Attribute synopsis
Common attributes and common linking attributes.

Description
The `package` element identifies a package of some sort. The precise kind of package is context dependent. It might be used, for example, to identify a Java package or an operating system distribution package.

Processing expectations
Formatted inline.

---

pagenums
The numbers of the pages in a book, for use in a bibliographic entry

Synopsis
pagenums ::= (text | phrase ^{db._phrase} | replaceable | *Graphic inlines* | *Indexing inlines* | *Linking inlines* | *Ubiquitous inlines*)*

Attribute synopsis
Common attributes and common linking attributes.

Description
A pagenums identifies a page or range of pages. This may be useful in the bibliography of a book, to indicate the number of pages, or in a citation to a journal article.

Processing expectations
Formatted inline. Sometimes suppressed.

Examples

See `bibliography` for an example using the `pagenums` element.

para A paragraph

Synopsis

para ::= (info? ^{db.titleforbidden.info}, (text | **bridgehead** | **revhistory** | *Bibliography inlines* | *Error inlines* | *Graphic inlines* | *GUI inlines* | *Indexing inlines* | *Keyboard inlines* | *Linking inlines* | *Markup inlines* | *Math inlines* | *Object-oriented programming inlines* | *Operating system inlines* | *Product inlines* | *Programming inlines* | *Publishing inlines* | *Technical inlines* | *Ubiquitous inlines* | *Admonition elements* | *Formal elements* | *Graphic elements* | *Informal elements* | *List elements* | *Publishing elements* | *Synopsis elements* | *Technical elements* | *Verbatim elements*)*)

Attribute synopsis

Common attributes and common linking attributes.

Additional constraints

- If this element is the root element, it must have a `version` attribute.

Description

A `para` is a paragraph. Paragraphs in DocBook may contain almost all inlines and most block elements. Sectioning and higher-level structural elements are excluded. DocBook offers two variants of paragraph: `simpara`, which cannot contain block elements, and `formalpara`, which has a title.

Some processing systems may find the presence of block elements in a paragraph difficult to handle. On the other hand, it is frequently most logical, from a structural point of view, to include block elements, especially informal block elements, in the paragraphs that describe their content. There is no easy answer to this problem.

Processing expectations

Formatted as a displayed block.

See Also

formalpara, simpara

Examples

An ordinary paragraph:

```
<article xmlns='http://docbook.org/ns/docbook'>
<title>Example para</title>

<para>The component suffered from three failings:
<itemizedlist>
<listitem><para>It was slow</para></listitem>
<listitem><para>It ran hot</para></listitem>
<listitem><para>It didn't actually work</para></listitem>
</itemizedlist>
Of these three, the last was probably the most important.
</para>

</article>
```

The component suffered from three failings:

- It was slow
- It ran hot
- It didn't actually work

Of these three, the last was probably the most important.

A formal paragraph:

```
<article xmlns='http://docbook.org/ns/docbook'>
<title>Example para</title>

<formalpara><title>A Test</title>
<para>This is a test.  This is only a test.  Had this been a real
example, it would have made more sense.
</para>
</formalpara>

</article>
```

A Test.
This is a test. This is only a test. Had this been a real example, it would have made more sense.

A simple paragraph:

```
<article xmlns='http://docbook.org/ns/docbook'>
<title>Example para</title>

<simpara>
Just the text, ma'am.
</simpara>

</article>
```

Just the text, ma'am.

---

paramdef

Information about a function parameter in a programming language

Synopsis
paramdef ::= (text | funcparams | initializer | parameter | phrase ^{db._phrase} | replaceable | type | *Graphic inlines* | *Indexing inlines* | *Linking inlines* | *Ubiquitous inlines*)*

Attribute synopsis
Common attributes and common linking attributes.

Additional attributes:

- choice (enumeration) = "opt" | "req" [default="opt"]

Description
In the syntax summary for a function in a programming language, `paramdef` provides the description of a parameter to the function. Typically, this includes the data type of

the parameter and its name. For parameters that are pointers to functions, it also includes a summary of the nested parameters.

Within the `paramdef`, the parameter name is identified with `parameter`, and the rest of the content is assumed to be the data type.

In the following definition, `str` is the name of the parameter and `char *` is its type:

```
<paramdef>char *<parameter>str</parameter></paramdef>
```

Sometimes a data type requires punctuation on both sides of the parameter. For example, the a parameter in this definition is an array of `char *`:

```
<paramdef>char *<parameter>a</parameter>[]</paramdef>
```

Processing expectations

Formatted inline. For a complete description of the processing expectations, see `funcsynopsis`.

Attributes

Common attributes and common linking attributes.

choice
> Indicates optionality

Enumerated values:	
"opt"	Formatted to indicate that it is optional
"req"	Formatted to indicate that it is required

See Also

`funcdef`, `funcparams`, `funcprototype`, `funcsynopsisinfo`, `function`, `parameter`, `return value`, `varargs`, `void`

Examples

```
<article xmlns='http://docbook.org/ns/docbook'>
<title>Example paramdef</title>

<funcsynopsis>
<funcprototype>
  <funcdef>int <function>max</function></funcdef>
  <paramdef>int <parameter>int1</parameter></paramdef>
  <paramdef>int <parameter>int2</parameter></paramdef>
</funcprototype>
</funcsynopsis>

</article>
```

```
int max(int1, int2);

int int1;
int int2;
```

parameter

A value or a symbolic reference to a value

Synopsis

parameter ::= (text | phrase ^{db._phrase} | replaceable | *Graphic inlines* | *Indexing inlines* | *Linking inlines* | *Ubiquitous inlines*)*

Attribute synopsis

Common attributes and common linking attributes.

Additional attributes:

- class (enumeration) = "command" | "function" | "option"

Description

A parameter identifies something passed from one part of a computer system to another. In this regard parameter is fairly generic, but it may have a more constrained semantic in some contexts (e.g., in a paramdef).

In a document that describes more than one kind of parameter—for example, parameters to functions and commands—the class attribute can be used to distinguish between them, if necessary.

Processing expectations

Formatted inline.

Attributes

Common attributes and common linking attributes.

class

> Identifies the class of parameter

Enumerated values:	
"command"	A command
"function"	A function
"option"	An option

See Also

computeroutput, constant, funcdef, funcparams, funcprototype, funcsynopsisinfo, function, literal, markup, option, optional, paramdef, prompt, replaceable, returnvalue, tag, userinput, varargs, varname, void

Examples

```
<article xmlns='http://docbook.org/ns/docbook'>
<title>Example parameter</title>

<para>Using the <parameter class='command'>-l</parameter> parameter on the
Linux <command>ls</command> command prints a long directory listing.
```

```
        </para>

        </article>
```

Using the -1 parameter on the Linux *ls* command prints a long directory listing.

---

part

Synopsis

part ::= ((((title & titleabbrev? & subtitle?), info? ^{db.titleforbidden.info}) | info ^{db.titlereq.info}), partintro?, (acknowledgements | appendix | article | bibliography | chapter | colophon | dedication | glossary | index | preface | refentry | reference | toc)+)

Attribute synopsis

Common attributes and common linking attributes.

Additional attributes:

- label
- status

Additional constraints

- If this element is the root element, it must have a **version** attribute.

Description

The **part**s segment a book into divisions. Each division can contain a number of component-level elements, such as **chapter**s.

Processing expectations

Formatted as a displayed block. Each **part** almost always introduces a forced page break. Sometimes parts start on the next recto page. Frequently, they also produce a part separator page, on which may be printed the content of the **partintro**.

Attributes

Common attributes and common linking attributes.

label
> Specifies an identifying string for presentation purposes

status
> Identifies the editorial or publication status of the element on which it occurs

See Also

appendix, article, book, chapter, colophon, dedication, partintro, preface, set

Examples

```
<part xmlns='http://docbook.org/ns/docbook'
      label="II">
<title>Programming with the Java API</title>
<partintro>
```

```
<para>The sections in Part II present real-world examples of
programming with Java.  You can study and learn from the
examples, and you can adapt them for use in your own programs.
</para>

<para>The example code in these chapters is available for downloading.
See <systemitem role="url">http://www.ora.com/catalog/books/javanut</systemitem>.
</para>

<literallayout>
<xref linkend="jnut-ch-04"/>
<xref linkend="jnut-ch-05"/>
<xref linkend="jnut-ch-06"/>
<xref linkend="jnut-ch-07"/>
<xref linkend="jnut-ch-08"/>
<xref linkend="jnut-ch-09"/>
</literallayout>
</partintro>
<chapter xml:id="jnut-ch-04"><title/><para>...</para></chapter>
<chapter xml:id="jnut-ch-05"><title/><para>...</para></chapter>
<chapter xml:id="jnut-ch-06"><title/><para>...</para></chapter>
<chapter xml:id="jnut-ch-07"><title/><para>...</para></chapter>
<chapter xml:id="jnut-ch-08"><title/><para>...</para></chapter>
<chapter xml:id="jnut-ch-09"><title/><para>...</para></chapter>
</part>
```

partintro
An introduction to the contents of a part

Synopsis
partintro ::= (((((title? & titleabbrev? & subtitle?), info? $^{db.titleforbidden.info}$) | info? $^{db.info}$),
(((annotation | bridgehead | remark | revhistory | *Indexing inlines* | *Admonition elements* | *Formal elements* | *Graphic elements* | *Informal elements* | *List elements* | *Paragraph elements* | *Publishing elements* | *Synopsis elements* | *Technical elements* | *Verbatim elements*)+, ((section+, simplesect*) | simplesect+ | (sect1+, simplesect*) | refentry+)?) | (section+, simplesect*) | simplesect
+ | (sect1+, simplesect*) | refentry+))

Attribute synopsis
Common attributes and common linking attributes.

Additional attributes:

- label
- status

Description

A `partintro` contains introductory text, often an overview of the content of the `part`.

Processing expectations

Formatted as a displayed block. Sometimes suppressed.

The `partintro` content is often printed on a part separator page.

Attributes

Common attributes and common linking attributes.

label
> Specifies an identifying string for presentation purposes

status
> Identifies the editorial or publication status of the element on which it occurs

See Also

`appendix`, `article`, `book`, `chapter`, `colophon`, `dedication`, `part`, `preface`, `set`

Examples

See `part` for an example that uses this element.

---

person
A person and associated metadata

Synopsis

person ::= (personname, (address | affiliation | email | personblurb | uri)*)

Attribute synopsis

Common attributes and common linking attributes.

Description

A `person` associates a personal name with other information about an individual.

Processing expectations

May be formatted inline or as a displayed block, depending on context.

Examples

```
<article xmlns='http://docbook.org/ns/docbook'>
<title>Example person</title>

<para>The principal author of this document is
<person><personname><firstname>Norman</firstname>
<surname>Walsh</surname></personname><email>ndw@nwalsh.com</email>
</person>.</para>

</article>
```

personblurb

A short description or note about a person

Synopsis

personblurb ::= (((title? & titleabbrev?), info? ^{db.titleforbidden.info}) | info ^{db.titleonly.info}), *Paragraph elements+*)

Attribute synopsis

Common attributes and common linking attributes.

Description

A short description of a person.

Processing expectations

Formatted as a displayed block. Sometimes suppressed.

See Also

author, authorgroup, collab, contrib, editor, othercredit, personname

Examples

See authorgroup for an example that uses this element.

---

personname

The personal name of an individual

Synopsis

personname ::= ((text | phrase ^{db._phrase} | replaceable | *Graphic inlines* | *Indexing inlines* | *Linking inlines* | *Ubiquitous inlines*)* | (firstname | honorific | lineage | othername | surname)+)

Attribute synopsis

Common attributes and common linking attributes.

Description

The personname identifies the personal name of an individual.

Processing expectations

May be formatted inline or as a displayed block, depending on context.

See Also

author, authorgroup, collab, contrib, editor, othercredit, personblurb

Examples

```
<article xmlns='http://docbook.org/ns/docbook'>
<title>Example personname</title>

<para>Starting in DocBook 4.2, personal names, like
<personname><firstname>Albert</firstname><surname>Einstein</surname></personname>,
can be marked up inline.</para>

</article>
```

Starting in DocBook 4.2, personal names, like Albert Einstein,can be marked up inline.

---

phone

Synopsis

phone ::= (text | phrase ^{db._phrase} | replaceable | *Graphic inlines* | *Indexing inlines* | *Linking inlines* | *Ubiquitous inlines*)*

Attribute synopsis

Common attributes and common linking attributes.

Description

A phone identifies a telephone number in an address.

Processing expectations

Formatted inline. Sometimes suppressed. In an address, this element may inherit the verbatim qualities of an address.

See Also

address, city, country, email, fax, otheraddr, pob, postcode, state, street

phrase (db._phrase)

Synopsis

phrase (db._phrase) ::= (text | phrase ^{db._phrase} | replaceable | *Graphic inlines* | *Indexing inlines* | *Linking inlines* | *Ubiquitous inlines*)*

Attribute synopsis

Common attributes and common linking attributes.

Description

This variant of phrase is used in places where the content model is restricted to only the "ubiquitous" inlines.

Processing expectations

Formatted inline.

See Also

abbrev, acronym, emphasis, foreignphrase, phrase (db.phrase), quote, wordasword

phrase (db.phrase)

Synopsis

phrase (db.phrase) ::= (text | *Bibliography inlines* | *Error inlines* | *Graphic inlines* | *GUI inlines* | *Indexing inlines* | *Keyboard inlines* | *Linking inlines* | *Markup inlines* | *Math inlines* | *Object-oriented programming inlines* | *Operating system inlines* | *Product inlines* | *Programming inlines* | *Publishing inlines* | *Technical inlines* | *Ubiquitous inlines*)*

Attribute synopsis

Common attributes and common linking attributes.

Description

The `phrase` element in DocBook has no specific semantic. It is provided as a wrapper around a selection of words smaller than a paragraph so that it is possible to provide an `xml:id` or other attributes for it.

For example, if you are making note of changes to a document using one of the effectivity attributes, you might use `phrase` to mark up specific sentences with revisions.

Processing expectations

Formatted inline.

See Also

`abbrev`, `acronym`, `emphasis`, `foreignphrase`, `phrase` (db._phrase), `quote`, `wordasword`

Examples

```
<para xmlns='http://docbook.org/ns/docbook'>Effectivity attributes can
be used to keep track of modifications to a document
<phrase revisionflag="deleted">at the word or sentence level</phrase>
<phrase revisionflag="added"> as long as the number and complexity of changes
is not too high</phrase>.
</para>
```

Effectivity attributes can be used to keep track of modifications to a document at the word or sentence level as long as the number and complexity of changes is not too high.

---

pob

A post office box in an address

Synopsis

pob ::= (text | phrase ^{db._phrase} | replaceable | *Graphic inlines* | *Indexing inlines* | *Linking inlines* | *Ubiquitous inlines*)*

Attribute synopsis

Common attributes and common linking attributes.

Description

A `pob` is a post office box number in an `address`.

Processing expectations

Formatted inline. In an `address`, this element may inherit the verbatim qualities of an address.

See Also

`address`, `city`, `country`, `email`, `fax`, `otheraddr`, `phone`, `postcode`, `state`, `street`

postcode
A postal code in an address

Synopsis
postcode ::= (text | phrase ^{db.–phrase} | replaceable | *Graphic inlines* | *Indexing inlines* | *Linking inlines* | *Ubiquitous inlines*)*

Attribute synopsis
Common attributes and common linking attributes.

Description
A postcode is a postal code (in the United States, a zip code) in an address.

Processing expectations
Formatted inline. In an address, this element may inherit the verbatim qualities of an address.

See Also
address, city, country, email, fax, otheraddr, phone, pob, state, street

---

preface
Introductory matter preceding the first chapter of a book

Synopsis
preface ::= ((((title & titleabbrev? & subtitle?), info? ^{db.titleforbidden.info}) | info ^{db.titlereq.info}), ((bibliography | glossary | index | toc)*, (((annotation | bridgehead | remark | revhistory | *Indexing inlines* | *Admonition elements* | *Formal elements* | *Graphic elements* | *Informal elements* | *List elements* | *Paragraph elements* | *Publishing elements* | *Synopsis elements* | *Technical elements* | *Verbatim elements*)+, ((section+, simplesect*) | simplesect+ | (sect1+, simplesect*) | refentry +)?) | (section+, simplesect*) | simplesect+ | (sect1+, simplesect*) | refentry+), (bibliography | glossary | index | toc)*))

Attribute synopsis
Common attributes and common linking attributes.

Additional attributes:

- label
- status

Additional constraints

- If this element is the root element, it must have a version attribute.

Description
A preface is a preface or a foreword in a book. The preface element may appear more than once and should be used for all introductory chapter-like material. For example, a book might have both a *Foreword* and an *Introduction*. Both should be tagged as prefaces in DocBook.

Processing expectations

Formatted as a displayed block. Usually introduces a forced page break and often starts on the next recto page. It is common for the page numbers in prefaces to be displayed as Roman numerals rather than Arabic numerals. The `preface`s are usually listed in the table of contents.

Attributes

Common attributes and common linking attributes.

label

Specifies an identifying string for presentation purposes

status

Identifies the editorial or publication status of the element on which it occurs

See Also

`appendix`, `article`, `book`, `chapter`, `colophon`, `dedication`, `part`, `partintro`, `set`

---

primary

The primary word or phrase under which an index term should be sorted

Synopsis

primary ::= (text | *Bibliography inlines* | *Error inlines* | *Graphic inlines* | *GUI inlines* | *Indexing inlines* | *Keyboard inlines* | *Linking inlines* | *Markup inlines* | *Math inlines* | *Object-oriented programming inlines* | *Operating system inlines* | *Product inlines* | *Programming inlines* | *Publishing inlines* | *Technical inlines* | *Ubiquitous inlines*)*

Attribute synopsis

Common attributes and common linking attributes.

Additional attributes:

- `sortas`

Description

In an `indexterm`, `primary` identifies the most significant word or words in the entry. All `indexterm`s must have a `primary`.

Processing expectations

Suppressed. This element provides data for processing but it is not rendered in the primary flow of text.

Attributes

Common attributes and common linking attributes.

sortas

Specifies the string by which the term is to be sorted; if unspecified, the term content is used

See Also

indexentry, indexterm, primaryie, secondary, secondaryie, see, seealso, seealsoie, seeie, tertiary, tertiaryie

primaryie

A primary term in an index entry, not in the text

Synopsis

primaryie ::= (text | *Bibliography inlines* | *Error inlines* | *Graphic inlines* | *GUI inlines* | *Indexing inlines* | *Keyboard inlines* | *Linking inlines* | *Markup inlines* | *Math inlines* | *Object-oriented programming inlines* | *Operating system inlines* | *Product inlines* | *Programming inlines* | *Publishing inlines* | *Technical inlines* | *Ubiquitous inlines*)*

Attribute synopsis

Common attributes.

Description

A primaryie identifies the most significant word or words in an indexentry. The index entrys occur in an index, not in the flow of the text. They are part of a formatted index, not markers for indexing.

If a document includes both indexterms and indexentrys, the indexentrys are usually constructed from the indexterms by some external process.

Processing expectations

Formatted as a displayed block. The primaryie starts a new entry in the index.

See Also

indexentry, indexterm, primary, secondary, secondaryie, see, seealso, seealsoie, seeie, tertiary, tertiaryie

printhistory

The printing history of a document

Synopsis

printhistory ::= *Paragraph elements+*

Attribute synopsis

Common attributes and common linking attributes.

Description

The printhistory of a document identifies when various editions and revisions were printed.

Processing expectations

Formatted as a displayed block. Sometimes suppressed.

See Also

date, edition, pubdate, releaseinfo, revhistory

Examples

```
<article xmlns='http://docbook.org/ns/docbook'>
<info>
  <title>Example printhistory</title>

  <printhistory>
    <para>September, 1996. First Printing.
    </para>
  </printhistory>
</info>

<para>…</para>

</article>
```

---

procedure   A list of operations to be performed in a well-defined sequence

Synopsis

procedure ::= ((((title? & titleabbrev?), info? ^{db.titleforbidden.info}) | info ^{db.titleonly.info}), (annotation | bridgehead | remark | revhistory | *Indexing inlines* | *Admonition elements* | *Formal elements* | *Graphic elements* | *Informal elements* | *List elements* | *Paragraph elements* | *Publishing elements* | *Synopsis elements* | *Technical elements* | *Verbatim elements*)*, step+)

Attribute synopsis

Common attributes and common linking attributes.

Description

A procedure encapsulates a task composed of steps (and possibly, substeps). Procedures are usually performed sequentially, unless individual steps direct the reader explicitly.

Often it is important to ensure that certain conditions exist before a procedure is performed, and that the outcome of the procedure matches the expected results. DocBook does not provide explicit semantic markup for these pre- and post-conditions. Instead, they must be described as steps (check the preconditions in the first step and the results in the last step), or described outside the body of the procedure.

The task element, added to DocBook in V4.3, provides some of this infrastructure.

Processing expectations

Formatted as a displayed block.

See Also

step, stepalternatives, substeps, task

Examples

```
<article xmlns='http://docbook.org/ns/docbook'>
<title>Example procedure</title>
```

```
<procedure><title>An Example Procedure</title>
<step>
  <para>    A Step
  </para>
</step>
<step>
  <para>    Another Step
  </para>
  <substeps>
    <step>
      <para>          Substeps can be nested indefinitely deep.
      </para>
    </step>
  </substeps>
</step>
<step>
  <para>    A Final Step
  </para>
</step>
</procedure>

</article>
```

Procedure 1. An Example Procedure

1. A Step
2. Another Step

   • Substeps can be nested indefinitely deep.

3. A Final Step

production

Synopsis
production ::= (lhs, rhs, constraint*)

Attribute synopsis
Common attributes (ID required) and common linking attributes.

Description
A production is a single production in an *Extended Backus-Naur Form* (EBNF) grammar.

Individual productions have two parts: a lefthand side (lhs) and a righthand side (rhs). Each nonterminal on the lefthand side is defined in terms of other nonterminals and literals on the righthand side.

See Also
constraint, lhs, productionrecap, productionset, rhs

productionrecap

Synopsis

productionrecap ::= empty

Attribute synopsis

Common attributes and common linking attributes.

Description

A productionrecap is a cross-reference to a production.

Processing expectations

A productionrecap is rendered exactly like the production to which it refers. The purpose of the productionrecap element is to allow a productionset to contain copies of productions defined elsewhere. This frequently makes it easier for readers to understand.

See Also

constraint, lhs, production, productionset, rhs

productionset

Synopsis

productionset ::= (((((title? & titleabbrev?), info? $^{db.titleforbidden.info}$) | info $^{db.titleonly.info}$), (production | productionrecap)+)

Attribute synopsis

Common attributes and common linking attributes.

Description

A productionset is a collection of *Extended Backus-Naur Form* (EBNF) productions.

EBNF is a notation for describing the grammar of context-free languages. Even if you aren't conversant in the programming language concepts of context-free languages and grammars, it's not really as hard to understand as it sounds.

Processing expectations

Formatted as a displayed block. The detailed processing expectations with respect to individual productions, lefthand sides, and righthand sides are quite complex.

The productions should be numbered.

See Also

constraint, lhs, production, productionrecap, rhs

Examples

A set of EBNF productions describes the legal arrangements of tokens in a language. Consider arithmetic expressions as a simple example.

The expression 3 + 4 is valid and so is 3 + 4 - 5, but 3 - + - 4 is not, nor is 3 + 4 6. We can use EBNF to describe all the possible legal arrangements.

That is expressed in DocBook like this:

```
<article xmlns='http://docbook.org/ns/docbook'>
<title>Example productionset</title>

<simplesect><title>EBNF Grammar</title>

<productionset><title>Arithemetic Expressions</title>
<production xml:id="ebnf.expression">
  <lhs>Expression</lhs>
  <rhs><nonterminal def="#ebnf.arith">ArithExpression</nonterminal> |
      <nonterminal def="#ebnf.mult">MultExpression</nonterminal>
  <lineannotation>Does this grammar actually get precedence right?
  </lineannotation>
  </rhs>
</production>
<production xml:id="ebnf.arith">
  <lhs>ArithExpression</lhs>
  <rhs><nonterminal def="#ebnf.expression">Expression</nonterminal>
      '+'
      <nonterminal def="#ebnf.mult">MultExpression</nonterminal> |
      <nonterminal def="#ebnf.expression">Expression</nonterminal>
      '-'
      <nonterminal def="#ebnf.mult">MultExpression</nonterminal>
  </rhs>
</production>
<production xml:id="ebnf.mult">
  <lhs>MultExpression</lhs>
  <rhs><nonterminal def="#ebnf.mult">MultExpression</nonterminal>
      '*'
      <nonterminal def="#ebnf.mult">MultExpression</nonterminal> |
      <nonterminal def="#ebnf.mult">MultExpression</nonterminal>
      '/'
      <nonterminal def="#ebnf.mult">MultExpression</nonterminal> |
      <nonterminal def="#ebnf.number">Number</nonterminal>
  </rhs>
  <constraint linkend="div0"/>
</production>
<production xml:id="ebnf.number">
  <lhs>Number</lhs>
  <rhs>[0-9]+</rhs>
</production>
</productionset>

<constraintdef xml:id="div0">
<title>Division by Zero</title>
<para>Division by zero is an error.</para>
</constraintdef>
</simplesect>

</article>
```

productname

Synopsis

productname ::= (text | phrase ^{db._phrase} | replaceable | *Graphic inlines* | *Indexing inlines* | *Linking inlines* | *Ubiquitous inlines*)*

Attribute synopsis

Common attributes and common linking attributes.

Additional attributes:

- class (enumeration) = "copyright" | "registered" | "service" | "trade"

Description

A productname is the formal name of any product. Identifying a product this way may be useful if you need to provide explicit disclaimers about product names or information.

For example, the copyright statement in most books includes a notice similar to this:

> Many of the designations used by manufacturers and sellers to distinguish their products are claimed as trademarks. Where those designations appear in this book, and O'Reilly Media, Inc. was aware of a trademark claim, the designations have been printed in caps or initial caps.

If every product name were coded as a productname, you could automatically generate a complete list of all the product names and mention them explicitly in the notice.

In running prose, the distinction between an application and a productname may be very subjective.

Processing expectations

Formatted inline.

Two of the values of the class attribute on productname, Trade and Registered, make assertions about trademarks. DocBook also has a trademark element; presumably the same markup is intended regardless of which one is used.

The service and copyright values should also generate the anticipated marks, if appropriate.

Attributes

Common attributes and common linking attributes.

class

Specifies the class of product name

Enumerated values:	
"copyright"	A name with a copyright
"registered"	A name with a registered copyright
"service"	A name of a service

Enumerated values:	
"trade"	A name which is trademarked

See Also
application, copyright, database, filename, hardware, trademark

Examples

```
<article xmlns='http://docbook.org/ns/docbook'>
<title>Example productname</title>

<para><productname class='registered'>Frobozz</productname>: it's not
just for breakfast anymore.
</para>

</article>
```

Frobozz®: it's not just for breakfast anymore.

```
<article xmlns='http://docbook.org/ns/docbook'>
<title>Example productname</title>

<para><trademark>Frobozz</trademark>: it's not
just for breakfast anymore.
</para>

</article>
```

Frobozz™: it's not just for breakfast anymore.

productnumber
A number assigned to a product

Synopsis
productnumber ::= (text | phrase $^{db.\_phrase}$ | replaceable | *Graphic inlines* | *Indexing inlines* | *Linking inlines* | *Ubiquitous inlines*)*

Attribute synopsis
Common attributes and common linking attributes.

Description
A productnumber identifies a "product number" in some unspecified numbering scheme. It's possible that product numbers for different products might not even come from the same scheme.

Processing expectations
Formatted inline. Sometimes suppressed.

DocBook does not control, or specify, the numbering scheme used for products.

See Also
biblioid, issuenum, seriesvolnums, volumenum

Examples

```
<article xmlns='http://docbook.org/ns/docbook'
         xmlns:xlink='http://www.w3.org/1999/xlink'>
<title>Example productnumber</title>

<para>You can order <citetitle>DocBook: The Definitive Guide</citetitle>
  directly from O'Reilly Media. Order product number
  <productnumber>978-0-596-80502-9</productnumber> by phone or
  <link xlink:href="http://www.oreilly.com/">on the Web</link>.
</para>

</article>
```

> You can order *DocBook: The Definitive Guide* directly from O'Reilly Media. Order product number 978-0-596-80502-9 by phone or on the Web (*http://www.oreilly.com/*).

---

programlisting

A literal listing of all or part of a program

Synopsis

programlisting ::= (info? ^{db.titleforbidden.info}, ((text | lineannotation | *Bibliography inlines* | *Computer-output inlines* | *Error inlines* | *Graphic inlines* | *GUI inlines* | *Indexing inlines* | *Keyboard inlines* | *Linking inlines* | *Markup inlines* | *Math inlines* | *Object-oriented programming inlines* | *Operating system inlines* | *Product inlines* | *Programming inlines* | *Publishing inlines* | *Technical inlines* | *Ubiquitous inlines* | *User-input inlines*)* | textobject))

Attribute synopsis

Common attributes and common linking attributes.

Additional attributes:

- continuation (enumeration) = "continues" | "restarts"
- linenumbering (enumeration) = "numbered" | "unnumbered"
- startinglinenumber (integer)
- language
- xml:space (enumeration) = "preserve"
- width (nonNegativeInteger)

Description

A programlisting is a verbatim environment for program source or source fragment listings. The programlistings are often placed in examples or figures so that they can be cross-referenced from the text.

Processing expectations

Formatted as a displayed block. This element is displayed "verbatim"; whitespace and line breaks within this element are significant. The programlistings are usually displayed in a fixed-width font.

Other markup within a `programlisting` is recognized. Contrast this with systems like LaTeX, in which verbatim environments disable markup recognition. If you want to disable markup recognition, you must use a *CDATA section*:

```
<programlisting>
<![CDATA[
This is a programlisting so white       space and line
breaks are significant.  But it is also a CDATA
section so <emphasis>tags</emphasis> and &entities;
are not recognized.  The only markup that is recognized
is the end-of-section marker, which is two
"]"'s in a row followed by a >.

]]>

</programlisting>
```

Two markup tags have special significance in `programlistings`: `co` and `lineannotation`. A `co` identifies the location of a `callout`. A `lineannotation` is a comment, added by the *documentor*—not the programmer.

Attributes

Common attributes and common linking attributes.

continuation

Determines whether line numbering continues from the previous element or restarts.

Enumerated values:	
"continues"	Line numbering continues from the immediately preceding element with the same name.
"restarts"	Line numbering restarts (begins at 1, usually).

language

Identifies the language (i.e., programming language) of the verbatim content.

linenumbering

Determines whether lines are numbered.

Enumerated values:	
"numbered"	Lines are numbered.
"unnumbered"	Lines are not numbered.

startinglinenumber

Specifies the initial line number.

width

Specifies the width (in characters) of the element.

xml:space

> Can be used to indicate explicitly that whitespace in the verbatim environment is preserved. Whitespace must always be preserved in verbatim environments whether this attribute is specified or not.

Enumerated values:	
"preserve"	Whitespace must be preserved.

See Also

`computeroutput`, `lineannotation`, `literallayout`, `screen`, `screenshot`, `synopsis`, `userinput`

---

programlistingco
A program listing with associated areas used in callouts

Synopsis
programlistingco ::= (info? ^{db.titleforbidden.info}, areaspec, programlisting, calloutlist*)

Attribute synopsis
Common attributes and common linking attributes.

Description
Callouts, such as numbered bullets, are an annotation mechanism. In an online system, these bullets are frequently "hot," and clicking on them sends you to the corresponding annotation.

A `programlistingco` is a wrapper around an `areaspec` and a `programlisting`. An `area spec` identifies the locations (coordinates) in the `programlisting` where the callouts occur. The `programlistingco` may also contain the list of annotations in a `callout list`, although the `calloutlist` may also occur outside the wrapper, elsewhere in the document.

It is also possible to embed `co` elements directly in the verbatim text, in order to avoid having to calculate the correct coordinates. If you decided to go this route, use a `programlisting` and a `calloutlist` without the `programlistingco` wrapper. A `programlistingco` must specify at least one coordinate.

For a complete description of callouts, see `callout`.

Processing expectations
Formatted as a displayed block. This element is displayed "verbatim"; whitespace and line breaks within this element are significant.

The mandatory processing expectations of a `programlistingco` are minimal: a system is expected to render the program listing and the callout list, if present.

If explicit `co` elements are embedded in a `programlisting`, they must generate appropriate callout marks.

In online environments, the processing system may be able to instantiate the linking relationships between the callout marks in the program listing and the annotations. Some systems may even be able to go a step further and generate the callout marks automatically from the coordinate information, but this level of sophistication is not mandatory.

See Also

areaspec, calloutlist, co, coref, imageobjectco, screenco

Examples

```
<article xmlns='http://docbook.org/ns/docbook'>
<title>Example programlistingco</title>

<programlistingco>
<areaspec>
<areaset xml:id="ex.plco.const">
  <area xml:id="ex.plco.c1" coords='4'/>
  <area xml:id="ex.plco.c2" coords='8'/>
</areaset>
<area xml:id="ex.plco.ret" coords='12'/>
<area xml:id="ex.plco.dest" coords='12'/>
</areaspec>
<programlisting>
sub do_nothing_useful {
    my($a, $b, $c);

    $a = new A;
    $a->does_nothing_either();
    $b = new B;
    $c = "frog";

    return ($a, $c);
}
</programlisting>
<calloutlist>
  <callout arearefs="ex.plco.const">
    <para>These are calls to the constructor
      <function>new</function> in the object classes.
    </para>
  </callout>
  <callout arearefs="ex.plco.ret">
    <para>This function returns a two-element list.
    </para>
  </callout>
  <callout arearefs="ex.plco.dest">
    <para>The <emphasis>destructor</emphasis>
      (<function>DESTROY</function>) for the object
      <literal>$b</literal> will be called automatically
      for this object since there can be no other references
      to it outside this function.
    </para>
  </callout>
</calloutlist>
```

```
</programlistingco>

</article>

sub do_nothing_useful {
    my($a, $b, $c);

    $a = new A;                              ❶

    $a->does_nothing_either();

    $b = new B;                              ❶

    $c = "frog";

    return ($a, $c);                         ❷❸
}
```

❶ These are calls to the constructor new in the object classes.

❷ This function returns a two-element list.

❸ The *destructor* (DESTROY) for the object $b will be called automatically for this object since there can be no other references to it outside this function.

---

prompt A character or string indicating the start of an input field in a computer display

Synopsis
prompt ::= (text | co | phrase db._phrase | replaceable | *Graphic inlines* | *Indexing inlines* | *Linking inlines* | *Ubiquitous inlines*)*

Attribute synopsis
Common attributes and common linking attributes.

Description
A prompt is a character or character string marking the beginning of an input field. The prompt element is generally used for command-line interfaces and not graphical user interfaces (GUIs). In GUIs, guilabel is usually more appropriate.

Processing expectations
Formatted inline.

See Also
computeroutput, constant, envar, filename, literal, markup, option, optional, parameter, replaceable, systemitem, tag, userinput, varname

Examples
```
<article xmlns='http://docbook.org/ns/docbook'>
<title>Example prompt</title>

<para>Enter your username when the system presents the
<prompt>login:</prompt> prompt.
```

```
    </para>

    </article>
```

Enter your username when the system presents the login: prompt.

---

property

Synopsis

property ::= (text | phrase ^{db._phrase} | replaceable | *Graphic inlines* | *Indexing inlines* | *Linking inlines* | *Ubiquitous inlines*)*

Attribute synopsis

Common attributes and common linking attributes.

Description

The notion of a **property** is very domain dependent in computer documentation. Some object-oriented systems speak of properties; the components from which GUIs are constructed have properties; and one can speak of properties in very general terms, as in "the properties of a relational database."

You might use **property** for any of these in your documentation.

Processing expectations

Formatted inline.

See Also

classname, symbol, token, type

Examples

```
    <article xmlns='http://docbook.org/ns/docbook'>
    <title>Example property</title>

    <para>When Emacs is running under X Windows, the <property>borderWidth</property>
    resource controls the width of the external border.
    </para>

    </article>
```

When Emacs is running under X Windows, the borderWidth resource controls the width of the external border.

---

pubdate

Synopsis

pubdate ::= (A date value. | A dateTime value. | A gYearMonth value. | A gYear value. | text)

Attribute synopsis

Common attributes and common linking attributes.

Description
The pubdate is the date of publication of a document.

Processing expectations
Formatted inline. Sometimes suppressed.

See Also
date, edition, printhistory, releaseinfo, revhistory

---

publisher

Synopsis
publisher ::= (publishername, address*)

Attribute synopsis
Common attributes and common linking attributes.

Description
A publisher associates a publishername and an address. Many publishers have offices in more than one city. A publisher can be used to list or distinguish between the multiple offices.

Processing expectations
May be formatted inline or as a displayed block, depending on context. Sometimes suppressed.

Examples
```
<article xmlns='http://docbook.org/ns/docbook'>
<info>
  <title>Example publisher</title>
  <publisher>
    <publishername>O'Reilly Media, Inc.</publishername>
    <address><street>101 ...</street>

    ...
    </address>
  </publisher>
</info>

<para>…</para>

</article>
```

---

publishername

Synopsis
publishername ::= (text | phrase ^{db._phrase} | replaceable | *Graphic inlines* | *Indexing inlines* | *Linking inlines* | *Ubiquitous inlines*)*

Attribute synopsis

Common attributes and common linking attributes.

Description

A publishername is the name of a publisher. Historically, this has been used in bibliographic meta-information to identify the publisher of a book or other document. It is also reasonable to identify the publisher of an electronic publication in this way.

Processing expectations

May be formatted inline or as a displayed block, depending on context. Sometimes suppressed.

See Also

orgname

---

qandadiv

A titled division in a qandaset

Synopsis

qandadiv ::= (((((title? & titleabbrev?), info? db.titleforbidden.info) | info db.titleonly.info), (annotation | bridgehead | remark | revhistory | *Indexing inlines* | *Admonition elements* | *Formal elements* | *Graphic elements* | *Informal elements* | *List elements* | *Paragraph elements* | *Publishing elements* | *Synopsis elements* | *Technical elements* | *Verbatim elements*)*, (qandadiv+ | qandaentry+))

Attribute synopsis

Common attributes and common linking attributes.

Description

A qandadiv is a section of a qandaset. A question-and-answer set might be divided into sections in order to group different sets of questions together, perhaps by topic.

A qandaset may contain any number of qandadiv or qandaentry elements, but it cannot contain a mixture of both at the same level.

Processing expectations

Formatted as a displayed block.

A table of contents for the question-and-answer set is sometimes generated, especially in online environments.

See Also

answer, qandaentry, qandaset, question

---

qandaentry

A question/answer set within a qandaset

Synopsis

qandaentry ::= (((((title? & titleabbrev?), info? db.titleforbidden.info) | info db.titleonly.info), question, answer*)

Attribute synopsis

Common attributes and common linking attributes.

Description

A qandaentry is an entry in a qandaset. Each qandaentry defines a question and (possibly) its answer or answers.

Processing expectations

Formatted as a displayed block. The questions are usually presented before the answers, and often the answers are indented to make the questions stand out.

See Also

answer, qandadiv, qandaset, question

---

qandaset

A question-and-answer set

Synopsis

qandaset ::= ((((title? & titleabbrev?), info? $^{\text{db.titleforbidden.info}}$) | info $^{\text{db.titleonly.info}}$), (annotation | bridgehead | remark | revhistory | *Indexing inlines* | *Admonition elements* | *Formal elements* | *Graphic elements* | *Informal elements* | *List elements* | *Paragraph elements* | *Publishing elements* | *Synopsis elements* | *Technical elements* | *Verbatim elements*)*, (qandadiv+ | qandaentry+))

Attribute synopsis

Common attributes and common linking attributes.

Additional attributes:

- defaultlabel (enumeration) = "none" | "number" | "qanda"

Description

A qandaset is a list consisting of questions and answers. A qandaset can be divided into sections.

Every entry in a qandaset must contain a question, but answers are optional (some questions have no answers), and may be repeated (some questions have more than one answer).

Common uses for qandasets include reader questionnaires and lists of Frequently Asked Questions (FAQs). For the purpose of a FAQ, DocBook V3.1 added the FAQ class to article.

Processing expectations

Formatted as a displayed block. The defaultlabel attribute has a significant influence on the presentation of questions and answers.

Attributes

Common attributes and common linking attributes.

defaultlabel
> Specifies the default labeling

Enumerated values:	
"none"	No labels
"number"	Numeric labels
"qanda"	"Q:" and "A:" labels

See Also
answer, qandadiv, qandaentry, question

Examples

```
<article xmlns='http://docbook.org/ns/docbook'>
<title>Example qandaset</title>

<qandaset defaultlabel='qanda'>
  <qandaentry>
    <question>
      <para>To be, or not to be?</para>
    </question>
    <answer>
      <para>That is the question.</para>
    </answer>
  </qandaentry>
</qandaset>

</article>

<article xmlns='http://docbook.org/ns/docbook'
    class="faq">
<title>Frequently Asked Questions About Fonts</title>

<qandaset>
  <qandadiv><title>General Information</title>

  <para>...</para>

  <qandadiv><title>Font Houses</title>

  <qandaentry><question><para>Who sells lots of fonts?</para></question>
  <answer><label>Seller</label><para>Adobe Systems, Inc.</para></answer>
  </qandaentry>

  <qandaentry><question><para>Who sells fonts and photos?</para></question>
  <answer><label>Seller</label><para>Veer</para></answer>
  </qandaentry>

  </qandadiv>
  </qandadiv>
</qandaset>
</article>
```

question

Synopsis

question ::= (label?, (annotation | bridgehead | remark | revhistory | *Indexing inlines* | *Admonition elements* | *Formal elements* | *Graphic elements* | *Informal elements* | *List elements* | *Paragraph elements* | *Publishing elements* | *Synopsis elements* | *Technical elements* | *Verbatim elements*)+)

Attribute synopsis

Common attributes and common linking attributes.

Description

A question in a qandaentry poses a question or states a problem that is addressed by the following answer(s). The answers are optional (some questions have no answers) and may be repeated (some questions have more than one answer).

Processing expectations

The questions are frequently introduced with a label, such as "A:". If a question has a label child element, the content of that label is used as the label for the question. The defaultlabel attribute on the nearest ancestor qandaset of a question can be used to indicate that a processing application should automatically generate a label for the question.

See Also

answer, qandadiv, qandaentry, qandaset

quote

Synopsis

quote ::= (text | *Bibliography inlines* | *Error inlines* | *Graphic inlines* | *GUI inlines* | *Indexing inlines* | *Keyboard inlines* | *Linking inlines* | *Markup inlines* | *Math inlines* | *Object-oriented programming inlines* | *Operating system inlines* | *Product inlines* | *Programming inlines* | *Publishing inlines* | *Technical inlines* | *Ubiquitous inlines*)*

Attribute synopsis

Common attributes and common linking attributes.

Description

A quote surrounds an inline quotation. Using an element for quotations is sometimes more convenient than entering the quotation marks directly, and makes it possible for a presentation system to alter the format of the quotation marks.

Block quotations are properly identified as blockquotes.

Processing expectations

Formatted inline. The quote element is expected to generate the proper quotation marks. These may be influenced by the lang attribute on an ancestor element. For example, a quote in French might use «guillemets» instead of English "quote marks."

See Also

abbrev, acronym, emphasis, foreignphrase, phrase, wordasword

Examples

```
<article xmlns='http://docbook.org/ns/docbook'>
<title>Example quote</title>

<para>This software is provided <quote>as is</quote>, without expressed
or implied warranty.
</para>

</article>
```

> This software is provided "as is", without expressed or implied warranty.

---

refclass
The scope or other indication of applicability of a reference entry

Synopsis

refclass ::= (text | application)*

Attribute synopsis

Common attributes and common linking attributes.

Description

The refclass element describes the applicability or scope of a refentry. A refclass might indicate that the entry was only applicable to a particular application, for example, or only to a particular vendor's operating system.

Processing expectations

May be formatted inline or as a displayed block, depending on context. Sometimes suppressed.

Formatting reference pages may require a fairly sophisticated processing system. Much of the meta-information about a reference page (its name, type, purpose, title, and classification) is stored in wrappers near the beginning of the refentry.

Common presentational features, such as titles and running heads, may require data from several of these wrappers plus some generated text. Other formatting often requires that these elements be reordered.

Examples

See refentry for an example using this element.

refdescriptor

A description of the topic of a reference page

Synopsis

refdescriptor ::= (text | *Bibliography inlines* | *Error inlines* | *Graphic inlines* | *GUI inlines* | *Indexing inlines* | *Keyboard inlines* | *Linking inlines* | *Markup inlines* | *Math inlines* | *Object-oriented programming inlines* | *Operating system inlines* | *Product inlines* | *Programming inlines* | *Publishing inlines* | *Technical inlines* | *Ubiquitous inlines*)*

Attribute synopsis

Common attributes and common linking attributes.

Description

Reference pages (`refentry`s) are usually identified by a short, succinct topic name, such as the name of a function or command. The `refname` (or one of the `refname`s, in the case of a reference page that has several) is generally used as the topic name. When none of the `refname`s is appropriate, `refdescriptor` is used to specify the topic name.

A `refdescriptor` is unnecessary when an appropriate `refname` can be selected automatically. At least one `refname` is required, so `refdescriptor` cannot be used in place of a name, only in addition to it.

Processing expectations

May be formatted inline or as a displayed block, depending on context.

Formatting reference pages may require a fairly sophisticated processing system. Much of the meta-information about a reference page (its name, type, purpose, title, and classification) is stored in wrappers near the beginning of the `refentry`.

Common presentational features, such as titles and running heads, may require data from several of these wrappers plus some generated text. Other formatting often requires that these elements be reordered.

If a `refdescriptor` is present, it should be used for the short topic name. This name usually appears in the running header along with the `manvolnum` in print media. It may also appear in tables of contents and the index.

See Also

`refentrytitle`, `refname`

Examples

See `reference` for an example using this element.

refentry

A reference page (originally a UNIX man-style reference page)

Synopsis

refentry ::= (*Indexing inlines**, info? db.titleforbidden.info, refmeta?, refnamediv+, refsynopsisdiv?, (refsection+ | refsect1+))

Attribute synopsis

Common attributes and common linking attributes.

Additional attributes:

- `label`
- `status`

Additional constraints

- If this element is the root element, it must have a `version` attribute.

Description

A `refentry` is a reference page. In UNIX parlance this has historically been called a "man page" (short for manual page).

A `refentry` is an appropriate wrapper for any small unit of reference documentation describing a single topic. Canonical examples are programming language functions and user commands (one `refentry` per function or command).‡

On some projects, the structure of reference pages may be rigorously defined right down to the number, order, and title of individual sections (some or all of which may be required).

Processing expectations

Formatted as a displayed block. It is not uncommon for `refentry`s to introduce a forced page break in print media.

Formatting reference pages may require a fairly sophisticated processing system. Much of the meta-information about a reference page (its name, type, purpose, title, and classification) is stored in wrappers near the beginning of the `refentry`.

Common presentational features, such as titles and running heads, may require data from several of these wrappers plus some generated text. Other formatting often requires that these elements be reordered.

Attributes

Common attributes and common linking attributes.

label
> Specifies an identifying string for presentation purposes

status
> Identifies the editorial or publication status of the element on which it occurs

Examples

```
<article xmlns='http://docbook.org/ns/docbook'>
<title>Example refentry</title>
```

---

‡ You're reading a `refentry` right now.

```
<refentry xml:id="ls">

  <refmeta>
    <refentrytitle>ls</refentrytitle>
    <manvolnum>1</manvolnum>
  </refmeta>

  <refnamediv>
    <refname>ls</refname>
    <refpurpose>list contents of a directory</refpurpose>
    <refclass>UNIX/Linux</refclass>
  </refnamediv>

  <refsynopsisdiv>
    <cmdsynopsis>
      <command>/usr/bin/ls</command>
      <arg choice="opt">
        <option>aAbcCdfFgilLmnopqrRstux1</option>
      </arg>
      <arg choice="opt" rep="repeat">file</arg>
    </cmdsynopsis>
  </refsynopsisdiv>

  <refsect1><title>Description</title>
  <para>For each file that is a directory, <command>ls</command>
  lists the contents of the directory; for each file that is an
  ordinary file, <command>ls</command> repeats its name and any
  other information requested.
  </para>
  <para>…</para>
  </refsect1>
</refentry>

</article>

<article xmlns='http://docbook.org/ns/docbook'>
<title>Example refentry</title>

<refentry xml:id="printf">

  <refmeta>
    <refentrytitle>printf</refentrytitle>
    <manvolnum>3S</manvolnum>
  </refmeta>

  <refnamediv>
    <refname>printf</refname>
    <refname>fprintf</refname>
    <refname>sprintf</refname>
    <refpurpose>print formatted output</refpurpose>
  </refnamediv>

  <refsynopsisdiv>

    <funcsynopsis>
      <funcsynopsisinfo>
```

```
        #include &lt;stdio.h&gt;
      </funcsynopsisinfo>
      <funcprototype>
        <funcdef>int <function>printf</function></funcdef>
        <paramdef>const char *<parameter>format</parameter></paramdef>
        <paramdef>...</paramdef>
      </funcprototype>

      <funcprototype>
        <funcdef>int <function>fprintf</function></funcdef>
        <paramdef>FILE *<parameter>strm</parameter></paramdef>
        <paramdef>const char *<parameter>format</parameter></paramdef>
        <paramdef>...</paramdef>
      </funcprototype>

      <funcprototype>
        <funcdef>int <function>sprintf</function></funcdef>
        <paramdef>char *<parameter>s</parameter></paramdef>
        <paramdef>const char *<parameter>format</parameter></paramdef>
        <paramdef>...</paramdef>
      </funcprototype>
    </funcsynopsis>

  </refsynopsisdiv>

  <refsect1><title>Description</title>
  <para><function>printf</function> places output on the standard
  output stream stdout.
  </para>
  <para>…</para>
  </refsect1>
</refentry>

</article>

<article xmlns='http://docbook.org/ns/docbook'>
<title>Example refentry</title>

<refentry xml:id="iovec">

  <refmeta>
    <refentrytitle>iovec</refentrytitle>
    <manvolnum>9S</manvolnum>
  </refmeta>

  <refnamediv>
    <refname>iovec</refname>
    <refpurpose>data storage structure for I/O using uio</refpurpose>
  </refnamediv>

  <refsynopsisdiv>
    <synopsis>
      #include &lt;sys/uio.h&gt;
    </synopsis>
  </refsynopsisdiv>
```

```
<refsect1><title>Interface Level</title>
<para>Architecture independent level 1 (DDI/DKI).
</para>
</refsect1>

<refsect1><title>Description</title>

<para>
  An <code>iovec</code> structure describes a data
  storage area for transfer in a
  <citerefentry><refentrytitle>uio</refentrytitle>
    <manvolnum>9S</manvolnum>
  </citerefentry>
  structure. Conceptually, it may be thought of as
  a base address and length specification.
</para>

</refsect1>
<refsect1><title>Structure Members</title>

<programlisting>
    caddr_t  iov_base;  /* base address of the data storage area */
                        /* represented by the iovec structure */
    int      iov_len;   /* size of the data storage area in bytes */
</programlisting>

<para>…</para>
</refsect1>
</refentry>

</article>
```

refentrytitle

The title of a reference page

Synopsis

refentrytitle ::= (text | *Bibliography inlines* | *Error inlines* | *Graphic inlines* | *GUI inlines* | *Index-ing inlines* | *Keyboard inlines* | *Linking inlines* | *Markup inlines* | *Math inlines* | *Object-oriented pro-gramming inlines* | *Operating system inlines* | *Product inlines* | *Programming inlines* | *Publishing in-lines* | *Technical inlines* | *Ubiquitous inlines*)*

Attribute synopsis

Common attributes and common linking attributes.

Description

A refentrytitle is the title of a reference page. It is frequently the same as the first refname or the refdescriptor, although it may also be a longer, more general title.

Processing expectations

Formatted as a displayed block.

Formatting reference pages may require a fairly sophisticated processing system. Much of the meta-information about a reference page (its name, type, purpose, title, and classification) is stored in wrappers near the beginning of the `refentry`.

Common presentational features, such as titles and running heads, may require data from several of these wrappers plus some generated text. Other formatting often requires that these elements be reordered.

See Also
`refdescriptor`, `refname`

Examples

See `refentry` for examples that use this element.

---

reference
A collection of reference entries

Synopsis
reference ::= ((((title & titleabbrev? & subtitle?), info? ^{db.titleforbidden.info}) | info ^{db.titlereq.info}), partintro?, refentry+)

Attribute synopsis
Common attributes and common linking attributes.

Additional attributes:

- `label`

- `status`

Additional constraints

- If this element is the root element, it must have a `version` attribute.

Description
A `reference` is a collection of `refentry`s. In a `book`, a `reference` can occur at either the part or the chapter level.

Reference pages are usually bound together by topic; in traditional UNIX documentation they are most frequently bound into volumes. See `manvolnum`.

Processing expectations
Formatted as a displayed block. A `reference` often introduces a forced page break and may start on the next recto page. Frequently, it also produces a separator page, on which may be printed the content of the `partintro`.

Attributes
Common attributes and common linking attributes.

label
> Specifies an identifying string for presentation purposes

status

Identifies the editorial or publication status of the element on which it occurs

Examples

```
<reference xmlns='http://docbook.org/ns/docbook'>
  <title>Reference Pages</title>

  <refentry>
    <refnamediv>
      <refdescriptor>GNU as</refdescriptor>
      <refname>as</refname>
      <refpurpose>the portable GNU assembler</refpurpose>
    </refnamediv>
    <refsynopsisdiv><title>SYNOPSIS</title>
    <synopsis>...</synopsis>
    </refsynopsisdiv>
    <refsect1><title>DESCRIPTION</title>
    <para>...</para>
    </refsect1>
  </refentry>

  <refentry>
    <refnamediv>
      <refname>awk</refname>
      <refpurpose>pattern scanning and text processing language</refpurpose>
    </refnamediv>
    <refsynopsisdiv><title>SYNOPSIS</title>
    <synopsis>...</synopsis>
    </refsynopsisdiv>
    <refsect1><title>DESCRIPTION</title>
    <para>...</para>
    </refsect1>
  </refentry>

  <!-- ... -->

</reference>
```

refmeta

Meta-information for a reference entry

Synopsis

refmeta ::= (*Indexing inlines**, refentrytitle, manvolnum?, refmiscinfo**, *Indexing inlines**)

Attribute synopsis

Common attributes and common linking attributes.

Description

A refmeta holds the title of the reference page, the number of the volume in which this reference page occurs, and possibly other miscellaneous information (typically used in printing the reference page).

Processing expectations

Suppressed. Most of the elements contained in `refmeta` are used in presentation, but they are not generally printed as part of the formatting of the `refmeta` wrapper—it merely serves to identify where they occur.

Examples

See `refentry` for examples that use this element.

refmiscinfo

Meta-information for a reference entry other than the title and volume number

Synopsis

refmiscinfo ::= (text | phrase ^{db._phrase} | replaceable | *Graphic inlines* | *Indexing inlines* | *Linking inlines* | *Ubiquitous inlines*)*

Attribute synopsis

Common attributes and common linking attributes.

Additional attributes:

- *At most one of:*
  — class (enumeration) = "source" | "version" | "manual" | "sectdesc" | "software"
  — *All or none of:*
    — class (enumeration) = "other"
    — otherclass

Description

The `refmiscinfo` element is an escape hatch for additional meta-information about a reference page. It may hold copyright information, release or revision information, descriptive text for use in a print header or footer, or any other information not explicitly provided for in `refmeta`.

Processing expectations

May be formatted inline or as a displayed block, depending on context.

Attributes

Common attributes and common linking attributes.

class

> Identifies the kind of miscellaneous information

Enumerated values:	
"source"	The name of the software product or component to which this topic applies
"version"	The version of the software product or component to which this topic applies
"manual"	The section title of the reference page (e.g., User Commands)

Enumerated values:	
"sectdesc"	The section title of the reference page (believed synonymous with "manual" but in wide use)
"software"	The name of the software product or component to which this topic applies (e.g., SunOS x.y; believed synonymous with "source" but in wide use)

class
Identifies the kind of miscellaneous information

Enumerated values:	
"other"	Indicates that the information is some "other" kind

otherclass
Identifies the nature of nonstandard miscellaneous information

refname
The name of (one of) the subject(s) of a reference page

Synopsis
refname ::= (text | *Bibliography inlines* | *Error inlines* | *Graphic inlines* | *GUI inlines* | *Indexing inlines* | *Keyboard inlines* | *Linking inlines* | *Markup inlines* | *Math inlines* | *Object-oriented programming inlines* | *Operating system inlines* | *Product inlines* | *Programming inlines* | *Publishing inlines* | *Technical inlines* | *Ubiquitous inlines*)*

Attribute synopsis
Common attributes and common linking attributes.

Description
A `refentry` is a small unit of reference documentation describing a single topic. The `refname` identifies the topic. Often this is the name of the command or function that the reference page describes.

Some reference pages describe a whole family of very closely related commands or functions. In this case, a `refentry` will have multiple `refnames`, one for each command or function. When a `refentry` has several `refnames`, it is likely to have a `refdescriptor` that identifies the whole family of functions.

Processing expectations
May be formatted inline or as a displayed block, depending on context.

Formatting reference pages may require a fairly sophisticated processing system. Much of the meta-information about a reference page (its name, type, purpose, title, and classification) is stored in wrappers near the beginning of the `refentry`.

Common presentational features, such as titles and running headers, may require data from several of these wrappers plus some generated text. Other formatting often requires that these elements be reordered.

See Also

refdescriptor, refentrytitle

Examples

See reference and refentry for examples that use this element.

---

refnamediv

Synopsis

refnamediv ::= (refdescriptor?, refname+, refpurpose, refclass*)

Attribute synopsis

Common attributes and common linking attributes.

Description

A refnamediv is the first mandatory section in a refentry. It is a peer to refsynopsis div and refsect1.

The elements in refnamediv identify the topic of the reference page (refdescriptor or refname), provide a concise summary (refpurpose), and classify the page (refclass).

Processing expectations

Formatted as a displayed block. A refnamediv usually generates a section heading, in the same typographic style as a refsect1 title, called "Name."

The content of this section is traditionally the refdescriptor or refname, and the refpurpose, separated by an em dash.

The refclass may be presented, or it may be suppressed and used only to select a group of reference pages to process. You might use the value of refclass to print all the reference pages appropriate to Solaris UNIX, for example.

Formatting reference pages may require a fairly sophisticated processing system. Much of the meta-information about a reference page (its name, type, purpose, title, and classification) is stored in wrappers near the beginning of the refentry.

Common presentational features, such as titles and running headers, may require data from several of these wrappers plus some generated text. Other formatting often requires that these elements be reordered.

See Also

refsect1, refsect2, refsect3, refsection, refsynopsisdiv

Examples

See reference and refentry for examples that use this element.

refpurpose

Synopsis

refpurpose ::= (text | *Bibliography inlines* | *Error inlines* | *Graphic inlines* | *GUI inlines* | *Indexing inlines* | *Keyboard inlines* | *Linking inlines* | *Markup inlines* | *Math inlines* | *Object-oriented programming inlines* | *Operating system inlines* | *Product inlines* | *Programming inlines* | *Publishing inlines* | *Technical inlines* | *Ubiquitous inlines*)*

Attribute synopsis

Common attributes and common linking attributes.

Description

The `refpurpose` is a concise summary of the topic of the reference page. A `refpurpose` is usually limited to a single, short sentence.

Processing expectations

Formatted inline. See `refnamediv`.

In a large **reference**, **refnames** and **refpurpose**s are sometimes used to construct a permuted index. A permuted index is a keyword-in-context concordance of lines, like the short definitions in this element reference; the keyword cycles alphabetically through the words of the (definition) lines.

Formatting reference pages may require a fairly sophisticated processing system. Much of the meta-information about a reference page (its name, type, purpose, title, and classification) is stored in wrappers near the beginning of the `refentry`.

Common presentational features, such as titles and running headers, may require data from several of these wrappers plus some generated text. Other formatting often requires that these elements be reordered.

Examples

See `reference` and `refentry` for examples that use this element.

---

refsect1

Synopsis

refsect1 ::= ((((title & titleabbrev? & subtitle?), info? ^{db.titleforbidden.info}) | info ^{db.titlereq.info}),
(((annotation | bridgehead | remark | revhistory | *Indexing inlines* | *Admonition elements* | *Formal elements* | *Graphic elements* | *Informal elements* | *List elements* | *Paragraph elements* | *Publishing elements* | *Synopsis elements* | *Technical elements* | *Verbatim elements*)+, refsect2*) | refsect2+))

Attribute synopsis

Common attributes and common linking attributes.

Additional attributes:

- `label`
- `status`

Additional constraints

- If this element is the root element, it must have a `version` attribute.

Description

Reference pages have their own hierarchical structure. A `refsect1` is a major division in a `refentry`, analogous to a `sect1` elsewhere in the document.

The value of a separate hierarchical structure is that it allows the content model of sections in reference pages to be customized differently than the content model of sections outside. For example, because of this split, it was easy to add a recursive sectioning element (`section`) as a peer to `sect1` in DocBook V3.1 without introducing it to `refentrys`, in which it would not be desirable.

Processing expectations

Formatted as a displayed block.

In some environments, the name, number, and order of major divisions in a reference page are strictly defined by house style. For example, one style requires that the first major section after the synopsis be the "Description," which it must have as its title.

In those cases, it may be useful to replace `refsect1` in the content model with a set of named sections (following the pattern of `refnamediv` and `refsynopsisdiv`).

Formatting reference pages may require a fairly sophisticated processing system. Much of the meta-information about a reference page (its name, type, purpose, title, and classification) is stored in wrappers near the beginning of the `refentry`.

Common presentational features, such as titles and running headers, may require data from several of these wrappers plus some generated text. Other formatting often requires that these elements be reordered.

Attributes

Common attributes and common linking attributes.

label
> Specifies an identifying string for presentation purposes

status
> Identifies the editorial or publication status of the element on which it occurs

See Also

`refnamediv`, `refsect2`, `refsect3`, `refsection`, `refsynopsisdiv`

refsect2

Synopsis
refsect2 ::= (((((title & titleabbrev? & subtitle?), info? $^{db.titleforbidden.info}$) | info $^{db.titlereq.info}$), (((annotation | bridgehead | remark | revhistory | *Indexing inlines* | *Admonition elements* | *Formal elements* | *Graphic elements* | *Informal elements* | *List elements* | *Paragraph elements* | *Publishing elements* | *Synopsis elements* | *Technical elements* | *Verbatim elements*)+, refsect3*) | refsect3+))

Attribute synopsis
Common attributes and common linking attributes.

Additional attributes:

- label
- status

Additional constraints

- If this element is the root element, it must have a **version** attribute.

Description
A refsect2 is a second-level section in a refentry, analogous to a sect2 elsewhere in the document. See refsect1.

Processing expectations
Formatted as a displayed block.

Attributes
Common attributes and common linking attributes.

label
   Specifies an identifying string for presentation purposes

status
   Identifies the editorial or publication status of the element on which it occurs

See Also
refnamediv, refsect1, refsect3, refsection, refsynopsisdiv

---

refsect3

Synopsis
refsect3 ::= (((((title & titleabbrev? & subtitle?), info? $^{db.titleforbidden.info}$) | info $^{db.titlereq.info}$), (annotation | bridgehead | remark | revhistory | *Indexing inlines* | *Admonition elements* | *Formal elements* | *Graphic elements* | *Informal elements* | *List elements* | *Paragraph elements* | *Publishing elements* | *Synopsis elements* | *Technical elements* | *Verbatim elements*)+))

Attribute synopsis
Common attributes and common linking attributes.

Additional attributes:

- `label`
- `status`

Additional constraints

- If this element is the root element, it must have a `version` attribute.

Description

A `refsect3` is a third-level section in a `refentry`, analogous to a `sect3` elsewhere in the document. See `refsect1`.

In DocBook, `refsect3` is the lowest-level section allowed in a `refentry`. There is no element analogous to a `sect4`.

Processing expectations
Formatted as a displayed block.

Attributes
Common attributes and common linking attributes.

label
> Specifies an identifying string for presentation purposes

status
> Identifies the editorial or publication status of the element on which it occurs

See Also

`refnamediv`, `refsect1`, `refsect2`, `refsection`, `refsynopsisdiv`

---

refsection

A recursive section in a refentry

Synopsis
refsection ::= ((((title & titleabbrev? & subtitle?), info? [db.titleforbidden.info]) | `info` [db.titlereq.info]), (((annotation | bridgehead | remark | revhistory | *Indexing inlines* | *Admonition elements* | *Formal elements* | *Graphic elements* | *Informal elements* | *List elements* | *Paragraph elements* | *Publishing elements* | *Synopsis elements* | *Technical elements* | *Verbatim elements*)+, refsection*) | `refsection+`))

Attribute synopsis
Common attributes and common linking attributes.

Additional attributes:

- `label`
- `status`

Additional constraints

- If this element is the root element, it must have a `version` attribute.

Description

Reference pages have their own hierarchical structure. A `refsection` is a recursive division in a `refentry`, analogous to a `section` elsewhere in the document.

The value of a separate hierarchical structure is that it allows the content model of sections in reference pages to be customized differently than the content model of sections outside.

Processing expectations
Formatted as a displayed block.

Attributes
Common attributes and common linking attributes.

label
> Specifies an identifying string for presentation purposes

status
> Identifies the editorial or publication status of the element on which it occurs

See Also
refnamediv, refsect1, refsect2, refsect3, refsynopsisdiv

---

refsynopsisdiv   A syntactic synopsis of the subject of the reference page

Synopsis
refsynopsisdiv ::= ((((title? & titleabbrev? & subtitle?), info? ^{db.titleforbidden.info}) | info? ^{db.info}), (((annotation | bridgehead | remark | revhistory | *Indexing inlines* | *Admonition elements* | *Formal elements* | *Graphic elements* | *Informal elements* | *List elements* | *Paragraph elements* | *Publishing elements* | *Synopsis elements* | *Technical elements* | *Verbatim elements*)+, (refsection+ | refsect2+)?) | refsection+ | refsect2+))

Attribute synopsis
Common attributes and common linking attributes.

Description
A `refsynopsisdiv` contains a syntactic synopsis of the function or command described by the `refentry`. When `refentrys` are used to describe other sorts of things, `refsynopsisdiv` should be used for whatever succinct, synopsis information seems appropriate.[§]

Processing expectations
Formatted as a displayed block. A `refsynopsisdiv` usually generates a section heading, in the same typographic style as a `refsect1 title`, called "Synopsis."

[§] In this book, each element of the schema is described on a reference page, and the `refsynopsisdiv` is used for the synopsis at the beginning of each entry.

Formatting reference pages may require a fairly sophisticated processing system. Much of the meta-information about a reference page (its name, type, purpose, title, and classification) is stored in wrappers near the beginning of the `refentry`.

Common presentational features, such as titles and running headers, may require data from several of these wrappers plus some generated text. Other formatting often requires that these elements be reordered.

See Also

arg, cmdsynopsis, group, refnamediv, refsect1, refsect2, refsect3, refsection, sbr, synopfragment, synopfragmentref

Examples

See `refentry` for an example using this element.

---

releaseinfo
Information about a particular release of a document

Synopsis

releaseinfo ::= (text | phrase ^{db._phrase} | replaceable | *Graphic inlines* | *Indexing inlines* | *Linking inlines* | *Ubiquitous inlines*)*

Attribute synopsis

Common attributes and common linking attributes.

Description

The `releaseinfo` element contains a brief description of the release or published version of a document or part of a document.

For example, the release information may state that the document is in beta, or that the software it describes is a beta version. It may also contain more specific information, such as the version number from a revision control system.

Processing expectations

May be formatted inline or as a displayed block, depending on context. Sometimes suppressed.

See Also

date, edition, printhistory, pubdate, revhistory

---

remark
A remark (or comment) intended for presentation in a draft manuscript

Synopsis

remark ::= (text | phrase ^{db._phrase} | replaceable | *Graphic inlines* | *Indexing inlines* | *Linking inlines* | *Ubiquitous inlines*)*

Attribute synopsis

Common attributes and common linking attributes.

Description

The `remark` element is designed to hold remarks—for example, editorial comments—that are useful while the document is in the draft stage, but are not intended for final publication.

Remarks are available almost anywhere and have a particularly broad content model. Your processing system may or may not support either the use of comments everywhere they are allowed or the full generality of the `remark` content model.

Prior to version 4.0 of DocBook, this element was named `comment`.

Processing expectations

May be formatted inline or as a displayed block, depending on context. Remarks are often printed only in draft versions of a document and suppressed otherwise. This may be controlled by the `status` attribute of an ancestor element (e.g., `chapter`), or by external processes, such as selecting an alternate stylesheet when publishing.

Examples

```
<article xmlns='http://docbook.org/ns/docbook'>
<title>Example remark</title>

<example xml:id="gut-qed">
<title>The Grand Unified Theory</title>

<para><remark>Some details are still a bit shaky</remark>
...
Q.E.D.
</para>
</example>

</article>
```

Example 27. The Grand Unified Theory

... Q.E.D.

replaceable

Content that may or must be replaced by the user

Synopsis

replaceable ::= (text | co | phrase ^{db._phrase} | replaceable | *Graphic inlines* | *Indexing inlines* | *Linking inlines* | *Ubiquitous inlines*)*

Attribute synopsis

Common attributes and common linking attributes.

Additional attributes:

- `class` (enumeration) = "command" | "function" | "option" | "parameter"

Description

A `replaceable` is used to mark text that describes *what* a user is supposed to enter, but not the *actual text* that the user is supposed to enter.

It is used to identify a class of object in the document, in which the user is expected to replace the text that identifies the class with some specific instance of that class. A canonical example is:

```
<replaceable>filename</replaceable>
```

in which the user is expected to provide the name of some specific file to replace the text "filename."

Processing expectations

Formatted inline. Usually, the text is given special typographic treatment, such as italics, as a clue to the user that this is replaceable text. Often the font used is described in a "conventions" section at the beginning of the document.

Attributes

Common attributes and common linking attributes.

class

> Identifies the nature of the replaceable text

Enumerated values:	
"command"	A command
"function"	A function
"option"	An option
"parameter"	A parameter

See Also

`command`, `computeroutput`, `constant`, `literal`, `markup`, `option`, `optional`, `parameter`, `prompt`, `tag`, `userinput`, `varname`

---

returnvalue

The value returned by a function

Synopsis

returnvalue ::= (text | phrase ^{db._phrase} | replaceable | *Graphic inlines* | *Indexing inlines* | *Linking inlines* | *Ubiquitous inlines*)*

Attribute synopsis

Common attributes and common linking attributes.

Description

A `returnvalue` identifies the value returned by a function or command.

Processing expectations
Formatted inline.

See Also
funcdef, funcparams, funcprototype, funcsynopsisinfo, function, paramdef, parameter, varargs, void

Examples

```
<article xmlns='http://docbook.org/ns/docbook'>
<title>Example returnvalue</title>

<para>The <function>open</function> function returns <returnvalue>2</returnvalue>
(<errorname>ENOFILE</errorname>) if the file does not exist.
</para>

</article>
```

The open function returns 2 (ENOFILE) if the file does not exist.

revdescription

An extended description of a revision to a document

Synopsis
revdescription ::= (annotation | bridgehead | remark | revhistory | *Indexing inlines* | *Admonition elements* | *Formal elements* | *Graphic elements* | *Informal elements* | *List elements* | *Paragraph elements* | *Publishing elements* | *Synopsis elements* | *Technical elements* | *Verbatim elements*)*

Attribute synopsis
Common attributes and common linking attributes.

Description
The revdescription associated with a revision is a summary of the changes made in that revision. A revdescription is intended for long, complete summaries. For a simple text-only summary, see revremark.

Processing expectations
May be formatted inline or as a displayed block, depending on context. Sometimes suppressed.

See Also
revhistory, revision, revnumber, revremark

revhistory

A history of the revisions to a document

Synopsis
revhistory ::= ((((title? & titleabbrev?), info? db.titleforbidden.info) | info db.titleonly.info), revision+)

Attribute synopsis
Common attributes and common linking attributes.

Description

A revhistory is a structure for documenting a history of changes, specifically, a history of changes to the document or section in which it occurs.

DocBook does not mandate an order for revisions: ascending order by date, descending order by date, and orders based on some other criteria are all equally acceptable.

Processing expectations

Formatted as a displayed block. A tabular or list presentation is most common.

The order of revisions within a revhistory (e.g., ascending or descending date order) is not mandated by DocBook.

See Also

date, edition, printhistory, pubdate, releaseinfo, revdescription, revision, revnumber, revremark

Examples

```
<article xmlns='http://docbook.org/ns/docbook'>
<title>Example revhistory</title>

<revhistory>

<revision>
  <revnumber>0.91</revnumber>
  <date>1996-12-11</date>
  <authorinitials>ndw</authorinitials>
  <revremark>Bug fixes</revremark>
</revision>

<revision>
  <revnumber>0.90</revnumber>
  <date>1996-11-30</date>
  <authorinitials>ndw</authorinitials>
  <revremark>First beta release</revremark>
</revision>

</revhistory>

</article>
```

revision

An entry describing a single revision in the history of the revisions to a document

Synopsis

revision ::= (revnumber?, date, (author | authorinitials)*, (revdescription | revremark)?)

Attribute synopsis

Common attributes and common linking attributes.

Description

A `revision` contains information about a single revision to a document. Revisions are identified by a number and a date. They may also include the initials of the author, and additional remarks.

Processing expectations

The `revisions` are often presented in a list or table. In a tabular presentation, each revision most likely forms a row in the table.

See Also

`revdescription`, `revhistory`, `revnumber`, `revremark`

Examples

See `revhistory` for an example that uses this element.

---

revnumber

A document revision number

Synopsis

revnumber ::= (text | phrase ^{db.–phrase} | replaceable | *Graphic inlines* | *Indexing inlines* | *Linking inlines* | *Ubiquitous inlines*)*

Attribute synopsis

Common attributes and common linking attributes.

Description

A `revnumber` identifies the revision number of a document. The revision number should uniquely identify a particular revision of a document.

Processing expectations

Formatted inline. DocBook does not require that `revnumber`s be sequential or make any demands on their format. They can be numeric, alphanumeric, or whatever suits your needs.

See Also

`revdescription`, `revhistory`, `revision`, `revremark`

Examples

See `revhistory` for an example that uses this element.

---

revremark

A description of a revision to a document

Synopsis

revremark ::= (text | phrase ^{db.–phrase} | replaceable | *Graphic inlines* | *Indexing inlines* | *Linking inlines* | *Ubiquitous inlines*)*

Attribute synopsis

Common attributes and common linking attributes.

Description

The `revremark` associated with a revision is a short summary of the changes made in that revision. If a longer, more complete summary is desired, see `revdescription`.

Processing expectations

May be formatted inline or as a displayed block, depending on context. Sometimes suppressed.

See Also

revdescription, revhistory, revision, revnumber

Examples

See `revhistory` for an example that uses this element.

---

rhs

The righthand side of an EBNF production

Synopsis

rhs ::= (text | lineannotation | nonterminal | sbr)*

Attribute synopsis

Common attributes and common linking attributes.

Description

The righthand side (`rhs`) of a production provides a definition for the `nonterminal` on the lefthand side (`lhs`) of the `production`.

See Also

constraint, lhs, production, productionrecap, productionset

---

row (db.entrytbl.row)

A row in a table

Synopsis

row (db.entrytbl.row) ::= entry+

Attribute synopsis

Common attributes and common linking attributes.

Additional attributes:

- `rowsep` (enumeration) = "0" | "1"
- `valign` (enumeration) = "bottom" | "middle" | "top"

Description

A `row` is a row in a table. It contains all of the cells (`entrys` or `entrytbls`) that appear in that row.

Processing expectations

This element is expected to obey the semantics of the *CALS Table Model Document Type Definition* [calsdtd].

Within a `row`, cells are arranged horizontally from the start of the row to the end. Cells can, but are not required to, specify the column in which they occur, so it is possible for a row to contain fewer cells than there are columns in the table. This introduces missing cells, which are assumed to be empty. These missing cells can occur anywhere in the row.

Once a cell has been allocated to a column, subsequent cells may not fill preceding columns. In other words, while three cells can specify that they occur in columns 1, 3, and 5, they cannot specify that they occur in columns 1, 5, and 3. Once a column is passed, you can never go back.

If cells do not specify the column in which they occur, they are placed in the next available column. Calculation of the next available column is complicated by horizontal and vertical spanning. Cells from preceding rows can have a vertical span that causes them to extend into the current row, thus occupying space in the current row. These logically occupied cells are skipped when looking for the next available column. Similarly, if a cell has a horizontal span, it logically occupies the columns that follow it. Cells can simultaneously span rows and columns.

Each of the following conditions is an error:

- A cell spans beyond the boundaries of the table.
- A row contains more cells than there are columns in the table.
- The arrangement of cells in a row forces one or more cells past the last column of the table.

Attributes

Common attributes and common linking attributes.

rowsep
> Specifies the presence or absence of the row separator

Enumerated values:	
"0"	No row separator rule.
"1"	Provide a row separator rule below.

valign
> Specifies the vertical alignment of text in an entry

Enumerated values:	
"bottom"	Aligned on the bottom of the entry
"middle"	Aligned in the middle
"top"	Aligned at the top of the entry

See Also

colspec, entry, entrytbl, informaltable, row (db.row), spanspec, table, tbody, tfoot, tgroup, thead

row (db.row)

A row in a table

Synopsis

row (db.row) ::= (entry | entrytbl)+

Attribute synopsis

Common attributes and common linking attributes.

Additional attributes:

- rowsep (enumeration) = "0" | "1"
- valign (enumeration) = "bottom" | "middle" | "top"

Description

A row is a row in a table. It contains all of the cells (entrys or entrytbls) that appear in that row.

Processing expectations

This element is expected to obey the semantics of the *CALS Table Model Document Type Definition* [calsdtd].

Within a row, cells are arranged horizontally from the start of the row to the end. Cells can, but are not required to, specify the column in which they occur, so it is possible for a row to contain fewer cells than there are columns in the table. This introduces missing cells, which are assumed to be empty. These missing cells can occur anywhere in the row.

Once a cell has been allocated to a column, subsequent cells may not fill preceding columns. In other words, while three cells can specify that they occur in columns 1, 3, and 5, they cannot specify that they occur in columns 1, 5, and 3. Once a column is passed, you can never go back.

If cells do not specify the column in which they occur, they are placed in the next available column. Calculation of the next available column is complicated by horizontal and vertical spanning. Cells from preceding rows can have a vertical span that causes them to extend into the current row, thus occupying space in the current row. These logically occupied cells are skipped when looking for the next available column.

Similarly, if a cell has a horizontal span, it logically occupies the columns that follow it. Cells can simultaneously span rows and columns.

Each of the following conditions is an error:

- A cell spans beyond the boundaries of the table.
- A row contains more cells than there are columns in the table.
- The arrangement of cells in a row forces one or more cells past the last column of the table.

Attributes
Common attributes and common linking attributes.

rowsep
Specifies the presence or absence of the row separator

Enumerated values:	
"0"	No row separator rule.
"1"	Provide a row separator rule below.

valign
Specifies the vertical alignment of text in an entry

Enumerated values:	
"bottom"	Aligned on the bottom of the entry.
"middle"	Aligned in the middle.
"top"	Aligned at the top of the entry.

See Also
colspec, entry, entrytbl, informaltable, row (db.entrytbl.row), spanspec, table, tbody, tfoot, tgroup, thead

---

sbr   An explicit line break in a command synopsis

Synopsis
sbr ::= empty

Attribute synopsis
Common attributes.

Description
For the most part, DocBook attempts to describe document structure rather than presentation. However, in some complex environments, there may be no reasonable set of processing expectations that can guarantee correct formatting.

There are two such environments in DocBook: cmdsynopsis and rhs. Within a long synopsis or long "righthand side," it may be necessary to specify the location of a line break explicitly.

The sbr element indicates the position of such a line break. It is purely presentational.

Processing expectations

An sbr causes a line break.

See Also

arg, cmdsynopsis, group, refsynopsisdiv, synopfragment, synopfragmentref

screen

Text that a user sees or might see on a computer screen

Synopsis

screen ::= (info? db.titleforbidden.info, ((text | lineannotation | Bibliography inlines | Computer-output inlines | Error inlines | Graphic inlines | GUI inlines | Indexing inlines | Keyboard inlines | Linking inlines | Markup inlines | Math inlines | Object-oriented programming inlines | Operating system inlines | Product inlines | Programming inlines | Publishing inlines | Technical inlines | Ubiquitous inlines | User-input inlines)* | textobject))

Attribute synopsis

Common attributes and common linking attributes.

Additional attributes:

- continuation (enumeration) = "continues" | "restarts"
- linenumbering (enumeration) = "numbered" | "unnumbered"
- startinglinenumber (integer)
- language
- xml:space (enumeration) = "preserve"
- width (nonNegativeInteger)

Description

A screen is a verbatim environment for displaying text that the user might see on a computer terminal. It is often used to display the results of a command.

Having less specific semantic overtones, screen is often used wherever a verbatim presentation is desired, but the semantic of programlisting is inappropriate.

Processing expectations

This element is displayed "verbatim"; whitespace and line breaks within this element are significant. The content of a screen element is usually displayed in a fixed-width font.

Attributes

Common attributes and common linking attributes.

continuation
> Determines whether line numbering continues from the previous element or restarts.

Enumerated values:	
"continues"	Line numbering continues from the immediately preceding element with the same name.
"restarts"	Line numbering restarts (begins at 1, usually).

language
> Identifies the language (i.e., programming language) of the verbatim content.

linenumbering
> Determines whether lines are numbered.

Enumerated values:	
"numbered"	Lines are numbered.
"unnumbered"	Lines are not numbered.

startinglinenumber
> Specifies the initial line number.

width
> Specifies the width (in characters) of the element.

xml:space
> Can be used to indicate explicitly that whitespace in the verbatim environment is preserved. Whitespace must always be preserved in verbatim environments whether this attribute is specified or not.

Enumerated values:	
"preserve"	Whitespace must be preserved.

See Also

computeroutput, lineannotation, literallayout, programlisting, screenshot, synopsis, userinput

Examples

```
<article xmlns='http://docbook.org/ns/docbook'>
<title>Example screen</title>

<screen>
 Volume in drive C is SYSTEM        Serial number is 2350:717C
 Directory of  C:\

10/17/97   9:04         &lt;DIR&gt;    bin
10/16/97  14:11         &lt;DIR&gt;    DOS
```

```
10/16/97  14:40        &lt;DIR&gt;    Program Files
10/16/97  14:46        &lt;DIR&gt;    TEMP
10/17/97   9:04        &lt;DIR&gt;    tmp
10/16/97  14:37        &lt;DIR&gt;    WINNT
10/16/97  14:25            119  AUTOEXEC.BAT
 2/13/94   6:21         54,619  COMMAND.COM
10/16/97  14:25            115  CONFIG.SYS
11/16/97  17:17     61,865,984  pagefile.sys
 2/13/94   6:21          9,349  WINA20.386
</screen>

</article>
```

```
Volume in drive C is SYSTEM        Serial number is 2350:717C
Directory of  C:\

10/17/97   9:04    <DIR>    bin
10/16/97  14:11    <DIR>    DOS
10/16/97  14:40    <DIR>    Program Files
10/16/97  14:46    <DIR>    TEMP
10/17/97   9:04    <DIR>    tmp
10/16/97  14:37    <DIR>    WINNT
10/16/97  14:25        119  AUTOEXEC.BAT
 2/13/94   6:21     54,619  COMMAND.COM
10/16/97  14:25        115  CONFIG.SYS
11/16/97  17:17 61,865,984  pagefile.sys
 2/13/94   6:21      9,349  WINA20.386
```

screenco

A screen with associated areas used in callouts

Synopsis

screenco ::= (info?$^{db.titleforbidden.info}$, areaspec, screen, calloutlist*)

Attribute synopsis

Common attributes and common linking attributes.

Description

The callouts, such as numbered bullets, are an annotation mechanism. In an online system, these bullets are frequently "hot," and clicking on them navigates to the corresponding annotation.

A screenco is a wrapper around an areaspec and a screen. An areaspec identifies the locations (coordinates) in the screen where the callouts occur. The screenco may also contain the list of annotations in a calloutlist, although the calloutlist may also occur outside of the wrapper, elsewhere in the document.

It is also possible to embed co elements directly in the verbatim text, in order to avoid the overhead of calculating the correct coordinates. If you decide to follow this route, use a screen and a calloutlist without the screenco wrapper. A screenco must specify at least one coordinate.

For a complete description of callouts, see callout.

Processing expectations

Formatted as a displayed block. This element is displayed "verbatim"; whitespace and line breaks within this element are significant.

The mandatory processing expectations of a **screenco** are minimal: a system is expected to render the program listing and the callout list, if present.

If explicit **co** elements are embedded in a **screen**, they must generate appropriate callout marks.

In online environments, the processing system may be able to instantiate the linking relationships between the callout marks in the program listing and the annotations. Some systems may even be able to go a step further and generate the callout marks automatically from the coordinate information, but this level of sophistication is not mandatory.

See Also

areaspec, calloutlist, co, coref, imageobjectco, programlistingco

Examples

```
<article xmlns='http://docbook.org/ns/docbook'>
<title>Example screenco</title>

<screenco>
<areaspec>
<area xml:id="dos" coords='5'/>
<area xml:id="autoexec.bat" coords='10'/>
<area xml:id="command.com" coords='11'/>
<area xml:id="config.sys" coords='12'/>
<area xml:id="wina20.386" coords='14'/>
</areaspec>
<screen> Volume in drive C is SYSTEM        Serial number is 2350:717C
 Directory of  C:\

10/17/97   9:04       &lt;DIR>     bin
10/16/97  14:11       &lt;DIR>     DOS
10/16/97  14:40       &lt;DIR>     Program Files
10/16/97  14:46       &lt;DIR>     TEMP
10/17/97   9:04       &lt;DIR>     tmp
10/16/97  14:37       &lt;DIR>     WINNT
10/16/97  14:25            119   AUTOEXEC.BAT
 2/13/94   6:21         54,619   COMMAND.COM
10/16/97  14:25            115   CONFIG.SYS
11/16/97  17:17     61,865,984   pagefile.sys
 2/13/94   6:21          9,349   WINA20.386</screen>
<calloutlist>
<callout arearefs="dos">
<para>This directory holds <trademark>MS-DOS</trademark>, the
operating system that was installed before <trademark>Windows
NT</trademark>.
</para>
</callout>
```

```
<callout arearefs="autoexec.bat command.com config.sys">
<para>System startup code for DOS.
</para>
</callout>

<callout arearefs="wina20.386">
<para>Some sort of <trademark>Windows 3.1</trademark> hack for some 386 processors,
as I recall.
</para>
</callout>
</calloutlist>
</screenco>

</article>
```

```
    Volume in drive C is SYSTEM        Serial number is 2350:717C
    Directory of  C:\

  10/17/97   9:04      <DIR>   bin
  10/16/97  14:11      <DIR>   DOS                   ❶
  10/16/97  14:40      <DIR>   Program Files
  10/16/97  14:46      <DIR>   TEMP
  10/17/97   9:04      <DIR>   tmp
  10/16/97  14:37      <DIR>   WINNT
  10/16/97  14:25            119  AUTOEXEC.BAT        ❷
   2/13/94   6:21         54,619  COMMAND.COM         ❸
  10/16/97  14:25            115  CONFIG.SYS          ❹
  11/16/97  17:17     61,865,984  pagefile.sys
   2/13/94   6:21          9,349  WINA20.386          ❺
```

❶   This directory holds MS-DOS™, the operating system that was installed before Windows NT™.

❷❸❹   System startup code for DOS.

❺   Some sort of Windows 3.1™ hack for some 386 processors, as I recall.

Compare this example with the example for co.

screenshot

A representation of what the user sees or might see on a computer screen

Synopsis

screenshot ::= (((((title? & titleabbrev? & subtitle?), info? $^{\text{db.titleforbidden.info}}$) | info? $^{\text{db.info}}$), mediaobject)

Attribute synopsis

Common attributes and common linking attributes.

Description

A screenshot is a graphical environment for displaying an image of what the user might see on a computer screen. It is often used to display application screenshots, dialog boxes, and other components of a graphical user interface.

Processing expectations

Formatted as a displayed block.

See Also

computeroutput, lineannotation, literallayout, programlisting, screen, synopsis, userinput

Examples

```
<article xmlns='http://docbook.org/ns/docbook'>
<title>Example screenshot</title>

<screenshot>
  <info>
    <bibliomisc role="resolution">640x480x256</bibliomisc>
  </info>
  <mediaobject>
    <imageobject>
      <imagedata fileref="copilot.gif"/>
    </imageobject>
  </mediaobject>
</screenshot>

</article>
```

---

secondary
A secondary word or phrase in an index term

Synopsis

secondary ::= (text | *Bibliography inlines* | *Error inlines* | *Graphic inlines* | *GUI inlines* | *Indexing inlines* | *Keyboard inlines* | *Linking inlines* | *Markup inlines* | *Math inlines* | *Object-oriented programming inlines* | *Operating system inlines* | *Product inlines* | *Programming inlines* | *Publishing inlines* | *Technical inlines* | *Ubiquitous inlines*)*

Attribute synopsis

Common attributes and common linking attributes.

Additional attributes:

* sortas

Description

A secondary contains a secondary word or phrase in an indexterm. The text of a secondary term is less significant than the primary term, but more significant than the tertiary term for sorting and display purposes.

In indexterms, you can only have one primary, secondary, and tertiary term. If you want to index multiple secondary terms for the same primary, you must repeat the primary in another indexterm. You cannot place several secondarys in the same primary.

Processing expectations

Suppressed. This element provides data for processing but is not rendered in the primary flow of text.

Attributes

Common attributes and common linking attributes.

sortas

Specifies the string by which the term is to be sorted; if unspecified, the term content is used

See Also

indexentry, indexterm, primary, primaryie, secondaryie, see, seealso, seealsoie, seeie, tertiary, tertiaryie

---

secondaryie   A secondary term in an index entry, rather than in the text

Synopsis

secondaryie ::= (text | *Bibliography inlines* | *Error inlines* | *Graphic inlines* | *GUI inlines* | *Indexing inlines* | *Keyboard inlines* | *Linking inlines* | *Markup inlines* | *Math inlines* | *Object-oriented programming inlines* | *Operating system inlines* | *Product inlines* | *Programming inlines* | *Publishing inlines* | *Technical inlines* | *Ubiquitous inlines*)*

Attribute synopsis

Common attributes.

Description

A secondaryie identifies a secondary word or words in an indexentry.

In indexentrys, you can specify as many secondary terms as are necessary. Secondary and tertiary terms can be mixed, following the primary.

Processing expectations

Formatted as a displayed block. The secondaryies occur below the primaryie, usually aligned with each other and indented from the primary.

See Also

indexentry, indexterm, primary, primaryie, secondary, see, seealso, seealsoie, seeie, tertiary, tertiaryie

---

sect1   A top-level section of a document

Synopsis

sect1 ::= ((((title & titleabbrev? & subtitle?), info? ^{db.titleforbidden.info}) | info ^{db.titlereq.info}), (((annotation | bridgehead | remark | revhistory | *Indexing inlines* | *Admonition elements* | *Formal elements* | *Graphic elements* | *Informal elements* | *List elements* | *Paragraph elements* | *Publishing elements* | *Synopsis elements* | *Technical elements* | *Verbatim elements*)+, ((sect2+, simplesect*) | simplesect+)?) | (sect2+, simplesect*) | simplesect+), (bibliography | glossary | index | toc)*)

Attribute synopsis

Common attributes and common linking attributes.

Additional attributes:

- `label`
- `status`

Additional constraints

- If this element is the root element, it must have a `version` attribute.

Description

A `sect1` is one of the top-level sectioning elements in a component. There are three types of sectioning elements in DocBook:

- Explicitly numbered sections, `sect1`...`sect5`, which must be properly nested and can only be five levels deep.
- Recursive `sections`, which are alternatives to the numbered sections and have unbounded depth.
- `simplesects`, which are terminal. The `simplesects` can occur as the "leaf" sections in either recursive sections or any of the numbered sections, or directly in components.

None of the sectioning elements is allowed to "float" in a component. You can place paragraphs and other block elements before a section, but you cannot place anything after it.

This means that you cannot have content in the `sect1` after the end of a `sect2`. This is consistent with the DocBook book model, because in a printed book it is usually impossible for a reader to detect the end of the enclosed second-level section and, therefore, all content after a second-level section appears in that section.

Processing expectations

Formatted as a displayed block. Sometimes sections are numbered.

Attributes

Common attributes and common linking attributes.

label
> Specifies an identifying string for presentation purposes

status
> Identifies the editorial or publication status of the element on which it occurs

See Also

bridgehead, sect2, sect3, sect4, sect5, section, simplesect

sect2

Synopsis

sect2 ::= (((((title & titleabbrev? & subtitle?), info? ^{db.titleforbidden.info}) | info ^{db.titlereq.info}), (((annotation | bridgehead | remark | revhistory | *Indexing inlines* | *Admonition elements* | *Formal elements* | *Graphic elements* | *Informal elements* | *List elements* | *Paragraph elements* | *Publishing elements* | *Synopsis elements* | *Technical elements* | *Verbatim elements*)+, ((sect3+, simple sect*) | simplesect+)?) | (sect3+, simplesect*) | simplesect+), (bibliography | glossary | index | toc)*)

Attribute synopsis

Common attributes and common linking attributes.

Additional attributes:

- label
- status

Additional constraints

- If this element is the root element, it must have a **version** attribute.

Description

A sect2 is a second-level section in a document.

Processing expectations

Formatted as a displayed block. Sometimes sections are numbered.

Attributes

Common attributes and common linking attributes.

label
> Specifies an identifying string for presentation purposes

status
> Identifies the editorial or publication status of the element on which it occurs

See Also

bridgehead, sect1, sect3, sect4, sect5, section, simplesect

---

sect3

Synopsis

sect3 ::= (((((title & titleabbrev? & subtitle?), info? ^{db.titleforbidden.info}) | info ^{db.titlereq.info}), (((annotation | bridgehead | remark | revhistory | *Indexing inlines* | *Admonition elements* | *Formal elements* | *Graphic elements* | *Informal elements* | *List elements* | *Paragraph elements* | *Publishing elements* | *Synopsis elements* | *Technical elements* | *Verbatim elements*)+, ((sect4+, simple sect*) | simplesect+)?) | (sect4+, simplesect*) | simplesect+), (bibliography | glossary | index | toc)*)

Attribute synopsis

Common attributes and common linking attributes.

Additional attributes:

- `label`
- `status`

Additional constraints

- If this element is the root element, it must have a `version` attribute.

Description

A `sect3` is a third-level section in a document.

Processing expectations

Formatted as a displayed block. Sometimes sections are numbered.

Attributes

Common attributes and common linking attributes.

label

    Specifies an identifying string for presentation purposes

status

    Identifies the editorial or publication status of the element on which it occurs

See Also

bridgehead, sect1, sect2, sect4, sect5, section, simplesect

---

sect4

A subsection within a sect3

Synopsis

sect4 ::= ((((title & titleabbrev? & subtitle?), info? ^{db.titleforbidden.info}) | info ^{db.titlereq.info}),
(((annotation | bridgehead | remark | revhistory | *Indexing inlines* | *Admonition elements* | *Formal elements* | *Graphic elements* | *Informal elements* | *List elements* | *Paragraph elements* | *Publishing elements* | *Synopsis elements* | *Technical elements* | *Verbatim elements*)+, ((sect5+, simple
sect*) | simplesect+)?) | (sect5+, simplesect*) | simplesect+), (bibliography | glossary | index |
toc)*)

Attribute synopsis

Common attributes and common linking attributes.

Additional attributes:

- `label`
- `status`

Additional constraints

- If this element is the root element, it must have a `version` attribute.

Description

A `sect4` is a fourth-level section in a document.

Processing expectations

Formatted as a displayed block. Sometimes sections are numbered.

Attributes

Common attributes and common linking attributes.

label

> Specifies an identifying string for presentation purposes

status

> Identifies the editorial or publication status of the element on which it occurs

See Also

bridgehead, sect1, sect2, sect3, sect5, section, simplesect

---

sect5

A subsection within a sect4

Synopsis

sect5 ::= (((((title & titleabbrev? & subtitle?), info? ^{db.titleforbidden.info}) | info ^{db.titlereq.info}), (((annotation | bridgehead | remark | revhistory | *Indexing inlines* | *Admonition elements* | *Formal elements* | *Graphic elements* | *Informal elements* | *List elements* | *Paragraph elements* | *Publishing elements* | *Synopsis elements* | *Technical elements* | *Verbatim elements*)+, simplesect*) | simplesect+), (bibliography | glossary | index | toc)*)

Attribute synopsis

Common attributes and common linking attributes.

Additional attributes:

- `label`
- `status`

Additional constraints

- If this element is the root element, it must have a `version` attribute.

Description

A `sect5` is a fifth-level section in a document. This is the lowest-level numbered sectioning element. There is no `sect6`.

Processing expectations

Formatted as a displayed block. Sometimes sections are numbered.

Attributes

Common attributes and common linking attributes.

label

> Specifies an identifying string for presentation purposes

status

Identifies the editorial or publication status of the element on which it occurs

See Also

bridgehead, sect1, sect2, sect3, sect4, section, simplesect

---

section

A recursive section

Synopsis

section ::= ((((title & titleabbrev? & subtitle?), info? ^{db.titleforbidden.info}) | info ^{db.titlereq.info}), (((annotation | bridgehead | remark | revhistory | *Indexing inlines* | *Admonition elements* | *Formal elements* | *Graphic elements* | *Informal elements* | *List elements* | *Paragraph elements* | *Publishing elements* | *Synopsis elements* | *Technical elements* | *Verbatim elements*)+, ((section+, simplesect*) | simplesect+ | refentry+)?) | (section+, simplesect*) | simplesect+ | refentry+), (bibliography | glossary | index | toc)*)

Attribute synopsis

Common attributes and common linking attributes.

Additional attributes:

- label
- status

Additional constraints

- If this element is the root element, it must have a **version** attribute.

Description

A **section** is one of the top-level sectioning elements in a component. There are three types of sectioning elements in DocBook:

- Explicitly numbered sections, **sect1...sect5**, which must be properly nested and can only be five levels deep.
- Recursive **sections**, which are an alternative to the numbered sections and have unbounded depth.
- **simplesects**, which are terminal. The **simplesects** can occur as the "leaf" sections in recursive sections or any of the numbered sections, or directly in components.

The **section** element may be more convenient than numbered sections in some authoring environments because instances can be moved around in the document hierarchy without renaming.

None of the sectioning elements is allowed to "float" in a component. You can place paragraphs and other block elements before a section, but you cannot place anything after it.

Processing expectations

Formatted as a displayed block. Sometimes sections are numbered.

Use of deeply nested sections may cause problems in some processing systems.

Attributes

Common attributes and common linking attributes.

label

> Specifies an identifying string for presentation purposes

status

> Identifies the editorial or publication status of the element on which it occurs

See Also

bridgehead, sect1, sect2, sect3, sect4, sect5, simplesect

Examples

```
<article xmlns='http://docbook.org/ns/docbook'>
<title>Example section</title>

<para>This <tag>article</tag> uses recursive sections.</para>

<section>
  <title>Like a Sect1</title>
  <subtitle>Or How I Learned to Let Go of Enumeration
            and Love to Recurse</subtitle>
  <info>
    <abstract>
      <para>A trivial example of recursive sections.</para>
    </abstract>
  </info>
  <para>This section is like a Sect1.</para>
  <section><title>Like a Sect2</title>
    <para>This section is like a Sect2.</para>
    <section><title>Like a Sect3</title>
      <para>This section is like a Sect3.</para>
      <section><title>Like a Sect4</title>
        <para>This section is like a Sect4.</para>
        <section><title>Like a Sect5</title>
          <para>This section is like a Sect5.</para>
          <section><title>Would be like a Sect6</title>
            <para>This section would be like a Sect6,
                  if there were one.</para>
            <section><title>Would be like a Sect7</title>
              <para>This section would be like a Sect7,
                    if there was one.</para>
            </section>
          </section>
        </section>
      </section>
    </section>
  </section>
</section>

</article>
```

see

Synopsis
see ::= (text | *Bibliography inlines* | *Error inlines* | *Graphic inlines* | *GUI inlines* | *Indexing inlines* | *Keyboard inlines* | *Linking inlines* | *Markup inlines* | *Math inlines* | *Object-oriented programming inlines* | *Operating system inlines* | *Product inlines* | *Programming inlines* | *Publishing inlines* | *Technical inlines* | *Ubiquitous inlines*)*

Attribute synopsis
Common attributes and common linking attributes.

Description
The use of see in an `indexterm` indicates that the reader should be directed elsewhere in the index when encountering this term.

The content of see identifies another term in the index which the reader should consult *instead* of the current term.

Processing expectations
Suppressed. This element provides data for processing but it is not rendered in the primary flow of text.

It is possible for multiple `indexterms`, taken together, to form an illogical index. For example, given the following `indexterms`:

```
<indexterm><primary>Extensible Markup Language</primary>
  <see>XML</see></indexterm>
<indexterm><primary>Extensible Markup Language</primary>
  <secondary>definition of</secondary>
</indexterm>
```

there's no way to construct a logical index because an entry in the index should never have both a see and other content.

DocBook cannot detect these errors. You will have to rely on an external process to find them.

See Also
indexentry, indexterm, primary, primaryie, secondary, secondaryie, seealso, seealsoie, seeie, tertiary, tertiaryie

seealso

Synopsis
seealso ::= (text | *Bibliography inlines* | *Error inlines* | *Graphic inlines* | *GUI inlines* | *Indexing inlines* | *Keyboard inlines* | *Linking inlines* | *Markup inlines* | *Math inlines* | *Object-oriented programming inlines* | *Operating system inlines* | *Product inlines* | *Programming inlines* | *Publishing inlines* | *Technical inlines* | *Ubiquitous inlines*)*

Attribute synopsis
Common attributes and common linking attributes.

Description

The use of `seealso` in an `indexterm` indicates that the reader should be directed elsewhere in the index for additional information.

The content of `seealso` identifies another term in the index that the reader should consult *in addition to* the current term.

Processing expectations

Suppressed. This element provides data for processing but is not rendered in the primary flow of text.

See Also

`indexentry`, `indexterm`, `primary`, `primaryie`, `secondary`, `secondaryie`, `see`, `seealsoie`, `seeie`, `tertiary`, `tertiaryie`

---

seealsoie

A "See also" entry in an index, rather than in the text

Synopsis

`seealsoie ::=` (text | *Bibliography inlines* | *Error inlines* | *Graphic inlines* | *GUI inlines* | *Indexing inlines* | *Keyboard inlines* | *Linking inlines* | *Markup inlines* | *Math inlines* | *Object-oriented programming inlines* | *Operating system inlines* | *Product inlines* | *Programming inlines* | *Publishing inlines* | *Technical inlines* | *Ubiquitous inlines*)*

Attribute synopsis

Common attributes.

Description

A `seealsoie` identifies a "See also" cross-reference in an `indexentry`. The `indexentrys` occur in an `index`, not in the flow of the text. They are part of a formatted index, not markers for indexing.

Processing expectations

Formatted as a displayed block. The `indexentrys` that include a `seealsoie` should be formatted normally, with the "See also" indented below the term.

A `seealsoie` is usually expected to generate the text "See also".

The `linkends` attribute should point other `indexentrys` in the same `index`. Online systems may use them to form hypertext links.

See Also

`indexentry`, `indexterm`, `primary`, `primaryie`, `secondary`, `secondaryie`, `see`, `seealso`, `seeie`, `tertiary`, `tertiaryie`

seeie
A "See" entry in an index, rather than in the text

Synopsis

seeie ::= (text | *Bibliography inlines* | *Error inlines* | *Graphic inlines* | *GUI inlines* | *Indexing inlines* | *Keyboard inlines* | *Linking inlines* | *Markup inlines* | *Math inlines* | *Object-oriented programming inlines* | *Operating system inlines* | *Product inlines* | *Programming inlines* | *Publishing inlines* | *Technical inlines* | *Ubiquitous inlines*)*

Attribute synopsis
Common attributes.

Description

A `seeie` identifies a "See" cross-reference in an `indexentry`. The `indexentrys` occur in an `index`, not in the flow of the text. They are part of a formatted index, not markers for indexing.

Processing expectations

Formatted as a displayed block. The `indexentrys` that include a `seeie` should be formatted normally, with the "See also" indented below the term. There should be no other entries for this term.

The `seeie` is usually expected to generate the text "See".

The `linkend` attribute should point to the referenced `indexentrys`, which should be in the same `index`. Online systems may use the link information to form a hypertext link.

See Also

indexentry, indexterm, primary, primaryie, secondary, secondaryie, see, seealso, seealsoie, tertiary, tertiaryie

---

seg
An element of a list item in a segmented list

Synopsis

seg ::= (text | *Bibliography inlines* | *Error inlines* | *Graphic inlines* | *GUI inlines* | *Indexing inlines* | *Keyboard inlines* | *Linking inlines* | *Markup inlines* | *Math inlines* | *Object-oriented programming inlines* | *Operating system inlines* | *Product inlines* | *Programming inlines* | *Publishing inlines* | *Technical inlines* | *Ubiquitous inlines*)*

Attribute synopsis
Common attributes and common linking attributes.

Description

A `segmentedlist` consists of a set of headings (`segtitles`) and a list of parallel sets of elements. Every `seglistitem` contains a set of elements that have a one-to-one correspondence with the headings. Each of these elements is contained in a `seg`.

Processing expectations

Segmented lists can be formatted in a number of ways. Two popular formats are tabular and as a list of repeated headings and elements. In a tabular presentation, each `seg` is

---

a cell in the body of the table. In the list presentation, each seg occurs next to the appropriate heading.

DocBook cannot detect errors caused by too many or too few segs in a seglistitem. You will have to rely on external processes to find those errors.

Examples

See segmentedlist for an example that uses this element.

---

seglistitem

A list item in a segmented list

Synopsis
seglistitem ::= seg+

Attribute synopsis
Common attributes and common linking attributes.

Additional constraints

- The number of seg elements must be the same as the number of segtitle elements in the parent segmentedlist.

Description
A segmentedlist consists of a set of headings (segtitles) and a list of parallel sets of elements. Each set of elements is stored in a seglistitem.

Processing expectations
Segmented lists can be formatted in a number of ways. Two popular formats are tabular and as a list of repeated headings and elements. In a tabular presentation, each seglistitem is a row in the table. In the list presentation, each seglistitem contains a block of heading/element pairs.

DocBook cannot detect errors caused by too many or too few segs in a seglistitem. You will have to rely on external processes to find those errors.

Examples

See segmentedlist for an example that uses this element.

---

segmentedlist

A segmented list, a list of sets of elements

Synopsis
segmentedlist ::= ((((title? & titleabbrev?), info? $^{\text{db.titleforbidden.info}}$) | info $^{\text{db.titleonly.info}}$), segtitle +, seglistitem+)

Attribute synopsis
Common attributes and common linking attributes.

Description

A `segmentedlist` consists of a set of headings (`segtitles`) and a list of parallel sets of elements. Every `seglistitem` contains a set of elements that have a one-to-one correspondence with the headings. Each of these elements is contained in a `seg`.

Processing expectations

Segmented lists can be formatted in a number of ways. Two popular formats are tabular and as a list of repeated headings and elements. In a tabular presentation, the `segmentedlist` is the table. In the list presentation, the `segmentedlist` surrounds the entire list of blocks of heading/element pairs.

Specifying the output format for lists is not part of the normative definition of DocBook. However, the tabular and list formats are supported in the open source DocBook stylesheets using the `list-presentation` attribute on the `<?dbhtml>` and `<?dbfo>` processing instructions. The examples on this reference page show how to use these processing instructions.

See Also

`calloutlist`, `itemizedlist`, `listitem`, `orderedlist`, `simplelist`, `variablelist`

Examples

```
<article xmlns='http://docbook.org/ns/docbook'>
<title>Example segmentedlist</title>

<para>The capitals of the states of the United States of America are:

<segmentedlist><title>State Capitals</title>
<?dbhtml list-presentation="list"?>
<?dbfo   list-presentation="list"?>
<segtitle>State</segtitle>
<segtitle>Capital</segtitle>
<seglistitem><seg>Alabama</seg><seg>Montgomery</seg></seglistitem>
<seglistitem><seg>Alaska</seg><seg>Juneau</seg></seglistitem>
<seglistitem><seg>Arkansas</seg><seg>Little Rock</seg></seglistitem>
</segmentedlist>

...

</para>

</article>
```

The capitals of the states of the United States of America are:
State Capitals

State: Alabama
Capital: Montgomery
State: Alaska
Capital: Juneau
State: Arkansas
Capital: Little Rock

...

```
<article xmlns='http://docbook.org/ns/docbook'>
<title>Example segmentedlist</title>

<para><segmentedlist><title>State Capitals</title>
<?dbhtml list-presentation="table"?>
<?dbfo    list-presentation="table"?>
<segtitle>State</segtitle>
<segtitle>Capital</segtitle>
<seglistitem><seg>Alabama</seg><seg>Montgomery</seg></seglistitem>
<seglistitem><seg>Alaska</seg><seg>Anchorage</seg></seglistitem>
<seglistitem><seg>Arkansas</seg><seg>Little Rock</seg></seglistitem>
</segmentedlist>

...

</para>

</article>
```

State Capitals

State	**Capital**
Alabama	Montgomery
Alaska	Anchorage
Arkansas	Little Rock
...	

segtitle

The title of an element of a list item in a segmented list

Synopsis

segtitle ::= (text | *Bibliography inlines* | *Error inlines* | *Graphic inlines* | *GUI inlines* | *Indexing inlines* | *Keyboard inlines* | *Linking inlines* | *Markup inlines* | *Math inlines* | *Object-oriented programming inlines* | *Operating system inlines* | *Product inlines* | *Programming inlines* | *Publishing inlines* | *Technical inlines* | *Ubiquitous inlines*)*

Attribute synopsis

Common attributes and common linking attributes.

Description

Each heading in a `segmentedlist` is contained in its own `segtitle`.

The relationship between `segtitle`s and `seg`s is implicit in the document; the first `segtitle` goes with the first `seg` in each `seglistitem`, the second `segtitle` goes with the second `seg`, and so on.

Processing expectations

Segmented lists can be formatted in a number of ways. Two popular formats are tabular and as a list of repeated headings and elements. In a tabular presentation, each `segtitle` is a column heading. In the list presentation, each `segtitle` is repeated before the corresponding `seg`.

Examples

See `segmentedlist` for an example that uses this element.

---

seriesvolnums

Synopsis

seriesvolnums ::= (text | phrase ^{db._phrase} | replaceable | *Graphic inlines* | *Indexing inlines* | *Linking inlines* | *Ubiquitous inlines*)*

Attribute synopsis

Common attributes and common linking attributes.

Description

A `seriesvolnums` contains the numbers of the volumes of the books in a series. It is a wrapper for bibliographic information.

Processing expectations

Formatted inline. Sometimes suppressed.

See Also

`biblioid`, `issuenum`, `productnumber`, `volumenum`

Examples

```
<article xmlns='http://docbook.org/ns/docbook'>
<title>Example seriesvolnums</title>

<bibliolist>
  <bibliomixed xml:id="Aho72">
    <bibliomset relation="book">
      <abbrev>Aho72</abbrev>
      <authorgroup>
        <author><personname>
          <firstname>Alfred V.</firstname>
          <surname>Aho</surname></personname>
        </author>
        <author><personname>
          <firstname>Jeffrey D.</firstname>
          <surname>Ullman</surname></personname>
        </author>
      </authorgroup>.
      <title>The Theory of Parsing, Translation, and Compiling:</title>
      <subtitle>Series in Automatic Computation</subtitle>
      <seriesvolnums>I: Parsing</seriesvolnums>.
      <address>Englewood Cliffs, New Jersey</address>:
      <publishername>Prentice Hall</publishername>,
      <pubdate>1972</pubdate>.
    </bibliomset>
  </bibliomixed>
</bibliolist>
```

```
</article>
```

[Aho72] Aho, Alfred V., and Jeffrey D. Ullman. *The Theory of Parsing, Translation, and Compiling: Series in Automatic Computation* I: Parsing. Englewood Cliffs, New Jersey: Prentice Hall, 1972.

set

Synopsis

set ::= ((((title & titleabbrev? & subtitle?), info? ^{db.titleforbidden.info}) | info ^{db.titlereq.info}), toc?, (book | set)+, setindex?)

Attribute synopsis

Common attributes and common linking attributes.

Additional attributes:

- label
- status

Additional constraints

- If this element is the root element, it must have a version attribute.

Description

A set is a collection of books. Placing multiple books in a set, as opposed to publishing each of them separately, has the advantage that ID/IDREF links can then be used across all books.

A set is the top of the DocBook structural hierarchy. Although sets can contain other sets, nothing else can contain them.

Processing expectations

Formatted as a displayed block. A set may generate additional front and back matter (e.g., tables of contents and setindexs) around the books it contains.

Attributes

Common attributes and common linking attributes.

label
    Specifies an identifying string for presentation purposes

status
    Identifies the editorial or publication status of the element on which it occurs

See Also

appendix, article, book, chapter, colophon, dedication, part, partintro, preface

Examples

```
<set xmlns='http://docbook.org/ns/docbook'>
<title>The Perl Series</title>
<info>
  <author>
    <orgname>O'Reilly Media</orgname>
  </author>
</info>

<book><title>Learning Perl</title>
<chapter><title>...</title><para>...</para></chapter>
</book>

<book><title>Programming Perl</title>
<chapter><title>...</title><para>...</para></chapter>
</book>

<book><title>Advanced Perl Programming</title>
<chapter><title>...</title><para>...</para></chapter>
</book>

</set>
```

setindex

An index to a set of books

Synopsis

setindex ::= (((title? & titleabbrev? & subtitle?), info? $^{\text{db.titleforbidden.info}}$) | info? $^{\text{db.info}}$), (anno tation | bridgehead | remark | revhistory | *Indexing inlines* | *Admonition elements* | *Formal elements* | *Graphic elements* | *Informal elements* | *List elements* | *Paragraph elements* | *Publishing elements* | *Synopsis elements* | *Technical elements* | *Verbatim elements*)*, (indexdiv* | indexentry*))

Attribute synopsis

Common attributes and common linking attributes.

Additional attributes:

- label
- status
- type

Additional constraints

- If this element is the root element, it must have a version attribute.

Description

A setindex contains the formatted index of a complete set of books. An index may begin with introductory material, followed by any number of indexentrys or indexdivs.

Processing expectations

Formatted as a displayed block. An index in a set usually causes a forced page break in print media.

In many processing systems, indexes are generated automatically or semiautomatically and never appear instantiated as DocBook markup.

Attributes

Common attributes and common linking attributes.

label
> Specifies an identifying string for presentation purposes

status
> Identifies the editorial or publication status of the element on which it occurs

type
> Specifies the target index for this term

shortaffil

A brief description of an affiliation

Synopsis

shortaffil ::= (text | phrase ^{db._phrase} | replaceable | *Graphic inlines* | *Indexing inlines* | *Linking inlines* | *Ubiquitous inlines*)*

Attribute synopsis

Common attributes and common linking attributes.

Description

A `shortaffil` contains an abbreviated or brief description of an individual's `affiliation`.

Processing expectations

May be formatted inline or as a displayed block, depending on context. Sometimes suppressed.

See Also

`affiliation`, `jobtitle`, `orgdiv`, `orgname`

shortcut

A key combination for an action that is also accessible through a menu

Synopsis

shortcut ::= (keycap | keycombo | keysym | mousebutton)+

Attribute synopsis

Common attributes and common linking attributes.

Additional attributes:

- *Exactly one of:*
  - `action` (enumeration) = "click" | "double-click" | "press" | "seq" | "simul"
  - *Each of:*

—action (enumeration) = "other"

—**otheraction**

Required attributes are shown in **bold**.

Description
A shortcut contains the key combination that is a shortcut for a menuchoice. Users who are familiar with the shortcuts can access the functionality of the corresponding menu choice, without navigating through the menu structure to find the right menu item.

Processing expectations
Formatted inline.

Attributes
Common attributes and common linking attributes.

action

Identifies the nature of the action taken. If keycombo contains more than one element, simul is the default; otherwise, there is no default.

Enumerated values:	
"click"	A (single) mouse click
"double-click"	A double mouse click
"press"	A mouse or key press
"seq"	Sequential clicks or presses
"simul"	Simultaneous clicks or presses

action

Identifies the nature of the action taken.

Enumerated values:	
"other"	Indicates a nonstandard action

otheraction

Identifies the nonstandard action in some unspecified way.

See Also
accel, guibutton, guiicon, guilabel, guimenu, guimenuitem, guisubmenu, keycap, key code, keycombo, keysym, menuchoice, mousebutton

Examples

```
<article xmlns='http://docbook.org/ns/docbook'>
<title>Example shortcut</title>

<para>You can exit from GNU Emacs with
<menuchoice>
```

```
<shortcut>
  <keycombo><keysym>C-x</keysym><keysym>C-c</keysym></keycombo>
</shortcut>
<guimenu>Files</guimenu>
<guimenuitem>Exit Emacs</guimenuitem>
</menuchoice>.
</para>

</article>
```

You can exit from GNU Emacs with Files → Exit Emacs (**C-x+C-c**).

---

sidebar
A portion of a document that is isolated from the main narrative flow

Synopsis

sidebar ::= (((((title? & titleabbrev?), info? ^{db.titleforbidden.info}) | info ^{db.titleonly.info}), (annotation | bridgehead | remark | revhistory | *Indexing inlines* | *Admonition elements* | *Formal elements* | *Graphic elements* | *Informal elements* | *List elements* | *Paragraph elements* | *Publishing elements* | *Synopsis elements* | *Technical elements* | *Verbatim elements*)+)

Attribute synopsis

Common attributes and common linking attributes.

Additional constraints

* sidebar must not occur among the children or descendants of sidebar.

Description

A sidebar is a short piece of text, rarely longer than a single column or page, that is presented outside the narrative flow of the main text.

Sidebars are often used for digressions or interesting observations that are related, but not directly relevant, to the main text.

Processing expectations

Formatted as a displayed block. Sometimes sidebars are boxed or shaded.

DocBook does not specify the location of the sidebar within the final displayed flow of text. The wrapper may float or remain where it is located.

See Also

abstract, blockquote, epigraph

Examples

```
<article xmlns='http://docbook.org/ns/docbook'>
<title>Example sidebar</title>

<section><title>An Example Section</title>

<para>Some narrative text.
</para>
```

```
<sidebar><title>A Sidebar</title>
<para>Sidebar content.
</para>
</sidebar>

<para>The continuing flow of the narrative text, as if the
sidebar was not present.
</para>

</section>

</article>
```

---

simpara

A paragraph that contains only text and inline markup, no block elements

Synopsis

simpara ::= (info? ^{db.titleforbidden.info}, (text | *Bibliography inlines* | *Error inlines* | *Graphic inlines* | *GUI inlines* | *Indexing inlines* | *Keyboard inlines* | *Linking inlines* | *Markup inlines* | *Math inlines* | *Object-oriented programming inlines* | *Operating system inlines* | *Product inlines* | *Programming inlines* | *Publishing inlines* | *Technical inlines* | *Ubiquitous inlines*)*)

Attribute synopsis

Common attributes and common linking attributes.

Description

A `simpara` is a "simple paragraph," one that may contain only character data and inline elements. The `para` element is less restrictive; it may also contain block-level structures (lists, figures, etc.).

Processing expectations

Formatted as a displayed block.

See Also

formalpara, para

Examples

```
<article xmlns='http://docbook.org/ns/docbook'>
<title>Example simpara</title>

<simpara>
Just the text, ma'am.
</simpara>

</article>
```

Just the text, ma'am.

simplelist

Synopsis

simplelist ::= member+

Attribute synopsis

Common attributes and common linking attributes.

Additional attributes:

- columns (integer)
- type (enumeration) = "horiz" | "vert" | "inline" [default="vert"]

Description

A simplelist is a list of words or phrases. It offers a convenient alternative to the other list elements for inline content.

Processing expectations

Ironically, the processing expectations of a simplelist are quite complex. The value of the type attribute determines if the list is presented inline, or in a row- or column-major table. In the table cases, the columns attribute determines the number of columns in the table.

Attributes

Common attributes and common linking attributes.

columns
> Specifies the number of columns for horizontal or vertical presentation

type
> Specifies the type of list presentation

Enumerated values:	
"horiz"	A tabular presentation in row-major order
"vert"	A tabular presentation in column-major order
"inline"	An inline presentation, usually a comma-delimited list

See Also

calloutlist, itemizedlist, listitem, orderedlist, segmentedlist, variablelist

Examples

```
<article xmlns='http://docbook.org/ns/docbook'>
<title>Example simplelist</title>

<para>Here is a <tag>SimpleList</tag>, rendered inline:
<simplelist type='inline'>
<member>A</member>
<member>B</member>
<member>C</member>
```

```
<member>D</member>
<member>E</member>
<member>F</member>
<member>G</member>
</simplelist>
</para>

</article>
```

Here is a `SimpleList`, rendered inline: A, B, C, D, E, F, G

```
<article xmlns='http://docbook.org/ns/docbook'>
<title>Example simplelist</title>

<para>Here is the same <tag>SimpleList</tag> rendered horizontally with
three columns:
<simplelist type='horiz' columns='3'>
<member>A</member>
<member>B</member>
<member>C</member>
<member>D</member>
<member>E</member>
<member>F</member>
<member>G</member>
</simplelist>
</para>

</article>
```

Here is the same `SimpleList` rendered horizontally with three columns:

A	B	C
D	E	F
G		

```
<article xmlns='http://docbook.org/ns/docbook'>
<title>Example simplelist</title>

<para>Finally, here is the list rendered vertically:
<simplelist type='vert' columns='3'>
<member>A</member>
<member>B</member>
<member>C</member>
<member>D</member>
<member>E</member>
<member>F</member>
<member>G</member>
</simplelist>
</para>

</article>
```

Finally, here is the list rendered vertically:

A	D	G
B	E	
C	F	

simplemsgentry

Synopsis

simplemsgentry ::= (msgtext, msgexplan+)

Attribute synopsis

Common attributes and common linking attributes.

Additional attributes:

- msgaud
- msglevel
- msgorig

Description

A simplemsgentry is a simpler alternative to msgentry. In a msgset, each simplemsgentry contains the text of a message and its explanation.

Processing expectations

Formatted as a displayed block.

Backward incompatibilities

In DocBook V5.0, the audience, level, and origin attributes are accidentally misspelled. The attribute "msgaud" should be spelled "audience"; the attribute "msglevel" should be spelled "level"; and the attribute "msgorig" should be spelled "origin". Those are the spellings in DocBook V4.5.

Unfortunately, the attribute name "audience" has subsequently been added to all elements as an effectivity attribute. Because there's no way to resolve that conflict now, the DocBook Technical Committee has decided to accept the error and leave the misspelled attribute names in place going forward.

Attributes

Common attributes and common linking attributes.

msgaud
> The audience to which the message is relevant

msglevel
> The level of importance or severity of a message

msgorig
> The origin of the message

simplesect

Synopsis

simplesect ::= ((((title & titleabbrev? & subtitle?), info? db.titleforbidden.info) | info db.titlereq.info),
(annotation | bridgehead | remark | revhistory | *Indexing inlines* | *Admonition elements* | *Formal el-*

ements | Graphic elements | Informal elements | List elements | Paragraph elements | Publishing elements | Synopsis elements | Technical elements | Verbatim elements)+)

Attribute synopsis

Common attributes and common linking attributes.

Additional attributes:

- `label`
- `status`

Description

A `simplesect` is one of the top-level sectioning elements in a component. There are three types of sectioning elements in DocBook:

- Explicitly numbered sections, `sect1`...`sect5`, which must be properly nested and can only be five levels deep.
- Recursive `sections`, which are alternatives to the numbered sections and have unbounded depth.
- `simplesects`, which are terminal. The `simplesects` can occur as the "leaf" sections in either recursive sections or any of the numbered sections, or directly in components.

None of the sectioning elements is allowed to "float" in a component. You can place paragraphs and other block elements before a section, but you cannot place anything after it.

The important semantic distinction of `simplesect` elements is that they never appear in the table of contents.

Processing expectations

Formatted as a displayed block. A `simplesect` element *never* appears in the table of contents.

Attributes

Common attributes and common linking attributes.

label
> Specifies an identifying string for presentation purposes

status
> Identifies the editorial or publication status of the element on which it occurs

See Also

`bridgehead, sect1, sect2, sect3, sect4, sect5, section`

Examples

```
<article xmlns='http://docbook.org/ns/docbook'>
<title>Example simplesect</title>

<section><title>Additional Coding</title>

<para>Support for the additional features requested will be provided.
</para>

<simplesect><title>Estimated Time</title>

<para>2 to 3 weeks.
</para>

</simplesect>
</section>

</article>
```

spanspec

Formatting information for a spanned column in a table

Synopsis
spanspec ::= empty

Attribute synopsis
Common attributes and common linking attributes.

Additional attributes:

- align (enumeration) = "center" | "char" | "justify" | "left" | "right"
- char
- charoff (decimal)
- colsep (enumeration) = "0" | "1"
- **nameend**
- **namest**
- rowsep (enumeration) = "0" | "1"
- **spanname**

Required attributes are shown in **bold**.

Description
A spanspec associates a name with a span between two columns in a table. In the body of the table, cells can refer to the span by name. Cells that refer to a span will span horizontally from the first column to the last column, inclusive.

Cells can also form spans directly, by naming the start and end columns themselves. The added benefit of a spanspec is that it can associate formatting information (such as alignment and table rule specifications) with the span. This information does not need to be repeated then, on each spanning cell.

Processing expectations
Suppressed. This element is expected to obey the semantics of the *CALS Table Model Document Type Definition* [calsdtd].

The namest and nameend attributes of a spanspec must refer to named colspecs in the same table. In other words, if the spanspec:

```
t<spanspec spanname="fullyear" namest="jan" nameend="dec"/>
```

exists in a table, colspecs named "jan" and "dec" must also exist in the same table.

Attributes
Common attributes and common linking attributes.

align
> Specifies the horizontal alignment of text in an entry

Enumerated values:	
"center"	Centered
"char"	Aligned on a particular character
"justify"	Left and right justified
"left"	Left justified
"right"	Right justified

char
> Specifies the alignment character when align is set to "char"

charoff
> Specifies the percentage of the column's total width that should appear to the left of the first occurrence of the character identified in char when align is set to "char"

colsep
> Specifies the presence or absence of the column separator

Enumerated values:	
"0"	No column separator rule.
"1"	Provide a column separator rule on the right.

nameend
> Specifies an ending column by name

namest
> Specifies a starting column by name

rowsep
> Specifies the presence or absence of the row separator

Enumerated values:	
"0"	No row separator rule.
"1"	Provide a row separator rule below.

spanname
> Provides a name for a span specification

See Also
colspec, entry, entrytbl, informaltable, row, table, tbody, tfoot, tgroup, thead

---

state
A state or province in an address

Synopsis
state ::= (text | phrase ^{db._phrase} | replaceable | *Graphic inlines* | *Indexing inlines* | *Linking inlines* | *Ubiquitous inlines*)*

Attribute synopsis
Common attributes and common linking attributes.

Description
A state is the name or postal abbreviation for a state (or province) in an address.

Processing expectations
Formatted inline. In an address, this element may inherit the verbatim qualities of an address.

See Also
address, city, country, email, fax, otheraddr, phone, pob, postcode, street

---

step
A unit of action in a procedure

Synopsis
step ::= ((((title? & titleabbrev?), info? ^{db.titleforbidden.info}) | info ^{db.titleonly.info}), (((annotation | bridgehead | remark | revhistory | *Indexing inlines* | *Admonition elements* | *Formal elements* | *Graphic elements* | *Informal elements* | *List elements* | *Paragraph elements* | *Publishing elements* | *Synopsis elements* | *Technical elements* | *Verbatim elements*)+, (stepalternatives | substeps)?, (annotation | bridgehead | remark | revhistory | *Indexing inlines* | *Admonition elements* | *Formal elements* | *Graphic elements* | *Informal elements* | *List elements* | *Paragraph elements* | *Publishing elements* | *Synopsis elements* | *Technical elements* | *Verbatim elements*)*) | ((stepalternatives | substeps), (annotation | bridgehead | remark | revhistory | *Indexing inlines* | *Admonition elements* | *Formal elements* | *Graphic elements* | *Informal elements* | *List elements* | *Paragraph elements* | *Publishing elements* | *Synopsis elements* | *Technical elements* | *Verbatim elements*)*)))

Attribute synopsis
Common attributes and common linking attributes.

Additional attributes:

- `performance` (enumeration) = "optional" | "required"

Description
A `step` identifies a unit of action in a `procedure`. If a finer level of granularity is required for some steps, you can embed `substeps` in a `step`. Embedded `substeps` contain `steps` so that substeps can be nested to any depth.

Processing expectations
Formatted as a displayed block. The `steps` are almost always numbered.

Attributes
Common attributes and common linking attributes.

performance
> Specifies if the content is required or optional

Enumerated values:	
"optional"	The content describes an optional step or steps.
"required"	The content describes a required step or steps.

See Also
procedure, stepalternatives, substeps

---

stepalternatives
Alternative steps in a procedure

Synopsis
stepalternatives ::= (`info?` db.titleforbidden.info, `step+`)

Attribute synopsis
Common attributes and common linking attributes.

Additional attributes:

- `performance` (enumeration) = "optional" | "required"

Description
Most `steps` in a `procedure` are sequential: do the first, then the second, then the third. Sometimes procedures provide an explicit ordering: do step 7 next.

The `stepalternatives` element was added to support the semantics of alternative steps: perform exactly one of the following steps. The reader is presumably given some criteria for deciding which one to choose, but the significant difference is that only one of the steps is performed.

Processing expectations

Formatted as a displayed block.

Attributes

Common attributes and common linking attributes.

performance

Specifies if the content is required or optional

Enumerated values:	
"optional"	The content describes an optional step or steps.
"required"	The content describes a required step or steps.

See Also

procedure, step, substeps

street

Synopsis

street ::= (text | phrase ^{db._phrase} | replaceable | *Graphic inlines* | *Indexing inlines* | *Linking inlines* | *Ubiquitous inlines*)*

Attribute synopsis

Common attributes and common linking attributes.

Description

In postal addresses, the street element contains the street address portion of the address. If an address contains more than one line of street address information, each line should appear in its own street.

Processing expectations

Formatted inline. In an address, this element may inherit the verbatim qualities of an address.

See Also

address, city, country, email, fax, otheraddr, phone, pob, postcode, state

subject

Synopsis

subject ::= subjectterm+

Attribute synopsis

Common attributes and common linking attributes.

Additional attributes:

- `weight`

Description

A "subject" categorizes or describes the topic of a document, or section of a document. In DocBook, a `subject` is defined by the `subjectterms` that it contains.

Subject terms should be drawn from a controlled vocabulary, such as the *Library of Congress Subject Headings*. If an outside vocabulary is not appropriate, a local or institutional subject set should be created.

The advantage of a controlled vocabulary is that it places the document into a known subject space. Searching the subject space with a particular subject term will find *all* of the documents that claim to have that subject. There's no need to worry about terms that are synonymous with the search item, or homophones of the search term.

All of the `subjectterms` in a `subject` should describe the same subject, and be from the *same controlled vocabulary*.

Processing expectations

May be formatted inline or as a displayed block, depending on context. Subjects are rarely displayed to a reader. Usually, they are reserved for searching and retrieval purposes.

Unlike `keywords`, which may be chosen freely, subject terms should come from a controlled vocabulary.

In order to ensure that typographic or other errors are not introduced into the subject terms, they should be compared against the controlled vocabulary by an external process.

Attributes

Common attributes and common linking attributes.

weight
> Specifies a ranking for this subject relative to other subjects in the same set

See Also

keyword, keywordset, `subjectset`, `subjectterm`

---

subjectset

A set of terms describing the subject matter of a document

Synopsis

subjectset ::= subject+

Attribute synopsis

Common attributes and common linking attributes.

Additional attributes:

- scheme (NMTOKEN)

Description

A subjectset is a container for a set of subjects. All of the subjects within a subject set should come from the *same* controlled vocabulary.

A document can be described using terms from more than one controlled vocabulary. In order to do this, you should use the scheme attribute to distinguish between controlled vocabularies.

Processing expectations

May be formatted inline or as a displayed block, depending on context. Subjects are rarely displayed to a reader. Usually, they are reserved for searching and retrieval purposes.

DocBook does not specify a relationship between subjectsets in different parts of a document or between a subjectset and the subjectsets of enclosing parts of the document.

Attributes

Common attributes and common linking attributes.

scheme

> Identifies the controlled vocabulary used by this set's terms

See Also

keyword, keywordset, subject, subjectterm

Examples

```
<article xmlns='http://docbook.org/ns/docbook'>
<info>
  <title>Example subjectset</title>
  <subjectset scheme="libraryofcongress">
    <subject>
      <subjectterm>Electronic Publishing</subjectterm>
    </subject>
    <subject>
      <subjectterm>SGML (Computer program language)</subjectterm>
    </subject>
  </subjectset>
</info>

<para>…</para>

</article>
```

subjectterm   A term in a group of terms describing the subject matter of a document

Synopsis

subjectterm ::= text

Attribute synopsis

Common attributes and common linking attributes.

Description

A `subjectterm` is an individual subject word or phrase that describes the subject matter of a document or the portion of a document in which it occurs.

Subject terms are not expected to contain any markup. They are external descriptions from a controlled vocabulary.

Processing expectations

May be formatted inline or as a displayed block, depending on context. Subject terms are rarely displayed to a reader. Usually, they are reserved for searching and retrieval purposes.

See Also

`keyword, keywordset, subject, subjectset`

---

subscript   A subscript (as in H_2O, the molecular formula for water)

Synopsis

subscript ::= (text | phrase ^{db._phrase} | replaceable | *Graphic inlines* | *Indexing inlines* | *Linking inlines* | *Ubiquitous inlines*)*

Attribute synopsis

Common attributes and common linking attributes.

Description

A `subscript` identifies text that is to be displayed as a subscript when rendered.

Processing expectations

Formatted inline. Subscripts are usually printed in a smaller font and shifted down with respect to the baseline.

See Also

`equation, informalequation, inlineequation, superscript`

Examples

```
<article xmlns='http://docbook.org/ns/docbook'>
<title>Example subscript</title>

<para>Thirsty?  Have some H<subscript>2</subscript>O.
</para>

</article>
```

Thirsty? Have some H_2O.

substeps

Synopsis
substeps ::= step+

Attribute synopsis
Common attributes and common linking attributes.

Additional attributes:

- performance (enumeration) = "optional" | "required"

Description
A procedure describes a sequence of steps that a reader is expected to perform. If a finer level of granularity is required for some steps, you can use substeps to embed substeps within a step.

The substeps element contains steps, so substeps can be nested to any depth.

Processing expectations
Formatted as a displayed block. The substeps are almost always numbered.

Attributes
Common attributes and common linking attributes.

performance
> Specifies if the content is required or optional

Enumerated values:	
"optional"	The content describes an optional step or steps.
"required"	The content describes a required step or steps.

See Also
procedure, step, stepalternatives

subtitle

Synopsis
subtitle ::= (text | *Bibliography inlines* | *Error inlines* | *Graphic inlines* | *GUI inlines* | *Indexing inlines* | *Keyboard inlines* | *Linking inlines* | *Markup inlines* | *Math inlines* | *Object-oriented programming inlines* | *Operating system inlines* | *Product inlines* | *Programming inlines* | *Publishing inlines* | *Technical inlines* | *Ubiquitous inlines*)*

Attribute synopsis
Common attributes and common linking attributes.

Description
A subtitle identifies the subtitle of a document, or portion of a document.

superscript

Processing expectations
Formatted as a displayed block.

See Also
`title`, `titleabbrev`

---

superscript
A superscript (as in x^2, the mathematical notation for x multiplied by itself)

Synopsis
superscript ::= (text | phrase ^{db._phrase} | **replaceable** | *Graphic inlines* | *Indexing inlines* | *Linking inlines* | *Ubiquitous inlines*)*

Attribute synopsis
Common attributes and common linking attributes.

Description
A `superscript` identifies text that is to be displayed as a superscript when rendered.

Processing expectations
Formatted inline. Superscripts are usually printed in a smaller font and shifted up with respect to the baseline.

See Also
`equation`, `informalequation`, `inlineequation`, `subscript`

Examples

```
<article xmlns='http://docbook.org/ns/docbook'>
<title>Example superscript</title>

<para>The equation e<superscript>πi</superscript> + 1 = 0 ties together
five of the most important mathematical constants.
</para>

</article>
```

The equation $e^{\pi i} + 1 = 0$ ties together five of the most important mathematical constants.

---

surname
An inherited or family name; in Western cultures, the last name

Synopsis
surname ::= (text | phrase ^{db._phrase} | **replaceable** | *Graphic inlines* | *Indexing inlines* | *Linking inlines* | *Ubiquitous inlines*)*

Attribute synopsis
Common attributes and common linking attributes.

412 | DocBook Element Reference

Description

A surname is an inherited or family name; in Western cultures, the last name. This is used for the patronymic or matronymic name or any name that is based on a person's situation at birth or due to marriage or adoption.

Processing expectations

Formatted inline. In an address, this element may inherit the verbatim qualities of an address.

See Also

affiliation, firstname, honorific, lineage, othername

---

symbol

A name that is replaced by a value before processing

Synopsis

symbol ::= (text | phrase db._phrase | replaceable | *Graphic inlines* | *Indexing inlines* | *Linking inlines* | *Ubiquitous inlines*)*

Attribute synopsis

Common attributes and common linking attributes.

Additional attributes:

- class (enumeration) = "limit"

Description

A symbol is a name that represents a value. It should be used in contexts in which the name will actually be replaced by a value before processing. The canonical example is a #defined symbol in a C program where the C preprocessor replaces every occurrence of the symbol with its value before compilation begins.

The Limit value of the class attribute identifies those symbols that represent system limitations (e.g., the number of characters allowed in a pathname or the largest possible positive integer). DocBook V3.1 introduced the constant element, which may be more suitable for some of these symbols.

Processing expectations

Formatted inline.

Attributes

Common attributes and common linking attributes.

class

Identifies the class of symbol

Enumerated values:	
"limit"	The value is a limit of some kind.

See Also
classname, property, token, type

Examples

```
<article xmlns='http://docbook.org/ns/docbook'>
<title>Example symbol</title>

<para>No filename may be more than <symbol class='limit'>MAXPATHLEN</symbol>
characters long.
</para>

</article>
```

No filename may be more than MAXPATHLEN characters long.

---

synopfragment
A portion of a cmdsynopsis broken out from the main body of the synopsis

Synopsis
synopfragment ::= (arg | group)+

Attribute synopsis
Common attributes and common linking attributes.

Description
A complex cmdsynopsis can be made more manageable with synopfragments. Rather than attempting to present the entire synopsis in one large piece, parts of the synopsis can be extracted and presented elsewhere. These extracted pieces are placed in synopfragments at the end of the cmdsynopsis.

At the point in which each piece was extracted, insert a synopfragmentref that points to the fragment. The content of the reference element will be presented inline.

Processing expectations
Formatted as a displayed block.

The presentation system is responsible for generating text that makes the reader aware of the link. This can be done with numbered bullets, or any other appropriate mechanism. Whatever mark is generated for the reference must also be generated for the fragment.

Online systems have additional flexibility. They may generate hot links between the references and the fragments, for example, or place the fragments in pop-up windows.

See Also
arg, cmdsynopsis, group, refsynopsisdiv, sbr, synopfragmentref

Examples

```
<article xmlns='http://docbook.org/ns/docbook'>
<title>Example synopfragment</title>
```

```
<cmdsynopsis>
  <command>cccp</command>
  <arg>-$</arg>
  <arg>-C</arg>
  <arg rep='repeat'>-D<replaceable>name</replaceable>
  <arg>=<replaceable>definition</replaceable></arg></arg>
  <arg>-dD</arg>
  <arg>-dM</arg>
  <sbr/>
  <arg rep='repeat'>-I <replaceable>directory</replaceable></arg>
  <arg>-H</arg>
  <arg>-I-</arg>
  <arg rep='repeat'>-imacros <replaceable>file</replaceable></arg>
  <sbr/>
  <arg rep='repeat'>-include <replaceable>file</replaceable></arg>
  <group>
    <synopfragmentref linkend="langs">languages</synopfragmentref>
  </group>
  <arg>-lint</arg>
  <sbr/>
  <group>
    <arg>-M</arg>
    <arg>-MD</arg>
    <arg>-MM</arg>
    <arg>-MMD</arg>
  </group>
  <arg>-nostdinc</arg>
  <arg>-P</arg>
  <arg>-pedantic</arg>
  <sbr/>
  <arg>-pedantic-errors</arg>
  <arg>-trigraphs</arg>
  <arg>-U<replaceable>name</replaceable></arg>
  <sbr/>
  <arg>-undef</arg>
  <arg choice="plain"><synopfragmentref linkend="warn">warnings
  </synopfragmentref></arg>
  <group choice='req'>
    <arg><replaceable>infile</replaceable></arg>
    <arg>-</arg>
  </group>
  <group choice='req'>
    <arg><replaceable>outfile</replaceable></arg>
    <arg>-</arg>
  </group>

  <synopfragment xml:id="langs">
    <group choice="plain">
      <arg>-lang-c</arg>
      <arg>-lang-c++</arg>
      <arg>-lang-objc</arg>
    </group>
  </synopfragment>

  <synopfragment xml:id="warn">
```

```
      <arg>-Wtrigraphs</arg>
      <arg>-Wcomment</arg>
      <arg>-Wall</arg>
      <arg>-Wtraditional</arg>
   </synopfragment>

</cmdsynopsis>

</article>
```

cccp [-$] [-C] [-D*name* [=*definition*]...] [-dD] [-dM]
[-I *directory*...] [-H] [-I-] [-imacros *file*...]
[-include *file*...] [*(1) languages*] [-lint]
[[-M] | [-MD] | [-MM] | [-MMD]] [-nostdinc] [-P] [-pedantic]
[-pedantic-errors] [-trigraphs] [-U*name*]
[-undef] *(2) warnings* {[*infile*] | [-]} {[*outfile*] | [-]}
(1) [-lang-c] | [-lang-c++] | [-lang-objc]
(2) [-Wtrigraphs] [-Wcomment] [-Wall] [-Wtraditional]

---

synopfragmentref

A reference to a fragment of a command synopsis

Synopsis
synopfragmentref ::= text

Attribute synopsis
Common attributes.

Additional constraints

- @linkend on synopfragmentref must point to a synopfragment.

Description
A complex cmdsynopsis can be made more manageable with synopfragments. Rather than attempting to present the entire synopsis in one large piece, parts of the synopsis can be extracted and presented elsewhere.

At the point where each piece was extracted, insert a synopfragmentref that points to the fragment. The content of the synopfragmentref will be presented inline.

The extracted pieces are placed in synopfragments at the end of the cmdsynopsis.

Processing expectations
Formatted as a displayed block.

The presentation system is responsible for generating text that makes the reader aware of the link. This can be done with numbered bullets, or any other appropriate mechanism.

Online systems have additional flexibility. They may generate hot links between the references and the fragments, for example, or place the fragments in pop-up windows.

See Also
arg, cmdsynopsis, group, refsynopsisdiv, sbr, synopfragment

Examples

See synopfragment for an example using this element.

---

synopsis   A general-purpose element for representing the syntax of commands or functions

Synopsis
synopsis ::= (info? ^{db.titleforbidden.info}, ((text | lineannotation | *Bibliography inlines* | *Computer-output inlines* | *Error inlines* | *Graphic inlines* | *GUI inlines* | *Indexing inlines* | *Keyboard inlines* | *Linking inlines* | *Markup inlines* | *Math inlines* | *Object-oriented programming inlines* | *Operating system inlines* | *Product inlines* | *Programming inlines* | *Publishing inlines* | *Technical inlines* | *Ubiquitous inlines* | *User-input inlines*)* | textobject))

Attribute synopsis
Common attributes and common linking attributes.

Additional attributes:

- continuation (enumeration) = "continues" | "restarts"
- linenumbering (enumeration) = "numbered" | "unnumbered"
- startinglinenumber (integer)
- language
- xml:space (enumeration) = "preserve"
- label

Description
A synopsis is a verbatim environment for displaying command, function, and other syntax summaries.

Unlike cmdsynopsis and funcsynopsis which have a complex interior structure, synopsis is simply a verbatim environment.

Processing expectations
This element is displayed "verbatim"; whitespace and line breaks within this element are significant. A synopsis element is usually displayed in a fixed-width font.

Attributes
Common attributes and common linking attributes.

continuation

Determines whether line numbering continues from the previous element or restarts.

Enumerated values:	
"continues"	Line numbering continues from the immediately preceding element with the same name.
"restarts"	Line numbering restarts (begins at 1, usually).

label
Specifies an identifying string for presentation purposes.

language
Identifies the language (i.e., programming language) of the verbatim content.

linenumbering
Determines whether lines are numbered.

Enumerated values:	
"numbered"	Lines are numbered.
"unnumbered"	Lines are not numbered.

startinglinenumber
Specifies the initial line number.

xml:space
Can be used to indicate explicitly that whitespace in the verbatim environment is preserved. Whitespace must always be preserved in verbatim environments whether this attribute is specified or not.

Enumerated values:	
"preserve"	Whitespace must be preserved.

See Also
cmdsynopsis, computeroutput, funcsynopsis, lineannotation, literallayout, program
listing, screen, screenshot, userinput

Examples

```
<article xmlns='http://docbook.org/ns/docbook'>
<title>Example synopsis</title>

<synopsis>chgrp [-R [-H | -L | -P]] [-f] group file...</synopsis>

</article>
```

```
    chgrp [-R [-H | -L | -P]] [-f] group file...
```

```
<article xmlns='http://docbook.org/ns/docbook'>
<title>Example synopsis</title>

<synopsis>int max(int int1, int int2);</synopsis>

</article>
```

```
    int max(int int1, int int2);
```

systemitem   A system-related item or term

Synopsis
systemitem ::= (text | co | phrase ^{db._phrase} | replaceable | *Graphic inlines* | *Indexing inlines* | *Linking inlines* | *Ubiquitous inlines*)*

Attribute synopsis
Common attributes and common linking attributes.

Additional attributes:

- class (enumeration) = "daemon" | "domainname" | "etheraddress" | "event" | "eventhandler" | "filesystem" | "fqdomainname" | "groupname" | "ipaddress" | "library" | "macro" | "netmask" | "newsgroup" | "osname" | "process" | "protocol" | "resource" | "server" | "service" | "systemname" | "username"

Description
A systemitem identifies any system-related item or term. The class attribute defines a number of common system-related terms.

Many inline elements in DocBook are, in fact, system related. Some of the objects identified by the class attribute on systemitem may eventually migrate out to become separate inline elements, and some inline elements may migrate into systemitem.

Processing expectations
Formatted inline.

Attributes
Common attributes and common linking attributes.

class
> Identifies the nature of the system item

Enumerated values:	
"daemon"	A daemon or other system process (syslogd)
"domainname"	A domain name (example.com)
"etheraddress"	An Ethernet address (00:05:4E:49:FD:8E)
"event"	An event of some sort (SIGHUP)
"eventhandler"	An event handler of some sort (hangup)
"filesystem"	A filesystem (ext3)
"fqdomainname"	A fully qualified domain name (my.example.com)
"groupname"	A group name (wheel)
"ipaddress"	An IP address (127.0.0.1)
"library"	A library (libncurses)

Enumerated values:	
"macro"	A macro
"netmask"	A netmask (`255.255.255.192`)
"newsgroup"	A newsgroup (`comp.text.xml`)
"osname"	An operating system name (`Hurd`)
"process"	A process (`gnome-cups-icon`)
"protocol"	A protocol (`FTP`)
"resource"	A resource
"server"	A server (`mail.example.com`)
"service"	A service (`ppp`)
"systemname"	A system name (`hephaistos`)
"username"	A username (`ndw`)

See Also
computeroutput, envar, filename, prompt, userinput

Examples

```
<article xmlns='http://docbook.org/ns/docbook'
         xmlns:xlink='http://www.w3.org/1999/xlink'>
<title>Example systemitem</title>

<para>For many years, O'Reilly's primary web server,
<link xlink:href="http://www.oreilly.com/">http://www.oreilly.com/</link>,
was hosted by <application>WN</application> on
<systemitem class="systemname">helio.oreilly.com</systemitem>.
</para>

</article>
```

For many years, O'Reilly's primary web server, *http://www.oreilly.com/*, was hosted by WN on `helio.oreilly.com`.

---

table (db.cals.table)   A formal table in a document

Synopsis
table (db.cals.table) ::= ((((title & titleabbrev?), info? db.titleforbidden.info) | info db.titleonlyreq.info), (alt? & *Indexing inlines** & textobject*), (mediaobject+ | tgroup+), caption? db.caption)

Attribute synopsis
Common attributes and common linking attributes.

Additional attributes:

- colsep (enumeration) = "0" | "1"

- floatstyle
- frame (enumeration) = "all" | "bottom" | "none" | "sides" | "top" | "topbot"
- label
- orient (enumeration) = "land" | "port"
- pgwide (enumeration) = "0" | "1"
- rowheader (enumeration) = "firstcol" | "norowheader"
- rowsep (enumeration) = "0" | "1"
- shortentry (enumeration) = "0" | "1"
- tabstyle
- tocentry (enumeration) = "0" | "1"

Additional constraints

- example must not occur among the children or descendants of table.
- figure must not occur among the children or descendants of table.
- equation must not occur among the children or descendants of table.
- informaltable must not occur among the children or descendants of table.
- caution must not occur among the children or descendants of table.
- important must not occur among the children or descendants of table.
- note must not occur among the children or descendants of table.
- tip must not occur among the children or descendants of table.
- warning must not occur among the children or descendants of table.

Description

This table element identifies a formal table (one without a title). DocBook allows either CALS or HTML tables, both of which describe tables geometrically using rows, columns, and cells.

Tables may include column headers and footers with thead and tfoot, respectively. Use the rowheader attribute to identify row headers.

Processing expectations

Formatted as a displayed block. This element is expected to obey the semantics of the *CALS Table Model Document Type Definition* [calsdtd].

Attributes

Common attributes and common linking attributes.

colsep
> Specifies the presence or absence of the column separator.

Enumerated values:	
"0"	No column separator rule.
"1"	Provide a column separator rule on the right.

floatstyle
: Specifies style information to be used when rendering the float.

frame
: Specifies how the table is to be framed. Note that there is no way to obtain a border on only the starting edge (left, in left-to-right writing systems) of the table.

Enumerated values:	
"all"	Frame all four sides of the table. In some environments with limited control over table border formatting, such as HTML, this may imply additional borders.
"bottom"	Frame only the bottom of the table.
"none"	Place no border on the table. In some environments with limited control over table border formatting, such as HTML, this may disable other borders as well.
"sides"	Frame the left and right sides of the table.
"top"	Frame the top of the table.
"topbot"	Frame the top and bottom of the table.

label
: Specifies an identifying string for presentation purposes.

orient
: Specifies the orientation of the table.

Enumerated values:	
"land"	90 degrees counterclockwise from the rest of the text flow.
"port"	The same orientation as the rest of the text flow.

pgwide
: Indicates if the element is rendered across the column or the page.

Enumerated values:	
"0"	The element should be rendered in the current text flow (with the flow column width).
"1"	The element should be rendered across the full text page.

rowheader
: Indicates whether or not the entries in the first column should be considered row headers.

Enumerated values:	
"firstcol"	Indicates that entries in the first column of the table are functionally row headers (analogous to the way that a thead provides column headers).
"norowheader"	Indicates that entries in the first column have no special significance with respect to column headers.

rowsep

Specifies the presence or absence of the row separator.

Enumerated values:	
"0"	No row separator rule.
"1"	Provide a row separator rule below.

shortentry

Indicates if the short or long title should be used in a list of tables.

Enumerated values:	
"0"	Indicates that the full title should be used.
"1"	Indicates that the short title (titleabbrev) should be used.

tabstyle

Specifies the table style.

tocentry

Indicates if the table should appear in a list of tables.

Enumerated values:	
"0"	Indicates that the table should not occur in the list of tables.
"1"	Indicates that the table should appear in the list of tables.

See Also

colspec, entry, entrytbl, equation, example, figure, informalequation, informalexample, informalfigure, informaltable, row, spanspec, table (db.html.table), tbody, tfoot, tgroup, thead

Examples

```
<article xmlns='http://docbook.org/ns/docbook'>
<title>Example table</title>

<table xml:id="ex.calstable" frame='all'>
<title>Sample CALS Table</title>
<tgroup cols='5' align='left' colsep='1' rowsep='1'>
<colspec colname='c1'/>
<colspec colname='c2'/>
```

```
<colspec colname='c3'/>
<colspec colnum='5' colname='c5'/>
<thead>
<row>
  <entry namest="c1" nameend="c2" align="center">Horizontal Span</entry>
  <entry>a3</entry>
  <entry>a4</entry>
  <entry>a5</entry>
</row>
</thead>
<tfoot>
<row>
  <entry>f1</entry>
  <entry>f2</entry>
  <entry>f3</entry>
  <entry>f4</entry>
  <entry>f5</entry>
</row>
</tfoot>
<tbody>
<row>
  <entry>b1</entry>
  <entry>b2</entry>
  <entry>b3</entry>
  <entry>b4</entry>
  <entry morerows='1' valign='middle'><para>Vertical Span</para></entry>
</row>
<row>
  <entry>c1</entry>
  <entry namest="c2" nameend="c3" align='center' morerows='1' valign='bottom'>
      Span Both</entry>
  <entry>c4</entry>
</row>
<row>
  <entry>d1</entry>
  <entry>d4</entry>
  <entry>d5</entry>
</row>
</tbody>
</tgroup>
</table>

</article>
```

Table 3. Sample CALS Table

Horizontal Span		a3	a4	a5
b1	b2	b3	b4	Vertical Span
c1	Span Both		c4	
d1			d4	d5
f1	f2	f3	f4	f5

table (db.html.table)

Synopsis

table (db.html.table) ::= (info? ^{db.titleforbidden.info}, caption ^{db.html.caption}, (col* | colgroup*),
thead? ^{db.html.thead}, tfoot? ^{db.html.tfoot}, (tbody ^{db.html.tbody}+ | tr+))

Attribute synopsis

Common attributes.

Additional attributes:

- floatstyle
- label
- orient (enumeration) = "land" | "port"
- pgwide (enumeration) = "0" | "1"
- summary
- width (enumeration) = xsd:integer | xsd:string (Pattern: "[0–9]+%")
- border (nonNegativeInteger)
- frame (enumeration) = "void" | "above" | "below" | "hsides" | "lhs" | "rhs" | "vsides" | "box" | "border"
- rules (enumeration) = "none" | "groups" | "rows" | "cols" | "all"
- cellspacing (enumeration) = xsd:integer | xsd:string (Pattern: "[0–9]+%")
- cellpadding (enumeration) = xsd:integer | xsd:string (Pattern: "[0–9]+%")
- tabstyle

Additional constraints

- example must not occur among the children or descendants of table.
- figure must not occur among the children or descendants of table.
- equation must not occur among the children or descendants of table.
- informaltable must not occur among the children or descendants of table.
- caution must not occur among the children or descendants of table.
- important must not occur among the children or descendants of table.
- note must not occur among the children or descendants of table.
- tip must not occur among the children or descendants of table.
- warning must not occur among the children or descendants of table.

Description

This table element identifies a formal (captioned) HTML table. DocBook allows either CALS or HTML tables, both of which describe tables geometrically using rows, columns, and cells.

HTML tables may include column headers and footers. To identify a row header, use a th in the row.

Why aren't HTML tables in the HTML namespace?

HTML tables were introduced in DocBook V4.3 which was not in a namespace and was defined normatively with a DTD. DTDs do not support namespaces very well. The Technical Committee decided to simply add the HTML element names to DocBook. This solution simplified specification, avoided issues of namespace support in DTDs, and solved the most compelling use case: cut-and-paste of simple, text-only HTML tables into DocBook.

Strictly speaking, it would be incorrect to put these elements in the XHTML namespace because the DocBook common attributes are allowed on all of them and the td and th elements have very different content models than their HTML counterparts.

Processing expectations

Formatted as a displayed block. This element is expected to obey the semantics described in *Tables (http://www.w3.org/TR/html401/struct/tables.html)*, as specified in *XHTML 1.0* [XHTML].

Attributes

Common attributes.

border
Specifies the width (in pixels only) of the frame around a table.

cellpadding
Specifies the amount of space between the border of the cell and its contents. If the value of this attribute is a pixel length, all four margins should be this distance from the contents. If the value of the attribute is a percentage length, the top and bottom margins should be equally separated from the content based on a percentage of the available vertical space, and the left and right margins should be equally separated from the content based on a percentage of the available horizontal space.

Enumerated values:

xsd:integer	An explicit padding
xsd:string (Pattern: "[0–9]+%")	A percentage padding

cellspacing
Specifies how much space the user agent should leave between the left side of the table and the lefthand side of the leftmost column, the top of the table and the top side of the topmost row, and so on for the right and bottom of the table. The attribute also specifies the amount of space to leave between cells.

Enumerated values:	
`xsd:integer`	An explicit spacing
`xsd:string` (Pattern: "[0–9]+%")	A percentage spacing

class

> Assigns a class name or set of class names to an element. Any number of elements may be assigned the same class name or names. Multiple class names must be separated by whitespace characters.

floatstyle

> Specifies style information to be used when rendering the float.

frame

> Specifies which sides of the frame surrounding a table will be visible.

Enumerated values:	
"void"	No sides; this is the default value
"above"	The top side only
"below"	The bottom side only
"hsides"	The top and bottom sides only
"lhs"	The lefthand side only
"rhs"	The righthand side only
"vsides"	The right and left sides only
"box"	All four sides
"border"	All four sides

label

> Specifies an identifying string for presentation purposes.

lang

> Specifies the base language of an element's attribute values and text content. The default value of this attribute is unknown.

onclick

> Occurs when the pointing device button is clicked over an element.

ondblclick

> Occurs when the pointing device button is double-clicked over an element.

onkeydown

> Occurs when a key is pressed down over an element.

onkeypress

> Occurs when a key is pressed and released over an element.

onkeyup
> Occurs when a key is released over an element.

onmousedown
> Occurs when the pointing device button is pressed over an element.

onmousemove
> Occurs when the pointing device is moved while it is over an element.

onmouseout
> Occurs when the pointing device is moved away from an element.

onmouseover
> Occurs when the pointing device is moved onto an element.

onmouseup
> Occurs when the pointing device button is released over an element.

orient
> Specifies the orientation of the table.

Enumerated values:	
"land"	90 degrees counterclockwise from the rest of the text flow.
"port"	The same orientation as the rest of the text flow.

pgwide
> Indicates if the element is rendered across the column or the page.

Enumerated values:	
"0"	The element should be rendered in the current text flow (with the flow column width).
"1"	The element should be rendered across the full text page.

rules
> Specifies which rules will appear between cells within a table. The rendering of rules is user agent dependent.

Enumerated values:	
"none"	No rules. This is the default value.
"groups"	Rules will appear between row groups (see thead, tfoot, and tbody) and column groups (see colgroup and col) only.
"rows"	Rules will appear between rows only.
"cols"	Rules will appear between columns only.
"all"	Rules will appear between all rows and columns.

style
> Specifies style information for the current element.

summary

Provides a summary of the table's purpose and structure for user agents rendering to nonvisual media such as speech and Braille.

tabstyle

Specifies the table style.

title

This attribute offers advisory information about the element for which it is set.

width

Specifies the desired width of the entire table and is intended for visual user agents. When the value is a percentage value, the value is relative to the user agent's available horizontal space. In the absence of any width specification, table width is determined by the user agent.

Enumerated values:

xsd:integer	An explicit width
xsd:string (Pattern: "[0–9]+%")	A percentage width

See Also

colspec, entry, entrytbl, equation, example, figure, informalequation, informalexample, informalfigure, informaltable, row, spanspec, table (db.cals.table), tbody, tfoot, tgroup, thead

Examples

```
<article xmlns='http://docbook.org/ns/docbook'>
<title>Example table</title>

<table xml:id="ex.htmltable">
<caption>Sample HTML Table</caption>
<thead>
  <tr>
    <td>Head 1</td>
    <td>Head 2</td>
  </tr>
</thead>
<tbody>
  <tr>
    <td>Body 1</td>
    <td>Body 2</td>
  </tr>
</tbody>
</table>

</article>
```

Table 4. Sample HTML Table

Head 1	Head 2
Body 1	Body 2

tag

A component of XML (or SGML) markup

Synopsis

tag ::= (text | phrase ^{db._phrase} | replaceable | *Graphic inlines* | *Indexing inlines* | *Linking inlines* | *Ubiquitous inlines*)*

Attribute synopsis

Common attributes and common linking attributes.

Additional attributes:

- class (enumeration) = "attribute" | "attvalue" | "element" | "emptytag" | "endtag" | "genentity" | "localname" | "namespace" | "numcharref" | "paramentity" | "pi" | "prefix" | "comment" | "starttag" | "xmlpi"
- namespace (anyURI)

Description

A tag identifies an XML or SGML markup construct. The utility of this element is almost wholly constrained to books about markup.

Processing expectations

Formatted inline.

A tag generates all the necessary punctuation before and after the construct it identifies. For example, it generates both the leading ampersand and the trailing semicolon when the class is genentity.

Attributes

Common attributes and common linking attributes.

class
> Identifies the nature of the tag content

Enumerated values:	
"attribute"	An attribute
"attvalue"	An attribute value
"element"	An element
"emptytag"	An empty element tag
"endtag"	An end tag
"genentity"	A general entity

Enumerated values:	
"localname"	The local name part of a qualified name
"namespace"	A namespace
"numcharref"	A numeric character reference
"paramentity"	A parameter entity
"pi"	A processing instruction
"prefix"	The prefix part of a qualified name
"comment"	An SGML comment
"starttag"	A start tag
"xmlpi"	An XML processing instruction

namespace
> Identifies the namespace of the tag content

See Also

`computeroutput`, `constant`, `literal`, `markup`, `option`, `optional`, `parameter`, `prompt`, `replaceable`, `userinput`, `varname`

task

A task to be completed

Synopsis

task ::= ((((title & titleabbrev? & subtitle?), info? ^{db.titleforbidden.info}) | info ^{db.titlereq.info}), task summary?, taskprerequisites?, procedure, example*, taskrelated?)

Attribute synopsis

Common attributes and common linking attributes.

Description

A `task` encapsulates a procedure providing an explicit location for summary information, identifying prerequisites for the task, examples, and pointers to related information.

Processing expectations

Formatted as a displayed block.

See Also

`procedure`, `taskprerequisites`, `taskrelated`, `tasksummary`

Examples

```
<article xmlns='http://docbook.org/ns/docbook'>
  <title>Example task</title>
  <task>
    <title>Changing a light bulb</title>
    <tasksummary>
      <para>How to change a light bulb</para>
```

```
      </tasksummary>
      <taskprerequisites>
        <para>Make sure you have a new light bulb.</para>
        <para>Make sure you have turned off the light switch.</para>
      </taskprerequisites>
      <procedure>
        <step><para>Remove the old light bulb.</para></step>
        <step><para>Insert the new light bulb.</para></step>
        <step><para>Turn on the new light bulb.</para></step>
        <step><para>Throw away the old light bulb.</para></step>
      </procedure>
    </task>

  </article>
```

taskprerequisites

The prerequisites for a task

Synopsis

taskprerequisites ::= ((((title? & titleabbrev?), info? $^{\text{db.titleforbidden.info}}$) | info $^{\text{db.titleonly.info}}$), (annotation | bridgehead | remark | revhistory | *Indexing inlines* | *Admonition elements* | *Formal elements* | *Graphic elements* | *Informal elements* | *List elements* | *Paragraph elements* | *Publishing elements* | *Synopsis elements* | *Technical elements* | *Verbatim elements*)+)

Attribute synopsis

Common attributes and common linking attributes.

Description

The taskprerequisites element is used to describe preparations that must be made before a task is attempted.

Processing expectations

Formatted as a displayed block.

See Also

task, taskrelated, tasksummary

Examples

See task for an example using this element.

taskrelated

Information related to a task

Synopsis

taskrelated ::= ((((title? & titleabbrev?), info? $^{\text{db.titleforbidden.info}}$) | info $^{\text{db.titleonly.info}}$), (annotation | bridgehead | remark | revhistory | *Indexing inlines* | *Admonition elements* | *Formal elements* | *Graphic elements* | *Informal elements* | *List elements* | *Paragraph elements* | *Publishing elements* | *Synopsis elements* | *Technical elements* | *Verbatim elements*)+)

Attribute synopsis

Common attributes and common linking attributes.

Description

The `taskrelated` element provides other, relevant information about a task (cross-references to other parts of the document, suggested next steps, etc.).

Processing expectations

Formatted as a displayed block.

See Also

`task`, `taskprerequisites`, `tasksummary`

tasksummary

A summary of a task

Synopsis

tasksummary ::= ((((title? & titleabbrev?), info? ^{db.titleforbidden.info}) | `info` ^{db.titleonly.info}), (*annotation* | `bridgehead` | `remark` | `revhistory` | *Indexing inlines* | *Admonition elements* | *Formal elements* | *Graphic elements* | *Informal elements* | *List elements* | *Paragraph elements* | *Publishing elements* | *Synopsis elements* | *Technical elements* | *Verbatim elements*)+)

Attribute synopsis

Common attributes and common linking attributes.

Description

A `tasksummary` provides introductory or summary information about a `task`.

Processing expectations

Formatted as a displayed block.

See Also

`task`, `taskprerequisites`, `taskrelated`

Examples

See `task` for an example using this element.

tbody (db.cals.entrytbl.tbody)

A wrapper for the rows of a table or informal table

Synopsis

tbody (db.cals.entrytbl.tbody) ::= `row` ^{db.entrytbl.row}+

Attribute synopsis

Common attributes and common linking attributes.

Additional attributes:

- `valign` (enumeration) = "bottom" | "middle" | "top"

Description

The `tbody` wrapper identifies the `rows` of a table that form the body of the table, as distinct from the header (`thead`) and footer (`tfoot`) rows.

In most tables, the tbody contains most of the rows.

Processing expectations
This element is expected to obey the semantics of the *CALS Table Model Document Type Definition* [calsdtd].

Attributes
Common attributes and common linking attributes.

valign
> Specifies the vertical alignment of text in an entry

Enumerated values:	
"bottom"	Aligned on the bottom of the entry
"middle"	Aligned in the middle
"top"	Aligned at the top of the entry

See Also
colspec, entry, entrytbl, informaltable, row, spanspec, table, tbody (db.cals.tbody), tfoot, tgroup, thead

---

tbody (db.cals.tbody)

A wrapper for the rows of a table or informal table

Synopsis
tbody (db.cals.tbody) ::= row $^{db.row}$+

Attribute synopsis
Common attributes and common linking attributes.

Additional attributes:

- valign (enumeration) = "bottom" | "middle" | "top"

Description
The tbody wrapper identifies the rows of a table that form the body of the table, as distinct from the header (thead) and footer (tfoot) rows.

In most tables, the tbody contains most of the rows.

Processing expectations
This element is expected to obey the semantics of the *CALS Table Model Document Type Definition* [calsdtd].

Attributes
Common attributes and common linking attributes.

valign
> Specifies the vertical alignment of text in an entry

See Also
colspec, entry, entrytbl, informaltable, row, spanspec, table, tbody (db.cals.entrytbl.tbody), tfoot, tgroup, thead

tbody (db.html.tbody)

A wrapper for the rows of an HTML table or informal HTML table

Synopsis
tbody (db.html.tbody) ::= tr+

Attribute synopsis
Attributes:

- align (enumeration) = "left" | "center" | "right" | "justify" | "char"
- char
- charoff (enumeration) = xsd:integer | xsd:string (Pattern: "[0–9]+%")
- valign (enumeration) = "top" | "middle" | "bottom" | "baseline"

Description
The tbody wrapper identifies the rows of a table that form the body of the table, as distinct from the header (thead) and footer (tfoot) rows.

In most tables, the tbody contains most of the rows.

Processing expectations
This element is expected to obey the semantics described in *Tables* (*http://www.w3.org/TR/html401/struct/tables.html*), as specified in *XHTML 1.0* [XHTML].

Attributes

align

Specifies the alignment of data and the justification of text in a cell.

Enumerated values:	
"left"	Left-flush data/Left-justify text. This is the default value for table data.
"center"	Center data/Center-justify text. This is the default value for table headers.
"right"	Right-flush data/Right-justify text.
"justify"	Double-justify text.
"char"	Align text around a specific character. If a user agent doesn't support character alignment, behavior in the presence of this value is unspecified.

char

Specifies a single character within a text fragment to act as an axis for alignment. The default value for this attribute is the decimal point character for the current language as set by the `lang` attribute (e.g., the period in English and the comma in French). User agents are not required to support this attribute.

charoff

When present, specifies the offset to the first occurrence of the alignment character on each line. If a line doesn't include the alignment character, it should be horizontally shifted to end at the alignment position. When `charoff` is used to set the offset of an alignment character, the direction of offset is determined by the current text direction (set by the `dir` attribute). In left-to-right texts (the default), offset is from the left margin. In right-to-left texts, offset is from the right margin. User agents are not required to support this attribute.

Enumerated values:	
`xsd:integer`	An explicit offset
`xsd:string` (Pattern: "[0–9]+%")	A percentage offset

class

Assigns a class name or set of class names to an element. Any number of elements may be assigned the same class name or names. Multiple class names must be separated by whitespace characters.

lang

Specifies the base language of an element's attribute values and text content. The default value of this attribute is unknown.

onclick

Occurs when the pointing device button is clicked over an element.

ondblclick

Occurs when the pointing device button is double-clicked over an element.

onkeydown

Occurs when a key is pressed down over an element.

onkeypress

Occurs when a key is pressed and released over an element.

onkeyup

Occurs when a key is released over an element.

onmousedown

Occurs when the pointing device button is pressed over an element.

onmousemove

Occurs when the pointing device is moved while it is over an element.

onmouseout

Occurs when the pointing device is moved away from an element.

onmouseover

Occurs when the pointing device is moved onto an element.

onmouseup

Occurs when the pointing device button is released over an element.

style

Specifies style information for the current element.

title

Offers advisory information about the element for which it is set.

valign

Specifies the vertical position of data within a cell.

Enumerated values:	
"top"	Cell data is flush with the top of the cell.
"middle"	Cell data is centered vertically within the cell. This is the default value.
"bottom"	Cell data is flush with the bottom of the cell.
"baseline"	All cells in the same row as a cell whose `valign` attribute has this value should have their textual data positioned so that the first text line occurs on a baseline common to all cells in the row. This constraint does not apply to subsequent text lines in these cells.

See Also

colspec, entry, entrytbl, informaltable, row, spanspec, table, tbody (db.cals.tbody), tfoot, tgroup, thead

---

td

Synopsis

td ::= ((text | *Bibliography inlines* | *Error inlines* | *Graphic inlines* | *GUI inlines* | *Indexing inlines* | *Keyboard inlines* | *Linking inlines* | *Markup inlines* | *Math inlines* | *Object-oriented programming inlines* | *Operating system inlines* | *Product inlines* | *Programming inlines* | *Publishing inlines* | *Technical inlines* | *Ubiquitous inlines*)* | (annotation | bridgehead | remark | revhistory | *Indexing inlines* | *Admonition elements* | *Formal elements* | *Graphic elements* | *Informal elements* | *List elements* | *Paragraph elements* | *Publishing elements* | *Synopsis elements* | *Technical elements* | *Verbatim elements*)*)

Attribute synopsis

Attributes:

- abbr
- axis
- headers

- scope (enumeration) = "row" | "col" | "rowgroup" | "colgroup"
- rowspan (nonNegativeInteger)
- colspan (nonNegativeInteger)
- align (enumeration) = "left" | "center" | "right" | "justify" | "char"
- char
- charoff (enumeration) = xsd:integer | xsd:string (Pattern: "[0–9]+%")
- valign (enumeration) = "top" | "middle" | "bottom" | "baseline"

Description
Identifies an entry in an HTML table.

Processing expectations
This element is expected to obey the semantics described in *Tables* (*http://www.w3.org/ TR/html401/struct/tables.html*), as specified in *XHTML 1.0* [XHTML].

Attributes

abbr
> Provides an abbreviated form of the cell's content and may be rendered by user agents when appropriate in place of the cell's content. Abbreviated names should be short since user agents may render them repeatedly. For instance, speech synthesizers may render the abbreviated headers relating to a particular cell before rendering that cell's content.

align
> Specifies the alignment of data and the justification of text in a cell.

Enumerated values:	
"left"	Left-flush data/Left-justify text. This is the default value for table data.
"center"	Center data/Center-justify text. This is the default value for table headers.
"right"	Right-flush data/Right-justify text.
"justify"	Double-justify text.
"char"	Align text around a specific character. If a user agent doesn't support character alignment, behavior in the presence of this value is unspecified.

axis
> May be used to place a cell into conceptual categories that can be considered to form axes in an *n*-dimensional space. User agents may give users access to these categories (e.g., the user may query the user agent for all cells that belong to certain categories, the user agent may present a table in the form of a table of contents, etc.). Please consult an HTML reference for more details.

char
> Specifies a single character within a text fragment to act as an axis for alignment. The default value for this attribute is the decimal point character for the current

language as set by the lang attribute (e.g., the period in English and the comma in French). User agents are not required to support this attribute.

charoff

When present, specifies the offset to the first occurrence of the alignment character on each line. If a line doesn't include the alignment character, it should be horizontally shifted to end at the alignment position. When charoff is used to set the offset of an alignment character, the direction of offset is determined by the current text direction (set by the `dir` attribute). In left-to-right texts (the default), offset is from the left margin. In right-to-left texts, offset is from the right margin. User agents are not required to support this attribute.

Enumerated values:	
`xsd:integer`	An explicit offset
`xsd:string` (Pattern: "[0–9]+%")	A percentage offset

class

Assigns a class name or set of class names to an element. Any number of elements may be assigned the same class name or names. Multiple class names must be separated by whitespace characters.

colspan

Specifies the number of columns spanned by the current cell. The default value of this attribute is one ("1"). The value zero ("0") means that the cell spans all columns from the current column to the last column of the column group (`colgroup`) in which the cell is defined.

headers

Specifies the list of header cells that provide header information for the current data cell. The value of this attribute is a space-separated list of cell names; those cells must be named by setting their `id` attribute. Authors generally use the `headers` attribute to help nonvisual user agents render header information about data cells (e.g., header information is spoken prior to the cell data), but the attribute may also be used in conjunction with stylesheets.

lang

Specifies the base language of an element's attribute values and text content. The default value of this attribute is unknown.

onclick

Occurs when the pointing device button is clicked over an element.

ondblclick

Occurs when the pointing device button is double-clicked over an element.

onkeydown

Occurs when a key is pressed down over an element.

onkeypress
> Occurs when a key is pressed and released over an element.

onkeyup
> Occurs when a key is released over an element.

onmousedown
> Occurs when the pointing device button is pressed over an element.

onmousemove
> Occurs when the pointing device is moved while it is over an element.

onmouseout
> Occurs when the pointing device is moved away from an element.

onmouseover
> Occurs when the pointing device is moved onto an element.

onmouseup
> Occurs when the pointing device button is released over an element.

rowspan
> Specifies the number of rows spanned by the current cell. The default value of this attribute is one ("1"). The value zero ("0") means that the cell spans all rows from the current row to the last row of the table section (`thead`, `tbody`, or `tfoot`) in which the cell is defined.

scope
> Specifies the set of data cells for which the current header cell provides header information. This attribute may be used in place of the `headers` attribute, particularly for simple tables.

Enumerated values:	
"row"	The current cell provides header information for the rest of the row that contains it.
"col"	The current cell provides header information for the rest of the column that contains it.
"rowgroup"	The header cell provides header information for the rest of the row group that contains it.
"colgroup"	The header cell provides header information for the rest of the column group that contains it.

style
> Specifies style information for the current element.

title
> Offers advisory information about the element for which it is set.

valign
> Specifies the vertical position of data within a cell.

Enumerated values:	
"top"	Cell data is flush with the top of the cell.

Enumerated values:	
"middle"	Cell data is centered vertically within the cell. This is the default value.
"bottom"	Cell data is flush with the bottom of the cell.
"baseline"	All cells in the same row as a cell whose `valign` attribute has this value should have their textual data positioned so that the first text line occurs on a baseline common to all cells in the row. This constraint does not apply to subsequent text lines in these cells.

term
The word or phrase being defined or described in a variable list

Synopsis
term ::= (text | *Bibliography inlines* | *Error inlines* | *Graphic inlines* | *GUI inlines* | *Indexing inlines* | *Keyboard inlines* | *Linking inlines* | *Markup inlines* | *Math inlines* | *Object-oriented programming inlines* | *Operating system inlines* | *Product inlines* | *Programming inlines* | *Publishing inlines* | *Technical inlines* | *Ubiquitous inlines*)*

Attribute synopsis
Common attributes and common linking attributes.

Description
The `term` in a `varlistentry` identifies the thing that is described or defined by that entry.

Processing expectations
Formatted as a displayed block. A `term` is usually formatted to make it stand out with respect to the text that follows. The best presentation depends on several factors, including the number and length of the terms. The `termlength` attribute on the containing `variablelist` may influence the presentation of `terms`. See `variablelist`.

termdef
An inline definition of a term

Synopsis
termdef ::= (text | *Bibliography inlines* | *Error inlines* | *Graphic inlines* | *GUI inlines* | *Indexing inlines* | *Keyboard inlines* | *Linking inlines* | *Markup inlines* | *Math inlines* | *Object-oriented programming inlines* | *Operating system inlines* | *Product inlines* | *Programming inlines* | *Publishing inlines* | *Technical inlines* | *Ubiquitous inlines*)*

Attribute synopsis
Common attributes and common linking attributes.

Additional attributes:

- `baseform`
- `sortas`

Additional constraints

- A `termdef` must contain exactly one `firstterm`.

Description

A `termdef` is an inline term definition. Some styles of documentation collect all terms together in a `glossary` of some sort, but another style is to place the definitions inline.

The `glossary` and `glosslist` elements support the former style, `termdef` the latter.

Every term should have an `xml:id` attribute to uniquely identify it. The content of the `termdef` is the definition of the term. Often it is valuable to word the definition so that it will stand alone, in case it becomes useful to extract all the terms into a separate glossary in addition to having them defined inline.

Every `termdef` must contain exactly one `firstterm`. The `firstterm` identifies the actual term defined by the `termdef`.

Processing expectations

Formatted inline.

Attributes

Common attributes and common linking attributes.

baseform

> Specifies the base form of the term, the one that appears in the glossary. This allows adjectival, plural, and other variations of the term to appear in the element. The element content is the default base form.

sortas

> Specifies the string by which the element's content is to be sorted; if unspecified, the content is used.

Examples

```
<article xmlns="http://docbook.org/ns/docbook"
    xmlns:xlink='http://www.w3.org/1999/xlink'>
<title>termdef</title>

<para>
  This paragraph contains an inline term definition.
  <termdef xml:id="dt-xml-processor">A software module
  called an <firstterm>XML processor</firstterm> is used
  to read XML documents and provide access to their
  content and structure.</termdef> The definition comes
  from <link xlink:href="http://www.w3.org/TR/REC-xml">the
  XML Recommendation</link>.
</para>

</article>
```

This paragraph contains an inline term definition. [Definition: A software module called an *XML processor* is used to read XML documents and provide access to their content and structure.] The definition comes from the XML Recommendation (*http://www.w3.org/TR/REC-xml*).

tertiary

Synopsis

tertiary ::= (text | *Bibliography inlines* | *Error inlines* | *Graphic inlines* | *GUI inlines* | *Indexing inlines* | *Keyboard inlines* | *Linking inlines* | *Markup inlines* | *Math inlines* | *Object-oriented programming inlines* | *Operating system inlines* | *Product inlines* | *Programming inlines* | *Publishing inlines* | *Technical inlines* | *Ubiquitous inlines*)*

Attribute synopsis

Common attributes and common linking attributes.

Additional attributes:

* `sortas`

Description

A `tertiary` element contains a third-level word or phrase in an `indexterm`. The text of a `tertiary` term is less significant than the `primary` and `secondary` terms for sorting and display purposes.

DocBook does not define any additional levels. You cannot use `indexterms` to construct indexes with more than three levels without extending the schema.

In `indexterms`, you can only have one primary, secondary, and tertiary term. If you want to index multiple tertiary terms for the same primary and secondary, you must repeat the primary and secondary in another `indexterm`. You cannot place several `tertiarys` in the same primary.

Processing expectations

Suppressed. This element provides data for processing but is not rendered in the primary flow of text.

Attributes

Common attributes and common linking attributes.

sortas

Specifies the string by which the term is to be sorted; if unspecified, the term content is used

See Also

`indexentry`, `indexterm`, `primary`, `primaryie`, `secondary`, `secondaryie`, `see`, `seealso`, `seealsoie`, `seeie`, `tertiaryie`

tertiaryie

Synopsis

tertiaryie ::= (text | *Bibliography inlines* | *Error inlines* | *Graphic inlines* | *GUI inlines* | *Indexing inlines* | *Keyboard inlines* | *Linking inlines* | *Markup inlines* | *Math inlines* | *Object-oriented programming inlines* | *Operating system inlines* | *Product inlines* | *Programming inlines* | *Publishing inlines* | *Technical inlines* | *Ubiquitous inlines*)*

Attribute synopsis

Common attributes.

Description

A `tertiaryie` identifies a third-level word or words in an `indexentry`.

In `indexentry`s, you can specify as many tertiary terms as are necessary. Secondary and tertiary terms can be mixed, following the primary.

Processing expectations

Formatted as a displayed block. A `tertiaryie` occurs below a `secondaryie`. If more than one `tertiaryie` occurs, they are usually aligned with each other and indented from the secondary.

See Also

indexentry, indexterm, primary, primaryie, secondary, secondaryie, see, seealso, seealsoie, seeie, tertiary

textdata

Synopsis
textdata ::= info? db.titleforbidden.info

Attribute synopsis

Common attributes.

Additional attributes:

- encoding
- *Each of:*
  - —format
  - —*Exactly one of:*
    - —**fileref** (anyURI)
    - —**entityref** (ENTITY)

Required attributes are shown in **bold**.

Description

This element points to an external entity containing text to be inserted.

Any markup in the text identified with textdata will be escaped. In other words, this element is for inserting things like program listings, not parts of an XML document. To break a document into separate physical files, use XInclude or external parsed entities.

Processing expectations

May be formatted inline or as a displayed block, depending on context.

There are two ways to provide content for textdata: entityref or fileref. It is best to use only one of these methods; however, if multiple sources are provided, entityref will be used in favor of fileref.

If the encoding is such that the processor will not be able to determine the encoding of the text, the encoding can be specified in the encoding attribute. For encodings registered (as charsets) (*http://www.iana.org/assignments/character-sets*) with the Internet Assigned Numbers Authority, recommended best practice suggests that they be referred to using their registered names.

Attributes

Common attributes.

encoding
> Identifies the encoding of the text in the external file

entityref
> Identifies the location of the data by external identifier (entity name)

fileref
> Identifies the location of the data by URI

format
> Specifies the format of the data

textobject

A wrapper for a text description of an object and its associated meta-information

Synopsis

textobject ::= (info? [db.titleforbidden.info], ((annotation | bridgehead | remark | revhistory | *Indexing inlines* | *Admonition elements* | *Formal elements* | *Graphic elements* | *Informal elements* | *List elements* | *Paragraph elements* | *Publishing elements* | *Synopsis elements* | *Technical elements* | *Verbatim elements*)+ | phrase [db.phrase] | textdata))

Attribute synopsis

Common attributes and common linking attributes.

Description

A textobject is a wrapper containing a textual description of a media object and its associated meta-information. A textobject is only allowed in mediaobject as a fallback. It cannot be the primary content.

There are two different forms of `textobject`, and it is not unreasonable for a media object to contain both of them.

In the first form, the content of a `textobject` is simply a `phrase`. This form is a mechanism for providing a simple "alt text" for a media object. The phrase might be used, for example, as the value of the `alt` attribute on an HTML `img`, with the primary content of the image coming from one of the other objects in the media object.

In the second form, the content of `textobject` is a longer, prose description. This form could be used when rendering to devices that are incapable of displaying any of the other alternatives.

Processing expectations

May be formatted inline or as a displayed block, depending on context. It might not be rendered at all, depending on its placement within a `mediaobject` or `inlinemediaobject` and the constraints on the publishing system. For a more detailed description of the semantics involved, see `mediaobject`.

See Also

`audioobject`, `caption`, `imageobject`, `inlinemediaobject`, `mediaobject`, `videoobject`

---

tfoot (db.cals.tfoot)
A table footer consisting of one or more rows

Synopsis

tfoot (db.cals.tfoot) ::= (`colspec`*, `row` $^{db.row}$+)

Attribute synopsis

Common attributes and common linking attributes.

Additional attributes:

- `valign` (enumeration) = "bottom" | "middle" | "top"

Description

The `tfoot` wrapper identifies the `rows` of a table that form the foot of the table, as distinct from the header (`thead`) and body (`tbody`) rows.

Footer rows are always rendered at the end of the table, despite their logical placement near the beginning.

Processing expectations

This element is expected to obey the semantics of the *CALS Table Model Document Type Definition* [calsdtd]. Footer rows are often presented in an alternate typographic style, such as boldface.

In paged media, if a table spans across multiple pages, footer rows are printed on the bottom of each page.

In our experience, relatively few formatters handle footer rows correctly.

Attributes

Common attributes and common linking attributes.

valign

>   Specifies the vertical alignment of text in an entry

Enumerated values:	
"bottom"	Aligned on the bottom of the entry
"middle"	Aligned in the middle
"top"	Aligned at the top of the entry

See Also

colspec, entry, entrytbl, informaltable, row, spanspec, table, tbody, tfoot (db.html.tfoot), tgroup, thead

---

tfoot (db.html.tfoot)
A table footer consisting of one or more rows in an HTML table

Synopsis

tfoot (db.html.tfoot) ::= tr+

Attribute synopsis

Attributes:

- align (enumeration) = "left" | "center" | "right" | "justify" | "char"
- char
- charoff (enumeration) = xsd:integer | xsd:string (Pattern: "[0–9]+%")
- valign (enumeration) = "top" | "middle" | "bottom" | "baseline"

Description

The tfoot wrapper identifies the rows of a table that form the foot of the table, as distinct from the header (thead) and body (tbody) rows.

Footer rows are always rendered at the end of the table, despite their logical placement near the beginning.

Processing expectations

This element is expected to obey the semantics described in *Tables* (*http://www.w3.org/TR/html401/struct/tables.html*), as specified in *XHTML 1.0* [XHTML]. Footer rows are often presented in an alternate typographic style, such as boldface.

In paged media, if a table spans across multiple pages, footer rows are printed on the bottom of each page.

In our experience, relatively few formatters handle footer rows correctly.

Attributes

align
> Specifies the alignment of data and the justification of text in a cell.

Enumerated values:	
"left"	Left-flush data/Left-justify text. This is the default value for table data.
"center"	Center data/Center-justify text. This is the default value for table headers.
"right"	Right-flush data/Right-justify text.
"justify"	Double-justify text.
"char"	Align text around a specific character. If a user agent doesn't support character alignment, behavior in the presence of this value is unspecified.

char
> Specifies a single character within a text fragment to act as an axis for alignment. The default value for this attribute is the decimal point character for the current language as set by the `lang` attribute (e.g., the period in English and the comma in French). User agents are not required to support this attribute.

charoff
> When present, specifies the offset to the first occurrence of the alignment character on each line. If a line doesn't include the alignment character, it should be horizontally shifted to end at the alignment position. When `charoff` is used to set the offset of an alignment character, the direction of offset is determined by the current text direction (set by the `dir` attribute). In left-to-right texts (the default), offset is from the left margin. In right-to-left texts, offset is from the right margin. User agents are not required to support this attribute.

Enumerated values:	
`xsd:integer`	An explicit offset
`xsd:string` (Pattern: "[0–9]+%")	A percentage offset

class
> Assigns a class name or set of class names to an element. Any number of elements may be assigned the same class name or names. Multiple class names must be separated by whitespace characters.

lang
> Specifies the base language of an element's attribute values and text content. The default value of this attribute is unknown.

onclick
> Occurs when the pointing device button is clicked over an element.

ondblclick
> Occurs when the pointing device button is double-clicked over an element.

onkeydown
> Occurs when a key is pressed down over an element.

onkeypress
> Occurs when a key is pressed and released over an element.

onkeyup
> Occurs when a key is released over an element.

onmousedown
> Occurs when the pointing device button is pressed over an element.

onmousemove
> Occurs when the pointing device is moved while it is over an element.

onmouseout
> Occurs when the pointing device is moved away from an element.

onmouseover
> Occurs when the pointing device is moved onto an element.

onmouseup
> Occurs when the pointing device button is released over an element.

style
> Specifies style information for the current element.

title
> Offers advisory information about the element for which it is set.

valign
> Specifies the vertical position of data within a cell.

Enumerated values:	
"top"	Cell data is flush with the top of the cell.
"middle"	Cell data is centered vertically within the cell. This is the default value.
"bottom"	Cell data is flush with the bottom of the cell.
"baseline"	All cells in the same row as a cell whose valign attribute has this value should have their textual data positioned so that the first text line occurs on a baseline common to all cells in the row. This constraint does not apply to subsequent text lines in these cells.

See Also
colspec, entry, entrytbl, informaltable, row, spanspec, table, tbody, tfoot (db.cals.tfoot), tgroup, thead

---

tgroup
A wrapper for the main content of a table, or part of a table

Synopsis

tgroup ::= (colspec*, spanspec*, thead? ^{db.cals.thead}, tfoot? ^{db.cals.tfoot}, tbody ^{db.cals.tbody})

Attribute synopsis

Common attributes and common linking attributes.

Additional attributes:

- `align` (enumeration) = "center" | "char" | "justify" | "left" | "right"
- `char`
- `charoff` (decimal)
- **`cols`** (positiveInteger)
- `colsep` (enumeration) = "0" | "1"
- `rowsep` (enumeration) = "0" | "1"
- `tgroupstyle`

Required attributes are shown in **bold**.

Description

A `tgroup` surrounds a logically complete portion of a table. Most tables consist of a single `tgroup`, but complex tables with widely varying column specifications may be easier to code using multiple `tgroups`.

The `tgroup` specifies the number of columns in the table, and contains all of the header, body, and footer rows, along with any additional column or span specifications necessary to express the geometry of the table.

Most of the properties of rows, columns, and cells inherit their default characteristics from the enclosing `tgroup`.

Processing expectations

This element is expected to obey the semantics of the *CALS Table Model Document Type Definition* [calsdtd].

Attributes

Common attributes and common linking attributes.

align
> Specifies the horizontal alignment of text in an entry.

Enumerated values:	
"center"	Centered
"char"	Aligned on a particular character
"justify"	Left and right justified
"left"	Left justified

Enumerated values:	
"right"	Right justified

char
> Specifies the alignment character when `align` is set to "char".

charoff
> Specifies the percentage of the column's total width that should appear to the left of the first occurrence of the character identified in `char` when `align` is set to "char".

cols
> The number of columns in the table. Must be an integer greater than zero.

colsep
> Specifies the presence or absence of the column separator.

Enumerated values:	
"0"	No column separator rule.
"1"	Provide a column separator rule on the right.

rowsep
> Specifies the presence or absence of the row separator.

Enumerated values:	
"0"	No row separator rule.
"1"	Provide a row separator rule below.

tgroupstyle
> Additional style information for downstream processing; typically the name of a style.

See Also

colspec, entry, entrytbl, informaltable, row, spanspec, table, tbody, tfoot, thead

---

th
A table header entry in an HTML table

Synopsis

th ::= ((text | *Bibliography inlines* | *Error inlines* | *Graphic inlines* | *GUI inlines* | *Indexing inlines* | *Keyboard inlines* | *Linking inlines* | *Markup inlines* | *Math inlines* | *Object-oriented programming inlines* | *Operating system inlines* | *Product inlines* | *Programming inlines* | *Publishing inlines* | *Technical inlines* | *Ubiquitous inlines*)* (annotation | bridgehead | remark | revhistory | *Indexing inlines* | *Admonition elements* | *Formal elements* | *Graphic elements* | *Informal elements* | *List elements* | *Paragraph elements* | *Publishing elements* | *Synopsis elements* | *Technical elements* | *Verbatim elements*)*)

Attribute synopsis

Attributes:

- `abbr`
- `axis`
- `headers`
- `scope` (enumeration) = "row" | "col" | "rowgroup" | "colgroup"
- `rowspan` (nonNegativeInteger)
- `colspan` (nonNegativeInteger)
- `align` (enumeration) = "left" | "center" | "right" | "justify" | "char"
- `char`
- `charoff` (enumeration) = `xsd:integer` | `xsd:string` (Pattern: "[0–9]+%")
- `valign` (enumeration) = "top" | "middle" | "bottom" | "baseline"

Description

Identifies a "head" entry in an HTML table.

Processing expectations

This element is expected to obey the semantics described in *Tables* (*http://www.w3.org/TR/html401/struct/tables.html*), as specified in *XHTML 1.0* [XHTML].

Attributes

abbr

> Provides an abbreviated form of the cell's content and may be rendered by user agents when appropriate in place of the cell's content. Abbreviated names should be short since user agents may render them repeatedly. For instance, speech synthesizers may render the abbreviated headers relating to a particular cell before rendering that cell's content.

align

> Specifies the alignment of data and the justification of text in a cell.

Enumerated values:	
"left"	Left-flush data/Left-justify text. This is the default value for table data.
"center"	Center data/Center-justify text. This is the default value for table headers.
"right"	Right-flush data/Right-justify text.
"justify"	Double-justify text.
"char"	Align text around a specific character. If a user agent doesn't support character alignment, behavior in the presence of this value is unspecified.

axis

> May be used to place a cell into conceptual categories that can be considered to form axes in an *n*-dimensional space. User agents may give users access to these

categories (e.g., the user may query the user agent for all cells that belong to certain categories, the user agent may present a table in the form of a table of contents, etc.). Please consult an HTML reference for more details.

char

Specifies a single character within a text fragment to act as an axis for alignment. The default value for this attribute is the decimal point character for the current language as set by the `lang` attribute (e.g., the period in English and the comma in French). User agents are not required to support this attribute.

charoff

When present, specifies the offset to the first occurrence of the alignment character on each line. If a line doesn't include the alignment character, it should be horizontally shifted to end at the alignment position. When `charoff` is used to set the offset of an alignment character, the direction of offset is determined by the current text direction (set by the `dir` attribute). In left-to-right texts (the default), offset is from the left margin. In right-to-left texts, offset is from the right margin. User agents are not required to support this attribute.

Enumerated values:	
`xsd:integer`	An explicit offset
`xsd:string` (Pattern: "[0–9]+%")	A percentage offset

class

Assigns a class name or set of class names to an element. Any number of elements may be assigned the same class name or names. Multiple class names must be separated by whitespace characters.

colspan

Specifies the number of columns spanned by the current cell. The default value of this attribute is one ("1"). The value zero ("0") means that the cell spans all columns from the current column to the last column of the column group (`colgroup`) in which the cell is defined.

headers

Specifies the list of header cells that provide header information for the current data cell. The value of this attribute is a space-separated list of cell names; those cells must be named by setting their `id` attribute. Authors generally use the `headers` attribute to help nonvisual user agents render header information about data cells (e.g., header information is spoken prior to the cell data), but the attribute may also be used in conjunction with stylesheets.

lang

Specifies the base language of an element's attribute values and text content. The default value of this attribute is unknown.

onclick
> Occurs when the pointing device button is clicked over an element.

ondblclick
> Occurs when the pointing device button is double-clicked over an element.

onkeydown
> Occurs when a key is pressed down over an element.

onkeypress
> Occurs when a key is pressed and released over an element.

onkeyup
> Occurs when a key is released over an element.

onmousedown
> Occurs when the pointing device button is pressed over an element.

onmousemove
> Occurs when the pointing device is moved while it is over an element.

onmouseout
> Occurs when the pointing device is moved away from an element.

onmouseover
> Occurs when the pointing device is moved onto an element.

onmouseup
> Occurs when the pointing device button is released over an element.

rowspan
> Specifies the number of rows spanned by the current cell. The default value of this attribute is one ("1"). The value zero ("0") means that the cell spans all rows from the current row to the last row of the table section (thead, tbody, or tfoot) in which the cell is defined.

scope
> Specifies the set of data cells for which the current header cell provides header information. This attribute may be used in place of the headers attribute, particularly for simple tables.

Enumerated values:	
"row"	The current cell provides header information for the rest of the row that contains it.
"col"	The current cell provides header information for the rest of the column that contains it.
"rowgroup"	The header cell provides header information for the rest of the row group that contains it.
"colgroup"	The header cell provides header information for the rest of the column group that contains it.

style
> Specifies style information for the current element.

title
>   Offers advisory information about the element for which it is set.

valign
>   Specifies the vertical position of data within a cell.

Enumerated values:	
"top"	Cell data is flush with the top of the cell.
"middle"	Cell data is centered vertically within the cell. This is the default value.
"bottom"	Cell data is flush with the bottom of the cell.
"baseline"	All cells in the same row as a cell whose `valign` attribute has this value should have their textual data positioned so that the first text line occurs on a baseline common to all cells in the row. This constraint does not apply to subsequent text lines in these cells.

thead (db.cals.entrytbl.thead)

A table header consisting of one or more rows

Synopsis

thead (db.cals.entrytbl.thead) ::= (colspec*, row ^{db.entrytbl.row}+)

Attribute synopsis

Common attributes and common linking attributes.

Additional attributes:

*   valign (enumeration) = "bottom" | "middle" | "top"

Description

The thead wrapper identifies the rows of a table that form the head of the table, as distinct from the body (tbody) and foot (tfoot) rows.

Header rows are always rendered at the beginning of the table.

Processing expectations

This element is expected to obey the semantics of the *CALS Table Model Document Type Definition* [calsdtd]. Header rows are often presented in an alternate typographic style, such as boldface.

In paged media, if a table spans across multiple pages, header rows are printed at the top of each new page.

Attributes

Common attributes and common linking attributes.

valign
>   Specifies the vertical alignment of text in an entry

Enumerated values:	
"bottom"	Aligned on the bottom of the entry
"middle"	Aligned in the middle
"top"	Aligned at the top of the entry

See Also
colspec, entry, entrytbl, informaltable, row, spanspec, table, tbody, tfoot, tgroup, thead (db.cals.thead)

thead (db.cals.thead)
A table header consisting of one or more rows

Synopsis
thead (db.cals.thead) ::= (colspec*, row $^{db.row}$+)

Attribute synopsis
Common attributes and common linking attributes.

Additional attributes:

- valign (enumeration) = "bottom" | "middle" | "top"

Description
The thead wrapper identifies the rows of a table that form the head of the table, as distinct from the body (tbody) and foot (tfoot) rows.

Header rows are always rendered at the beginning of the table.

Processing expectations
This element is expected to obey the semantics of the *CALS Table Model Document Type Definition* [calsdtd]. Header rows are often presented in an alternate typographic style, such as boldface.

In paged media, if a table spans across multiple pages, header rows are printed at the top of each new page.

Attributes
Common attributes and common linking attributes.

valign
> Specifies the vertical alignment of text in an entry

Enumerated values:	
"bottom"	Aligned on the bottom of the entry
"middle"	Aligned in the middle
"top"	Aligned at the top of the entry

See Also

colspec, entry, entrytbl, *informaltable*, row, spanspec, *table*, tbody, tfoot, tgroup, thead (db.cals.entrytbl.thead)

---

thead (db.html.thead)

A table header consisting of one or more rows in an HTML table

Synopsis

thead (db.html.thead) ::= **tr+**

Attribute synopsis

Attributes:

- align (enumeration) = "left" | "center" | "right" | "justify" | "char"
- char
- charoff (enumeration) = xsd:integer | xsd:string (Pattern: "[0–9]+%")
- valign (enumeration) = "top" | "middle" | "bottom" | "baseline"

Description

The thead wrapper identifies the rows of a table that form the head of the table, as distinct from the body (tbody) and foot (tfoot) rows.

Header rows are always rendered at the beginning of the table.

Processing expectations

This element is expected to obey the semantics described in *Tables (http://www.w3.org/TR/html401/struct/tables.html)*, as specified in *XHTML 1.0* [XHTML]. Header rows are often presented in an alternate typographic style, such as boldface.

In paged media, if a table spans across multiple pages, header rows are printed at the top of each new page.

Attributes

align

> Specifies the alignment of data and the justification of text in a cell.

Enumerated values:	
"left"	Left-flush data/Left-justify text. This is the default value for table data.
"center"	Center data/Center-justify text. This is the default value for table headers.
"right"	Right-flush data/Right-justify text.
"justify"	Double-justify text.
"char"	Align text around a specific character. If a user agent doesn't support character alignment, behavior in the presence of this value is unspecified.

char
> Specifies a single character within a text fragment to act as an axis for alignment. The default value for this attribute is the decimal point character for the current language as set by the lang attribute (e.g., the period in English and the comma in French). User agents are not required to support this attribute.

charoff
> When present, specifies the offset to the first occurrence of the alignment character on each line. If a line doesn't include the alignment character, it should be horizontally shifted to end at the alignment position. When charoff is used to set the offset of an alignment character, the direction of offset is determined by the current text direction (set by the dir attribute). In left-to-right texts (the default), offset is from the left margin. In right-to-left texts, offset is from the right margin. User agents are not required to support this attribute.

Enumerated values:

xsd:integer	An explicit offset
xsd:string (Pattern: "[0–9]+%")	A percentage offset

class
> Assigns a class name or set of class names to an element. Any number of elements may be assigned the same class name or names. Multiple class names must be separated by whitespace characters.

lang
> Specifies the base language of an element's attribute values and text content. The default value of this attribute is unknown.

onclick
> Occurs when the pointing device button is clicked over an element.

ondblclick
> Occurs when the pointing device button is double-clicked over an element.

onkeydown
> Occurs when a key is pressed down over an element.

onkeypress
> Occurs when a key is pressed and released over an element.

onkeyup
> Occurs when a key is released over an element.

onmousedown
> Occurs when the pointing device button is pressed over an element.

onmousemove
> Occurs when the pointing device is moved while it is over an element.

onmouseout
> Occurs when the pointing device is moved away from an element.

onmouseover
> Occurs when the pointing device is moved onto an element.

onmouseup
> Occurs when the pointing device button is released over an element.

style
> Specifies style information for the current element.

title
> Offers advisory information about the element for which it is set.

valign
> Specifies the vertical position of data within a cell.

Enumerated values:	
"top"	Cell data is flush with the top of the cell.
"middle"	Cell data is centered vertically within the cell. This is the default value.
"bottom"	Cell data is flush with the bottom of the cell.
"baseline"	All cells in the same row as a cell whose valign attribute has this value should have their textual data positioned so that the first text line occurs on a baseline common to all cells in the row. This constraint does not apply to subsequent text lines in these cells.

See Also

colspec, entry, entrytbl, informaltable, row, spanspec, table, tbody, tfoot, tgroup, thead (db.cals.thead)

tip
A suggestion to the user, set off from the text

Synopsis

tip ::= (((((title? & titleabbrev?), info? db.titleforbidden.info) | info db.titleonly.info), (annotation | bridgehead | remark | revhistory | *Indexing inlines* | *Admonition elements* | *Formal elements* | *Graphic elements* | *Informal elements* | *List elements* | *Paragraph elements* | *Publishing elements* | *Synopsis elements* | *Technical elements* | *Verbatim elements*)+)

Attribute synopsis
Common attributes and common linking attributes.

Additional constraints

- caution must not occur among the children or descendants of tip.
- important must not occur among the children or descendants of tip.
- note must not occur among the children or descendants of tip.
- tip must not occur among the children or descendants of tip.

- warning must not occur among the children or descendants of tip.

Description
A tip is an admonition set off from the main text.

In some types of documentation, the semantics of admonitions are clearly defined (caution might imply the possibility of harm to equipment whereas warning might imply harm to a person), but DocBook makes no such assertions.

Processing expectations
Formatted as a displayed block. Often outputs the generated text "Tip" or some other visible indication of the type of admonition, especially if a title is not present. Sometimes outputs a graphical icon or other symbol as well.

See Also
caution, important, note, warning

Examples
```
<article xmlns='http://docbook.org/ns/docbook'>
<title>Example tip</title>

<tip>
<para>If you tie your shoelaces, you're less likely to trip and
fall down.
</para>
</tip>

</article>
```

 If you tie your shoelaces, you're less likely to trip and fall down.

---

title
The text of the title of a section of a document or of a formal block-level element

Synopsis
title ::= (text | *Bibliography inlines* | *Error inlines* | *Graphic inlines* | *GUI inlines* | *Indexing inlines* | *Keyboard inlines* | *Linking inlines* | *Markup inlines* | *Math inlines* | *Object-oriented programming inlines* | *Operating system inlines* | *Product inlines* | *Programming inlines* | *Publishing inlines* | *Technical inlines* | *Ubiquitous inlines*)*

Attribute synopsis
Common attributes and common linking attributes.

Description

The title element is widely used in DocBook. It identifies the titles of documents and parts of documents, and is the required caption on formal objects. It is also allowed as an optional title or caption on many additional block elements.

Processing expectations

Formatted as a displayed block. Titles are often repeated in several locations: for example, at the location where the object occurs, in the table of contents, and in running headers and footers.

DocBook does not offer any mechanism for indicating where a line break should occur in long titles. Titles are often repeated and no single line break is likely to be correct in all of the places where a title is used. Instead, you will have to rely on your processing system to provide a mechanism, such as a processing instruction, for identifying the location of forced line breaks.

See Also

subtitle, titleabbrev

Examples

```
<article xmlns='http://docbook.org/ns/docbook'>
<title>Example title</title>

<section>
  <title>A Top Level Section</title>

  <para>Actual content.</para>
</section>

</article>
```

titleabbrev

The abbreviation of a title

Synopsis

titleabbrev ::= (text | *Bibliography inlines* | *Error inlines* | *Graphic inlines* | *GUI inlines* | *Indexing inlines* | *Keyboard inlines* | *Linking inlines* | *Markup inlines* | *Math inlines* | *Object-oriented programming inlines* | *Operating system inlines* | *Product inlines* | *Programming inlines* | *Publishing inlines* | *Technical inlines* | *Ubiquitous inlines*)*

Attribute synopsis

Common attributes and common linking attributes.

Description

A titleabbrev holds an abbreviated version of a title. One common use of titleabbrev is for the text used in running headers or footers, when the proper title is too long to be used conveniently.

Processing expectations

May be formatted inline or as a displayed block, depending on context. Abbreviated titles are usually used only in specific contexts, such as headers and footers, and are suppressed everywhere else.

See Also

subtitle, title

Examples

```
<chapter xmlns='http://docbook.org/ns/docbook'>
<info>
  <title>How to Configure the Menu Subsystem
  of the Graphical User Interface</title>
  <titleabbrev>Configuring Menus</titleabbrev>
</info>

<para>Actual content.
</para>
</chapter>
```

---

toc

A table of contents

Synopsis

toc ::= ((((title? & titleabbrev?), info? $^{db.titleforbidden.info}$) | info $^{db.titleonly.info}$), (annotation | bridgehead | remark | revhistory | *Indexing inlines* | *Admonition elements* | *Formal elements* | *Graphic elements* | *Informal elements* | *List elements* | *Paragraph elements* | *Publishing elements* | *Synopsis elements* | *Technical elements* | *Verbatim elements*)*, (tocdiv | tocentry)*)

Attribute synopsis

Common attributes and common linking attributes.

Additional constraints

- If this element is the root element, it must have a `version` attribute.

Description

The toc element defines a table of contents, or more generally, a list of titles in a document.

Processing expectations

Formatted as a displayed block.

In real life, tocs are usually generated automatically by the presentation system and never have to be represented explicitly in the document source.

See Also

tocdiv, tocentry

Examples

```
<book xmlns='http://docbook.org/ns/docbook'>
<title>DocBook: The Definitive Guide</title>
<subtitle>TOC Markup Example</subtitle>

<toc>
  <title>Table of Contents</title>
  <tocdiv>
    <title>Preface</title>
    <tocentry>Why Read This Book?</tocentry>
    <tocentry>This Book's Audience</tocentry>
    <!-- ... -->
  </tocdiv>
  <tocdiv>
    <title>Part I. Introduction</title>
    <tocdiv>
      <title>Chapter 1. Getting Started with DocBook</title>
      <tocdiv>
        <title>A Short DocBook History</title>
        <tocentry>The HaL and O'Reilly Era</tocentry>
        <tocentry>The Davenport Era</tocentry>
        <tocentry>The OASIS Era</tocentry>
      </tocdiv>
      <tocdiv>
        <title>DocBook V5.0</title>
        <tocdiv>
          <title>What's New in DocBook V5.0?</title>
          <tocentry>Renamed and removed elements</tocentry>
          <!-- ... -->
        </tocdiv>
      </tocdiv>
    </tocdiv>
    <tocdiv>
      <title>Chapter 2. Creating DocBook Documents</title>
      <tocdiv>
        <title>Making an XML Document</title>
        <tocentry>An XML Declaration</tocentry>
        <!-- ... -->
      </tocdiv>
    </tocdiv>
  </tocdiv>
</toc>

<preface>
  <title>Preface</title>
  <para>DocBook provides a system for writing structured documents using
  <acronym>XML</acronym>. ...</para>

  <!-- ... -->

  <section>
    <title>Why Read This Book?</title>

    <para>This book is designed to be the clear, concise, normative reference to
```

```
    the DocBook schema. This book is the official documentation for DocBook.
    </para>

    <!-- ... -->
  </section>
</preface>

<!-- ... -->

</book>
```

---

tocdiv
A division in a table of contents

Synopsis
tocdiv ::= ((((title? & titleabbrev? & subtitle?), info? ^{db.titleforbidden.info}) | info? ^{db.info}), (annotation | bridgehead | remark | revhistory | *Indexing inlines* | *Admonition elements* | *Formal elements* | *Graphic elements* | *Informal elements* | *List elements* | *Paragraph elements* | *Publishing elements* | *Synopsis elements* | *Technical elements* | *Verbatim elements*)*, (tocdiv | tocentry)+)

Attribute synopsis
Common attributes.

Additional attributes:

- pagenum

Description
A tocdiv is a division in a manually constructed table of contents, or more generally, a list of titles.

Processing expectations
Formatted as a displayed block.

In real life, lists of titles are usually generated automatically by the presentation system and never have to be represented explicitly in the document source.

Attributes
Common attributes.

pagenum
   Indicates the page on which this element occurs in some version of the printed document

See Also
toc, tocentry

tocentry

A component title in a table of contents

Synopsis

tocentry ::= (text | *Bibliography inlines* | *Error inlines* | *Graphic inlines* | *GUI inlines* | *Indexing inlines* | *Keyboard inlines* | *Linking inlines* | *Markup inlines* | *Math inlines* | *Object-oriented programming inlines* | *Operating system inlines* | *Product inlines* | *Programming inlines* | *Publishing inlines* | *Technical inlines* | *Ubiquitous inlines*)*

Attribute synopsis

Common attributes.

Additional attributes:

* pagenum

Description

A `tocentry` is an entry in a manually constructed table of contents, or more generally, a list of titles.

Processing expectations

Formatted as a displayed block.

In real life, lists of titles are usually generated automatically by the presentation system and never have to be represented explicitly in the document source.

Attributes

Common attributes.

pagenum
> Indicates the page on which this element occurs in some version of the printed document

See Also

toc, tocdiv

token

A unit of information

Synopsis

token ::= (text | phrase ^{db.–phrase} | replaceable | *Graphic inlines* | *Indexing inlines* | *Linking inlines* | *Ubiquitous inlines*)*

Attribute synopsis

Common attributes and common linking attributes.

Description

A `token` identifies a unit of information. Usually, "tokens" are the result of some processing pass that has performed lexical analysis and divided a data set into the smallest units of information used for subsequent processing.

Exactly what constitutes a token varies by context.

Processing expectations

Formatted inline.

See Also

classname, property, symbol, type

Examples

```
<article xmlns='http://docbook.org/ns/docbook'>
<title>Example token</title>

<para>In parsing, line ends are turned into the <token>CRLF</token>, all other
whitespace becomes <token>WHITESP</token>.
</para>

</article>
```

In parsing, line ends are turned into the CRLF, all other whitespace becomes WHITESP.

---

tr

A row in an HTML table

Synopsis

tr ::= (td | th)+

Attribute synopsis

Attributes:

- align (enumeration) = "left" | "center" | "right" | "justify" | "char"
- char
- charoff (enumeration) = xsd:integer | xsd:string (Pattern: "[0–9]+%")
- valign (enumeration) = "top" | "middle" | "bottom" | "baseline"

Description

Identifies a row in an HTML table.

Processing expectations

This element is expected to obey the semantics described in *Tables* (*http://www.w3.org/ TR/html401/struct/tables.html*), as specified in *XHTML 1.0* [XHTML].

Attributes

align

Specifies the alignment of data and the justification of text in a cell.

Enumerated values:	
"left"	Left-flush data/Left-justify text. This is the default value for table data.
"center"	Center data/Center-justify text. This is the default value for table headers.
"right"	Right-flush data/Right-justify text.

Enumerated values:	
"justify"	Double-justify text.
"char"	Align text around a specific character. If a user agent doesn't support character alignment, behavior in the presence of this value is unspecified.

char

Specifies a single character within a text fragment to act as an axis for alignment. The default value for this attribute is the decimal point character for the current language as set by the `lang` attribute (e.g., the period in English and the comma in French). User agents are not required to support this attribute.

charoff

When present, specifies the offset to the first occurrence of the alignment character on each line. If a line doesn't include the alignment character, it should be horizontally shifted to end at the alignment position. When `charoff` is used to set the offset of an alignment character, the direction of offset is determined by the current text direction (set by the `dir` attribute). In left-to-right texts (the default), offset is from the left margin. In right-to-left texts, offset is from the right margin. User agents are not required to support this attribute.

Enumerated values:	
`xsd:integer`	An explicit offset
`xsd:string` (Pattern: "[0–9]+%")	A percentage offset

class

Assigns a class name or set of class names to an element. Any number of elements may be assigned the same class name or names. Multiple class names must be separated by whitespace characters.

lang

Specifies the base language of an element's attribute values and text content. The default value of this attribute is unknown.

onclick

Occurs when the pointing device button is clicked over an element.

ondblclick

Occurs when the pointing device button is double-clicked over an element.

onkeydown

Occurs when a key is pressed down over an element.

onkeypress

Occurs when a key is pressed and released over an element.

onkeyup

Occurs when a key is released over an element.

onmousedown
> Occurs when the pointing device button is pressed over an element.

onmousemove
> Occurs when the pointing device is moved while it is over an element.

onmouseout
> Occurs when the pointing device is moved away from an element.

onmouseover
> Occurs when the pointing device is moved onto an element.

onmouseup
> Occurs when the pointing device button is released over an element.

style
> Specifies style information for the current element.

title
> Offers advisory information about the element for which it is set.

valign
> Specifies the vertical position of data within a cell.

Enumerated values:	
"top"	Cell data is flush with the top of the cell.
"middle"	Cell data is centered vertically within the cell. This is the default value.
"bottom"	Cell data is flush with the bottom of the cell.
"baseline"	All cells in the same row as a cell whose valign attribute has this value should have their textual data positioned so that the first text line occurs on a baseline common to all cells in the row. This constraint does not apply to subsequent text lines in these cells.

trademark   A trademark

Synopsis
trademark ::= (text | phrase $^{db.\_phrase}$ | replaceable | *Graphic inlines* | *Indexing inlines* | *Linking inlines* | *Ubiquitous inlines*)*

Attribute synopsis
Common attributes and common linking attributes.

Additional attributes:

- class (enumeration) = "copyright" | "registered" | "service" | "trade"

Description
A trademark identifies a legal trademark.

One of the values of the `class` attribute on `trademark` is `Copyright`. DocBook also has a `copyright` element, but it is confined to meta-information. A copyright in running text is best represented as `<trademark class=copyright>`.

Processing expectations
Formatted inline.

In addition to `trademark`, two of the values of the `class` attribute on `productname` make assertions about trademarks; presumably the same markup is intended for both `trademark` and `productname` when they make assertions about trademarks.

Attributes
Common attributes and common linking attributes.

class
> Identifies the class of trademark

Enumerated values:	
"copyright"	A copyright
"registered"	A registered copyright
"service"	A service
"trade"	A trademark

See Also
`copyright`, `legalnotice`, `productname`

Examples

```
<article xmlns='http://docbook.org/ns/docbook'>
<title>Example trademark</title>

<para><trademark class='registered'>Nutshell Handbook</trademark> is a
registered trademark of O'Reilly Media, Inc.
</para>

</article>
```

Nutshell Handbook® is a registered trademark of O'Reilly Media, Inc.

type
The classification of a value

Synopsis
type ::= (text | phrase ^{db._phrase} | replaceable | *Graphic inlines* | *Indexing inlines* | *Linking inlines* | *Ubiquitous inlines*)*

Attribute synopsis
Common attributes and common linking attributes.

Description

In general usage, type identifies one member of a class of values.

In documenting computer programs, it identifies specifically a "type," as might be declared with typedef in the C programming language.

Processing expectations

Formatted inline.

See Also

classname, property, symbol, token

Examples

```
<article xmlns='http://docbook.org/ns/docbook'>
<title>Example type</title>

<para>The <function>geteuid</function> function returns a <type>uid_t</type> that
contains the user's <emphasis>effective</emphasis> user ID.
</para>

</article>
```

The geteuid function returns a uid_t that contains the user's *effective* user ID.

---

uri   A Uniform Resource Identifier

Synopsis

uri ::= (text | phrase ^{db._phrase} | replaceable | *Graphic inlines* | *Indexing inlines* | *Linking inlines* | *Ubiquitous inlines*)*

Attribute synopsis

Common attributes and common linking attributes.

Additional attributes:

- type

Description

The uri element identifies a Uniform Resource Identifier (URI) in content.

Processing expectations

Formatted inline. The uri element does not automatically generate a link to the URI it identifies.

DocBook does not mandate any values for the type attribute, but several useful values have been suggested:

- xmlnamespace for an XML namespace name; for example, *http://docbook.org/ns/docbook*
- saxfeaturename for a SAX feature name; for example, *http://xml.org/sax/features/namespaces*

- saxpropertyname for a SAX property name; for example, *http://xml.org/sax/properties/declaration-handler*
- soapaction for a SOAP action; see *SOAP Version 1.2 Part 2: Adjuncts (http://www.w3.org/TR/soap12-part2/#ActionFeature)*
- rddlpurpose for an RDDL purpose; see *Resource Directory Description Language (RDDL) (http://rddl.org/)*
- rddlnature for an RDDL nature; see *Resource Directory Description Language (RDDL) (http://rddl.org/)*
- homepage for a home page; for example, *http://nwalsh.com/*
- weblog for a web log; for example, *http://norman.walsh.name/*
- webpage for a web page; for example, *http://docbook.org/schemas/*
- website for a website; for example, *http://docbook.org*

Attributes

Common attributes and common linking attributes.

type
> Identifies the type of URI specified

---

userinput

Data entered by the user

Synopsis

userinput ::= (text | *Computer-output inlines* | *Graphic inlines* | *GUI inlines* | *Indexing inlines* | *Keyboard inlines* | *Linking inlines* | *Markup inlines* | *Operating system inlines* | *Technical inlines* | *Ubiquitous inlines* | *User-input inlines*)*

Attribute synopsis

Common attributes and common linking attributes.

Description

The userinput element identifies words or phrases that the user is expected to provide as input to a computer program.

Note that userinput is not a verbatim environment, but an inline.

Processing expectations

Formatted inline. Often presented in a fixed-width font.

See Also

computeroutput, constant, envar, filename, lineannotation, literal, literallayout, markup, option, optional, parameter, programlisting, prompt, replaceable, screen, screenshot, synopsis, systemitem, tag, varname

Examples

```
<article xmlns='http://docbook.org/ns/docbook'>
<title>Example userinput</title>
```

```
<para>At the system prompt, enter <userinput>xyzzy</userinput> to gain
supervisor access to the system.
</para>

</article>
```

At the system prompt, enter **xyzzy** to gain supervisor access to the system.

---

varargs

Synopsis

varargs ::= empty

Attribute synopsis

Common attributes and common linking attributes.

Description

A varargs indicates that a function takes a variable number of arguments.

Processing expectations

The varargs element produces generated text that indicates that the function takes a variable number of arguments. The exact generated text may vary. One common result is (...).

See Also

funcdef, funcparams, funcprototype, funcsynopsisinfo, function, paramdef, parameter, returnvalue, void

Examples

```
<article xmlns='http://docbook.org/ns/docbook'>
<title>Example varargs</title>

<funcsynopsis>
<funcsynopsisinfo>
#include &lt;varargs.h&gt;
</funcsynopsisinfo>
<funcprototype>
  <funcdef>int <function>max</function></funcdef>
  <varargs/>
</funcprototype>
</funcsynopsis>

</article>
```

#include <varargs.h>

int max(...);

variablelist

A list in which each entry is composed of a set of one or more terms and an associated description

Synopsis

variablelist ::= ((((title? & titleabbrev?), info? ^{db.titleforbidden.info}) | info ^{db.titleonly.info}), (annotation | bridgehead | remark | revhistory | *Indexing inlines* | *Admonition elements* | *Formal elements* | *Graphic elements* | *Informal elements* | *List elements* | *Paragraph elements* | *Publishing elements* | *Synopsis elements* | *Technical elements* | *Verbatim elements*)*, varlistentry+)

Attribute synopsis

Common attributes and common linking attributes.

Additional attributes:

- spacing (enumeration) = "compact" | "normal"
- termlength

Description

A variablelist is a list consisting of terms and their definitions or descriptions.

Processing expectations

Formatted as a displayed block.

There are many ways to present a variable list. DocBook does not mandate any particular presentation. The termlength attribute may influence the presentation of terms. The termlength attribute is often specified as a number of characters, but other forms are possible. This is an interchange issue.

Attributes

Common attributes and common linking attributes.

spacing

Specifies (a hint about) the spacing of the content

Enumerated values:	
"compact"	The spacing should be "compact".
"normal"	The spacing should be "normal".

termlength

Indicates a length beyond which the presentation system may consider a term too long and selects an alternate presentation for that term, item, or list

See Also

calloutlist, itemizedlist, listitem, orderedlist, segmentedlist, simplelist

Examples

```
<article xmlns='http://docbook.org/ns/docbook'>
  <title>Example variablelist</title>

 <variablelist><title>Font Filename Extensions</title>
```

```
<varlistentry>
  <term><filename>TTF</filename></term>
  <listitem>
    <para>TrueType fonts.</para>
  </listitem>
</varlistentry>
<varlistentry>
  <term><filename>PFA</filename></term>
  <term><filename>PFB</filename></term>
  <listitem>
    <para>
      PostScript fonts. <filename>PFA</filename> files are common
      on <acronym>UNIX</acronym> systems, <filename>PFB</filename>
      files are more common on Windows systems.
    </para>
  </listitem>
</varlistentry>
</variablelist>

</article>
```

Font Filename Extensions

TTF
> TrueType fonts.

PFA, PFB
> PostScript fonts. *PFA* files are common on UNIX systems, *PFB* files are more common on Windows systems.

---

varlistentry

A wrapper for a set of terms and the associated description in a variable list

Synopsis
varlistentry ::= (term+, listitem)

Attribute synopsis
Common attributes and common linking attributes.

Description
A varlistentry is an entry in a variablelist. Each varlistentry contains one or more terms and their description or definition.

Processing expectations
Formatted as a displayed block.

A term is usually formatted to make it stand out with respect to the text that follows. The best presentation depends on several factors, including the number and length of the terms. See variablelist.

varname

Synopsis

varname ::= (text | phrase ^{db._phrase} | replaceable | *Graphic inlines* | *Indexing inlines* | *Linking inlines* | *Ubiquitous inlines*)*

Attribute synopsis

Common attributes and common linking attributes.

Description

A varname identifies a variable name in a programming or expression language. Variables most often get their values from literals, replaceable values, constants, or symbols.

Processing expectations

Formatted inline.

See Also

command, computeroutput, constant, literal, markup, option, optional, parameter, prompt, replaceable, tag, userinput

Examples

```
<article xmlns='http://docbook.org/ns/docbook'>
<title>Example varname</title>

<para>In Perl, <varname>@ARGV</varname> contains the command-line parameters
used when the script was run.
</para>

</article>
```

In Perl, @ARGV contains the command-line parameters used when the script was run.

---

videodata

Synopsis

videodata ::= info? ^{db.titleforbidden.info}

Attribute synopsis

Common attributes.

Additional attributes:

- align (enumeration) = "center" | "char" | "justify" | "left" | "right"
- contentdepth
- contentwidth
- depth
- *Each of:*

— format

— *Exactly one of:*

— **fileref** (anyURI)

— **entityref** (ENTITY)

- scale (positiveInteger)
- scalefit (enumeration) = "0" | "1"
- valign (enumeration) = "bottom" | "middle" | "top"
- width

Required attributes are shown in **bold**.

Description

This element points to an external entity containing video data.

Processing expectations

May be formatted inline or as a displayed block, depending on context. Rendering a video is usually accomplished by reserving a rectangular area on the display and "running" the video in that frame.

There are two ways to provide content for `videodata`: `entityref` or `fileref`. It is best to use only one of these methods. However, if multiple sources are provided, `entityref` will be used in favor of `fileref`.

Attributes

Common attributes.

align
Specifies the (horizontal) alignment of the video data

Enumerated values:	
"center"	Centered horizontally
"char"	Aligned horizontally on the specified character
"justify"	Fully justified (left and right margins or edges)
"left"	Left aligned
"right"	Right aligned

contentdepth
Specifies the depth of the content rectangle

contentwidth
Specifies the width of the content rectangle

depth
Specifies the depth of the element

entityref
> Identifies the location of the data by external identifier (entity name)

fileref
> Identifies the location of the data by URI

format
> Specifies the format of the data

scale
> Specifies the scaling factor

scalefit
> Determines if anamorphic scaling is forbidden

Enumerated values:	
"0"	False (do not scale to fit; anamorphic scaling may occur)
"1"	True (scale to fit; anamorphic scaling is forbidden)

valign
> Specifies the vertical alignment of the video data

Enumerated values:	
"bottom"	Aligned on the bottom of the region
"middle"	Centered vertically
"top"	Aligned on the top of the region

width
> Specifies the width of the element

videoobject

A wrapper for video data and its associated meta-information

Synopsis
videoobject ::= (info? db.titleforbidden.info, videodata)

Attribute synopsis
Common attributes and common linking attributes.

Description
A videoobject is a wrapper containing videodata and its associated meta-information.

Processing expectations
May be formatted inline or as a displayed block, depending on context. It might not be rendered at all, depending on its placement within a mediaobject or inlinemediaob ject and the constraints on the publishing system. For a more detailed description of the semantics involved, see mediaobject.

See Also
audioobject, caption, imageobject, inlinemediaobject, mediaobject, textobject

Examples

```
<article xmlns='http://docbook.org/ns/docbook'>
<title>Example videoobject</title>

<mediaobject>
  <videoobject>
    <videodata fileref='movie.avi'/>
  </videoobject>
  <imageobject>
    <imagedata fileref='movie-frame.gif'/>
  </imageobject>
  <textobject>
    <para>This video illustrates the proper way to assemble an
    inverting time distortion device.
    </para>
    <warning>
      <para>It is imperative that the primary and secondary temporal
      couplings not be mounted in the wrong order. Temporal
      catastrophe is the likely result. The future you destroy
      may be your own.
      </para>
    </warning>
  </textobject>
</mediaobject>

</article>
```

void
An empty element in a function synopsis indicating that the function in question takes no arguments

Synopsis
void ::= empty

Attribute synopsis
Common attributes and common linking attributes.

Description
The void element indicates explicitly that a function has no arguments.

Processing expectations
The void element produces generated text that indicates the function has no arguments (or returns nothing). The exact generated text may vary. One common result is void.

See Also
funcdef, funcparams, funcprototype, funcsynopsisinfo, function, paramdef, parameter, returnvalue, varargs

volumenum

The volume number of a document in a set (as of books in a set or articles in a journal)

Synopsis

volumenum ::= (text | phrase ^{db._phrase} | replaceable | *Graphic inlines* | *Indexing inlines* | *Linking inlines* | *Ubiquitous inlines*)*

Attribute synopsis

Common attributes and common linking attributes.

Description

A volumenum identifies the volume number of a book in a set, or a periodical. It is a wrapper for bibliographic information.

Processing expectations

Formatted inline. Sometimes suppressed.

See Also

biblioid, issuenum, productnumber, seriesvolnums

warning

An admonition set off from the text

Synopsis

warning ::= (((((title? & titleabbrev?), info? ^{db.titleforbidden.info}) | info ^{db.titleonly.info}), (annotation | bridgehead | remark | revhistory | *Indexing inlines* | *Admonition elements* | *Formal elements* | *Graphic elements* | *Informal elements* | *List elements* | *Paragraph elements* | *Publishing elements* | *Synopsis elements* | *Technical elements* | *Verbatim elements*)+)

Attribute synopsis

Common attributes and common linking attributes.

Additional constraints

- caution must not occur among the children or descendants of warning.
- important must not occur among the children or descendants of warning.
- note must not occur among the children or descendants of warning.
- tip must not occur among the children or descendants of warning.
- warning must not occur among the children or descendants of warning.

Description

A warning is an admonition, usually set off from the main text.

In some types of documentation, the semantics of admonitions are clearly defined (caution might imply the possibility of harm to equipment whereas warning might imply harm to a person), but DocBook makes no such assertions.

Processing expectations

Formatted as a displayed block. Often outputs the generated text "Warning" or some other visible indication of the type of admonition, especially if a title is not present. Sometimes outputs a graphical icon or other symbol as well.

See Also

caution, important, note, tip

Examples

```
<article xmlns='http://docbook.org/ns/docbook'>
<title>Example warning</title>

<warning>
<para>Striking your thumb with a hammer may cause severe pain and discomfort.
</para>
</warning>

</article>
```

 Striking your thumb with a hammer may cause severe pain and discomfort.

---

wordasword

A word meant specifically as a word and not representing anything else

Synopsis

wordasword ::= (text | phrase $^{db.\_phrase}$ | replaceable | *Graphic inlines* | *Indexing inlines* | *Linking inlines* | *Ubiquitous inlines*)*

Attribute synopsis

Common attributes and common linking attributes.

Description

A lot of technical documentation contains words that have overloaded meanings. Sometimes it is useful to be able to use a word without invoking its technical meaning. The wordasword element identifies a word or phrase that might otherwise be interpreted in some specific way, and asserts that it should be interpreted simply as a word.

It is unlikely that the presentation of this element will be able to help readers understand the variation in meaning; good writing will have to achieve that goal. The real value of wordasword lies in the fact that full-text searching and indexing tools can use it to avoid false positives.

Processing expectations

Formatted inline.

See Also

abbrev, acronym, emphasis, foreignphrase, phrase, quote

Examples

```
<article xmlns='http://docbook.org/ns/docbook'>
<title>Example wordasword</title>
```

```
<para>A <wordasword>Term</wordasword> in algebra has a very different
meaning than a <tag>term</tag> in DocBook.
</para>

</article>
```

A *Term* in algebra has a very different meaning than a `term` in DocBook.

---

xref

Synopsis
xref ::= empty

Attribute synopsis
Common attributes and common linking attributes.

Additional attributes:

- `endterm` (IDREF)
- `xrefstyle`

Description
The `xref` element forms a cross-reference from the location of the `xref` to the element to which it points. Unlike `link` and the other cross-referencing elements, `xref` is empty. The processing system has to generate appropriate cross-reference text for the reader.

Processing expectations
Under ordinary circumstances, the `xref` points to some element with its `linkend` attribute and the processing system generates appropriate cross-reference text. There are three ways for the author to influence the generated text:

1. If the `endterm` attribute is specified on `xref`, the content of the element pointed to by `endterm` will be used as the text of the cross-reference.
2. Otherwise, if the object *pointed to* has a specified `xreflabel`, the content of that attribute will be used as the cross-reference text.
3. Finally, the author may specify a keyword (or other information) in the `xrefstyle` attribute. Unlike `endterm` and `xreflabel` which have rigid semantics, the content of the `xrefstyle` attribute is simply additional information for the processing system. What effect it has, if any, is dependent on the processing system.

Attributes
Common attributes and common linking attributes.

endterm
> Points to the element whose content is to be used as the text of the link

xrefstyle
> Specifies a keyword or keywords identifying additional style information

See Also
anchor, link, olink

Examples

```
<book xmlns='http://docbook.org/ns/docbook'>
<title>An Example Book</title>

<chapter xml:id="ch01"><title>XRef Samples</title>
<para>This paragraph demonstrates several features of <tag>XRef</tag>.
</para>

<itemizedlist>
  <listitem><para>A straight link generates the cross-reference text:
    <xref linkend="ch02"/>.
  </para></listitem>
  <listitem><para>A link to an element with an
    <tag class="attribute">XRefLabel</tag>:
  <xref linkend="ch03"/>.
  </para></listitem>
  <listitem><para>A link with an <tag class="attribute">EndTerm</tag>:
    <xref linkend="ch04" endterm="ch04short"/>.
  </para></listitem>
</itemizedlist>
</chapter>

<chapter xml:id="ch02">
  <title>The Second Chapter</title>
  <para>Some content here</para>
</chapter>

<chapter xml:id="ch03" xreflabel="Chapter the Third">
  <title>The Third Chapter</title>
  <para>Some content here</para>
</chapter>

<chapter xml:id="ch04">
  <title>The Fourth Chapter</title>
  <titleabbrev xml:id="ch04short">Chapter 4</titleabbrev>
  <para>Some content here</para>
</chapter>
</book>
```

year

The year of publication of a document

Synopsis
year ::= (text | phrase $^{db.\_phrase}$ | replaceable | *Graphic inlines* | *Indexing inlines* | *Linking inlines* | *Ubiquitous inlines*)*

Attribute synopsis
Common attributes and common linking attributes.

Description

A year element identifies a year. It is used in **copyright** to identify the year or years in which copyright is asserted.

Processing expectations

Formatted inline.

Examples

See **copyright** for an example that uses this element.

---

mml:*

Synopsis

mml:* ::= Any element from the *http://www.w3.org/1998/Math/MathML* namespace

Attribute synopsis

Attributes:

- *Zero or more of:*
  — *Any attribute*

Description

This position in a content model can be occupied by any element in the MathML namespace.

The Mathematical Markup Language (*http://www.w3.org/TR/MathML2/*) Recommendation from the W3C defines the Mathematical Markup Language, or MathML. MathML is an XML application for describing mathematical notation and capturing both its structure and its content.

A complete description of MathML is outside the scope of this reference.

Attributes

any attribute
    Any attribute, including any attribute in any namespace

Examples

```
<article xmlns='http://docbook.org/ns/docbook'
    xmlns:mml="http://www.w3.org/1998/Math/MathML">
<title>Example mml-math</title>

<informalequation>
<mml:math>
  <mml:msup>
    <mml:mi>x</mml:mi>
    <mml:mn>3</mml:mn>
  </mml:msup>
</mml:math>
```

```
</informalequation>

</article>
```

x^3

---

svg:*

Synopsis

svg:* ::= Any element from the *http://www.w3.org/2000/svg* namespace

Attribute synopsis

Attributes:

- *Zero or more of:*
  - *Any attribute*

Description

This position in a content model can be occupied by any element in the SVG namespace.

The Scalable Vector Graphics (*http://www.w3.org/TR/SVG/*) Recommendation from the W3C defines the features and syntax for SVG, a language for describing two-dimensional vector and mixed vector/raster graphics in XML.

A complete description of SVG is outside the scope of this reference.

Attributes

any attribute
    Any attribute, including any attribute in any namespace

Examples

```
<article xmlns='http://docbook.org/ns/docbook'
    version="5.0">
<title>Example svg-svg</title>

<mediaobject>
  <imageobject>
    <imagedata>
      <svg xmlns="http://www.w3.org/2000/svg"
       width="100" height="100" version="1.1">
    <rect x="20" y="20" width="80" height="80"
        style="fill:blue; stroke:green; stroke-width: 2;
            fill-opacity: 0.5; stroke-opacity: 0.9"/>
      </svg>
    </imagedata>
  </imageobject>
</mediaobject>

</article>
```

Synopsis
. ::=

- Any element from any namespace except:
    — *http://docbook.org/ns/docbook*
    — *http://www.w3.org/1999/xhtml*

Attribute synopsis
Attributes:

- *Zero or more of:*
    — *Any attribute*

Description
This position in a content model can be occupied by any element from any namespace.

Attributes

any attribute
   Any attribute, including any attribute in any namespace

## PART III

Appendixes

Installation

Installing DocBook

If you use editing software that already supports DocBook, then DocBook should be installed with that software. Although at this writing, DocBook V5.0 is new, many tools already support V5.0. The DocBook Wiki (*http://wiki.docbook.org/*) has a list of editing and other tools that support DocBook, along with other relevant information and links to further information.

If you are not using a tool that directly supports DocBook, then you will need to install one or more of the DocBook schemas directly. This appendix describes how to do that.

The most recent version of the DocBook V5.x schemas can be found at *http://docbook .org/schemas/5x.html*. At the time this was written the most recent version was V5.0. The directory for V5.0 (*http://docbook.org/xml/5.0/*) contains the RELAX NG schema, DTD, W3C XML schema, Schematron rules, tools to convert DocBook V4.x to V5.0, and a sample catalog file.

Installing the DocBook Schemas

The schemas may be installed in any convenient directory. If you download the file *docbook-5.0.zip* and unpack it, it will create a directory structure that puts each schema in its own directory. This directory structure matches the structure in the sample *catalog.xml* file, so you should be able to set up the catalog file (described in "XML Catalogs and DocBook" on page 490) with minimal effort.

Once you have unpacked the schemas, you will need to set them up so that your tools can use them. While each tool has its own procedure for accessing schemas, many use *XML Catalogs: OASIS Standard V1.1* [XML-CAT] as a common means to locate schemas, stylesheets, and other files. The next section describes how to set up a catalog for DocBook using the sample *catalog.xml* file from the distribution.

XML Catalogs and DocBook

SGML instances require either a public or system identifier to specify the schema. Public identifiers are abstract identifiers that must be mapped to a schema file to be useful. For the SGML versions of DocBook, the distribution included a catalog file, *docbook.cat* that provided mappings for all of the public identifiers referenced by DocBook. Unlike SGML, which allows an instance to use only a public identifier, XML requires a system identifier in the form of a URI. For the XML version of DocBook, the distribution contains a sample catalog file using the *XML Catalogs: OASIS Standard V1.1* [XML-CAT], which is used by many XML tools.

To quote the standard, an XML catalog "defines an entity catalog that maps both external identifiers and arbitrary URI references to URI references." This means that you can define mappings through an XML catalog that tell tools where you have put the schemas (and other files, like the stylesheets) on your system. Those tools can then access them without having to resolve a remote URL.

Installing and setting up the DocBook XML catalog

One way to set up a catalog for DocBook is install the DocBook stylesheets (see "Installing the DocBook Stylesheets" on page 492), which also sets up a catalog. You can also use the sample catalog from the schema distribution, which can be found at: *http://docbook.org/xml/5.0/catalog.xml*. The sample is a starting place, but it will almost surely not work "out of the box." To make it work, you need to make the catalog available to your tools, and you will also need to update the catalog entries to point to the right location on your system. Here is an example based on the sample file:

```
<catalog prefer="public"
        xml:base="file:///usr/share/xml/docbook/schema/rng/5.0/">
    <public publicId="-//OASIS//DTD DocBook XML 5.0//EN"
            uri="dtd/docbook.dtd"/>
    <system systemId="http://docbook.org/xml/5.0/dtd/docbook.dtd"
            uri="dtd/docbook.dtd"/>
    <uri name="http://www.oasis-open.org/docbook/xml/5.0/rng/docbook.rng"
        uri="rng/docbook.rng"/>
</catalog>
```

In this example, the public and system elements describe where to find the DTD associated with named public and system identifiers. The uri element describes where to find the RELAX NG schema. In all three cases, the uri attribute identifies a relative path to the file. The absolute path is constructed by concatenating the value of the xml:base attribute on the catalog element to the value of the uri attribute. If there is no xml:base attribute, the value of the uri attribute is used as is.

To make the catalog work on your system, set the xml:base attribute to the directory on your system that contains the schema directories. That should be the only change you need to make to the sample catalog.

If you already have other XML schemas installed, you probably already have a catalog file. On Linux systems, this is often in */etc/xml/catalog.xml*. In that case, you can add the following line to that file, replacing */usr/share/xml/docbook/catalog.xml* with the location of the DocBook catalog file on your system:

```
<nextCatalog catalog="file:///usr/share/xml/docbook/catalog.xml">
```

Some XML and XSL applications use the environment variable `XML_CATALOG_FILES`, which contains a delimited list of catalog filenames. Here is an example:

```
XML_CATALOG_FILES=/usr/share/xml/docbook/catalog.xml:/etc/xml/catalog
```

(On a Windows system, use semicolons instead of colons to delimit the filenames.)

Many applications also provide a configuration option that allows you to set the location of a catalog file. Check the documentation for your tool for details.

This description only scratches the surface of XML Catalogs. For a full description, go to the *XML Catalogs: OASIS Standard V1.1* [XML-CAT] or Bob Stayton's *DocBook XSL: The Complete Guide* [Stayton07].

Getting the ISO entity sets

Modern schema languages (including RELAX NG and W3X XML Schema) do not include the ISO Entity Sets. Therefore, you need to use other means if you want to use these or other sets of entities. For the ISO Entity Sets, some editors give you the ability to easily select needed characters and insert them into a document.

You can also directly include entity definitions in the prolog of your document. The World Wide Web Consortium (W3C) maintains the ISO Entity Set Definitions (*http://www.w3.org/2003/entities/*) and you can reference them from the document prolog as shown here:

```
<?xml version="1.0" encoding="utf-8"?>
<!DOCTYPE article [
<!ENTITY % isopub SYSTEM "http://www.w3.org/2003/entities/iso8879/isopub.ent">
%isopub;
]>
<article xmlns="http://docbook.org/ns/docbook" version="5.0">
<title>DocBook V5.0 &ndash; the superb documentation format</title>
…
</article>
```

For your convenience there is also a flattened entity definition file which contains all entity definitions.

```
<?xml version="1.0" encoding="utf-8"?>
<!DOCTYPE article [
<!ENTITY % allent SYSTEM "http://www.w3.org/2003/entities/2007/w3centities-f.ent">
%allent;
]>
<article xmlns="http://docbook.org/ns/docbook" version="5.0">
```

```
<title>DocBook V5.0 &ndash; the superb documentation format</title>
...
</article>
```

Installing the DocBook Stylesheets

Members of the OASIS DocBook Technical Committee and other interested people have developed a set of XSL stylesheets that can be used to transform DocBook into various forms, including: HTML, FO (for print), HTML Help, Java Help, ePub, and other formats.

The definitive guide to using the stylesheets is Bob Stayton's *DocBook XSL: The Complete Guide* [Stayton07]. The description below is sufficient to install and run the stylesheets in their standard form. However, to do any serious work with the stylesheets or to customize them, you should read Stayton's book.

Procedure A-1. Procedure for Installing DocBook XSL Stylesheets

1. Download the latest stylesheets from *http://sourceforge.net/projects/docbook/*. Look for a file with the name: docbook-xsl-ns-*X.YY.Z*.zip, where *X.YY.Z* is the version number of the latest stable release of the stylesheets.

2. Unpack the distribution into a directory on your system. The exact location is your choice. On Windows systems you might use a folder named: *C:\docbook\stylesheets*. On a Linux/UNIX-based system you might use a directory named */usr/share/xml/docbook/stylesheets*, or a directory under your home directory. As long as you have permissions to create and write in the directory, it doesn't matter where it is.

3. When you unpack the distribution, it will create a directory named *docbook-xsl-ns-X.YY.Z* that will contain the stylesheets.

4. This is all you need to do to install the distribution, however, on Linux/UNIX systems, you can run an install script that will set up catalogs for you. Look for a file named *INSTALL* for details.

You will also need an XSLT processor. If you are running Linux, you may already have xsltproc or Saxon installed on your system. If not, most Linux distributions will let you install one of these packages through their application installer.

If you are running Windows or Mac, you can find information about these applications at:

- xsltproc: *http://xmlsoft.org/XSLT/xsltproc2.html*
- Saxon: *http://saxon.sourceforge.net/*

DocBook Variants and Future Directions

DocBook Variants

The DocBook community has developed several variants that, while not part of the normative specification, have proven to be useful. These include:

Simplified DocBook

Simplified DocBook is a proper subset of DocBook. Therefore, any valid instance will also be valid against the full DocBook schema. The objective is to provide a significantly smaller schema that is useful for articles and other small documents. As of the publication of this book, the latest version of Simplified DocBook was based on DocBook V4.5. Further information can be found at *http://www.docbook .org/schemas/simplified*.

DocBook website

The DocBook website schema is a customization of the schema designed for building websites. There is also support in the DocBook stylesheets for this schema. As of the publication of this book, there is a version of the schema based on DocBook V5.0 under development. Information about the DocBook website and how to use it can be found in *DocBook XSL: The Complete Guide* [Stayton07] and at *http:// www.dpawson.co.uk/docbook/website/*. The latter has information about the Doc-Book V5.0 version of the schema.

DocBook slides

This schema is a customization for making slide sets. The schema and stylesheets can be found at *http://docbook.sourceforge.net* as part of the open source DocBook stylesheet distribution.

Future Directions

With the introduction of DocBook V5.0, there have been several new initiatives started to take advantage of the increased flexibility and customizability of the standard. Two of these initiatives have become subcommittees of the OASIS DocBook Technical Committee:

OASIS DocBook Publisher's Subcommittee
> This subcommittee is chartered to develop and maintain official variants of DocBook in support of the publishing industry. In May, 2009, this subcommittee released The DocBook Publishers Schema Version 1.0 (*http://docs.oasis-open.org/docbook/specs/publishers-1.0-spec-cd-01.html*), a draft based on the DocBook V5.0 standard.

OASIS DocBook eLearning Subcommittee
> This subcommittee will develop enhancements to the DocBook standard for eLearning applications, including materials for online learning, instructor-led training and other related educational activities.

DocBook Assembly Mechanism

In addition to these two subcommittees, there is a current effort to create markup for an "assembly" capability to better support development of documents using a modular approach.

Most modular methodologies use a topic-oriented approach, where writers create independent units of information that are meant to stand alone. Topics are then collected into a library in much the same way that programmers create libraries of functions. Authors select the topics they need to assemble the documentation for a particular system from the library.

In order to support modular methodologies, you need support for marking up individual topics, which DocBook does well. You also need support for some kind of "map" or "assembly" file that identifies which topics are required for a particular deliverable, and at least for print deliverables, what order they should be presented in.

The proposed DocBook assembly would serve this purpose. While still under consideration as this book is being written, the general outline of an assembly is clear. It would identify a collection of resources (which could include topics and other modules), an ordering of those resources for a particular document, a set of relationships between resources, and the transformations that are to be applied to the collection.

While DocBook already supports many aspects of topic-oriented writing, the assembly mechanism is being designed to provide a more capable and intuitive model for this type of methodology.

Resources

The quantity of information about XML grows daily. This appendix collects the references mentioned explicitly in this book and identifies additional resources related to DocBook and XML.

Latest Versions of DocBook Schemas

Since July, 1998, the DocBook Technical Committee of OASIS (Organization for the Advancement of Structured Information Standards) at *http://www.oasis-open.org/* has been responsible for the advancement and maintenance of the DocBook schemas, including any schemas from a subcommittee that are approved by the DocBook Technical Committee.

The latest releases of DocBook can be obtained from the official DocBook home page at *http://www.oasis-open.org/docbook/*. All normative versions of the DocBook standard, including derivatives like the Publisher's schema, are available at this site.

Information about the most commonly used, non-normative customizations of the DocBook schema, such as Simplified DocBook and DocBook Website, can be found at *http://docbook.org/*.

 The only schemas that are considered normative standards are those that have been approved through the OASIS process by the DocBook Technical Committee.

DocBook and XML Resources on the Web

The following websites and lists are excellent starting places for information about DocBook and XML:

The most recent version of this book
> The most recent online version of this book can be found at *http://docbook.org/*.

DocBook mailing lists
> OASIS maintains two public DocBook mailing lists:

> *docbook@lists.oasis-open.org*
>> This list is for general questions, comments, and discussion about DocBook, including questions about the schemas, syntax, semantics, and markup.
>>
>> An archive is maintained at: *http://lists.oasis-open.org/archives/docbook/*.

> *docbook-apps@lists.oasis-open.org*
>> This list is for questions, comments, and discussion about implementing Doc-Book, including questions about formatting, processing, using the stylesheets, and editing.
>>
>> An archive is maintained at: *http://lists.oasis-open.org/archives/docbook-apps/*.

> You can subscribe to either list at: *http://www.oasis-open.org/mlmanage/*.

DocBook stylesheets
> The DocBook stylesheets (*http://docbook.sourceforge.net/*) are a set of stylesheets for use with an XSLT engine like *xsltproc* or Saxon. The stylesheets can transform DocBook XML documents (including documents using DocBook 5.0 and earlier versions) into output formats like HTML, PDF, various help formats, and the ePub ebook format. The stylesheets are open source software maintained by the DocBook community.

DocBook Wiki
> The DocBook Wiki (*http://wiki.docbook.org*) contains a wide variety of DocBook information, from FAQs to lists of consultants.

Robin Cover's "Cover Pages"
> A large list of XML resources: *http://xml.coverpages.org*.

`comp.text.xml`
> Newsgroup devoted to XML issues. This newsgroup can be accessed through Google Groups at: *http://groups.google.com/group/comp.text.xml*.

FAQ
> A good XML FAQ is available at *http://xml.silmaril.ie/*.

XML.com
> XML.com (*http://www.xml.com/*), run by O'Reilly Media, is a site devoted to news and information about XML.

Introductory Material on the Web

These documents provide a good starting place for learning about XML.

[XML-Intro] TEI, ed. "A Gentle Introduction to XML." Text Encoding Initiative (TEI), March 2002, *http://www.tei-c.org/Guidelines/P4/html/SG.html*.

[XML-Tech] Norman Walsh. "A Technical Introduction to XML." February 1998, *http://nwalsh.com/docs/articles/xml/*.

[RNG-Intro] Clark, James, and Makoto Murata. "RELAX NG Tutorial." OASIS Open, December 2001, *http://www.relaxng.org/tutorial.html*.

References and Technical Notes on the Web

[XML-CAT] Walsh, Norman, ed. *XML Catalogs: OASIS Standard V1.1*. Organization for the Advancement of Structured Information Standards (OASIS), 7 October 2005, *http://www.oasis-open.org/committees/download.php/14809/xml-catalogs .html*.

[CALS] Severson, Eric, and Harvey Bingham, ed. *Table Interoperability: Issues for the CALS Table Model*. Organization for the Advancement of Structured Information Standards (OASIS), 21 November 1995, OASIS Technical Research Paper 9501:1995, *http://www.oasis-open.org/html/a501.htm*.

[calsdtd] Bingham, Harvey, ed. *CALS Table Model Document Type Definition*. Organization for the Advancement of Structured Information Standards (OASIS), 19 October 1995, OASIS Technical Memorandum TM 9502:1995, *http://www.oasis-open .org/html/a502.htm*.

[cals-xchg] Bingham, Harvey, ed. *Exchange Table Model Document Type Definition*. Organization for the Advancement of Structured Information Standards (OASIS), 8 May 1996, OASIS Technical Resolution TR 9503:1995, *http://www.oasis-open.org/ specs/a503.htm*.

[TGN] *Thesaurus of Geographic Names Online*. J. Paul Getty Trust, *http://www.getty .edu/research/tools/vocabulary/tgn*.

World Wide Web Consortium (W3C) Recommendations

[HTML] Raggett, Dave, et al., ed. *HTML 4.01 Specification*. World Wide Web Consortium, 24 December 1999, *http://www.w3.org/TR/html401/*.

[MathML] Carlisle, David, et al., ed. *Mathematical Markup Language (MathML) Version 2.0*. Second Edition, World Wide Web Consortium, 21 October 2003, *http:// www.w3.org/TR/MathML/*.

[XHTML] W3C HTML Working Group, ed. *XHTML 1.0 The Extensible HyperText Markup Language*. Second Edition, W3C Recommendation, 26 January 2000, revised 1 August 2002, *http://www.w3.org/TR/xhtml1*.

[XLink] DeRose, Steve, Eve Maler, and David Orchard, ed. *XML Linking Language (XLink) Version 1.0*. World Wide Web Consortium, 27 June 2001, *http://www.w3.org/TR/xlink/*.

[XML] Bray, Tim, et al., ed. *Extensible Markup Language (XML) 1.0*. Fifth Edition, World Wide Web Consortium, 26 November 2008, *http://www.w3.org/TR/xml*.

[XML-ID] Marsh, Jonathan, et al., ed. *xml:id Version 1.0*. World Wide Web Consortium, 9 September 2005, *http://www.w3.org/TR/xml-id/*.

[XML-NS] Bray, Tim, et al., ed. *Namespaces in XML*. Third Edition, World Wide Web Consortium, 8 December 2009, *http://www.w3.org/TR/xml-names/*.

[XPath] Berglund, Anders, et al., ed. *XML Path Language (XPath) 2.0*. World Wide Web Consortium, 23 January 2007, *http://www.w3.org/TR/xpath20/*.

[XQuery] Boad, Scott, et al., ed. *XQuery 1.0: An XML Query Language*. World Wide Web Consortium, 23 January 2007, *http://www.w3.org/TR/xquery/*.

[XSLT-1] Clark, James, ed. *XSL Transformations (XSLT) Version 1.0*. World Wide Web Consortium, 16 December 1999, *http://www.w3.org/TR/xslt*.

[XSLT-2] Kay, Michael, ed. *XSL Transformations (XSLT) Version 2.0*. World Wide Web Consortium, 23 January 2007, *http://www.w3.org/TR/xslt20/*.

Related Standards

[DCMI] Dublin Core Metadata Initiative. *Dublin Core Metadata Element Set, Version 1.1*. Dublin Core Metadata Initiative, January 2008, *http://dublincore.org/documents/dces/*. Now also an ISO standard: ISO 15836:2009.

[NVDL] ISO. *Namespace-based Validation Dispatching Language (NVDL)*. International Organization for Standardization, ISO/IEC 19757-4, 1 June 2006, *http://www.nvdl.org/*.

[Unicode] Allen, Julie D., et al., ed. *The Unicode Standard Version 5.2.0*. The Unicode Consortium, December 2009, *http://www.unicode.org/standard/standard.html*.

Internet RFCs

RFCs ("Request for Comments") are standards documents produced by the Internet Engineering Task Force (IETF).

[RFC-1630] Berners-Lee, Tim. *Universal Resource Identifiers in WWW*. Network Working Group, Internet Engineering Task Force (IETF), June 1994, *http://www.apps.ietf.org/rfc/rfc1630.html*.

[RFC-1736] Kunze, J. *Functional Recommendations for Internet Resource Locators.* Network Working Group, Internet Engineering Task Force (IETF), February 1995, *http://www.apps.ietf.org/rfc/rfc1736.html.*

[RFC-1737] Sollins, K. *Functional Requirements for Uniform Resource Names.* Network Working Group, Internet Engineering Task Force (IETF), December 1994, *http://www.apps.ietf.org/rfc/rfc1737.html.*

[RFC-1738] Berners-Lee, T., L. Masinter, and M. McCahill. *Uniform Resource Locators (URL).* Network Working Group, Internet Engineering Task Force (IETF), December 1994, *http://www.apps.ietf.org/rfc/rfc1738.html.*

[RFC-3066] Alvestrand, H. *Tags for the Identification of Languages.* Network Working Group, Internet Engineering Task Force (IETF), December 1994, *http://www.apps.ietf.org/rfc/rfc3066.html.*

Books and Printed Resources

[Fitz04] Fitzgerald, Michael. *XML Hacks: 100 Industrial-Strength Tips and Tools.* Sebastopol, CA:O'Reilly, July 2004, ISBN: 978-0596007119.

[Harold03] Harold, Elliotte Rusty. *Effective XML: 50 Specific Ways to Improve Your XML.* Boston:Addison-Wesley, October 2003, ISBN: 978-0321150400.

[Harold04] Harold, Elliotte Rusty, and W. Scott Means. *XML in a Nutshell.* Sebastopol, CA:O'Reilly, October 2003, ISBN: 978-0596007645.

[Kay08] Kay, Michael. *XSLT 2.0 and XPath 2.0 Programmer's Reference.* Indianapolis, IN:Wrox, May 2008, ISBN: 978-0470192740.

[Maler95] Maler, Eve, and Jeanne El Andaloussi. *Developing SGML DTDs: From Text to Model to Markup.* Prentice Hall, December 1995, ISBN: 978-0596004200. This book is out of print. However, the information on document schema modeling is still relevant and has not been superseded to date. Although the book is out of print, the authors have made an online version available at: *http://www.xmlgrrl.com/publications/DSDTD/index.html*

[Ray03] Ray, Erik. *Learning XML.* Second Edition, Sebastopol, CA:O'Reilly, September 2003, ISBN: 978-0596004200.

[Stayton07] Stayton, Bob. *DocBook XSL: The Complete Guide.* Fourth Edition, Sagehill Enterprises, 2007, ISBN: 978-0974152134. The essential guide to the DocBook XSL stylesheets.

[Tidwell08] Tidwell, Doug. *XSLT.* Second Edition, Sebastopol, CA:O'Reilly, June 2008, ISBN: 978-0596527211.

[Vlist03] van der Vlist, Eric. *RELAX NG.* Sebastopol, CA:O'Reilly, July 2003, ISBN: 978-0596004217.

XML Tools

Here is information about some of the tools mentioned in this book. If you are running Linux, you may be able to load some of these tools using a package manager like Synaptic, yum, or apt. Needless to say, this is not a comprehensive list; there are other capable tools available. However, these are a good starting place.

RELAX NG
> A variety of tools that support RELAX NG can be found at: *http://relaxng.org/*. These include:

MSV
> Sun Multi-Schema XML Validator (from Sun Microsystems). MSV is an open source program that validates RELAX NG as well as other schema languages including W3C XML Schema.
>
> *https://msv.dev.java.net/*

Jing
> An open source RELAX NG validator that supports both compact and XML syntax.
>
> *http://www.thaiopensource.com/relaxng/jing.html*

Trang
> An open source program that is a companion to Jing, Trang converts between various XML schema languages. It supports both compact and XML syntax for RELAX NG, XML 1.0 DTDs, and W3C XML Schemas, though it only supports W3C XML Schemas for output.
>
> *http://www.thaiopensource.com/relaxng/trang.html*

EMACS nXML mode
> This is an open source addon for emacs that supports syntax-directed editing using a RELAX NG compact mode schema. It validates as you type and will show you at any point what the valid set of elements, attributes, and attribute values is. It also supports automatic completion of partially typed elements, attributes, and attribute values.
>
> *http://www.thaiopensource.com/nxml-mode/*

Saxon
> Saxon is an XSLT processor. The basic processor is available as an open source product, and there are also commercial versions that offer additional features. The latest versions of Saxon support both XSLT 1.0 and 2.0.
>
> *http://saxon.sourceforge.net/*

xsltproc
> Xsltproc is an open source XSLT processor that supports XSLT 1.0.
>
> *http://xmlsoft.org/XSLT/xsltproc2.html*

<oXygen/> XML Editor

The <oXygen/> XML Editor is a popular commercial editor. The latest versions support DocBook V5.0, including both the RELAX NG and Schematron rules. It is also integrated with the DocBook stylesheets.

http://oxygenxml.com

XMLmind XML Editor (XXE)

The XMLmind XML Editor is a popular commercial editor that comes in two varieties, a personal edition and a professional edition. The personal edition is free for non-commercial use. Both versions support DocBook V5.0.

http://www.xmlmind.com/xmleditor/

Interchanging DocBook Documents

One of the early factors that motivated the development of DocBook was the desire for companies to interchange documents. In particular, UNIX vendors wanted to be able to interchange common UNIX documentation.

A great deal of effort went into making sure that DocBook could handle most (probably all) of the documents that were likely to be exchanged. This avoids the guaranteed problem of interchanging documents created with extended schemas.

However, simply using DocBook or a subset of it is not enough to ensure successful interchange. If you send someone your DocBook files, you must also tell the recipient about the markup your documents use, any additional markup conventions, and any processing expectations that impose constraints.

This appendix provides a sample interchange questionnaire to help draw your attention to those areas that might cause problems.

For maximum portability, delivered DocBook documents should be accompanied by a filled-out interchange questionnaire. Because each situation is unique, you may need to supply additional information (such as layout specifications) in order to deliver a complete package.

DocBook and XML Usage

1. What version of the schema are you using?

2. Did you use any markup features of the schema that have been flagged as obsolete (to be removed at the next major version of DocBook)? If so, which ones?

3. Did you extend DocBook in any way, inside or outside the provided customization mechanisms? How? All extensions must be negotiated with the recipient.

4. Did you remove markup from DocBook to create a subset? If you used a subset of DocBook, supply the subset you used.

5. Did you use the supplied catalog or another one, or none at all? If you used a catalog other than the one supplied, provide it.

6. Did you use SVG, MathML, XInclude, XLink, or any other XML schema?

7. Did you use character sets other than UTF-8? If so, which ones? How did you use them?

Processing Requirements and Markup Interpretation

8. What formatting that you applied do you require your interchange partner to apply? For example, where and how must text be generated in order for the documents to make sense?

9. Did you supply your stylesheet and information regarding its format and version?

10. How did you create tables of contents, lists of titles, and indexes? Are they stored in DocBook form? If so, did you generate them (and according to what rules) or create them by hand?

11. If you used the xml:lang common attribute, why, and to what effect?

12. If you used the remap common attribute, why, and to what effect?

13. If you used the role common attribute, why, and to what effect?

14. If you used the effectivity attributes, which did you use, why, and to what effect?

15. What values did you give to the label attribute and how are they to be interpreted for rendering?

16. What values did you give to the mark and override attributes for lists and how are they to be interpreted for rendering?

17. Did you use the renderas attribute on sections and/or bridgeheads?

18. Did you supply all keyword values you used for attributes whose declared values are not enumerated tokens, along with the expected processing for the occurrence of each keyword?

19. Did you use markup to control width, size, and/or positioning settings (such as "fold-out" or "centered") for graphics, line specific regions, and tables? If so, how?

20. For rendering of sidebars, must these appear in the flow of the text where they appear in your files, or may they float?

21. Did you use callouts? If so, what are the processing expectations for callout marks?

22. Did you use itemizedlists? If so, what are the processing expectations for the marks on list items and nested lists?

23. For mediaobject and inlinemediaobject, what method(s) did you use for providing graphic data: element content, fileref attribute, or entityref attribute?

24. For mediaobject and inlinemediaobject, what method(s) did you use for selecting between alternative presentations?

25. How did you specify column widths in tables? Did you use vertical spans? Did you use horizontal spans?

26. Did you use entrytbls?

---

27. If you used the `type` attribute on the link elements, why, and to what effect?

28. If you used the `xref`, do your interchange partners need additional information about the semantics of the link? Have you provided it, perhaps with `role`?

29. Did you use the `subject` attribute on `glossdef`? If so, did you use a thesaurus of terms? If so, what is it?

30. If you used the `class` attribute on `refmiscinfo`, why and to what effect?

31. If you used `link` and provided URLs that are queries, what back-end processing is required to resolve those queries?

32. Is there a `fileref` or `entityref` attribute on every `audiodata`, `imagedata`, and `video data` element. If one is not present, what is the expectation?

33. If your `bibliographys` or `glossarys` have special processing expectations, such as the ability to display only those entries that are cited, have you described them?

34. If your `bibliographys` contain `biblioentrys`, what are the processing expectations? Which fields are selected for display? What punctuation is added, and where?

35. Do `glossterms` or other elements have implicit linking relationships that must be obeyed or handled in presentation?

36. Did you use any processing instructions? Why and what for? Are they in entities?

37. What copy fitting have you already done, and for what outputs?

38. Are the `revisions` in your `revhistorys` sorted in any particular way?

39. If you use any of the `*synopsis` elements, describe how you define and markup "arguments," "options," "parameters," etc.

Miscellaneous

40. Have you checked your files for viruses?

41. If you used `bridgehead`, have you joined a recovery support group?

GNU Free Documentation License

GNU Free Documentation License
Version 1.1, March 2000

0. PREAMBLE

The purpose of this License is to make a manual, textbook, or other
written document "free" in the sense of freedom: to assure everyone
the effective freedom to copy and redistribute it, with or without
modifying it, either commercially or noncommercially. Secondarily,
this License preserves for the author and publisher a way to get
credit for their work, while not being considered responsible for
modifications made by others.

This License is a kind of "copyleft", which means that derivative
works of the document must themselves be free in the same sense. It
complements the GNU General Public License, which is a copyleft
license designed for free software.

We have designed this License in order to use it for manuals for free
software, because free software needs free documentation: a free
program should come with manuals providing the same freedoms that the
software does. But this License is not limited to software manuals;
it can be used for any textual work, regardless of subject matter or
whether it is published as a printed book. We recommend this License
principally for works whose purpose is instruction or reference.

1. APPLICABILITY AND DEFINITIONS

This License applies to any manual or other work that contains a
notice placed by the copyright holder saying it can be distributed
under the terms of this License. The "Document", below, refers to any
such manual or work. Any member of the public is a licensee, and is

addressed as "you".

A "Modified Version" of the Document means any work containing the Document or a portion of it, either copied verbatim, or with modifications and/or translated into another language.

A "Secondary Section" is a named appendix or a front-matter section of the Document that deals exclusively with the relationship of the publishers or authors of the Document to the Document's overall subject (or to related matters) and contains nothing that could fall directly within that overall subject. (For example, if the Document is in part a textbook of mathematics, a Secondary Section may not explain any mathematics.) The relationship could be a matter of historical connection with the subject or with related matters, or of legal, commercial, philosophical, ethical or political position regarding them.

The "Invariant Sections" are certain Secondary Sections whose titles are designated, as being those of Invariant Sections, in the notice that says that the Document is released under this License.

The "Cover Texts" are certain short passages of text that are listed, as Front-Cover Texts or Back-Cover Texts, in the notice that says that the Document is released under this License.

A "Transparent" copy of the Document means a machine-readable copy, represented in a format whose specification is available to the general public, whose contents can be viewed and edited directly and straightforwardly with generic text editors or (for images composed of pixels) generic paint programs or (for drawings) some widely available drawing editor, and that is suitable for input to text formatters or for automatic translation to a variety of formats suitable for input to text formatters. A copy made in an otherwise Transparent file format whose markup has been designed to thwart or discourage subsequent modification by readers is not Transparent. A copy that is not "Transparent" is called "Opaque".

Examples of suitable formats for Transparent copies include plain ASCII without markup, Texinfo input format, LaTeX input format, SGML or XML using a publicly available DTD, and standard-conforming simple HTML designed for human modification. Opaque formats include PostScript, PDF, proprietary formats that can be read and edited only by proprietary word processors, SGML or XML for which the DTD and/or processing tools are not generally available, and the machine-generated HTML produced by some word processors for output purposes only.

The "Title Page" means, for a printed book, the title page itself, plus such following pages as are needed to hold, legibly, the material this License requires to appear in the title page. For works in formats which do not have any title page as such, "Title Page" means the text near the most prominent appearance of the work's title, preceding the beginning of the body of the text.

2. VERBATIM COPYING

You may copy and distribute the Document in any medium, either commercially or noncommercially, provided that this License, the copyright notices, and the license notice saying this License applies to the Document are reproduced in all copies, and that you add no other conditions whatsoever to those of this License. You may not use technical measures to obstruct or control the reading or further copying of the copies you make or distribute. However, you may accept compensation in exchange for copies. If you distribute a large enough number of copies you must also follow the conditions in section 3.

You may also lend copies, under the same conditions stated above, and you may publicly display copies.

3. COPYING IN QUANTITY

If you publish printed copies of the Document numbering more than 100, and the Document's license notice requires Cover Texts, you must enclose the copies in covers that carry, clearly and legibly, all these Cover Texts: Front-Cover Texts on the front cover, and Back-Cover Texts on the back cover. Both covers must also clearly and legibly identify you as the publisher of these copies. The front cover must present the full title with all words of the title equally prominent and visible. You may add other material on the covers in addition. Copying with changes limited to the covers, as long as they preserve the title of the Document and satisfy these conditions, can be treated as verbatim copying in other respects.

If the required texts for either cover are too voluminous to fit legibly, you should put the first ones listed (as many as fit reasonably) on the actual cover, and continue the rest onto adjacent pages.

If you publish or distribute Opaque copies of the Document numbering more than 100, you must either include a machine-readable Transparent copy along with each Opaque copy, or state in or with each Opaque copy a publicly-accessible computer-network location containing a complete Transparent copy of the Document, free of added material, which the general network-using public has access to download anonymously at no charge using public-standard network protocols. If you use the latter option, you must take reasonably prudent steps, when you begin distribution of Opaque copies in quantity, to ensure that this Transparent copy will remain thus accessible at the stated location until at least one year after the last time you distribute an Opaque copy (directly or through your agents or retailers) of that edition to the public.

It is requested, but not required, that you contact the authors of the Document well before redistributing any large number of copies, to give them a chance to provide you with an updated version of the Document.

4. MODIFICATIONS

You may copy and distribute a Modified Version of the Document under the conditions of sections 2 and 3 above, provided that you release the Modified Version under precisely this License, with the Modified Version filling the role of the Document, thus licensing distribution and modification of the Modified Version to whoever possesses a copy of it. In addition, you must do these things in the Modified Version:

A. Use in the Title Page (and on the covers, if any) a title distinct from that of the Document, and from those of previous versions (which should, if there were any, be listed in the History section of the Document). You may use the same title as a previous version if the original publisher of that version gives permission.

B. List on the Title Page, as authors, one or more persons or entities responsible for authorship of the modifications in the Modified Version, together with at least five of the principal authors of the Document (all of its principal authors, if it has less than five).

C. State on the Title page the name of the publisher of the Modified Version, as the publisher.

D. Preserve all the copyright notices of the Document.

E. Add an appropriate copyright notice for your modifications adjacent to the other copyright notices.

F. Include, immediately after the copyright notices, a license notice giving the public permission to use the Modified Version under the terms of this License, in the form shown in the Addendum below.

G. Preserve in that license notice the full lists of Invariant Sections and required Cover Texts given in the Document's license notice.

H. Include an unaltered copy of this License.

I. Preserve the section entitled "History", and its title, and add to it an item stating at least the title, year, new authors, and publisher of the Modified Version as given on the Title Page. If there is no section entitled "History" in the Document, create one stating the title, year, authors, and publisher of the Document as given on its Title Page, then add an item describing the Modified Version as stated in the previous sentence.

J. Preserve the network location, if any, given in the Document for public access to a Transparent copy of the Document, and likewise the network locations given in the Document for previous versions it was based on. These may be placed in the "History" section. You may omit a network location for a work that was published at least four years before the Document itself, or if the original publisher of the version it refers to gives permission.

K. In any section entitled "Acknowledgements" or "Dedications", preserve the section's title, and preserve in the section all the substance and tone of each of the contributor acknowledgements and/or dedications given therein.

L. Preserve all the Invariant Sections of the Document, unaltered in their text and in their titles. Section numbers or the equivalent are not considered part of the section titles.

M. Delete any section entitled "Endorsements". Such a section may not be included in the Modified Version.

N. Do not retitle any existing section as "Endorsements" or to conflict in title with any Invariant Section.

If the Modified Version includes new front-matter sections or appendices that qualify as Secondary Sections and contain no material copied from the Document, you may at your option designate some or all of these sections as invariant. To do this, add their titles to the list of Invariant Sections in the Modified Version's license notice. These titles must be distinct from any other section titles.

You may add a section entitled "Endorsements", provided it contains nothing but endorsements of your Modified Version by various parties--for example, statements of peer review or that the text has been approved by an organization as the authoritative definition of a standard.

You may add a passage of up to five words as a Front-Cover Text, and a passage of up to 25 words as a Back-Cover Text, to the end of the list of Cover Texts in the Modified Version. Only one passage of Front-Cover Text and one of Back-Cover Text may be added by (or through arrangements made by) any one entity. If the Document already includes a cover text for the same cover, previously added by you or by arrangement made by the same entity you are acting on behalf of, you may not add another; but you may replace the old one, on explicit permission from the previous publisher that added the old one.

The author(s) and publisher(s) of the Document do not by this License give permission to use their names for publicity for or to assert or imply endorsement of any Modified Version.

5. COMBINING DOCUMENTS

You may combine the Document with other documents released under this License, under the terms defined in section 4 above for modified versions, provided that you include in the combination all of the Invariant Sections of all of the original documents, unmodified, and list them all as Invariant Sections of your combined work in its license notice.

The combined work need only contain one copy of this License, and multiple identical Invariant Sections may be replaced with a single copy. If there are multiple Invariant Sections with the same name but different contents, make the title of each such section unique by adding at the end of it, in parentheses, the name of the original author or publisher of that section if known, or else a unique number. Make the same adjustment to the section titles in the list of Invariant Sections in the license notice of the combined work.

In the combination, you must combine any sections entitled "History" in the various original documents, forming one section entitled "History"; likewise combine any sections entitled "Acknowledgements", and any sections entitled "Dedications". You must delete all sections entitled "Endorsements."

6. COLLECTIONS OF DOCUMENTS

You may make a collection consisting of the Document and other documents released under this License, and replace the individual copies of this License in the various documents with a single copy that is included in the collection, provided that you follow the rules of this License for verbatim copying of each of the documents in all other respects.

You may extract a single document from such a collection, and distribute it individually under this License, provided you insert a copy of this License into the extracted document, and follow this License in all other respects regarding verbatim copying of that document.

7. AGGREGATION WITH INDEPENDENT WORKS

A compilation of the Document or its derivatives with other separate and independent documents or works, in or on a volume of a storage or distribution medium, does not as a whole count as a Modified Version of the Document, provided no compilation copyright is claimed for the compilation. Such a compilation is called an "aggregate", and this License does not apply to the other self-contained works thus compiled with the Document, on account of their being thus compiled, if they are not themselves derivative works of the Document.

If the Cover Text requirement of section 3 is applicable to these copies of the Document, then if the Document is less than one quarter of the entire aggregate, the Document's Cover Texts may be placed on covers that surround only the Document within the aggregate. Otherwise they must appear on covers around the whole aggregate.

8. TRANSLATION

Translation is considered a kind of modification, so you may distribute translations of the Document under the terms of section 4. Replacing Invariant Sections with translations requires special permission from their copyright holders, but you may include translations of some or all Invariant Sections in addition to the original versions of these Invariant Sections. You may include a translation of this License provided that you also include the original English version of this License. In case of a disagreement between the translation and the original English version of this License, the original English version will prevail.

9. TERMINATION

You may not copy, modify, sublicense, or distribute the Document except as expressly provided for under this License. Any other attempt to copy, modify, sublicense or distribute the Document is void, and will automatically terminate your rights under this License. However, parties who have received copies, or rights, from you under this License will not have their licenses terminated so long as such parties remain in full compliance.

10. FUTURE REVISIONS OF THIS LICENSE

The Free Software Foundation may publish new, revised versions
of the GNU Free Documentation License from time to time. Such new
versions will be similar in spirit to the present version, but may
differ in detail to address new problems or concerns. See
http://www.gnu.org/copyleft/.

Each version of the License is given a distinguishing version number.
If the Document specifies that a particular numbered version of this
License "or any later version" applies to it, you have the option of
following the terms and conditions either of that specified version or
of any later version that has been published (not as a draft) by the
Free Software Foundation. If the Document does not specify a version
number of this License, you may choose any version ever published (not
as a draft) by the Free Software Foundation.

ADDENDUM: How to use this License for your documents

To use this License in a document you have written, include a copy of
the License in the document and put the following copyright and
license notices just after the title page:

> Copyright (c) YEAR YOUR NAME.
> Permission is granted to copy, distribute and/or modify this document
> under the terms of the GNU Free Documentation License, Version 1.1
> or any later version published by the Free Software Foundation;
> with the Invariant Sections being LIST THEIR TITLES, with the
> Front-Cover Texts being LIST, and with the Back-Cover Texts being LIST.
> A copy of the license is included in the section entitled "GNU
> Free Documentation License".

If you have no Invariant Sections, write "with no Invariant Sections"
instead of saying which ones are invariant. If you have no
Front-Cover Texts, write "no Front-Cover Texts" instead of
"Front-Cover Texts being LIST"; likewise for Back-Cover Texts.

If your document contains nontrivial examples of program code, we
recommend releasing these examples in parallel under your choice of
free software license, such as the GNU General Public License,
to permit their use in free software.

Glossary

attribute

Attributes augment the element on which they appear; they also provide additional information about the element.

Attributes appear as name-value pairs in the element's start tag. For example, to assign the value `hostname` to the `role` attribute of `systemitem`, you would use the markup: `<systemitem role="hostname">`.

callout

A pointer, verbal or graphical or both, to a *component* of an illustration or a text object.

character reference

A character reference is a mechanism for inserting an arbitrary Unicode character into a document. They're most often used for characters that aren't available on the author's keyboard or font. Syntactically, they have the form `&#number;` where "number" is the Unicode codepoint of the character expressed as a decimal number. Hexadecimal numbers can also be used with character references of the form `&#xnumber;`.

For example, you can type `&#169;` (or `&#xa9;`) to insert a © symbol.

cooked

"Cooked" data, as distinct from "raw," is a collection of elements and character data that's ready for presentation. The processor is not expected to rearrange, select, or suppress any of the elements, but simply present them as specified.

See also `raw`.

Document Type Declaration (DTD)

A set of declarations that defines the names of the elements and their attributes, and that specifies rules for their combination or sequence.

effectivity

A term used to identify attributes used for profiling or conditional processing. DocBook contains a set of effectivity attributes that allow you to flag elements as being "effective" under particular conditions. For example, you might set the value of the `os` effectivity attribute to "linux" to indicate that this element is applicable to the Linux operating system. With the DocBook stylesheets, if you set the `profile.os` parameter to "linux" this element will be included. If you set the parameter to some other value, the element will be excluded. Further information about using the DocBook stylesheets for profiling can be found in Bob Stayton's *DocBook XSL: The Complete Guide*.

element

Elements define the hierarchical structure of a document. Most elements have start and end tags and contain some part of the document content. Empty elements have only a start tag and have no content.

entity

A name assigned (by means of a declaration) to some chunk of data so that it can be referred to by that name; the data can be of various kinds (e.g., a special character or a chapter or a set of declarations in a DTD), and the way in which it is referred to depends on the type of data and where it is being referenced.

external entity

An external entity is a general entity that refers to another document. External entities are often used to incorporate parsable text documents, like legal notices or chapters, into larger units, like chapters or books.

external subset

Element, attribute, and other declarations that compose (part of) a document type definition that are stored in an external entity, and referenced from a document's Document Type Declaration using a system identifier and optionally a public identifier.

float

Text objects such as sidebars, figures, tables, and graphics are said to float when their actual place in the document is not fixed. For presentation on a printed page, for instance, a graphic may float to the top of the next page if it is too tall to fit on the page in which it actually falls, in the sequence of words and the sequence of other like objects in a document.

formal public identifier

A public identifier that conforms to the specification of formal public identifiers in ISO 8879.

general entity

An entity referenced by a name that starts with an ampersand (&) and ends with a semicolon. Most of the time general entities are used in document instances, not in the schema. There are two types, external and internal entities, and they refer either to special characters or to text objects such as commonly repeated phrases or names or chapters.

internal entity

A general entity that references a piece of text (including its markup and even other internal entities), usually as a keyboard shortcut.

internal subset

Element, attribute, and other declarations that compose (part of) a document type definition that are stored in a document, within the Document Type Declaration.

meta-information

Meta-information is information about a document, such as the specification of its author or its date of composition, as opposed to the content of a document itself.

NVDL

NVDL is the Namespace-based Validation Dispatching Language; see *http://www.nvdl .org/*.

processing instruction

An essentially arbitrary string preceded by a question mark and delimited by angle brackets that is intended to convey information to an application that processes an XML instance. For example, the processing instruction `<?linebreak>` might cause the formatter to introduce a line break at the position where the processing instruction occurs.

In XML documents, processing instructions should have the form:

```
<?pitarget param1="value1" param2="value2"?>
```

The *pitarget* should be a name that the processing application will recognize. Additional information in the processing instruction should be added using "attribute syntax."

public identifier

An abstract identifier for an XML document, DTD, or external entity.

raw

"Raw" data is just a collection of elements, with no additional punctuation or information about presentation. To continue the cooking metaphor, raw data is just a set of ingredients. It's up to the processor to select appropriate elements, arrange them for display, and add required presentational information.

See also cooked.

RELAX NG

RELAX NG is a grammar-based schema language for XML; see *http://relaxng.org/*.

Schematron

Schematron is a language for making assertions about patterns found in XML documents; see *http://www.schematron.com/*.

SGML

Standard Generalized Markup Language is an international standard (ISO 8879) that specifies the rules for the creation of platform-independent markup languages for electronic texts.

stylesheet

A file that specifies the presentation or appearance of a document; there are several standards for such stylesheets, including CSS, FOSIs, DSSSL, and XSL.

system identifier

In SGML, a local, system-dependent identifier for a document, DTD, or external entity. Usually a filename on the local system.

In XML, a system identifier is required to be a URI.

tag

An XML element name enclosed in angle brackets (<>), used to mark up the semantics or structure of a document. <para> is a tag in DocBook used to mark the beginning of a paragraph.

URI

Uniform Resource Identifier, the W3C's codification of the name and address syntax of present and future objects on the Internet. In its most basic form, a URI consists of a scheme name (such as file, http, ftp, news, mailto, gopher) followed by a colon, followed by a path whose nature is determined by the scheme that precedes it (see RFC 1630).

URI is the umbrella term for URNs, URLs, and all other Uniform Resource Identifiers.

URL

Uniform Resource Locator, a name and address for an existing object accessible over the Internet. http://www.docbook.org is an example of a URL (see RFC 1738).

W3C

The World Wide Web Consortium (*http://www.w3.org/*).

wrapper

Some elements, such as chapter, have important semantic significance. Other elements serve no obvious purpose except to contain a number of other elements. For example, info has no important semantics; it merely serves as a container for the meta-information about a book. Elements that are just containers are sometimes called "wrappers."

XML

The Extensible Markup Language (*http://www.w3.org/TR/REC-xml*), a subset of SGML designed specifically for use over the Web.

XSL

Extensible Stylesheet Language (XSL), an evolving language for stylesheets to be attached to XML documents. The stylesheet is itself an XML document.

Index

A

abbrev element, 29
accel element, 31
accessibility, 10
acronym element, 29
adding attributes, 68
adding elements, 67–68
address element, 26
addresses, Internet syntax, 517
admonitions, 24
   DocBook types, 25
anchor element, 30
angle brackets
   XML tags, 517
answer element, 27
appearance
   cooked data, 515
   raw data, 516
   stylesheets, 517
appendix element, 20
   typical structure, 35
application element, 33, 34
article
   creating, 36
   examples, 36
article element, 20
assembly mechanism, 494
attributes, 515
   adding, 68
   adding a value to an enumeration, 69
   common, 77
      subsetting, 66
   common linking, 80
   customizing, 55

effectivity, 78, 515
elements, referencing, 71
removing, 66–67
semantics, 72
title, 9
version, 9
attribution element, 28
author element, 21

B

back matter, 39
bibliodiv element, 21
biblioentry element, 42
bibliographies, creating, 42
bibliography element, 20, 21
bibliolist element, 25
bibliomixed element, 43
block elements, 20, 24
   formal and informal elements, 26
   graphic, 27
   inline elements vs., 24
block quotations, 24
blockquote element, 28
book element, 20
books
   components, 20
   DocBook, making, 35
   example, 18, 35
   typical structure, 20, 35
bridgehead element, 21

C

callout element, 25
calloutlist element, 25

We'd like to hear your suggestions for improving our indexes. Send email to *index@oreilly.com*.

J

Jing, 46, 500
journal articles, 36

K

keycap element, 32
keycode element, 32
keycombo element, 32
keysym element, 32
keyword sets (meta-information), 21

L

languages
    stylesheet, 51
line breaks, preserving, 25
line-specific environments, 24, 25
link element, 30
linkend attribute, 30
    glossterm tag, 41
linking, 7–8
    attributes, 80
    glossary terms to glossary entries, 41
    ulink removed, 8
lists, 24
    elements, 25
literal element, 30, 32, 34
literallayout element, 26

M

mailing lists, OASIS, 496
manpage (UNIX), 36
manual page, creating, 36
manvolnum, 37
markup
    back matter, books and articles, 39
    elements, 30
    glossaries, 41
markup element, 30
mathematics (DocBook), 31
MathML, 12
    incorporating, 31
    W3C recommendation, 497
mathphrase element, 31
mediaobject element, 27
menuchoice element, 32
meta-information, 516
    DocBook book, 35

elements, 21
    reference page, 36
    wrappers, 517
modules
    redeclarations, 65
mousebutton element, 32
msgset element
    removing, 62
msgtext element, 32, 33
MSV (Multi-Schema Validator), 46, 500

N

names
    Internet, syntax, 517
Namespace-based Validation Dispatching
        Language (see NVDL)
namespaces, 31
    DocBook, 10, 56
    W3C recommendation, 498
    XInclude, 18
navigation, component-level elements, 20
nesting
    section elements, 21
newsgroup, comp.text.xml, 496
note element, 25
numbered sections, levels, 21
NVDL, 46, 516
    ISO standard, 498
nXML mode (emacs), 500

O

OASIS, 3
    DocBook Technical Committee, 5
    entity sets (ISO standard), obtaining, 491
    mailing lists, 496
olink element, 30
Open Software Foundation, 3
operating systems
    configurations, software support, 37
    inline elements, 33
option element, 33, 34
optional element, 34
options, 24
    marking up, 28
orderedlist element, 25
, 501
    documents, validating, 46
    Schematron support, 46

constraints, 9
   validating, 46
screen element, 26
screenco element, 26
screenshot element, 26, 27
secondary level index entries, 40
section element, 21
sections
   elements, 20
   elements, removing, 63
   refentry, levels, 37
see and see also index entries, 40
segmentedlist element, 25
semantics (elements), describing, 71
sets, 20
SGML, 517
   public identifiers, 516
   system identifiers, 517
   XML and, 517
shortcut element, 32
sidebars, 24
simplelist element, 25
simplesect element, 21
Simplified DocBook, 493
singular index markers, 39
special characters, encoding as entities, 516
standards
   CALS table model, 497
   Dublin Core Metadata Element Set, 498
   HTML 4.01, 497
   IETF RFCs, 498
   MathML 2.0, 497
   NVDL, 498
   OASIS CALS tables, 497
   OASIS XML catalogs, 497
   Unicode, 498
   XHTML 1.0, 497
   XLink 1.0, 498
   XML 1.0, 498
   XML namespaces, 498
   xml:id 1.0, 498
   XPath, 498
   XQuery, 498
   XSLT 1.0, 498
   XSLT 2.0, 498
start tags
   attribute ID, containing, 515
   empty element, 515
   errors, 47

   misspelling, 48
   out of context, 49
starting index terms (ranges), 40
stylesheets, 517
   examples, 52
   installing, 492
   languages, 51–54
   publishing documents, 51
   sourceforge.net, 54, 496
subscript element, 31
subscripts and superscripts, 24
subsets (DocBook schema), 57
subsetting common attributes, 66
Sun Multi-Schema XML Validator (MSV) (see MSV)
superscript element, 31
SVG, 12
symbol element, 33, 34
synopses, 24
   elements (reference pages), 71
   reference topics, 37
   synopsis elements, removing, 63
synopsis element, 26
system identifiers
   external subset, 516
   SGML, 517
   XML, 16, 517
systemitem element, 33

T

table element, 26
tables, 24
   mixing CALS and HTML, 9
tables of contents, 20
   creating, 39
   markup, 9
tag element, 31
tags, 517
   context errors, 49
task element, 28
tertiary level index entries, 40
testing
   schema customizations, 61
text
   float, 516
   inline elements, 29
text editors
   unstructured, parsing and, 45
text screen captures, 26

About the Author

Norman Walsh is a principal technologist at Mark Logic Corporation, where he assists in the design and deployment of advanced content applications. Norm is also an active participant in a number of standards efforts worldwide: he is chair of the DocBook Technical Committee at OASIS. At the W3C, he is chair of the XML Processing Model Working Group and also cochair of the XML Core Working Group.

About the Editor

Richard L. Hamilton has more than 10 years of experience leading writing teams and documentation tools teams at AT&T, Novell, and Hewlett-Packard. He is an independent consultant specializing in the application of XML technology to technical documentation, and is also a member of the OASIS DocBook Technical Committee. He is the author of *Managing Writers: A Real World Guide to Managing Technical Documentation*, published in January 2009 by XML Press.

Colophon

The animal on the cover of *DocBook 5: The Definitive Guide* is a wood duck (*Aix sponsa*), also known as a Carolina duck. Often considered one of the most beautiful ducks in North America, the male wood duck has a metallic purple and green head with white streaks extending from its bill around the eyes and down to its blue and green, gold-flecked wings. It has a white neck, a chestnut-colored chest, a white or red bill, and yellow-orange legs and feet. Females have more brown, gray, and subdued hues.

The cover image is from the Dover Pictorial Archive. The cover font is Adobe ITC Garamond. The text font is Linotype Birka; the heading font is Adobe Myriad Condensed; and the code font is LucasFont's TheSansMonoCondensed.